Caring for School-Age Children

Fourth Edition

Join us on the web at

EarlyChildEd.delmar.com

Caring for School-Age Children

Fourth Edition

PHYLLIS CLICK
JENNIFER PARKER

THOMSON

DELMAR LEARNING

Australia Canada Mexico Singapore Spain United Kingdom United States

THOMSON

DELMAR LEARNING

Caring for School Age Children, Fourth Edition
Phyllis Click and Jennifer Parker

Vice President,
Career Education SBU:
Dawn Gerrain

Director of Editorial:
Sherry Gomoll

Acquisitions Editor:
Erin O'Connor

Developmental Editor:
Patricia Osborn

Editorial Assistant:
Stephanie Kelly

Director of Production:
Wendy A. Troeger

Production Manager:
J.P. Henkel

Production Editor:
Joy Kocsis

Production Assistant:
Angela Iula

Technology Project Manager:
Sandy Charette

Director of Marketing:
Wendy E. Mapstone

Channel Manager:
Kristin McNary

Marketing Coordinator:
David White

Cover Design:
Joseph Villanova

Composition:
Pre-Press Company, Inc.

Library of Congress Cataloging-in-Publication Data

Click, Phyllis.
  Caring for school age children / Phyllis M. Click, Jennifer Parker.-- 4th ed.
      p. cm.
  Includes bibliographical references and index.
  ISBN-13 978-1-4018-9770-3
  ISBN-10 1-4018-9770-3
  1. School-age child care--United States. I. Parker, Jennifer (Lynch Parker) II. Title.
  HQ778.6.C55 2005
  305.234--dc22

                                          2005000019

NOTICE TO THE READER

CONTENTS

PREFACE

This fourth edition of *Caring for School-Age Children* is an easy-to-use course of study for those who are preparing for a career in early childhood education or a reference for those who are already employed as teachers, aides, caregivers, leaders, or recreation supervisors.

It will also help those in administrative positions, such as directors, principals, managers, or coordinators. In addition, parents of school-age children will find useful information for understanding their youngsters and for participating in the operation of their children's child care center. The textbook can be used as the basis for a college or university course or for a series of in-service training sessions sponsored by boards of education or community agencies. It will also be useful for administrators of out-of-school programs who wish to upgrade the skills of staff members through in-service training sessions.

Rationale

At the time the first edition of this book was written, there was little information for those interested in before- and after-school programs. This fourth edition of *Caring for School-Age Children* reflects a continuing and increasing national interest in providing quality programs for the large numbers of children who spend their out-of-school time in a group setting. Educators have a heightened awareness of the dangers that might confront children when they have unsupervised hours after school, whether they are home alone or out in neighborhoods. We firmly believe that it is absolutely imperative that children should be able to be safe during their after-school hours and that they obtain the education and training they need to become happy, productive adults.

Therefore, information throughout this book is based on the most recent information concerning developmentally appropriate practice with school-age children and on the adult role as a professional. We both have many years of experience teaching both adult and child learners. Jennifer Parker currently teaches courses for early childhood professionals and is involved in developing quality programs for after-school care. We both have brought our knowledge and experience to the writing of this edition in order to help others achieve the goal of quality programs for children through the education of caregivers and teachers.

Organization

The order of the sections and chapters in this new edition remains the same as in the third edition. Section I, The People in Child Care, introduces the reader first to the caregivers, then the children, and finally, the families. The caregivers are portrayed in the first chapter because the reader either already is or will be a caregiver. We discuss the characteristics of an effective caregiver, the education and experience needed, and ways in which the adults affect children's development. Chapter 2 presents an overview of development of children ages 5 to 12, as well as a discussion of children in groups. Chapter 3 is devoted to families, their makeup, their culture, recent changes in configuration , and the ways in which these factors affect the children.

Section II, How Children Grow and Develop, presents information about children's stages of growth and the factors that affect their development. The first three chapters in this section contain extensive coverage of children's physical, cognitive, and psychosocial development. Chapter 7 in Section II titled Helping Children Develop Social Competence includes strategies and activities to help children be more effective socially, resolve conflicts, increase their self-image, and become more cooperative. This chapter also covers specific behaviors or characteristics that create problems for children and includes ways to effectively guide children toward acceptance of others and in changing their own behaviors.

Section III, The Background, includes chapters on program planning and creating an environment. Section IV, The Curriculum, covers the day-to-day activities of a child care program. Each chapter has a segment on how that part of the curriculum contributes to or supports the development of the children for whom it is designed. The activities begin with a stated purpose and include a list of materials to have available. Chapter 12 reflects the newest thinking about children. This chapter, Science and Math, views the child as a natural scientist and mathematician. It shows how that approach can be used to plan exciting activities that engage children in constructing knowledge about the world.

The final section, Section V, Resources and Regulations, includes a chapter on using community resources and another that discusses quality and standards for child care programs. Here the reader can learn about the ways early childhood professionals are trying to upgrade the quality of experiences children have in their out-of-school time. Accreditation, credentialing, and evaluation are discussed.

Features

Profiles of caregivers and families are featured throughout the book. These vignettes allow the reader to glimpse the lives of real people who are involved in programs. They also serve as attention-getters allowing the reader to relate to others' stories. "If she or he can start a new career at age 50, perhaps I can, too." There is a list of key terms at the end of each chapter and a glossary defining those terms. Students will find it helpful to test their knowledge by answering the review questions and considering the questions following the case study presented at the end of each chapter. One of the most important features is extensive information about the use of the Internet for researching further information.

The sequence of chapters provides the reader with a logical progression of topics that has been field-tested by many instructors using the book. Instructors can adopt the order as is or change it to suit the needs of a particular setting. Review questions and activities at the end of each chapter also make it applicable to a self-study plan by individual students.

Many chapters include appropriate Web sites, and at the end of the book, Appendix B provides a complete list of Internet links for child care information.

The authors and Thomson Delmar Learning affirm that the Web site URLs referenced herein were accurate at the time of printing. Each has been checked for this edition. However, due to the fluid nature of the Internet, we cannot guarantee their accuracy for the life of the edition.

New to This Edition

As requested by reviewers, we have added new material to this edition. Chapter 2 has an added discussion of bullying. Children sometimes test their power in an effort to define their self-image by being aggressive toward their peers. Boys take direct forms: hitting, teasing, and threatening. Girls use indirect forms such as gossiping, spreading rumors, or enforcing social isolation. Chapter 2 suggests ways that children and adults can deal with the problem so that children can become empowered without hurting others in the process. In Chapter 7 we added a discussion of general strategies for helping children with special needs. The reader is cautioned to realize that each child is unique, including those with a disability. This topic, added to the strategies for helping children with specific disabilities, will help students learn to incorporate these children into the group setting. A section on managing transitions has been added to Chapter 8. The student will learn to have curriculum areas ready before a transition is made and to minimize waiting. They will learn the importance of alerting children to an impending change and to involve the children in making the transitions go smoothly. Also in this chapter there is a discussion of summer programs. How is the curriculum different when the children are in the group all day rather than just before and after school? What are the things that make summers enjoyable for the children? Chapter 12 includes a greatly expanded discussion of math and its place in a child care program. Math is seen as a part of everyday experiences and can be integrated into a wide variety of activities. A discussion of how children construct knowledge while engaged in science or math activities reinforces the reader's understanding of the theories of Piaget and Vygotsky. This chapter also includes new math activities.

A brand new Appendix C, Lesson Plans, presents plans for art, music, math, and science activities. Each plan describes the activity, lists the materials needed, outlines the procedure for carrying out the activity, and discusses the role of the adult leader. Readers can use these plans directly in their day-to-day curriculum in their child care settings.

Online Companion™

An exciting feature, *Online Companion™,* accompanies *Caring for School-Age Children.* It is designed for use by the student reader and provides a link to early childhood education on the Internet. The Online Companion™ contains many features to help focus your understanding of caring for school age children:

Discussion Forum For each of the sections, a short presentation of the issue is followed by critical thinking questions students can consider and discuss with others via e-mail or a chat room. Some examples are ethical considerations for staff members, bullying among children, and organized, competitive sports.

Case Studies For each section there are case studies of children, caregivers, or parents. Each will portray problems caregivers frequently encounter or an issue that is frequently discussed. Critical thinking questions are posed to help students consolidate their learning.

Power Point Presentations A new section of the Online Companion™ includes Power Point presentations for each chapter that an instructor can use to enhance classroom lectures.

The *Online Companion™* can be found at http://www.earlychilded.delmar.com.

For the Instructor

For the instructor, there are supplementary materials in the form of an *Instructor's Manual* and a *Computerized Test Bank.* The instructor's manual is a chapter-by-chapter plan for organizing a course using this textbook. Features include a brief statement of the focus of each chapter, a chapter outline, classroom activities to enhance student learning, additional case studies that can be used for discussion, assignments to further learning, and guidelines for answering the review questions in the textbook. In addition, there is a midterm and final exam composed of multiple-choice and short-answer questions. A final feature of the instructor's manual is a list of videos to enhance classroom activities. The *Computerized Test Bank* can be used by instructors to create sample exams for students. It contains multiple-choice, true/false, short answer, and completion questions for each chapter.

About the Authors

Phyllis Click obtained her bachelor's and master's degrees from the University of California at Berkeley in psychology and child development. Throughout a long career, her interest in providing the best possible environment for young children led her to work in a variety of settings from preschools to summer camps for older children as well as programs for children with special needs. For several years she developed and taught in a preschool for children diagnosed with autism. Later she began working with adults, teaching college students, administering grant programs, and designing a curriculum for a private college for prospective teachers.

Now retired, she has been a consultant, helping others to start or administer programs and has published extensively. Her publications include another textbook for administrators of child care programs, articles in professional journals, and ancillary materials for other authors' textbooks. She has participated in research studies that are written up in anthologies. She belongs to the National Association for the Education of Young Children, the California School-Age Consortium, and the Association for Childhood Education International.

Jennifer Parker is currently an associate professor teaching early childhood education classes at Moorpark College, and she was instrumental in adding a school-age component to the child development degree program there. She is currently working to expand the degree program to include a paraprofessional certificate for students wishing to work as elementary classroom aides. Her classes include students with diverse backgrounds and experience, ranging from beginning, entry-level to those who are currently teaching in early childhood programs. Her course load also includes teaching master teachers skills in supervision and mentoring. She coordinates a mentor teacher program in which she selects and trains caregivers to mentor student teachers in their field placements.

She received her master's degree from California State University, Northridge, and has had extensive experience working with children, families, and adults. She founded a parent support program for infants and toddlers in a developmentally appropriate environment and has been a lead kindergarten teacher in an on-campus demonstration school. She is currently a member of Ventura County Child Care Planning Council, the executive committee for two First 5 Neighborhoods for Learning, the National Association for the Education of Young Children, and the California School-Age Consortium.

Acknowledgments

Thanks to all those who generously gave of their time to allow us to gather information for the Caregiver Profiles that appear at the beginning of each chapter. Some were students in a class at Moorpark College, while others were employed in local child care programs.

Thanks also to Erin O'Connor, Acquisition Editor, for continuing to support this book through its various revisions. And finally, thanks to Patricia Osborn, Developmental Editor, and all the other Thomson Delmar Learning staff members who carry the project from one step to another until the final pages are put together.

Our special thanks go to the reviewers who offered many excellent suggestions for additions to previous editions and those who reviewed the draft version of the updated edition. We appreciate their thoughtful comments.

Linda Aulgur, PhD
Westminster College
Fulton, MO

Sylvia Brooks, EdD
University of Delaware
Newark, DE

Mary Lou Brotherson, PhD
Nova Southeastern University
Fort Lauderdale, FL

Mary Henthorne
Western Wisconsin Technical College
La Crosse, WI

Beverly Hugener, MA
Reid State Technical College
Evergreen, AL

Elaine Boski-Wilkinson, MEd
Collin County Community College
Plano, TX

Patricia Weaver, MEd
Fayetteville Technical Community College
Fayetteville, NC

The authors hope that this new edition will help those who are concerned for the welfare of the millions of children who spend their out-of-school time in organized-care programs.

Our children deserve the best.

The People in Child Care

CHAPTER 1

Caregivers: Who Are They?

Objectives

After studying this chapter, the student should be able to:

- Describe the characteristics of an effective caregiver/teacher
- State education and experience requirements of a caregiver/teacher
- Relate children's needs to a caregiver's role

C A R E G I V E R   P R O F I L E

Sierra is 18 and lives at home with her parents and a younger brother. She has an older brother who is 24 but does not live in the household. She was three years old when she and the older boy were adopted. Sierra lived with her biological parents for two years, then was put in a foster home, and she was there for a year before being adopted. She remembers the foster home but not her birth parents. She did keep in touch with one biological grandmother.

Sierra's passion to be with children led to her present job at a YMCA after-school program. She says, "Getting paid to do something I love is so great, I don't even consider it work!" What she finds most enjoyable is talking with the children, learning about them and their personality, or getting to know them as individuals.

Sierra decided on this kind of work because she had a very hard time dealing with being adopted. She occasionally visited her biological grandmother, and after each visit Sierra became withdrawn. Her parents knew something was troubling her so arranged for her to meet with a psychologist. She hated going to the psychologist because the woman would try to get her to talk about being in the foster home. Sierra didn't want to be reminded that she was adopted. Because of her own experiences, Sierra wants to work at some kind of job where she can help children. She is preparing herself for future jobs by taking college classes. She doesn't want to be a psychologist but thinks she will probably become a teacher. She feels that her ability to relate to children is her most important quality. She is willing to listen to children, and in turn they come to her when they have problems. "I have patience and I have a heart."

What Do Children Really Need from Caregivers?

If you are already working in school-age child care, you may occasionally question your choice of profession. Or if you are just considering child care as a career, you may wonder if this is the right place for you. Children can be tiring, frustrating, and demanding. They can also be humorous, marvelously exciting, and fun. This chapter should help you decide whether you are the right person for these children and for the job.

First, try to answer the question "What do children need from caregivers?" What did you want from the adults in your life? Children need security—a feeling they can trust adults and be trusted. They want freedom to be independent, while at the same time they like clear limits that define what they can or cannot do. They like adults who are flexible and can respond to new situations and interests with enthusiasm. They need affection, caring, and acceptance of their individual differences. They want to solve their own problems and to feel empowered, but have an adult's help available when needed. They want to be challenged to use their skills and abilities. Probably, most of all, they want to feel competent and successful.

What Are They Called?

Many different titles are used to designate the adults who spend time with children in after-school programs. There is still no universally accepted designation that satisfies the need to indicate the importance of this type of work. Some adults prefer to be called teachers because they certainly do teach. Others emphasize their caring role and therefore prefer to be called caregivers or guides. This term may be unacceptable to many children in after-school settings because they feel they do not need to "be cared for." Those who emphasize the recreational aspect of after-school programs use recreational supervisor, or counselor. Still others use the title of leader, aide, assistant, or child care worker. Daniel (1995) has suggested using developmentalist, while Betty Caldwell, past president of NAEYC (National Association for the Education of Young Children), has coined the term educare. Until a universally accepted new word is coined reflecting the multifaceted aspects of working with school-age children, each of the preceding should be acceptable.

Characteristics of the Effective Caregiver/Teacher

If you want to be a caregiver or teacher of school-age children, you need certain characteristics. Do not be discouraged if you do not have every single quality in the following list. You will acquire some of these attributes as you gain more experience.

Someone Who Really Likes School-Age Children

Liking school-age children should certainly be the first important characteristic for a caregiver because few people relate well to children of all ages. "Liking" school-age children means many things. It means being interested in these children, enjoying conversations with them, and being with them. It means appreciating each child's unique qualities and accepting their differences.

Someone Who Encourages Children to Be Independent

School-age children are striving to be autonomous. They want to do things for themselves and to solve their own problems. Often adults want children to be compliant and obedient. They may feel threatened when children say, "I want to do it my way." Others feel frightened by what might happen when children are allowed to do what they want. It is important that children develop a sense that they can do things for themselves and that they be given the opportunity to grow in independence.

Someone Who Understands Child Development

You should have a good knowledge of how children develop during middle childhood. You need to know what children are like at each stage of development throughout the elementary years. What are their physical abilities? What are they capable of learning? What do these children need? How do they form their identity and acquire moral values?

It is important to be aware of the causes of behavior so you can better understand why a particular child responds the way he does. Why does one child go along willingly with the group and another want to be alone? Why are the six-year-olds in your group suddenly rebelling against your ideas or directions? Why are some children easy to get along with some days, but impossible on others? To understand the "whys" of behavior, you need to know the emotional stresses most children go through at various stages of childhood.

When you do understand child development, it is easier to realize that often just the passage of time will change behavior. In other words, they are just going through an expected phase in their development. Soon it will change as they move into the next stage. Beyond that, what behaviors may create problems for children themselves? What are the things that make it difficult for them to have friends or to accomplish what they want to do? Then, and this is the hard part, how can you help each child change his behavior for more mature actions? A knowledge of development will help you find the answers.

You need knowledge of child development to understand how to provide guidance and control in positive ways. How you control a toddler is very different from how you treat a nine-year-old. The toddler needs clear, firm limits to protect her from harm. The nine-year-old must feel empowered to control her own behavior. Therefore, you allow as

Children are encouraged to work independently, but an adult is available to help when needed.

much freedom as possible while teaching her to set her own limits. It is a subtle kind of guidance that respects the child's desire to be competent.

Understanding development is basic to planning any activities in school-age child care. You need to know what children are capable of doing or learning. With that knowledge you can plan age-appropriate activities at which children are likely to succeed. Sometimes the children themselves have ideas for projects that are way beyond their capabilities. You must guide them to choose things they can do while challenging them to progress to the next level of developmental abilities.

Someone Who Is a Good Role Model

Although parents still continue to be important, school-age children will be looking to you as a model. They watch what you do and listen to your words. They sometimes imitate you as they develop their own standards for behavior. Therefore, you should have the characteristics you want children to have. Honesty, dependability, fairness, and trustworthiness are some of the words you might consider. You could add flexibility, caring, tolerance, and patience. You could also include a happy disposition and optimistic outlook.

Whenever possible, child care groups should have both male and female leaders. The majority of elementary school teachers are female. Boys spend a large part of their day without a male role model. When these children are being raised by single mothers, they are further deprived. A male leader in child care can help to fill the gap. Girls, too, need male child care workers to help them develop their own identities in relation to males. Both girls and boys need both genders to help them learn to trust adults outside their own home.

Someone Who Has Lots of Interests

You should know a lot about many things. Your own curiosity and interests should lead you to seek out information you can share with children. They will be fascinated by what you know about stars, electricity, dinosaurs, or many other topics. Know also where to look for answers to their questions. Know how to find information in your local library and have some ideas about what is available in your community. You can also help children to use the Internet for research on subjects that interest them. When you share children's excitement about learning, you encourage rather than discourage their own desire to discover.

You should be able to do a lot of things. Any skills you have can be shared. If you are adept at woodworking, you can teach children how to use tools. If you know how to knit or crochet, children can learn those skills as well. If you do not have many skills, find out how you can develop some. You can read about how to do some of these things. There are many "how to" books that will help you. You can also learn from someone who already has these skills.

You should be willing to learn from children. Often there is more than one way of doing things. A child may show you a way you would not have thought of yourself. But you have to be willing to consider alternatives rather than feeling there is one absolute right way. Many children have information and skills they can share with the group. Be willing to listen to children and provide opportunities for others to listen as well.

What characteristics do men bring to a child care program?

Someone Who Allows Freedom While Setting Limits

School-age children are trying to move from dependence on adults to independence. Consequently, they need the freedom to make their own decisions, and to set their own rules. This freedom bolsters their self-esteem. You have to be willing to give up or share control when it is appropriate. For instance, you may want to set rules that involve safety but allow them to write their own code of conduct in the group.

On the other hand, when limits are needed, you have to be able to set them firmly and consistently. You have to be able to say "no" and mean it. That is not always as easy as it sounds. Children test how far they can go before you stop them, and they want to feel secure in the knowledge that you will not let them go too far. You should be clear that it is not all right to run around the pool area, for example. Explain why the rule is necessary, then enforce it. You will gain their respect and trust.

Sometimes you have to balance individual freedoms with group rights. One child cannot be allowed to work at a noisy project alone when the group is listening to a story. If a group of children wants to play with blocks, one child cannot be allowed to take all the blocks. However, other times individual rights must be considered. Some children need to have exclusive use of materials or space for a period of time. Others want to be able to choose another child as a partner for an activity. You need a great deal of sensitivity to children to decide when to meet individual or group needs.

Someone Who Has Good Communication Skills

Communication includes both the ability to convey messages and to listen. You should be able to do both well. When you give children directions, they should be stated clearly. There should be no ambiguity about your meaning. "You have five minutes to finish what you are doing before snack time" is a clear statement. "It will be snack time in a few minutes" leaves room for confusion. What is a few minutes? Five? Three? Ten? You should also be able to express your feelings honestly. "I don't like it when you call me names" lets a child know exactly how you feel. In addition, good communication skills involve the ability to write in an organized, concise manner. You may need to write out information for children, for parents, or for other staff members.

The other side of communication is the willingness to listen. Children often need to talk about school, their families, or their friends. You should be willing to listen and be interested in what they have to say. Children are not the only ones who appreciate a good listener. Parents and other staff members occasionally need a "friendly ear." There is one last reminder about communication. It is important when you work with children not to talk down to them. Use language that is appropriate for their level of understanding.

Someone Who Can Guide Children in Social Problem Solving

Children without social skills do not have friends, and that often leads to either aggressive or passive behaviors. These are the children who become bullies or sit quietly in the background alone. They need help to change their behaviors so they can make and keep friends. A sensitive adult can help these children understand what is preventing them from achieving their goals or making friends.

The most effective ways to help children learn the techniques that allow them to have friends include discussing strategies in small groups and modeling friendships among the adults. Individual children can be coached. You can review the behaviors that led to the child's being excluded and then suggest alternative behaviors. Encourage the child to practice the behaviors, and then evaluate the results. Sometimes it even helps to set up a private signal system, such as a hand sign, a word, or a phrase. If aggressive behavior has prevented the child from being part of a group, signal him to remind him to try an alternate method. Conflict resolution is discussed further in Chapter 7.

Someone Who Enjoys Physical Activity

You should like to play active games and sports with children. Children who attend elementary school spend a large part of their day sitting down. When they come to child care, they need to be involved in activities that allow them to move around. They want to be able to play games outdoors, climb, run, jump, skate, or do whatever else is available. Both you and the children will get a great deal of pleasure doing some of these together. That takes a lot of energy and good health on your part.

What do you think the caregiver is saying to this child?

Someone Who Cares about Families

All children you work with are part of a family. As described in Chapter 3, these families will have many distinct characteristics. They may be like your own family or very different. It is up to you to get to know family members. Find out what they are like and what they want for their children. Become familiar with their cultural values and the standards they set for their family, then be supportive and avoid criticizing them. Find ways to strengthen their role as parents. You should see child care as a family service, not just a place for children.

You should be the kind of person parents can talk to. If you are young and have not had children yourself, you may find this difficult. But remember, what parents probably want most is an indication that you know their children and care about them. They want to hear what their children did during the day and how their children are getting along. Sometimes they may want to talk about their children's problems. Do not feel you have to have solutions but just be willing to listen. Often it is enough just to listen to a parent talk about the difficulties of working and having time for children. They do not always want advice, just understanding.

Caregivers should have a good relationship with parents.

Someone Who Understands the Role of a Caregiver

You are both a parent and a teacher when you work in an after-school program. Your job has aspects of both relationships. At times your role is to be a listener. When children arrive at child care, they may need someone to talk to about their day or to discuss problems. At other times you become a disciplinarian who sets limits or administers appropriate consequences when limits are overstepped. You have to see that they get their homework done. These are things a parent does. At other times you become an instructor. In the course of a day's activities, you will often teach them some of the same things they learn in school. They need help with math concepts when they work on projects. They may need help reading a recipe while cooking a snack. You may encourage them to pursue their interest in astronomy, then praise their accomplishments. You explain instructions when they play a game. Your role, therefore, is a combination of teacher and parent but is also different. Your primary role is to see that children are well cared for while their parents are at work.

Someone Who Is Able to Work as Part of a Team

You should be able to get along with other adults as well as you do with children. Other staff members within your center depend on you or have to coordinate their activities with yours. Therefore, you have to be willing to share responsibilities, space, and materials. Sometimes you have to be ready to do more than is expected of you. You should see working with children as a profession, not just a job. When you do, you will respect fellow workers and be respected by them.

Being part of a team may also mean working with elementary school personnel. This can be difficult because caregivers often seem to be invisible, not seen as part of the school. When your center is within a school system, you are likely to be housed on the school grounds. You will have to work out the arrangements for sharing indoor and outdoor space. You may have to order materials through the school office. In order to foster a good working relationship, initiate ways to inform school personnel about your program. Let the principal know about any special activities. Offer to put up a display of children's artwork. Talk to parents at a PTA meeting. Get to know the teachers and inform them of children's activities in child care. A healthy relationship with school personnel is worth the effort it takes to establish and maintain.

Education and Experience

Each child care center will have its own requirements for staff members. Criteria for employment are usually based on guidelines mandated by local or state licensing regulations as well as by the funding sources that support the program. In addition, each situation will have demands based on the needs of the program or the children to be served. In general two broad areas of education and experience are usually required in school-age child care.

This caregiver uses visual clues to teach quantity.

Some center directors look for personnel who have strong backgrounds in early child-hood education. Staff members must be knowledgeable in the development of young children. Directors also want people who have expertise and experience in planning a curriculum for "school-agers." Many caregivers who fit these requirements have completed courses in early childhood education and have worked in preschool programs. In addition, they may have had the opportunity to work with five- or six-year-olds. More and more colleges and universities are offering courses in school-age child care.

Other directors seek personnel who have strong backgrounds in recreation. These staff members know a lot of games suitable to this age level. Staff members should be aware of activities that are safe for young children. Caregivers with this kind of background probably have taken courses in physical education and recreation. They may have had experience supervising playground situations or working in summer camps.

As you look at these two areas of background and experience, it probably occurs to you that a good caregiver needs both. You are absolutely right. It would certainly be ideal if that were so. In most child care situations, however, the problem is resolved by hiring staff who have skills that complement one another. In each group one person may have an early childhood education background and one comes from recreation programs.

To further achieve an ideal staff balance in a child care program, it would be necessary to have a staff that is comparable ethnically to the surrounding community. It also helps to have people of different age levels. A staff member over the age of 30 who has had children will bring a different perspective to the care of children than a 20-year-old.

By now you should have a picture of the kind of person who will make a good teacher or caregiver of school-age children. Let us take one last look at the role of a caregiver in children's development.

The Caregiver's Role in Children's Development

In general terms, your role as caregiver is to foster all aspects of children's development. The ways in which you do that have been implied by the description of characteristics needed for the job. However, look at it in another way. Children have specific needs; your job is to help fulfill them.

- Children need security; you provide a secure environment.
- Children need to trust themselves and others; you show you can be trusted and that you trust them.
- Children need to be independent; you allow freedom within limits.
- Children need to develop interests; you encourage and foster those interests.
- Children need a positive self-image; you appreciate their similarities and differences.
- Children need to feel competent; you provide opportunities for them to be successful.
- Children need to acquire values; you offer a positive role model for them to imitate.
- Children need to belong to a group; you include each child and encourage friendships.
- Children need to solve their own problems; you allow them to solve their problems but help when needed.

As you can see, having a part in the development of young children is an awesome task. But should you choose this as a career, you will find it is never boring, for you are constantly challenged. You will find that children force you to grow in order to keep up with their demands. It is certainly a job that will keep you learning for many years into the future.

Ethical Considerations

As an early childhood educator, whether you are experienced or just starting out, you will be faced with situations that call for a difficult decision. For example, you suspect that a child in your class is being exposed to sexually explicit experiences. Or a fellow teacher is taking home paper and paint to use with her own child. How do you decide what the right way is to respond to either of these situations or even whether to do anything at all? Your own personality or personal attributes will affect how you react to situations, how you think, and what you feel. Early childhood educators tend to be caring, empathetic people who try to be fair. The trouble is that these qualities are not always enough to guide you when you are faced with ethical dilemmas. Your values also play a part in helping to decide what to do. Values are the qualities that people believe to be intrinsically desirable and that they strive to achieve in themselves. Personal values are the basis for professional values. However, not everyone has the same values, and others may not understand the choices you make. A good example is the dilemma you face when a parent asks you to discipline her child in a way that is counter to your values. You may truly believe your way is the right way, but the parent may have just as strong a conviction.

Your sense of morality also affects your decisions. Morality is the perception of what is good or right. Morality also includes beliefs about how people should behave and the kind of obligations they have to one another. During the early years children are taught by their parents or their religion that it is wrong to lie or to steal and that it is right to be truthful and treat others kindly. This becomes the core of their moral sense as adults.

However, as professionals caregivers need another standard by which to decide how to resolve problems. They need a code of ethics that outlines responsibilities in ways that everyone can agree on. Ethics is the study of right, wrong, duty, and obligation. Ethics and morality are closely related and in fact are often used interchangeably, but ethics implies a conscious deliberation regarding moral choices.

NAEYC has developed a Code of Ethical Conduct that "offers guidelines for responsible behavior and sets forth a common basis for resolving the principal ethical dilemmas encountered in early childhood care and education" (Feeney & Freeman, 1999). The code focuses on the daily interactions with children from birth through age 8 and their families in preschools, child care centers, kindergartens, and primary classrooms. The code consists of four sections, each addressing a particular area of professional relationships. The sections are (1) children, (2) families, (3) colleagues, and (4) community and society. Each section addresses responsibilities, ideals, and principles. The intent is to portray exemplary professional practice and define practices that are required, prohibited, and permitted.

A sample of paragraphs from Section I: Ethical responsibilities to children, will give you a sense of the content of the Code:

> Childhood is a unique and valuable stage in the life cycle. Our paramount responsibility is to provide safe, healthy, nurturing, and responsive settings for children. We are committed to supporting children's development, respecting individual differences, helping children learn to live and work cooperatively, and promoting health, self-awareness, competence, self-worth, and resiliency.

Ideals

I-1.1 To be familiar with the knowledge base of early childhood care and education and to keep current through continuing education and in-service training.

I-1.2 To base program practices upon current knowledge in the field of child development and related disciplines and upon particular knowledge of each child.

I-1.3 To recognize and respect the uniqueness and the potential of each child.

I-1.4 To appreciate the special vulnerability of children.

The full text of the Code of Ethical Conduct can be found in *Ethics and the Early Childhood Educator* listed in the references at end of this chapter.

Summary

School-age children have some specific needs. To be trusted, to be independent, to have challenges, to be accepted for who they are, and to be successful are a few.

Many different titles are used to designate the adults who spend time with children in after-school programs: teacher, caregiver, guide, recreational supervisor, counselor, leader, aide, assistant, and child care worker. All should be acceptable.

Those who care for school-age children should be people who

- like school-age children
- understand child development
- are good role models
- have a lot of interests
- allow freedom while setting limits
- have good communication skills
- can guide children in social problem solving
- enjoy physical activity
- care about families
- understand the role of caregiver
- are able to work as part of a team

Child care programs may require personnel who have a background in either early childhood education or recreation. Both are helpful. All should have knowledge of what is developmentally appropriate for children.

In general, the role of a caregiver with school-age children is to foster all aspects of children's development. Caregivers sometimes have to make decisions that require them to consider their own values or sense of what is right or wrong. NAEYC has developed a Code of Ethical Conduct that offers guidelines for responsible behavior.

Key Terms

caregiver	morality
developmentalist	recreational supervisor
educare	values
ethics	

Student Activities

1. Visit two different kinds of school-age programs. Choose, for instance, one that is operated by a city recreation department and one that is part of a corporation. In what ways are the children's activities the same or different in these two programs?
2. Observe several child care teachers as they interact with children. How do their styles differ? Describe the one you would use as your own model for interactions with children.
3. Interview the director of a school-age child care program. What are the qualities he or she looks for when hiring new staff members?
4. In class do "Quick Writes." Be prepared to share them with classmates when finished. Spend one minute responding to "One teacher was my favorite because _____." Highlight three main characteristics and then prioritize them. Finally, state why the first priority item is the most important.
5. Write an advertisement for the perfect school-age caregiver.

Review Questions

1. List the reasons child care workers need a knowledge of child development.
2. Describe the qualities of a good role model for school-age children.
3. This chapter suggests a child care teacher should have a lot of interests. Explain the reasons for that statement.
4. Effective communication has two parts. What are they?
5. Describe ways to foster your relationship with parents.
6. Why is it important that caregivers be able to work together as a team?
7. What kinds of education and experience should be required to qualify as a caregiver?

Case Study

Alberto is nine and speaks with a slight accent because his home language is Spanish. He is often the butt of teasing and does not seem to know how to make friends. He frequently sits by himself in the reading area or at the science table. The caregivers in the group tend to leave him alone because he isn't creating any problems, but they do intervene when the other children tease him. They send the tormentors to a quiet place for a time-out. One caregiver really wants to help Alberto make at least one friend but doesn't know how.

1. How could you help Alberto react in such a way as to stop the teasing?
2. What would be a more effective way to help the teasers to change their behavior?
3. What are three things you could do to help Alberto make a friend?

References

Daniel, J. (1995). Advancing the care and education paradigm: A case for developmentalists. *Young Children, 50*(2), 2.

Feeney, S., & Freeman, N. K. (1999). *Ethics and the early childhood educator: Using the NAEYC Code*. Washington, DC: NAEYC.

Suggested Readings

Bender, J., Flatter, C. H., & Sorrentino, J. M. (2000). *Half a childhood: Quality programs for out-of-school hours* (2nd ed.). Nashville: School-Age Notes.

California State Department of Education. (1994). *Kid's time, a school-age program guide*. Sacramento: Author.

Elicker, J., & Fortner-Wood, C. (1995). Adult-child relationships in early childhood programs. *Young Children, 51*(1), 69–78.

Gratz, R., & Boulton, P. (1996). Erikson and early childhood educators: Looking at ourselves and our profession developmentally. *Young Children, 51*(5), 74–78.

Kaiser, B., & Rasminsky, J. S. (2003). Opening the culture door. *Young Children, 58*(4), 53–56.

Musson, S. (1994). *School-age care, theory and practice*. Don Mills, Ont.: Addison-Wesley.

Stapen, C. (1988). Caring for your child-care person. *Working Woman, 13,* 148.

Whitebook, M., Howes, C., Phillips, D., & Pemberton, C. (1989). Who cares? Child care teachers and the quality of care in America. *Young Children, 45*(1), 41–45.

CHAPTER 2

The Children

Objectives

After completing this chapter, the student should be able to:

- Discuss the ways in which children develop friendships
- State the factors that are important to children's sense of self
- State the ways child care leaders can help children form friendships and develop a healthy sense of self

CAREGIVER PROFILE

Yumiko is 43 and works as a playground supervisor in an elementary school where she has been for four years. She has previously done a variety of jobs, such as selling ladies clothing and making jewelry. She got her present job when her son started school. She walked onto the campus, and the child care director asked her if she wanted a job. She immediately said "Yes" and has worked there ever since.

Yumiko comes from a family with four children in which she was third to the oldest. One of her siblings had some problems, and she tried to help. In her present school setting she is very aware of children who have problems. She sees that when problems occur in the classroom, the child is sent to the office. She worries that this does nothing to help resolve the problems.

One of the things she enjoys about her job is being able to help children. When she has to "bench" a child on the playground for some reason, she tries to help that child find better ways of behaving. When children are teasing each other, she has them talk and find other ways of getting along. Her lifelong interest in helping children with their behavior has led to a dream of becoming a psychologist or perhaps a special education teacher. Right now she is taking one step at a time and wants to finish her associate degree.

Being a parent has helped Yumiko to understand that children behave the way they do for a reason. "If you can understand the reason, you can help the child change." She feels her assets for working with children are that she is sensitive, caring, and firm but gentle. She says the children also know that she is honest and fair.

In thinking about the future, she feels her biggest challenge will be to find the right job.

Development of Self

Middle childhood is an important period when children develop a sense of who they are, what they can do, and how others perceive them. It is a time when the focus of their daily lives is on school and their self-esteem is closely tied to school success. Most children enter kindergarten eager to learn and are optimistic in their evaluation of self and their expectations for academic success (Stipek & MacIver, 1989). When they first begin reading and writing, they have little idea of how successful they will be and cannot accurately assess their own competency. Young children assume they are successful because they put

"Mom, me, Dad, and Rascal, my dog." Carissa, age 6

a lot of effort into their activities. As they get older and more experienced, they become more realistic. They learn that different people have different abilities, enabling them to achieve at varying levels. They may find they are good at reading but not so capable at math.

A second way children develop a sense of self is through their feelings of power. One source of power is their status with their peers. They measure and compare themselves to others. Are they liked and looked up to? Are they similar to their peers in appearance, dress, and abilities? If they answer in the affirmative, they feel more powerful. A second source of power is inner control over their own behavior, in other words, being able to behave in ways that their parents and society view favorably. They also have good self-esteem if they are accomplishing their goals and expanding their skills.

At times school-age children test their power and their place in a group by bullying others. **Bullying** is unprovoked aggression that is intended to inflict injury or discomfort on the victim and can be either direct or indirect. Boys more often use a direct form: hitting, teasing, threatening, humiliating, mobbing, or taunting. Girls tend to engage in indirect methods such as gossiping, spreading rumors, or enforcing social isolation. A recent survey by the World Health Organization reported that 30 percent of students said they bullied others or were the target of bullies themselves (Bowman, 2001). Students who engage in bullying behaviors often seem to care little for the feelings of their victims.

Children who are victims of bullying may be physically different from their peers in size, race, and in the way they dress. They often feel helpless, anxious, insecure, cautious, and suffer from low self-esteem. They may be labeled with various insensitive names such as sissy or dork, may not have friends, and may become socially isolated. The effects of bullying carry over to their schoolwork where they have trouble concentrating and have poor academic performance. Bullies, themselves, are also hurt by the behavior. They do not learn to manage their emotions or how to cope when difficulties arise. They fail to develop empathy for others and don't learn how to have real relationships with other people. Instead they continue to blame others for their problems and never take responsibility for their own behavior.

The best way for children to deal with a bully is stand up to him or her or even sometimes to turn the situation into a joke. The bully sees that his behavior is not getting the result he might have wanted. If the victim is unable to stand up to the bully, adults need to intervene and stop the behavior immediately, followed by increased supervision to stop potential incidents before they begin. Add activities to the curriculum that promote individual competencies, self-confidence, and emotional management techniques. Some of the activities outlined in Chapter 7, such as "Fighting Fair," "Getting to Know You," and "Y'All Come Up," are a few of the examples. It is also important for caregivers to emphasize respecting others, using their own behavior as a role model. Finally, collaboration with parents will help to reinforce the antibullying message.

At times, aggressive behavior turns into "rough and tumble play" and is particularly prevalent in boys. To the outsider, the attacking, teasing, threatening, pushing, or wrestling looks the same as hostile aggression. Caregivers can observe signs that distinguish rough and tumble play from hostile aggression. Usually the children have positive facial expressions or may be laughing. They do not use their full force and they do not hit hard. They push just hard enough to make an impact on the other child. They can be observed to alternate roles, each being on top or being the aggressor. At the end of the play, they happily go on together to participate in other activities.

A final standard by which school-age children evaluate themselves is in terms of good or bad behavior. In Chapter 6 Lawrence Kohlberg describes moral behavior in middle childhood as being nice to others, behaving in ways that others approve of, and obeying rules or laws. Teachers and peers use these standards to label children as good/nice or bad/not nice. Reputations acquired during middle childhood may affect an individual's behavior into adolescence and adulthood.

Race may also play a part in how children perceive themselves and others. Holmes (1995) studied kindergarten children in several schools in southern California. She found that the content of children's self-concepts and the way children perceive themselves and convey information about themselves is linked to their cognitive maturation. At the kindergarten level, children concentrated on specific, observable characteristics: gender, skin color, eye color, and language. The children described themselves by saying, "I have brown skin" or "My eyes are brown." According to Holmes, older children at a higher cognitive level will portray themselves as having personal preferences or personality traits—"I'm pretty good at sports and have a lot of friends."

Holmes found that socialization experiences were important factors affecting children's subjective feelings about themselves. Children who had repeated negative experiences with others from a group different from their own may incorrectly assume that the negativism was due to their being African American or because they spoke Spanish rather than English, for example.

In the same way, when children had limited interactions with others from a different group from their own and those interactions were negative, they tended to categorize all persons from that group as being alike. They saw the group as homogeneous even though their experience had been with only a few members. One negative encounter led to a wrong conclusion about the group, thus giving rise to stereotyping and prejudice.

"This is me." Sarah, age 6

Implications for Child Care Staff Members

Children's feelings about themselves develop not in a vacuum but rather within the context of their daily experiences and their contacts with others. Many factors influence the development of self-esteem and social competence. According to Katz and McClellan (1997), these factors are "the children's attachments to their primary caregivers within the family; the modeling, guidance, and support of parents and teachers; the opportunity to observe peers and interact with them; and children's relationships with non-family adults involved in their care and education and those involved in the neighborhood and community in which they spend a large proportion of their time" (p. 13). Caregivers can encourage children's positive feelings about themselves by:

- Providing authentic feedback to children rather than empty praise. Help them evaluate their own skills realistically and to set feasible goals for themselves. "You were having a hard time learning to use the saw, but you figured out how to do it. Look how well you were able to cut a straight line for the side of your birdhouse."
- Providing supportive intervention to children who have been rejected or are having difficulty gaining acceptance by their peers. Offer help to upgrade skills that bring acceptance in the classroom or playground. Teach children how to be successful. "I

Snack time can be an opportunity for socializing.

can see that you were hurt that you weren't chosen for their team. Suppose I help you practice so that you will be able to play better." Or "Not everyone can be a good basketball player. Remember how great you are when we put on plays."

- Accepting children's feelings rather than deny or belittle their importance. Be a sensitive listener. "I can see you're pretty mad about something today. If you feel like talking about it, I'm ready to listen."
- Providing positive encounters with persons from different racial or ethnic backgrounds.
- Scheduling adult visitors who can talk about their culture or experiences. Ask an adult to present a craft or music activity representative of their culture.
- Encouraging interracial groups to work together on activities that require cooperation and compromise. Invite children from an ethnically different child care group to participate in an activity such as a swim meet, a game, or a picnic. Expect each group to work on planning for the activity.

Peer Groups: "The Society of Children"

Beginning in the preschool period, when children first understand the meaning of the word *friend*, the need to have friends becomes increasingly important. As children's cognitive abilities change, so does their concept of friendship and its purpose. At first there is a mutual dependence on friends to share activities, carry on conversations, and provide support for attempts at independence from parents. Young school-age children choose friends who are the same gender, have similar interests, and share similar values. There is very little cross-gender fraternization and, in fact, even some antagonism toward members of the opposite sex. Girls pal around with girls, tell each other secrets, watch movies, and talk on the telephone. The leader of a group of girls is chosen for her managerial skills, for having new ideas, and for being thoughtful, friendly, and organized (Edwards, 1994). Boys get together to skateboard, play video games, share a hobby, or compete in organized sports.

Older school-age children rely on friends for intimate conversations about problems, dreams, and expectations. Friends are seen as people who will remain loyal and can be relied on when life is difficult. The circle of friends gradually becomes smaller as children become more selective about the qualities of a friend. Often, by age 10 both boys and girls have a single best friend, although this exclusivity tends to occur more frequently with girls. By the end of middle childhood, many girls have only one best friend on whom they depend for all their social needs (Gilligan, Murphy, & Tappan, 1990). By age 9 everyone knows who is best friends with whom and would not think of trying to disrupt the pair.

This fraternity of friend relationships makes it difficult for children who have not found a companion. It is also heart wrenching when one of a pair becomes more mature than the other and moves on to other alliances. The deserted partner experiences difficulty in finding a new companion.

Middle childhood is also a period when children form themselves into cliques, clubs, or gangs with the primary purpose of gaining independence from adults. Each group has its own vocabulary, dress code, rules, and activities (Opie & Opie, 1959). The group provides a mutual support system and a sense of solidarity as children learn to sharpen

School-age children choose friends who have the same interests.

their social skills. Those who belong build self-esteem, but those who are excluded have difficulties socially and often academically as well.

Adler and Adler (1998) followed 200 elementary-age children in their community. They found that children were very aware of the importance of cliques and the power they give the members who belong. Some of the influence is positive, helping children learn appropriate social behavior and the consequences of misbehavior. Clique members tend to have similar characteristics. During middle childhood they have similar interests or come from similar backgrounds. When the cliques continue into high school, they are identified as the jocks, the nerds, the druggies, the artists, or the intellectuals. Cliques provide children with a social identity and a sense of belonging.

Adler and Adler (1998) found that cliques can be extremely limiting, prescribing very specific ways of behaving, dressing, or associating with others outside the group. Those outside the group can be derided for wearing the wrong clothes, being of a different race or religion, or being too studious. They may even carry on "negative campaigns" against chosen targets, heaping verbal abuse and humiliation on them. In order to stay in the group and be accepted, as well as gain the feelings of power that result, members go along with this behavior. The consequence is that bigotry and racism become part of children's value system as well as increase their need to conform to standards that may conflict with values they have been taught at home.

In the case of gangs, the purpose may be even more negative. Not only do gangs operate outside the realm of adults, but they may even be antisocial. The result is that members engage in vandalism or criminal activities that put them in legal jeopardy.

The need to form groups may be observed in the child care setting as well as in the community. The number of individuals involved is usually smaller than in school or in the neighborhood, but the same dynamics can be seen. Friendships form and break up. Groups congregate and then change. But the need to belong remains strong in all children, with those who are not included feeling left out and unhappy.

Some children seem to make friends easily and are sought out while others find it extremely difficult. Certain social skills are necessary and may be in the formative stage during middle childhood. The first is the ability to understand that others may have views different from their own. Younger children are egocentric, believing that they are the center of the universe and that friends are there to satisfy them. "He's my friend because he plays with me" or "He's my friend because he shares his toys with me." Older children begin to realize that others have needs and feelings, too. In order to make and maintain a friendship, they must make compromises to accommodate the other's needs or feelings. They may have to negotiate whether they want to go to a party or just hang out at the mall if they want to be together.

A second essential skill for making friends is the ability to recognize that others have separate identities and feelings of their own. Although children tend to choose friends who are like themselves, each has different characteristics and ways of reacting. It is a difficult lesson to learn that sometimes a best friend can be cross and want to be alone.

Finally, children have to understand that each encounter with others is part of a relationship. They tend to isolate incidents and fail to see the importance of their behavior in specific situations. If they lash out at another child in anger, they do not immediately recognize that this behavior will have consequences for their ability to form a friendship with that person. They must learn that in order to have friends they must curb certain behaviors.

Implications for Child Care Staff Members

Teachers and caregivers in after-school programs can have a significant impact on children's ability to make friends and be part of a group.

- Allow children opportunities to spend time with a friend without the pressure of having to engage in an activity. Let them "just hang out" in a corner of the room or an outdoor area.
- Encourage children to take another's point of view. Ask "How do you think he feels when you call him that name?"
- Help children recognize their own psychological characteristics and that others can accept those qualities. An adult who says "Thanks for helping me understand that sometimes you just want to be alone" does that.
- Nurture children's ability to examine the basis for friendships. Lead discussions about what makes a good friend and how to maintain friendships.
- Help individual children develop a plan to change behaviors that interfere with friendships.
- Discuss alternative ways of behaving, encourage the child to test out the behavior, and then evaluate the results. Give honest appraisal and rewards for positive outcomes.

"We're best friends forever."

"When you asked how you could help rather than just pushing into his activity, he made a place for you."

* Discourage attempts to exclude individual children from activities. Suggest ways each can contribute.

Overview of Developmental Stages

The following summary of typical developmental characteristics of children during middle childhood should provide further help in understanding the children in your care. However, the list is merely a prediction of when these behaviors will occur. There will be wide variations from child to child, with some behaviors happening earlier in some children and later in others.

Five- to Seven-Year-Old Children

Family Relationships

* are more independent of parents, but still need rules
* need assurance of being loved
* have a sense of duty and take on family responsibilities
* develop a conscience

Peers

* begin to see others' points of view
* rely on their peer group for self-esteem
* criticize differences in others
* have two or three best friends
* exhibit little interaction between boys and girls
* can learn to share and take turns
* can participate in organized games

School

* want approval from teacher for achievement
* are eager to learn and be successful in school
* are influenced by teacher's attitudes and values

Emotions

* begin to inhibit aggression and resolve problems with words
* use humor, often expressed in riddles, practical jokes, or nonsense
* learn to postpone immediate rewards for delayed gratification
* become sensitive to what others think
* become concerned with issues of right and wrong or fair and unfair

Thinking

* are usually clear about differences between fantasy and reality
* can sustain interest for long periods of time

- give more thought and judgment to decisions
- have a good memory for concrete ideas and can remember two things for short periods of time
- can understand and abide by rules
- have a natural curiosity and often ask "why" questions

Language

- learn that words and pictures represent real objects
- can remember and relate past and present events
- sometimes use language aggressively
- understand more language than they use in their communication
- may tease others whose language is different from their own

Physical Development

- are developing at different rates, girls faster than boys
- have good small-muscle and eye-hand coordination
- are able to handle simple tools and materials
- have a high energy level

Eight- to Ten-Year-Old Children

Family Relationships

- need parental guidance and support for school achievements
- rely on parents for help in assuming personal and social responsibilities

Peers

- are overly concerned about conforming to peer-imposed rules
- are competitive
- become antagonistic toward the opposite gender, leading to quarrels or teasing
- develop gender differences in interests
- form same-gender cliques
- spend a lot of energy in physical game playing

School

- are more competitive in school activities
- still need teacher approval and attention
- believe academic achievement is important

Emotions

- react to feelings of others and are sensitive to criticism
- look for friendly relationships with adults
- make value judgments about own behavior and set standards for self
- are aware of the importance of belonging
- exhibit strong conformation to gender role

- are independent and self-sufficient
- begin to develop moral values

Thinking

- are capable of sustained interest; can make plans, then carry them out
- can begin to think logically about practical problems
- begin to understand cause and effect
- understand abstract concepts such as time and the value of money

Language

- exhibit abilities to use language or to read vary widely
- use language to communicate ideas, spend a lot of time in discussion
- can use more abstract words
- often resort to slang and profanity

Physical Development

- view physical skills as important in determining status and self-concept
- exhibit gender differences; girls are taller, stronger, and more skillful in small-muscle activities
- have a high energy level
- begin a growth spurt in girls toward end of this period
- take responsibility for their own personal hygiene

Eleven- to Thirteen-Year-Old Children

Family Relationships

- ready to make own decisions outside of the family
- aware that parental influence is decreasing
- sometimes rebellious but still need input on family values

Peers

- rely on peer group to model and set standards for behavior
- choose friends based on common interests
- seek information about appropriate gender roles from peers
- may conform rigidly to role assigned by peer group
- place greater importance on team games
- devlop divergent interests based on gender
- may develop crushes and hero worship
- are often self-conscious and may become boisterous to cover anxiety
- are interested in opposite gender; girls are more interested than boys
- are faced with decisions regarding behavior: sex, drugs, and alcohol

School

- worry when in a new school setting
- begin to question adult authority, particularly in school

- often focus on school for social experience
- are reluctant to attend child care; are bored or think they can care for themselves

Emotions

- may lack self-confidence, be shy or introspective
- worry about what others think, especially peers
- may be moody
- may experience great stress caused by physical changes heralding puberty
- develop own value systems, although influenced by peers
- seek self-identity, may result in rebellious behavior

Thinking

- can now move from dependence on concrete thinking to abstract concepts
- can apply logic and solve problems
- can consider more than one solution to problems
- enjoy problem-solving games and puzzles

Language

- have a good command of spoken and written language
- can use language to discuss feelings, thus bringing about self-understanding
- are often argumentative and contradict adults

Physical Development

- Boys begin adolescent growth spurt.
- Adolescent growth peaks in girls, who experience changes in body proportions.
- In girls, secondary gender characteristics develop: breasts, menstruation.
- Early maturing is related to positive self-image.
- Boys have improved motor development and coordination and can excel at sports.
- Girls and boys master physical skills that are necessary for playing games.

Summary

Middle childhood is an important period when children develop a sense of who they are, what they can do, and how others perceive them. Because the focus of their daily lives is school, their self-esteem is closely tied to school success.

A second way children develop a sense of self is in terms of feelings of power. One source of power is their status with their peers. Another is an inner control over their own behavior.

Acceptance by their peers is a third way children refine their sense of self. School-age children can be aggressive as they test their own power and use bullying or teasing to assert their dominance. Children who are often the target of this behavior have a difficult time, further eroding their self-esteem.

The final standard by which school-age children evaluate themselves is in terms of good or bad behavior. Often reputations acquired during middle childhood may affect the individual's behavior into adolescence and adulthood.

Race also plays a part in how children perceive themselves and others. Children first describe themselves in terms of observable characteristics. Socialization experiences are important factors affecting children's subjective feelings about group members.

Negative encounters with persons of a different race or ethnic background can lead to a belief that all persons of that group have similar characteristics. This is the basis for stereotyping and prejudice.

Beginning in the preschool period, when children first learn the meaning of the word *friend,* the need to have a friend becomes increasingly important. Young school-age children choose friends of the same gender and age who have similar interests and values. Older children rely on friends for intimate conversations about problems, dreams, and expectations.

Children usually have one best friend and by age 9 everyone knows who is best friends with whom. Later in middle childhood, children form cliques, clubs, or gangs with the main purpose of gaining independence from adults.

Cliques provide children with a sense of belonging and a feeling of power. Cliques can be limiting in that they prescribe specific ways of dressing or behaving. In the case of gangs, the purpose may be to not only operate outside the realm of adult supervision but even be antisocial. They may engage in illegal activities.

However, the need to form friendships and to belong is strong. In order to make friends, certain skills are necessary: the ability to understand that others have different points of view, the ability to recognize that others have separate identities, and the ability to understand that each encounter is part of a relationship.

Key Terms

bullying	gang
clique	rough and tumble play

Student Activities

1. Observe children on a school playground or in a park. Notice how they group themselves. Are there mixed-gender or single-gender groups? How many children are in each group? What are they playing? Write a short paper describing your observations, relating what you saw to the information in this chapter. Compare your findings with those of your classmates.
2. In small groups, discuss your own perceptions of the following:
   a. an ethnic group different from your own
   b. people who do not speak English
   Describe the experiences that have led you to your perceptions. Were some of your perceptions based on prejudices? What can you do to change your beliefs?
3. Ask the children in your child care group to draw a picture of themselves. Bring the pictures to class. Choose two to share with classmates. Show the pictures and tell what you think the pictures say about the children's self-esteem.

Review Questions

1. Describe the changes that take place in children's assessment of their school achievement.
2. This chapter stated that children derive some of their sense of self through feelings of power. What are the sources of that power?
3. Explain the importance of peers in determining children's sense of self.
4. State three ways in which child care leaders can help children increase their self-esteem.
5. Compare the criteria for choosing friends among young school-age children with those of older children.
6. What is the primary purpose of groups, clubs, and gangs? Are there other purposes?
7. What are the positive aspects of belonging to a clique or group? What are the negatives?
8. List and explain the three skills children need in order to make friends.
9. This chapter suggested that child care staff members allow children opportunities to "just hang out" with a friend. Why is that important?
10. What would you say to a child to achieve the following:
    a. encourage her to take another's point of view
    b. help him recognize his own psychological characteristics
    c. evaluate her attempts to change behaviors that interfere with friendships

Case Study

Justin is an eight-year-old Vietnamese boy who was adopted by his Caucasian parents when he was only three months old. His two older siblings had been born into the family before he was chosen. The siblings are both boys and much larger than Justin, and they are both very involved in school sports. Justin wants to follow in their footsteps but finds it difficult to match their success. In his after-school program, Justin loves to paint and creates some beautiful watercolor paintings, which his caregiver displays on the bulletin board. However, Justin still longs to join in when the other children are playing baseball. He is usually the last one to be chosen for a team and is booed or called names when he strikes out. When this happens, he goes back to the bench and looks like he can hardly keep from crying. He doesn't cry but is reluctant to try again when it is his turn at bat.

1. What do you think are the causes of Justin's lack of confidence in his own abilities? What are some things his caregiver can do to help him feel better about himself?
2. Are there ways the parents can help?
3. What group games could caregivers facilitate that would encourage teamwork and ultimately help Justin feel a valued part of the team?

References

Adler, P. A., & Adler, P. (1998). *Peer power: Preadolescent culture and identity.* Piscataway, NJ: Rutgers University Press.

Bowman, D. H. (2001). *Survey of students documents the extent of bullying.* Education Week on the Web, May 2, 2001.

Edwards, C. P. (1994). Leadership in groups of school-age girls. *Developmental Psychology, 30*(6), 920–927.

Gilligan, C., Murphy, J. M., & Tappan, M. B. (1990). Moral development beyond adolescence. In C. N. Alexander & E. J. Langer (Eds.), *Higher stages of human development* (pp. 208–225). New York: Oxford University Press.

Holmes, R. N. (1995). *How young children perceive race.* Thousand Oaks, CA: Sage.

Katz, L. G., & McClellan, D. E. (1997). *Fostering children's social competence.* Washington, DC: NAEYC.

Kohlberg, L. (1963). Development of children's orientation towards a moral order Part 1: Sequence in the development of moral thought. *Vita Numana, 6,* 11-36.

Opie, I., & Opie, P. (1959). *The lore and language of children.* New York: Clarendon.

Stipek, D. J., & MacIver, D. (1989). Developmental change in children's assessment of intellectual competence. *Child Development, 60,* 521–538.

Web Resources

U.S. Department of Health and Human Services antibullying program. http://www.hhs.gov   In search field, type "antibullying program."

Nemours Foundation for articles on general health and bullying for children and adults. http://kidshealth.org

Information to help parents and teachers to decrease incidents of bullying in group settings. http://www.pta.org   Search for "bullying."

CHAPTER 3

Families: Where Children Are Nurtured

Objectives

After studying this chapter, the student should be able to:

- State changing definitions of a family
- Describe family forms
- Discuss the effects of each family composition on children
- Review the role of caregivers in relation to parents

Angelique is 21 and married with two daughters, ages three years and 11 weeks. She has worked for two years in a child care center that is connected with a hospital. The center services children from infants through school age. Angelique works three days a week for four hours, sometimes in the infant room but most of the time with the second graders. She supervises when the children are outside and works with the children in activities that have been planned by other staff members. She decided to become a school-age caregiver because she loves older children. "I have always been interested in being an elementary teacher. I come from a large and unique family. I have one biological brother, two half-sisters, three half-brothers, and two stepbrothers. I feel having such a large family has helped me realize that I want to teach children." One of the things she likes best about her job is getting involved with the children, especially having conversations with them. She says they are interested in sports as she is, and she also likes to help them think.

When asked what her primary qualities are for working in child care, she said that she is energetic, understanding, and sympathetic. She also says the children respond to her because she likes to have fun with them and encourages them to use their minds. Because she grew up in such a large and diverse family, she feels she has learned to share, and this allows her to work well with her colleagues. In fact, one of the things she likes best about working in this particular center is the relationship with other staff members. She feels they are compatible and work well together.

The Changing Family

Historically, humans have always grouped themselves together in tribes, clans, networks, or families. In her book *Families,* Howard (1978) writes, "The trouble we take to arrange ourselves in some semblance of families is one of the imperishable habits of the human race." Although people continue to group together, as society changes, the definition of family changes. The meaning most widely used by scholars in the past signified parents and their biological children whether dwelling together or not. Legal experts have also stressed the biological relationships but broadened the definition to include any persons related by blood. This definition is becoming less meaningful in today's surrogate parenting situations. Another definition would include a group of kin and others living together day by day. Some contemporary researchers broaden the definition even further. They state that a family is an attitude—an identification with and among a group of individuals who support and nurture one another. Kevin and Elizabeth, whose family portraits appear in this chapter, even included their pets as important members of their families. Families can also be defined by their function. A well-functioning family supports its members in developing their full potential. The family nurtures children in the following five ways (Berger, 2000):

- Meeting basic needs for food, clothes, and shelter
- Encouraging learning through guidance and motivation
- Developing self-esteem by helping children to feel competent
- Nurturing friendships with peers
- Creating an atmosphere of harmony and stability in the home.

When most of us hear the word *family,* we still think first of the nuclear (intact) family or the extended family. The nuclear family is made up of mother, father, and children if any. The extended family has these members plus grandparents, cousins, aunts, and uncles. The number of children who live in extended families has declined. According to the 2000 census, the average family size in the United States is 3.14 members.

The single-parent family is headed by either the father or the mother and is indicative of changes in family composition. In 2002, nearly 14 million children lived in a single-parent household headed by the mother, and almost 3 million lived with the father only. The rapid rise in this type of family is partially due to the number of children born to unmarried women (U.S. Census Bureau, 2002).

Because many divorced couples remarry, many children live in reconstituted, or blended, families. Other terms that describe these families are *recoupled, refamilied,* and *binuclear.* These terms designate families that bring together children of one or both former marriages or associations as well as children born of the new marriage. They are the "his, hers, and our" children.

An increasing number of households include grandparents or are headed by a grandmother or grandfather. In 2002, 5.6 million children were living in a household where a grandparent was present (U.S. Census Bureau, 2002). These adults provide valuable assistance, particularly in families that have experienced a divorce. They can emotionally support children during difficult times, perhaps add some income, and provide child care. In some cases, grandmothers become the only adult in the household if both parents are deceased, incarcerated, or on drugs. One study surveying children in various family configurations found that those living with both grandparents had more behavior problems, such as dependence, disobedience, and aggression. They were also found to have poorer language skills (Hawkins & Eggebeen, 1991).

Another family form that is becoming more visible is the interracial family, where the parents come from different ethnic groups. In the past few decades the number of these marriages has been on the rise. Some people call them "rainbow families" because they mix persons of two or more ethnic groups. In addition, interracial families are created when parents choose to adopt a child from a racial or ethnic group different from their own.

A fairly recent development is the single-gender family composed of gay or lesbian couples or single parents. Some of the children in these relationships are the result of previous marriages to heterosexual partners. More liberal adoption laws have allowed some children to be adopted into these families. Some children have been produced through artificial insemination.

In addition to understanding family forms, it is important to note that existing families change as the members grow and develop or as their circumstances shift. The first

Many children grow up in a household with either their father or their mother.

child may have grown up in a nuclear family, but his sibling is being reared by a single parent. A child whose divorced mother remarries may suddenly find herself with several new siblings. Whatever the form, the family is the first and, therefore, the most important determinant in children's development.

Effect of Home Environment on Children

In the past it was assumed that the optimum environment for children's development was the two-parent family, one in which the father went to work and the mother stayed home to care for the children. However, social scientists are reexamining that idea because fewer families still fit that pattern. In many households both parents are working outside the home.

Children in the United States live under a variety of family environmental circumstances. The following are a few of the latest statistics according to the U.S Census Bureau in 2002:

- 69 percent of children lived with both parents
- 23 percent with only their mother
- 5 percent with only their father
- 8 percent of children lived with a grandparent present

Some research still seems to favor the intact, two-parent family as providing for the optimum development of children (McLanahan, 1997; Simons, 1996). Children who grow up

"Radio, Dad, me, brother, brother, Mom." Kevin, age 5.

with two loving parents who have nurtured them from birth have fewer problems, do better in school, and are less likely to use drugs or get arrested when they are teenagers. Other research indicates that additional factors may influence student achievement, particularly parental expectations (Shim, Fenlenr, & Shim, 2000). The advantages these children enjoy stem from the fact that two adults share child-rearing tasks. Each can support the other parent or even take on tasks that may be difficult for one of them. Two-parent families often have a financial advantage over other family forms. In many, both parents are wage earners, allowing them to provide better housing, health care, and education for their offspring. When the mother is proud of her work, children have a role model for making their own choices in adulthood. All of these positives for the intact family neither guarantee optimum development of children nor eliminate the possibility that other family forms can offer many of the same benefits.

Children who attend child care have some advantages as well. They can participate in supervised activities and have new experiences. They can make friends within a wider circle than is available in their neighborhood. They learn to get along with adults other than their parents. Children who stay by themselves after school may also feel they have advantages. Many relish the freedom to come home and do what they want. They grow in independence and self-esteem as they master emergency situations or do household chores.

In spite of the advantages, there remains concern over the tremendous stress that many working parents feel. Their most frequently voiced complaint is that they never have enough time. They do not have enough time for housework, to spend with the children, or for each other. Fatigue and stress may cause family friction or result in adults taking out their frustrations on the children. Children may feel isolated because the adults have little energy left for being parents. Children may also feel abandoned or that their parents care more about work than about them. If children do not attend child care but stay home alone after school, they may feel lonely and sometimes frightened.

When parents divorce, another kind of stress is added to children's lives. Approximately 50 percent of children under the age of 18 are affected by divorce. This can have a profound and lasting impact on their behavior. These children may exhibit acting-out behaviors such as aggression or conflicts with authorities. Acting out may also be seen as withdrawal from contacts with others, depression, or anxiety. In addition to changes in behavior, children of divorce often perform less well academically. Their grades go down, and they are less motivated to achieve. A few studies show that boys have more difficulty adjusting to divorce than girls, but multiple-gender studies find that boys do less well than girls only in their social adjustment (Amato & Rezac, 1994). There are also some age-related differences in children's development. Preschoolers are more concerned about maintaining relationships with both parents. In middle childhood, children tend to assume responsibility for the divorce and have unrealistic expectations of their own ability to affect their parents' behavior. They may believe they can get their parents back together again. High school children tend to relate the divorce to their own identity and their ability to maintain relationships and make wise life choices (Kurdek, 1989).

However, if contact is maintained with both parents and if income and living conditions remain stable, these children do as well as those in an intact family. The reality is that in many divorce situations, the mother becomes the custodial parent, and family income is often far lower than during the marriage.

Children of mothers who have never been married can raise well-adjusted children, but the odds are against fatherless children. These children are deprived of the special kind of child rearing fathers can provide. Kyle Pruett (1987), a professor of psychiatry at Yale University and author of *The Nurturing Father,* says that whether roughhousing with a five-year-old or disciplining a delinquent teen, fathers have a different parenting style. Boys and girls both need fathers. Boys need a role model. Girls need a father with whom they can practice heterosexual relationships.

Probably the most serious difficulty for the single-parent family, especially when headed by the mother, is the low economic status. Women still receive lower salaries than men, often causing these families to live at or below poverty level. Single parents often suffer from "role overload" as they try to nurture their children, offer sensible discipline, and provide adequate financial support. Stressors increase with more than one child or when illness strikes.

Frequently, when the words *single parent* are used, people often assume that they apply to mothers. However, a growing number of men are granted custody of children. According to a 2002 count by the U.S. Bureau of the Census, there were 3,297,000 single-father households. When fathers are motivated to provide a loving, nurturing environment, both boys and girls in father-only families do as well as those living with their mother ("*Single Fathers,*" 1995). However, boys are placed more frequently with their father than are girls, and they seem to do even better in a father-only family than if they lived with their mother. Part of the reason may be that fathers seek custody because they want to care for their children; mothers are often given custody whether they want it or not. Another reason that children do well in a father-headed household is that they often respond well to the male as an authority figure and are less likely to get into trouble. Finally, the income level of a father-led family is more likely to be higher than that of a single mother. The children benefit from a higher standard of living.

Sometimes single parents resolve some of the problems of caring for their youngsters alone by moving in with their own parents. Although there are advantages to this arrangement, there are also additional stresses on the adults and the children..This

"My family." Tai, age 7

is less true in cultural or ethnic groups where the extended family structure is more commonplace. The adults in these families find ways to mitigate the problems of several generations living under one roof.

When divorced adults find new spouses, the remarriage and resulting blended family are usually seen as an opportunity to start over and to resolve the difficulties of a previous union or of being a single parent. For the children, the experience can be positive, negative, or mixed. If the children have been living with their mother, the economic situation improves. Boys are sometimes helped by the presence of a stepfather, especially if he takes a personal interest in them. When the father remarries, there may be a more equal sharing of household chores and routines. Children in blended families often find they have more models and choices. In addition, they may have the opportunity to live in new places and have new experiences. All of these are positives.

Many adjustments are difficult, however, and vary with the ages of the children. Younger children suffer more from loss of a close relationship with both parents. Some children continue to have problems of identity and self-worth in this type of marriage. School-age children may go through a period of lower academic achievement.

Although interracial families are becoming more accepted, some still face difficulties. Many children are proud of their dual heritage and feel good about themselves when they are young and their world consists mostly of the home and family. Unfortunately, when they go to school or out into the community, some are the target of discrimination. Where the family lives may be a determinant. Many mixed families choose to live in large urban areas or neighborhoods where they will be accepted. Small towns and rural areas tend to be less tolerant of differences. The economic status and educational background of the parents may also determine a family's comfort in a particular community. It is easier if they fit in economically. More educated adults choose their friends to avoid people who cause problems. There is also a growing number of magazines and books that help parents raise children in a biracial family.

"My family." Elizabeth, age 10

One of the biggest problems for children growing up in an interracial family is developing their own identity. They must learn to define themselves as being of one group or another or even a melding of the two. They may be pressured by parents or other adults to accept their identity as one or the other ethnic group. They are sometimes discouraged from associating with children outside of one of their background groups. When these children are encouraged to accept their biracial origins, they usually develop a positive self-image. It also helps when parents teach them to appreciate the cultural richness of both sides of their family.

Single-gender families may also be the target of discrimination. Although homosexuality is no longer considered a pathological state, many people still view these relationships with hostility. Children may feel something is wrong with them when they are the targets of negative attitudes. They may also consider themselves different from schoolmates who have a "mom and a dad." Despite these issues, a number of studies show that children in these situations can and do adjust when given adequate adult support. If children have an opportunity to seek out additional role models, they have an easier time developing their own identity.

Although family composition does have an effect on children's development, the essential ingredients for emotionally healthy children can be found in any group. Successful families have the following common characteristics:

- They are affectionate. Members express their love and caring for one another.
- They have a sense of place. They either have a stable environment or have a commitment to their place of origin.

- They pass on their cultural heritage.
- They connect with posterity. They honor their elders.
- They promote and perpetuate family rituals. Parents pass on traditions from their own past and encourage a sense of family continuity.
- They communicate with one another.
- They respect differences among their members.

As you can see, the ingredients for an effective family can exist no matter who makes up the group. Remember that as you work with children and families in your child care center.

Poverty

According to the Children's Defense Fund (2004), one in six children lived in families where the annual income is below the government poverty level. The number rose from 11,600,000 in 1999 to 12,100,000 in 2002. Female-headed households are most likely to live in poverty, either totally without child support from the father or receiving amounts that are inadequate to bolster the family income. The impact of poverty on children can be devastating, affecting them for the rest of their lives.

Children living in substandard conditions are likely to suffer from malnutrition and disease, are subject to abuse or neglect, and are injured or die more frequently from accidents than children in better environments. Poor children frequently live in housing where they are exposed to lead poisoning due to drinking water from lead pipes or breathing lead paint dust.

In addition to health risks, children in some low-income neighborhoods are behind in academic achievement because their schools are poorly equipped and maintained, class sizes are large, and teachers are poorly paid and may be undermotivated.

Perhaps the most devastating of all is the toll that poverty takes on children's psychosocial development. Middle childhood is a time when children become acutely aware

"My family and TV." Rachel, age 5

of their circumstances compared to those they see portrayed in movies or on television. When their own neighborhoods are run-down and dangerous, they develop feelings of hopelessness and depression.

Helping Children and Their Parents

Probably your most important function as a caregiver is to support the bond between parents and their children. Working parents agonize over how they can provide the best kind of upbringing for their children and still earn a living. They are sad they cannot spend as much time with their family as they would like. Many find it hard to get back to being a parent at the end of the day after the pressures of their job. You can help them bridge the gap between their daytime activities and their role as parents.

The key word is communicate! If you see the parents frequently, talk with them. If you seldom see some parents, you will have to find other means to communicate. Parent handbooks or newsletters provide an opportunity to present aspects of the program, make suggestions for parent-child activities, or announce coming events. A bulletin board in an entry area where all parents will see it can be used to give information and also to display children's artwork or show photos of children. Some centers set up their own Web site and have e-mail addresses. Parents can log on to the Web site to get information about the program, coming events, or special services. Staff members can receive inquiries from parents by e-mail and answer in the same way. You can also use telephone calls to keep in contact with parents. It is important to take the time to ask parents how they see their child's experience in child care or to check on a child that has been absent. Sometimes phone calls can be just a means to say "Hello, I've missed seeing you for a while." That may open up a dialogue that will be invaluable in your ongoing relationship with that parent.

Some centers have found a parent survey to be an effective way to reach parents to determine their concerns or needs. Ask parents what they need to know about the program or their children's development. Additional questions might determine other ways that the center could support parents. Once the information has been gathered, staff can decide on ways to respond. Parents appreciate knowing about any changes in their children since they left them in the morning. They want to know if the children are troubled or ill or are showing changes in behavior. You can both then work together to determine causes and bring about needed change. And communication is not one-way. Ask parents to let you know when there are variations in the home situation or when they see changes in their children.

Another means for keeping in contact with parents is through a family journal. Every child is provided with a notebook in which both caregivers and parents can write notes to one another. The caregiver can direct inquiries such as "What has John been reading at home lately? He tells me he loves to read at home" or "Tell me the favorite things your child likes to do on weekends." The notebook can become a valuable tool for maintaining contact as well as providing a record of a child's progress.

Schedule social events that allow parents to get to know staff members and other parents in a relaxed, fun situation. Many parents would welcome a potluck dinner on a Friday evening. They can meet their children at the center and have dinner. As an added bonus, make it a multicultural dinner, with everyone bringing a dish specific to his or her culture or that has been a family tradition. As recipes are shared and traditions discussed, everyone

It is important for caregivers to support the bond between parents and their children.

Bulletin boards can provide important information for parents.

should gain an appreciation for how many families are alike even though their backgrounds are radically different.

Help parents see their children's behavior realistically. Working parents often feel guilty about leaving their children in the care of others. When problems arise, they immediately think, "If I didn't have to work, these things wouldn't happen." That may or may not be so. Help them to understand that some behaviors are developmentally predictable. Children will go through those stages whether the parent works or not. Often, time alone will resolve the situation. Sometimes simple changes within the family work miracles.

Encourage parents to use their own knowledge of their children to bring about changes. Do not be too quick to offer advice based on your own experiences. Your family and your own child may be quite different. Instead, help parents to think through the problem and come up with their own solutions. Discuss your observations of the behaviors, then ask them what happens at home. Encourage them to consider the causes. Let them suggest ways the problem might be alleviated. Obviously, if they have no suggestions, you can voice your own.

Recognize that parents sometimes express anger toward you as an outlet for their own fatigue. Try not to take it personally. The anger may be a way of expressing guilt about not having more time or energy to spend with the child. In addition, the cost of child care consumes a large portion of one parent's income. Parents may be feeling "I am paying a lot of money for this care. The least you can do is to see that he gets his homework done." If you understand the reasons for the parents' frustrations, you can deal with them more easily. Recognition of the fatigue helps. Most parents will respond to "It sounds like you have had a really hard day" or "Yes, it is hard to get him to do his homework. Do you have any suggestions as to how I can be any more successful?" Accept differences in family organizations. Examine your own prejudices about what makes a family. If you grew up in a happy, intact family, you may see that as the only alternative. Instead, be open to recognizing the strengths of each family you work with. It will help if you increase your knowledge about the changes that have taken place in the last decade by reading further in the books listed at the end of this chapter.

Encourage families to share their cultural and ethnic traditions with your center. This will be especially important to children in interracial families. Visit the children's community and talk to the residents. Learn about the cultures through books, pictures, music, and observation. Actively involve the parents by asking them to share stories, songs, drawings, and experiences that portray important aspects of their culture. One of the best times to involve parents is during holidays. Some parents may be able to spend time in the classroom showing children the way they celebrate. Others may be willing to bring you books, toys, or artifacts that are typical of their background. Still others may welcome an opportunity to get together at a workshop to make presents or decorations for the holiday.

Help all children to increase their own self-esteem. As you read earlier parts of this chapter, you learned that this is more vital for children in some families than in others. But caregivers know that children who feel good about themselves have a better chance of getting along and of becoming happy, functioning adults. So be aware of the ways you can let children know they are liked and successful. A later chapter provides specific strategies and activities.

As a child care worker, you share the responsibility for children's welfare and education not only with parents but also with elementary school teachers. In a model situation, each of you would have close contact with the other. However, this does not always happen. Although you may see parents daily when they deliver or pick up the child, you seldom have contact with elementary school personnel. If your child care center is located on a public school campus, it is easier to bring about a close working relationship. If your center is outside a school, it is harder to establish a liaison with teachers. When it is impossible for you to work directly with teachers, you can monitor the child's progress in other ways. Ask parents how their children are doing in school. Make sure you know what homework children have each day and encourage them to get it done. Be aware of when report cards come out and inquire how children did.

Know when to refer parents for outside help. Find out what is available in your community so that you can suggest sources. Make referrals when the service needed is not something your center can provide. Medical or social services are examples. Make referrals when the problem with the child or within the family is acute or long-standing.

Establishing a close relationship with parents can bring about immense rewards for you and the families you work with. Parents will find they are not alone in trying to provide the best for their children. You will find that getting to know parents adds to your ability to help their children.

Summary

As society has changed, the definition of a family has evolved. Several types of families are now recognized. The nuclear family consists of mother, father, and children. An extended family includes other relatives.

Single-parent families make up a growing sector. Either mother or father cares for the child or children exclusively or for a large portion of the time. Reconstituted or blended families are another growing phenomenon.

Divorced parents remarry and combine their families, sometimes conceiving additional children. Interracial families may combine persons from widely different races or cultures.

Single-gender couples have been able to incorporate children into their partnerships. The family is a system that affects children's development at every age level.

The nuclear family no longer always has a stay-at-home mother who cares for the children while the father goes to work. Both parents frequently work, leaving children to care for themselves or be cared for by others.

Single-parent families are often compared unfavorably with two-parent families.

More recent information indicates that children can adjust to the loss of daily contact with one parent.

Divorce can have a profound effect on children's lives. These children may exhibit acting-out behaviors such as aggression, conflicts with authorities, withdrawal from contacts with others, and depression or anxiety. They may also perform less well academically.

Boys seem to have more difficulty than girls do in their social adjustment. Age also determines the kinds of problems children exhibit. In middle childhood, children tend to assume responsibility for the divorce, while high school children relate the divorce to their own identity and ability to maintain relationships.

Although adults see remarriage as an opportunity to start over, children in blended families may experience some difficulties.

Children of mixed-race marriages and single-gender couples may be the target of discrimination.

Close contact between parent, school, and caregivers is vital. Working parents suffer stresses and pressures. Caregivers can help by being understanding. Regular avenues of communication must be established.

Key Terms

extended family   reconstituted or blended family
interracial family   single-gender family
nuclear family   single-parent family

Student Activities

1. Prepare a collage depicting your own family. You can do this on a large piece of poster board, using cutout pictures, words, and phrases from magazines. Display this collage to your class. Ask class members to discuss the family portrayed in the collage. Verify or refute your classmates' impressions.
2. Visit a child care center at the time parents are coming to pick up their children. Write a short paper on your impressions of parent-teacher-child relationships.
3. Bring to class an object that is meaningful to your family and representative of some aspect of your culture. It can be a picture, poem, or story, an article of clothing, or a handcrafted object. Show it to classmates and discuss its significance to you. Following the completion of all the presentations, discuss what you have learned. Have you learned something new about your own culture or about another?
4. Interview a single parent and a family with both a mother and a father. Ask them to describe the situations that create the most stress for themselves and their children. Are there similarities between the two families? What are the differences?
5. Invite several parents from different family configurations to discuss their children's child care arrangement. Ask the students to develop a set of questions to determine how the parents see what is happening in the care setting. The students might ask what the parents like about the program. Are there things they would like to see happen that are not occurring? Summarize the findings at the conclusion of the activity.

Review Questions

1. How has the definition of the word *family* changed?
2. List and describe three family forms.
3. What is the most serious difficulty for the single-parent family headed by a woman?
4. What are the advantages to children when a parent remarries?
5. What are the problems faced by children in interracial families?
6. List three characteristics of an effective family.
7. What is your most important function as a caregiver?

8. What are the advantages for children who live with a father-only household?
9. How does poverty affect children?
10. List some ways that child care staff members can share the responsibility for children's welfare with parents and elementary school teachers.

Case Study

For Mrs. Jolie and her family, the day begins long before it gets light. She and her children are on early, tight schedules to get to their various daytime commitments. Mrs. Jolie must travel 40 miles to her job as a middle school teacher and must leave the house at 6:45. Often her oldest daughter leaves even earlier, at 6:30, for before-school activities at her high school. Victor, age 10, is supposed to be picked up at 6:55 by the transporter service his mother has hired. This morning when it doesn't arrive, he tries to reach his mother, but she is still en route to her school. At 7:20 he calls the key leader at his child care center. Chris, the leader, tells him not to panic and to keep cool, and they will work to contact his mother. He assures Victor his mom will have a solution. Chris leaves a message for Mrs. Jolie at her school's office. She returns his call immediately on arriving at her school and quickly arranges other transportation for Victor.

Mrs. Jolie was really upset that this happened and said she felt guilty she had to leave her children to go to work. She has been divorced for only six months and knows that it has been hard on the children.

1. How would you assess the children's ability to cope with a divorce and a working mother?
2. Is there anything additional Mrs. Jolie can do to prevent another upsetting incident like this?
3. What can you say to Mrs. Jolie?

References

Amato, P. R., & Rezac, S. J. (1994). Contact with non-resident parents, interparental conflict, and children's behavior. *Journal of Family Issues, 15,* 191–207.

Berger, K. S. (2000). *The developing person through childhood and adolescence* (5th ed.). New York: Worth.

Children's Defense Fund. (2004). *The state of America's children,* 2004. Washington, DC: Author.

Hawkins, A. J., & Eggebeen, D. J. (1991). Are fathers fungible? *Journal of Marriage and the Family, 51,* 958–972.

Howard, J. (1978). *Families*. New York: Simon & Schuster.

Kurdek, L. (1989). Relationship quality for newly married husbands and wives: Marital history, stepchildren and individual predictors. *Journal of Marriage and the Family, 52,* 1053–1064.

McLanahan, S. S. (1997). Parent absence or poverty: Which matters more? In G. J. Duncan & J. Brooks-Gunn (Eds.), *Consequences of growing up poor* (pp. 35–48). New York: Russell Sage Foundation.

Pruett, K.D. (1987). The nurturing father: Journey toward the complete man. New York: Warner.

Shim, M. K., Felenr, R. D., & Shim, E. (2000). *The effects of family structure on academic achievement.* Paper presented at the annual meeting of the American Educational Research Association. (Document Reproduction Service ERIC) No. ED455300.

Simons, R. L. (1996). Understanding differences between divorced and intact families. Thousand Oaks, CA: Sage.

Single fathers: Doing it all. (1995). *Ebony, 50,* 60.

U.S. Bureau of the Census. (2002, March). *Children's living arrangements and characteristics.* Washington, DC: Author.

Suggested Readings

Brand, S. (1996). Making parent involvement a reality: Helping teachers develop partnerships. *Young Children, 51*(2), 76–81.

McLanahan, S. (1994). *Growing up with a single parent.* Cambridge, MA: Harvard University Press.

Miller, P. A., Ryan, P., & Morrison, W. (1999). Practical strategies for helping children of divorce in today's classroom. *Childhood Education, 75*(5), 285–289.

Saracho, O. N., & Spodek, B. (1983). *Understanding the multicultural experience in early childhood education.* Washington, DC: National Association for the Education of Young Children.

Thompson, R. A., Scalora, M. J., Castrianno, L., & Limber, S. P. (1992). Grandparent visitation rights: Emergent psychological and psycholegal issues. In D. K. Kagehiro & W. S. Laufer (Eds.), *Handbook of psychology and law.* New York: Springer-Verlag.

Wallerstein, J. (1993). *Children after divorce. Human development.* Guilford, CT: Duskin.

Web Resources

The Child Advocate serves the needs of children, families and professionals while addressing mental health, medical, educational, legal and legislative issues. www.childadvocate.net

NPIN.org provides educational software and services for middle school, high school, and college students. Creative, innovative and interactive products that empower students of all ages. http://npin.org

Parents Action for Children formerly the I Am Your Child Foundation http://iamyourchild.org

How Children Grow and Develop

CHAPTER 4

Development in Middle Childhood: Physical

Objectives

After completing this chapter, the student should be able to:

- Discuss the importance of understanding child development
- Distinguish between development and learning
- Relate major changes and variations in growth patterns among children
- Describe ways in which child care leaders can enhance children's physical development

Lizette is 19 and enrolled in a community college near her home. She lives with her mom and dad and her 10-year-old brother. Her brother attends an after-school program, and Lizette thought she would have a lot of fun working in child care. She has always enjoyed teaching her sibling and watching him grow. She has now been at her job for three months, and most of the time she is with third- to fifth-graders. Her responsibilities include making sure the children are safe when they are on the playground, helping with homework, setting up art projects, and organizing group games. She expects children to respect one another, and she sees changes as they get older. "I especially like the interaction with the kids. They tell me about what happened to them that day at school and ask what I think about it."

Lizette feels that one of her best characteristics is the willingness to listen to children. The parents of one little girl are going through a divorce, and she talks to Lizette about it. The children know she is there for them and that she will listen. Other characteristics that make her able to work well with children are that she is consistent yet fun. She expects them to abide by the rules, and the children know that she will always follow through, but that they can still have fun together. She also feels that her family has taught her that with understanding and caring you can work through any problem. It evidently works since her parents have been married for 27 years. "Also, my brother is nine years younger, and I have learned to be patient and motherly." Both of her parents work, and when they were younger, Lizette had to be partly responsible for her brother. There was a caregiver in the home, but her mother told Lizette that if she saw the caregiver doing something that was wrong, she should say something. So at an early age she learned to be responsible.

Lizette wants to be an elementary teacher, probably third or fourth grade. "I like that age level because they're not real little anymore, and they're starting to become their own person." She knows that she will need to continue her education in order to obtain a teaching credential.

Importance of Understanding Child Development

The years between 5 and 12 bring about changes in children that make them more independent of adult assistance in the conduct of their daily activities. Children master new physical skills fairly easily when they have opportunities to practice those skills. Illnesses and death occur less frequently than during infancy and preschool years or later in adolescence.

What skills are these children using?

Gender differences in physical development and ability are minimal. Most children feel competent to manage their school and home lives and still want to perform in ways that earn recognition from adults.

A knowledge of the universal predictable stages of growth as well as an understanding of individual patterns of timing are absolutely essential for anyone involved in planning and operating a child care program. The quality of a program may depend on a variety of factors, but a major determinant is the extent to which activities and procedures are appropriate for the developmental level of the participating children. The learning environment and program activities should be based on an assessment of children's cognitive, social, emotional, and physical abilities at each stage of their development and also provide challenges to promote further development. A knowledge of child development enables adults to choose effective techniques for guiding an individual child's behavior and planning strategies for group interactions. Further, a knowledge of child development enables child care leaders to communicate more effectively with parents about a child's progress.

Development and Learning

The study of human development examines how individuals grow and change over the period of a lifetime, how they remain the same, and how some individuals may vary from typical patterns. Several characteristics of individuals are programmed by genetic makeup at the time of conception, whereas others are the result of environmental conditions and experiences. The relative importance of one over the other, known as *nature vs. nurture,* is a topic for debate among developmental researchers.

Nature refers to a variety of characteristics such as eye color and body type, which are inherited from parents. Physical limitations and certain diseases are also inherited, as well as some personality characteristics such as activity level or verbal ability. Nurture refers to all the experiences and influences people are exposed to from the moment of conception on throughout a lifetime.

The dichotomy of influences on human development is also portrayed as *maturation vs. learning.* Maturation indicates the progression of changes that takes place as people age. Learning refers to the processes by which environmental influences and experiences bring about permanent changes in thinking, feeling, and behavior.

The basic question is the same no matter what labels are used. How much of development and human behavior is the result of genetic inheritance, and how much is the result of all of life's experiences? Most developmentalists believe that both are important and that in fact the interaction between them is the determining factor in a person's pattern of growth.

Physical Development

Middle childhood is a time when children grow more slowly than they did in the preschool years, and they will not experience another growth spurt until they approach adolescence.

Height and Weight

Typically, children gain about 5 pounds per year and 2 1/2 inches. By the time they are 10 years old, most will weigh 70 pounds and be 54 inches tall (Lowrey, 1986). Up to the age of 9, boys and girls are about the same size, but then girls start to pull ahead in both height and weight. Around age 9 or 10 girls begin a growth spurt that precedes adolescence. By the end of the elementary years, girls are generally taller and heavier than boys. School-age children seem slimmer than they did during the preschool years because their body proportions change, and they begin to look more like adults. Their arms and legs get longer, their torsos elongate, and their faces are thinner.

Yet there are wide variations in their appearance. Variations in body size could be due to malnutrition. Children who are well nourished will be taller than their contemporaries growing up in poverty. Genetics also plays a large part in determining size as well as rate of maturity. Although adults may understand that variations in size and timing of maturity are normal, it is often difficult for children to accept these differences. Physical development can affect peer relationships because children often choose friends who have a pleasing appearance and are physically, academically, or socially capable (Hartup, 1983). Children who are shorter, taller, or heavier than their peers, as well as those who are less capable, are often rejected.

School-age children master many physical skills.

Obesity

Obesity is a growing problem among children. It can seriously affect a child emotionally as well as physically. The most recent study from the National Health and Nutrition Examination Survey (for 1999 to 2000) shows 30 percent of children between the ages of 6 and 19 are overweight (CDC, 2002). Whether a child is overweight rather than just childishly chubby can be determined by figuring the ratio of weight to height, a measure called body-mass index, or BMI. BMI is found by dividing weight in kilograms by height in meters squared (BMI = kg/m2). At age 8 a child is overweight if his BMI is 18 and at age 12 if the BMI is 23 (Hubbard, 1995).

Overweight children are subject to health risks such as higher blood pressure and blood cholesterol levels. These children may also have orthopedic or respiratory problems. The greatest risk is that they will become overweight adults, prone to developing heart disease at a young age, high blood pressure, gallbladder disease, arthritis, and some forms of cancer.

At least 10 percent of all children in the United States are 20 pounds above the average for their peers. More exact measurements of the percentage of body fat at various points of the body show that the percentage of overweight children may be higher than 10 percent and has increased in the last few years (Gortmaker, Dietz, Sobol, & Wekler, 1987).

In addition, serious psychological distress can occur because these children may be the object of teasing and rejection by their classmates. This results in lowered self-esteem, depression, and various kinds of behavior problems. Their unhappiness leads them to further curtail participation with their peers and to overeat to compensate for their unhappiness.

Thus, patterns are established that carry over into adulthood; overweight children are frequently overweight adults (Serdula et al., 1993). It is estimated that 60 percent to 80 percent of obese children become overweight adults (Lucas, 1991).

Causes of Obesity

There is no one cause of obesity; rather, it is an interaction between several possible conditions. Patterns are often established in infancy and continue into adulthood.

- *Heredity.* Several factors that contribute to obesity are inherited: body type, height and bone structure, the amount and distribution of fat, metabolic rate, and activity level.
- *Activity level.* Children who are more active are less likely to be overweight because they burn more calories. Although activity level is influenced by heredity, an individual's willingness to engage in active play also affects weight. For some children, the unavailability of safe places to play will also be a factor.
- *Television watching.* Families who watch television frequently have a higher incidence of obesity (Dietz & Gortmaker, 1985). Children are not only inactive when they watch television but are also bombarded with commercials for foods that are high in fat and sugar. These are the foods they choose to snack on while they watch television.
- *High-calorie foods.* Overweight children are not necessarily overeaters. However, much of the food they consume is high in calories. Many children take in large quantities of high-calorie soft drinks and chips, as well as high-fat hamburgers and French-fried potatoes. Often, too, parents give in to demands from their children for the high-calorie snack foods shown on television ads.
- *Attitudes toward food.* In some families, children are encouraged to consume large portions of food as a measure of the family's prosperity or a parent's love for their children. Often, too, food becomes a symbol for love and comfort, causing children to overeat when under stress or unhappy. Parents who offer special foods as a reward or comfort set up a lifelong habit that can lead to obesity.
- *Specific event.* A traumatic event in a child's life can be a precipitating factor in the onset of increased weight gain. Hospitalization, parental divorce, the death of someone close to the child, or even a move to a new neighborhood can all cause distress and a need for a substitute gratification in the form of food.
- *Physiological problems.* A small number of cases of obesity in children can be traced to abnormalities in the growth process or metabolism (Lowrey, 1986). The obesity is only one part of the problem that usually includes disturbances in normal physical and mental growth. Only about 1 percent of childhood obesity can be attributed to this cause, however.

Implications for Child Care Staff Members

Within any group of school-age children, particularly if there is a wide age span, there will be children of many sizes and shapes. Children compare their own appearance with their peers and as a result often think they are too tall, too little, too heavy, or too thin. In addition, children who vary noticeably from their peers tend to get teased and labeled with unflattering names. Differing from the norm can cause a great deal of anguish and loss of self-esteem.

- An important task for adults who have responsibility for children's welfare is to assure them they are accepted no matter how they look and to help their peers be accepting. Further, they need to know that they will change as they grow and develop.
- Obese children need special attention to help them change their eating patterns and activity level. They can learn about good nutrition and how to prepare good-tasting, low-calorie foods. See Chapter 14 for ideas that can be used in child care. Although increased activity is the best way to lose weight, obese children have a difficult time participating in active sports or games. They are often rejected as team members and are teased if they try to join in games. It is important to encourage them to start somewhere: walking to school, bicycling, or participating in the exercises suggested in Chapter 14.
- The children's families need help to change the environment that created the obesity, whether it lies in the foods they eat, in the parental interactions, or in the kinds of activities children are encouraged to engage in. Remember that talking about food and weight is a sensitive issue for many parents. Therefore, in a nonjudgmental way, provide parents with information about nutrition. Help them find ways to discipline or reward their children other than with food. Provide suggestions for active things the family can do together.
- Caregivers are responsible for planning and preparing nutritious snacks that are not high in fat, salt, or sugar. Use the Food Guide Pyramid as a basis for choosing.

Health Conditions

During middle childhood children may suffer from a variety of health conditions. According to a 1992 study, 31 percent of children under age 18, or 20 million children nationwide, have chronic health problems (Newacheck & Taylor, 1992). Nine million children (12 percent) under 18 have asthma and it is most frequently diagnosed in boys. The most frequently reported conditions are respiratory allergies, which are suffered by 12 percent of children (Blackwell, Vickerie, & Wondimy, 2003). Less common are diabetes, sickle cell disease, and cerebral palsy.

Conditions that are not chronic but are prevalent during the school years are communicable diseases and hearing, vision, or ambulatory limitations. Early sexual behavior leads to preadolescent pregnancies and sexually transmitted disease, including HIV and AIDS. Drug and alcohol abuse are also occurring at the elementary school level.

Poverty contributes to the poor health status of many children. According to the Children's Defense Fund (2004), 12.1 million children under age 18 were living in poverty in 2002. Nearly 14 percent of these children have no health insurance coverage. Because of their living conditions, they are subject to poor nutrition, inadequate preventive care, and little treatment for chronic conditions.

Implications for Child Care Staff Members

Caregivers can do a great deal to help children learn to maintain a healthy lifestyle as well as help parents be responsible for ensuring that children's health needs are met.

- Help children evaluate the messages they receive from their environment concerning health. Provide activities that encourage them to question images of people having fun while smoking cigarettes, eating "junk" foods, or consuming alcoholic beverages.
- Include program activities that stress good nutrition. Allow children to participate in choosing and preparing food.
- Offer only nutritious meals and snacks. Offer supplementary nutrition to children who may be undernourished.
- Provide space within the physical facility for activities that encourage health and fitness.
- Model behavior that demonstrates fitness. Do not smoke or consume non-nutritious foods.
- Become informed about community health services and resources. Refer parents to appropriate facilities.

Motor Skills

During the elementary school period children develop a wide variety of motor skills, particularly when they have ample opportunities to practice and are encouraged to try new things. Five-year-olds endlessly practice running, jumping, and throwing. Gradually their timing and coordination increase, enabling them to become noticeably more proficient. They soon learn to judge the time to swing a bat in order to hit a ball or estimate the distance a ball will travel when thrown in order to catch it. Along with developing physical skills, children are also acquiring new ways to get along with their peers and beginning to understand the importance of rules. The interaction of these developing abilities accounts for the popularity of sports during middle childhood.

Gross-Motor Skills

Several skills that children acquire in middle childhood occur in play activities typical of this period. Developmentally appropriate practices for school-age children should include opportunities to develop both gross- and fine-motor skills (Albrecht & Plantz, 1993).

- *Running.* By age 5 or 6 most children have mastered the form and power required to run. They have learned to start, stop, and turn and can integrate these into their play activities.

A game of tag can help to develop gross-motor skills.

- *Jumping.* Jumping requires a complex set of skills including balance, maintenance of equilibrium, and form. Jumping is usually not attempted by children until they have become fairly proficient in basic locomotion, but by age 5 most children have a good mastery of jumping skills.
- *Throwing.* At age 5 or 6, there is a perceptible change in children's ability to throw. They learn to transfer their weight from one foot to the other during throwing. This weight shift, coupled with a horizontal movement of the arms and body, allows children to efficiently propel a ball forward. Most six-year-olds are able to perform an overhand throw.

Further practice and refinement of gross-motor skills allow children to participate in the popular activities of childhood: swimming, biking, roller-skating, ice-skating, jumping rope, baseball, and basketball.

Fine-Motor Skills

During middle childhood, most children master a variety of tasks requiring the use of small muscles. They learn to cut easily with scissors, draw, write or print accurately, and sew or knit. As their coordination increases further, they can learn to play musical instruments, engage in hobbies such as model making, or play games such as jacks.

"I like to play baseball." Lark, age 8.

Differences in Motor Skills

Boys and girls are fairly equal in their physical abilities during the middle childhood years except that boys have greater forearm strength and girls have greater flexibility. Boys are often better at baseball, while girls excel in gymnastics. More and more girls are willing to try sports like baseball, and when they are given ample opportunities to practice, they, too, can catch and throw a ball accurately and hit well. Likewise, with training, boys can do well in activities that require flexibility, such as gymnastics.

Certain motor skills do not depend on the amount of practice a youngster engages in. Some depend on body size, brain maturation, or inherent talents. A good example of a skill dependent on brain maturation is reaction time. A child's brain continues to mature into adolescence; therefore, older children usually do better where this skill is necessary.

Inherent traits are also important in determining how well a particular child performs a motor skill. Body size, particularly height, gives some children an advantage when playing basketball. Children also vary in their ability to coordinate body movements. Some children find it easy to kick a soccer ball with accuracy while others find it almost impossible. Heredity accounts for children's basic skill at these activities, but practice and experience can increase their proficiency.

With practice, children can participate in difficult sport activities.

Implications for Child Care Staff Members

Middle childhood is a time when children want to feel competent at whatever they do. In school they must use small muscles to be successful, while out of school they need well-developed gross-motor skills to participate in the sports, vigorous games, and strenuous individual activities that are so much a part of the school-age years. Because practice and experience help children enhance their inherited abilities and acquire new skills, it is extremely important that child care offer as many opportunities as possible. Child care leaders can:

- Provide a wide variety of activities requiring different skills and skills at varying levels
- Allow children ample time to practice and refine new skills
- Encourage both genders to participate in all activities
- Offer children encouragement for their efforts rather than praise their achievements
- Encourage children to teach their skills to others
- Discourage competition

Girls have greater flexibility than boys.

Summary

A knowledge of the universal predictable stages of growth, as well as an understanding of individual patterns of timing, are essential for anyone involved in planning and operating a child care program. The quality of the program may depend to a large degree on the extent to which all activities, procedures, and interactions are developmentally appropriate for the children who participate.

Human growth is affected by both maturation and learning. Maturation refers to a variety of abilities, characteristics, and limits that are inherited from parents. Learning refers to processes by which environmental influences and experiences bring about permanent change in thinking, feeling, and behavior. Children grow more slowly during middle childhood than they did in the preschool years. They may gain 5 pounds and 2 1/2 inches. Boys and girls are about the same size up until age 9, when girls begin a preadolescent growth spurt. Variations in size are due to nutrition and heredity.

Obesity is a growing problem among children and can affect a child emotionally as well as physically. Overweight children are often unhappy because they are rejected or teased by their peers.

Causes of obesity are heredity, activity level, types of food consumed, and attitudes toward food. In addition, specific events and psychological problems trigger overeating.

Child care leaders can help children accept the way they look and also to understand that as they grow, they will change. Obese children need special attention to encourage them to change eating habits and to be more active.

School-age children may suffer from a variety of health conditions, both chronic and nonchronic. Child care staff members can help children and parents learn to be responsible for meeting their health needs.

During middle childhood, children rapidly acquire a variety of new motor skills. Gross-motor skills include running, jumping, and throwing. Fine-motor skills include the ability to cut easily with scissors, draw, write or print accurately, and sew or knit. Boys and girls are fairly equal in their physical abilities during middle childhood except that boys have greater forearm strength and girls have greater flexibility. With training and opportunities to practice, the differences are lessened.

Child care leaders can provide many opportunities for children to participate in a wide variety of activities requiring the use of large or small muscles. Leaders should also allow plenty of time for children to practice, encourage both genders to participate in all activities, encourage efforts rather than achievements, and encourage children to teach their skills to others.

Key Terms

BMI
learning
maturation

nature
nurture

Student Activities

1. Ask the children in your child care group to draw a picture of themselves and one best friend. Do they show themselves as taller or shorter than the friend? Is there any noticeable difference between the attractiveness of their own image and that of the friend?

2. Write a paragraph describing your appearance when you were 6. Include the kinds of activities you engaged in during your out-of-school time. Next, describe yourself when you were 11. In what ways did your development follow the description in this chapter? In what ways did it differ?

3. Watch two hours of Saturday morning children's television programs. Count and list the commercials for food that are shown. How many are for high-fat, high-sugar, or high-salt foods? Do they show children having fun while consuming these foods? Discuss the impact these commercials might have on children.

4. Survey the neighborhood near your home or child care center. Are there places where children can play outdoors? How do you think the environment affects the children who live there? What could be done to increase opportunities for physical activities? Share your information with your classmates.

Review Questions

1. Why is it important for child care leaders to have a knowledge of predictable stages of growth and an understanding of individual patterns of timing?
2. Differentiate between maturation and learning.
3. What is another way to describe the dichotomy of influences on human development?
4. How much will an average well-nourished child gain in weight and height per year? The typical 10-year-old will weigh _____ pounds and be _____ inches tall.
5. Boys and girls are about the same size for part of the middle childhood years. At what age do girls begin to increase in size faster than boys?
6. List the causes of obesity in children.
7. In what ways can child care personnel help children who differ from the norm in body size or who are obese?
8. List eight motor skills developed by children during middle childhood. In what ways do children use these skills in their daily lives at school or at home?
9. In what ways do the motor skills of boys and girls differ?
10. What can child care leaders do to help children enhance their inherited abilities and acquire new skills?

Case Study

Nine-year-old Ian is often called names by some of the other children. They refer to him as "Tubby," "Fatso," or "Lardo." He gets very angry and starts hitting, although sometimes he ends up crying in frustration. His caregiver has noticed that he seems to have an ample supply of snacks that he carries in his backpack—often chips and candy bars. He wants to have those for snack time rather than the food the center provides. When his request is refused, he stomps away from the table and refuses to eat anything. Occasionally he is seen sneaking food from his locker.

1. How would you respond when Ian stomps away from the table?
2. What can you say to his parents?
3. What can you do to help Ian change his eating pattern at child care?

References

Albrecht, K., & Plantz, M. (1993). *Developmentally appropriate practice in school-age child care programs*. Dubuque, IA: Kendall/Hunt.

Blackwell, D. L., Vickerie, J. I., & Wondimy, E. A. (2003). Summary health statistics for U.S. children. National Health Interview Survey. National Center for Health Statistics. *Vital Health Statistics 10, 213*.

CDC (Centers for Disease Control and Prevention). (2002). http://www.cdc.gov.

Children's Defense Fund. (2004). *The state of America's children, 2004*. Washington, DC: Author.

Dietz, W., Jr., & Gortmaker, S. (1985). Do we fatten our children at the television set? Obesity and television viewing in children and adolescents. *Pediatrics, 75*, 807–812.

Gortmaker, S. L., Dietz, W. H., Sobol, A. M., & Wehler, C. A. (1987). Increasing pediatric obesity in the United States. *American Journal of Diseases of Children, 141,* 535–540.

Hartup, W. (1983). Peer relations. In P. H. Mussen (Ed.), *Handbook of child psychology: Vol. 4. Socialization, personality and social development* (pp. 103–196). New York: Wiley.

Hubbard, V. S. (1995). Future directions in obesity research. In L. W. Y. Cheung & J. B. Richmond (Eds.), *Child health, nutrition, and physical activity.* Champaign, IL: Human Kinetics.

Lowrey, G. (1986). *Growth and development of children* (8th ed.). Chicago: Year Book Medical.

Lucas, A. (1991). Eating disorders. In M. Lewis (Ed.), *Child and adolescent psychiatry: A comprehensive textbook.* Baltimore: Williams & Wilkins.

Newacheck, P., & Taylor, W. (1992). Childhood chronic illness. Prevention, severity, and impact. *American Journal of Public Health, 82*(3), 364–371.

Serdula, M., Ivory, D., Coates, R., Freedman, D., Williamson, D., & Byers, T. (1993). Do obese children become obese adults? A review of the literature. *Preventive Medicine, 22,* 167–177.

CHAPTER 5

Development in Middle Childhood: Cognitive

Objectives

After completing this chapter, the student should be able to:

- Discuss the major principles of several cognitive theories
- List the concerns expressed by critics of each theory as well as the points of agreement
- Describe ways child care leaders can use each theory to enhance children's development
- Discuss the ways in which children develop and use language

Kari is 20 years old. She works in child care at an elementary school and has been there about a year. At first she was assigned to a group of K–3 children but now works with children who are in the fourth and fifth grades. She really likes the older age level but is glad she has been able to experience both ages. She plans activities for circle time, prepares craft projects, and organizes group games.

Kari has had a lot of experience with children because she comes from a large family. Originally, she had two younger brothers, one who was two years younger and the other, five years younger. When their father died, Kari was six. Eventually her mother remarried a man who had two children—a boy nine months older than Kari and a girl two years older. Her mother and stepfather had a girl who is ten years younger than Kari.

In addition to her job and family interactions, Kari baby-sits several days a week with a little girl who is three. Kari wants to do something to help children, as either a teacher, psychologist, or psychiatrist. It was very hard for her when her dad died and she didn't have anybody to talk to. She feels that many children are like her and have so many things they need to get out. "I think, though, my experiences have made me a stronger person, someone who is really patient with children." She wants to learn more about how children think and constantly finds children fascinating. She knows she will have to continue her education in order to reach her goals.

Cognitive Theories

Cognitive theories are used to explain all the mental processes that enable children to think or acquire knowledge and the way these processes affect how they perceive and understand their experiences. How individual children function depends partly on hereditary factors and partly on their experiences. As children's brains grow and mature, they are able to use different cognitive skills to gather and process information.

The thinking processes of school-age children are markedly different from those of preschoolers. By middle childhood, children can selectively focus on tasks; that is, they are able to screen out distractions and concentrate on the relevant parts of the information at hand. This capacity helps them to remember and also to reason in logical steps in order to solve a problem. School-age children also learn strategies for increasing memory. These are called storage strategies. They rehearse the information, organize it into memorable units, or use mnemonic devices such as rhymes or mental images to aid in remembering. Language develops rapidly and is used to communicate ideas, interact with others, and

Children's thinking changes, and they are able to use logic to solve problems.

develop competencies required by the society in which they live. All of these abilities enable children to perform tasks beyond the reach of younger children.

Jean Piaget

The Swiss psychologist Piaget was an important contributor to the understanding of how children think and learn. He began his work with children by helping to develop the first intelligence test. Piaget's task was to interview children and find the age at which most children could answer the test questions correctly. Instead, Piaget became curious about children's incorrect responses to items on the test and observed that children who were the same age gave similar answers. This observation began a lifelong search to understand children's thought processes and how they change with age. Piaget (1952) concluded that cognitive development follows predictable patterns through four major stages. Each stage has certain characteristics that form the basis for how children approach and process intellectual tasks. Everyone proceeds through these stages at their own rate, some slower, some faster, but everyone goes through them. Each stage is built on the skills of the previous stage. Piaget called the period from birth to two years the sensorimotor period. During this time, infants use all their senses to explore and learn about the world around them. They put objects in their mouths, become attentive to sounds, poke or pat objects, react to tastes, and follow out-of-reach objects with their eyes. The information they gather is experience based; they can understand only what they experience directly. Limited memory of an object or experience is retained when the object is removed or the experience ended.

By contrast, preschool children, two to seven years old, are in the preoperational period in which they can begin to think symbolically. They can remember experiences and objects independently of the immediate encounter. This is evident in their rapidly developing ability to use language. Words help them to remember past events or to talk about an object. They also begin to engage in pretend play, not always needing the real props to support the play. Preschool children can play out elaborate scenarios in which they relive familiar interactions with parents or with siblings.

Piaget observed that during the preoperational period children often come to the wrong conclusions. He believed that this was because they could not perform "operations." By operations Piaget meant the ability to internalize an action, that is, carry it out in the mind and understand it can go in one direction or reverse into the opposite direction. The preoperational child cannot perform these operations.

Piaget observed the difficulty children had with one of his conservation experiments. He placed two identical cylinders with equal amounts of liquid before four-year-olds. He then added two cylinders, one tall and slim, the other short. He poured the liquid from one glass into the tall cylinder and from the other into the short one. When asked which glass had more, most children would indicate the taller one. They could not mentally reverse the event to realize that when poured back into the original containers, the amounts were equal. In addition to an inability to imagine reversibility, children can focus on only one dimension of a form at a time. In the case of the liquids, they focused on the height of the fluid in the glasses. Piaget called this centering.

Another characteristic of preoperational children is that they believe everyone thinks and acts the same way they do. They are egocentric—incapable of understanding how others think or feel.

Between the ages of 7 and 11, children are in the concrete operations stage. They begin to think symbolically and can imagine reversing processes. The word *concrete* means that children can carry out this process only when the information is presented concretely.

If a child is asked how many pieces of fruit there are if she has two apples and a friend gives her one, she will be able to figure out the answer. She can imagine two apples and then one additional one. She has experienced apples, can imagine them, and execute the solution. It would be somewhat more difficult for her to figure out the answer to the question "What is half of a dozen?"

During this period children become less egocentric and much more social. Increased language skills enable them to interact more effectively with their peers and to begin to understand the views of others. The need to be a part of a group or to have friends requires discussion and negotiations over play activities. In the process, children learn that others do not always think or feel the same way they do.

Piaget's last stage, formal operations, occurs between the ages of 11 and 15. During this period adolescents are able to consider hypothetical problems without concrete examples. They are also not limited by having to consider the here and now but can imagine situations they have not yet experienced or that are abstract. Thus, adolescents begin to ponder questions about the effects of global warming or the importance of preserving wilderness areas for future generations to enjoy. They question the wisdom of using war as a way to resolve conflicts or what to do about the starving peoples of less-developed countries.

Children learn by doing.

Several general principles underlie the concepts of Piaget's theory and are important to fully understand his perception of how children think and learn.

- Children are active participants in the development of their own intelligence. Piaget believed that children actually *construct* their knowledge of the world through their activities. Experiences are the raw ingredients from which they organize and structure their knowledge, implying that the process takes place within the child rather than being transmitted from the outside. Through experimenting with the objects and experiences in their environment, children actually create their own intelligence.
- The development of intelligence is the result of a progression through stages. Each stage builds a foundation for the next stage. There is no finite division of the stages because each stage may carry vestiges of the previous period. Thus, school-age children may function at a preschool level at times or in certain situations.
- Due to differences in maturation rate, individuals progress through the stages at different rates. However, each individual goes through the same stages in the same order.

Evaluation of Piaget's Theory

Piaget's ideas changed the way children's intellectual development is perceived, focusing more on how children come to know rather than on what they know (Berger, 2000). Yet there are criticisms from those who point to the formal nature of his experiments. These critics state that when children are closely watched in everyday situations, different interpretations of their abilities are possible. Some skills that Piaget relegates to later stages are clearly present in earlier ones. Therefore, critics contend that Piaget must have been wrong about just how early some cognitive skills develop.

Another concern of those who have looked closely at Piagetian theory is that children's abilities are not homogeneous within a given stage. In fact, each stage is entered gradually with vestiges of the previous stage remaining for a period of time. Additional factors affect children's ability to think consistently at an expected level for their stage of development. Hereditary differences in abilities and aptitudes, as well as timing of maturation, play an important part. Environmental factors, such as the kinds of experiences children are exposed to and the kind of education they receive, also influence the rate of intellectual development.

The criticisms of Piaget's theory do not negate the importance of his ideas, however. It is commonly accepted that children proceed developmentally from one stage to the next, changing their thinking processes as their maturity and experiences dictate. They continue to learn, taking in new information, organizing it, and deciding how it fits in with previous information.

Implications for Child Care Staff Members

Piaget never claimed to be an educator, yet his theory is widely used to formulate educational programs for children. His theory provides a framework from which appropriate learning experiences can be designed. It enables educators to:

- Provide many different objects and experiences for children to explore so they can incorporate them into their symbolic thinking process at a later time. There needs to be a balance between unstructured materials and guided ones. Art materials, sand and water, and building materials are examples of unstructured activities. Experiences such as cooking, in which children must follow a recipe, and classifying or seriating a group of objects are guided activities.
- Plan activities that are age appropriate for the level of ability of most members of the group. In addition, teachers can add activities that meet the needs of individual children.
- Allow plenty of time for children to explore freely and engage in play activities. Through play children have an opportunity to test out their own ideas and find out what is true and what is not.
- Provide experiences that allow children to solve their own problems and make decisions.
- Set up situations in which children can exchange ideas, thus learning that others may think differently from themselves.

Behaviorist Learning Theory

Watson (1967) saw the need for a more exact study of psychology. He believed that in order to be a true science, hypotheses should be tested and measured. The only way that could be done was to measure those things that could be observed: behaviors and words

"Me doing my reading book." Sarah, age 6.

rather than feelings or thoughts. His concepts were popular because they were different from the psychoanalytic theory prevalent at the time.

Watson studied Pavlov's (1960) classical conditioning experiments with animals and then used those ideas to formulate his own theory of human conditioning. In classical conditioning, a stimulus (anything that elicits a response, either a reflex or voluntary action) is repeatedly followed by a specific response (behavior). Dogs salivate when they see their food. Pavlov added a ringing bell along with the presentation of the food. After several repetitions, the dogs would salivate when they heard the bell. The result is a connection that allows the response to occur without the need for the stimulus. An example is a person's response to a favorite food. When presented with that food, the sight and the smell cause a person to salivate in preparation for tasting. When viewing pictures of that food in a magazine or on television, the person often has the same reaction—salivating.

Watson was also influenced by the writings of Locke (1959), who saw human infants as a tabula rasa, a blank tablet on which life experiences write a script. According to Watson, human behavior could be shaped by controlling events children were exposed to and by offering rewards for proper responses. Give children appropriate rewards and the desired behavior will follow. A parent who says "You are being so patient waiting while I pay for our groceries" is giving an appropriate reward to her child.

Skinner (1953) used both Watson's and Locke's (1959) ideas to formulate his theory. He proposed that infants are "empty organisms" that can be filled with carefully controlled experiences. He agreed that behavior can be changed by conditioning but saw another type of conditioning that plays a larger role. He called it **operant conditioning**. Children play an active part by operating or acting on their environment and are reinforced for their behaviors. When a behavior is followed by a pleasant response (reward), it is likely to be repeated. If the consequence of a behavior is unpleasant, it is not likely to be repeated. Therefore, a system of positive or negative reinforcers can be used to shape an individual's behavior. Teachers who tell children they have done a good job putting away their materials are using a positive reinforcer. At the next cleanup time, the children are more likely to go about the task willingly.

Bandura (1977) contributed another dimension to the understanding of how learning takes place. He felt that some behaviors cannot be explained as a simple conditioned response to a direct stimulus but occur through less direct learning. He believes children observe others behaving in given ways and then pattern their own behavior accordingly. This type of social learning is more likely to occur when a person is uncertain or unsure in a situation and when the object of observation is admired or seen as powerful. Called **modeling**, it is a technique that parents and teachers use to increase the likelihood of acceptable behavior in children. In other words, parents model the behavior they expect of children. It may also explain why four-year-olds pretend to be Superman or why teenagers want to dress like their favorite rock star. They are imitating the behavior of people they admire.

Social learning changes as individuals mature. Children are attentive to the behaviors of others, store the information for future retrieval, possibly mentally rehearse the behavior, and then use the information when needed. The consequences of behaviors are also noted. Children can then test out alternative behaviors and choose the one with the best outcome. A school-age child observes that when she gets mad and leaves a game, her friends do not ask her to play next time. She will try to curb her anger in order to be included.

Evaluation of Behaviorism

Learning theories have contributed a great deal to the study of how behaviors are shaped (Berger, 2000). The emphasis on the connection between stimulus and the resulting observable response allows a different interpretation of some kinds of behaviors. Previous notions that behavior is the result of deep-seated emotional problems could be revised by observing the environmental causes of some behaviors. Behavior can then be changed by changing the environment's response. As an example, when adults praise children for acceptable behavior rather than focusing on punishing unacceptable behavior, children can change. "Thank you for sitting quietly at story time, Jamal" often is more effective than saying "Sit down and be quiet or I'll have to remove you from the story area." After a few repetitions, Jamal is likely to cease his disruption.

Learning theory has also contributed to a more scientific study of human development. Researchers are pressured to refine their hypotheses, define their terms, devise replicable tests for their hypotheses, and avoid reliance on concepts that they cannot test.

Conversely, there are valid criticisms of learning theory. The emphasis on observable behavior and external influences does not take into account the inner life of children. Some behaviors result from complex relationships between biological maturation, an individual's thought processes, and the struggle to make sense of new experiences. Only considering observable behaviors creates an incomplete picture of the wide range of influences on human behavior.

When behaviorist learning theory was first proposed, researchers made claims that behavior modification through a system of rewards and punishments was manipulative. Present-day critics still voice the same concerns and also object to the kinds of reinforcers that parents or teachers sometimes use.

Implications for Child Care Staff Members

Behaviorist theory provides some specific guidelines for adults who work with children:

- Carefully arrange the learning environment. Because the importance of the environment is stressed in behaviorist learning theory, anyone who works with children can use this information to arrange the setting to bring about positive responses. The placement of furniture, the ways in which activities are presented, and the ways in which adults interact with children all have to be carefully considered with expected results in mind.
- Use appropriate reinforcers to bring about desired results. Carefully consider the implications of reinforcers, and choose those that will enhance positive, rather than negative, behaviors.
- Model the behavior that you expect of children.
- Provide opportunities for social learning to take place among peers. Children are powerful models and can have extensive influence on one another.
- Help children find alternative behaviors to those that generate negative responses from others.

Sociocultural Theory

Vygotsky, writing in the early 1900s, was a pioneer in the study of sociocultural influences on learning. Only recently have his writings become available, Vygotsky (1978, 1987). Vygotsky's theory assumes that social interaction and children's direct participation in authentic cultural activities is necessary for their optimum development. Several main ideas follow this basic assumption.

Cross-Cultural Variation

Cultures differ in the kinds of opportunities they provide children to develop the competencies they need. Every culture has hopes and expectations for the children growing up within that society. These expectations are expressed in terms of competencies or things children need to know or be able to do. A child in rural China will be encouraged to learn vastly different skills from one living in a housing project in New York. Vygotsky believed that knowledge and skills are taught by the older and more mature members of a group. In daily interactions within families, school, child care center, and neighborhood groups, children are constantly being shown models or are being told directly. Children in rural China work beside their parents, learning how to nurture the crops or perform the daily tasks necessary for their existence. Children in New York are taught by their parents how to behave within the neighborhood environment, but they also learn from their friends as they play.

Scaffolding

Children constantly add to their knowledge and skills through learning and play activities (Berk & Winsler, 1995). Vygotsky saw that this was possible because of the presence of a support system or scaffold in the form of the social environment. Both parents and teachers plan a series of activities from simple to more complex, thus allowing children to acquire the knowledge and tools they need in manageable steps. The scaffold may also be a suggestion or question. It might include encouragement to continue the task even though the child is frustrated. An example can be seen in a child who cannot complete a difficult puzzle. The teacher may place a piece close to where it fits or may suggest looking for pieces that are a particular color. Another example is the parent who helps a child learn to ride a two-wheeler bike. The adult puts on training wheels, holds the handlebars, and runs beside the child. As the child's confidence grows the adult lets go of the handlebars, but continues to be close by. The final step may be removal of the training wheels.

Other family members may also provide the scaffold for learning new skills. Children may watch older siblings performing a task, then try to imitate the behavior. Sometimes the older brother or sister shows the younger siblings how to do something, then encourages them to attempt the task. When children go to child care or enter school, peers or older children are often part of the cooperative learning environment supporting growth. When children work together on tasks there is an opportunity for the less skilled to learn from the more skilled participant.

Language

Language plays a crucial role in the development of cognitive abilities because it is the basis for social interactions between adult and child or between children. Through communication children can be guided to acquire the practical skills needed in their society. Communication also allows individuals to make mental contacts with others and provides a means for interpreting, storing, and using social experiences.

Zone of Proximal Development

The zone of proximal development is the hypothetical environment in which learning and development take place (Berk & Winsler, 1995). It can be further described as the region between what children can learn by themselves and what they can learn through the guidance and tutoring of a more competent member of society. Through carefully chosen and planned activities, children gradually move from assisted performance to independent performance. Crucial to this process is sensitivity to each child's level of competence and a means to encourage them to move to the next level. When teachers or parents help children acquire a new skill, they may begin with a demonstration, then carefully guide them through the steps and encourage them as they perform on their own.

Evaluation of Sociocultural Theory

Sociocultural theory has added a new dimension to the study of children's development, particularly in understanding diversity (Berger, 2000). It has increased knowledge of the ways in which cognitive development varies depending on the values and makeup of different societies. It further emphasizes the importance of understanding each culture's values and beliefs and their effect on children's competencies.

Although the importance of Vygotsky's theory is recognized, present-day researchers are cautious in trying to generalize research findings from one culture to another (Cole, 1992). On the other hand, researchers recognize that children's competencies should be examined through procedures that are relevant within their culture.

One limitation of sociocultural theory is that it does not take into account developmental processes that are not social. Some processes are the result of biological maturation.

Another limitation is that Vygotsky did not consider how much children affect their own learning environment. According to Rogoff (1990), children often choose their own activities or their mentors. They often reject or resist help and support from parents or teachers.

Implications for Child Care Staff Members

Most child care centers serve children who come from more than one cultural group and who, as adults, will live in an increasingly diverse society. It is important, therefore, that they learn to function comfortably in a multicultural environment without losing their identity within their own group. Child care staff members can help them achieve that goal in the following ways:

- Learn more about different cultures and be sensitive to cultural values, ways of interacting, and linguistic differences.
- Include families, integrating their values and culture into teaching and learning experiences.
- Learn about their expectations for their children.
- Encourage children to learn about and appreciate cultures other than their own.
- Help children to acquire the competencies that are important in their culture as well as those that are necessary in broader society.
- Carefully choose and plan activities that gradually move children from assisted performance to independent performance.
- Cultivate each child's communication skills as an important tool of learning.
- Establish a meaningful relationship with every child because it is through the interaction between adult and child that much learning takes place.
- Encourage cooperative learning in small groups so children can learn from each other.

Which theorist said that children learn from each other?

Intelligence and Learning

Attempts to understand and measure intelligence have existed for many years. Tests were developed to try to quantify intelligence in relation to chronological age. Items on tests such as the Stanford-Binet focus on general knowledge, reasoning ability, mathematical skill, memory, vocabulary, and spatial perception. More recently, theories of multiple intelligences have interested professionals who are concerned with the education of young children. Sternberg (1996) delineates three types of intelligence: academic (measured by achievement or IQ tests), creative (measured by imaginative undertakings), and practical (seen in everyday tasks and interactions). Gardner (1983) describes seven distinct intelligences: body-kinesthetic, spatial, linguistic, logical-mathematical, musical, interpersonal (social understanding), and intrapersonal (self-understanding). Later, Gardner (1999) added naturalist intelligence, the ability to recognize and classify features of the environment. According to Gardner, everyone has a basic aptitude for each of the intelligences, but most people are stronger in one area than in other areas. One person may have exceptional musical ability but have limited spatial skill and therefore gets lost easily.

Implications for Child Care Staff Members

Theories of multiple intelligence are important to anyone who works with children because they can help us understand why some children do so well in some areas but have difficulty in others. It also explains why learning experiences should provide children the opportunity to use all their senses and to express their abilities in a variety of ways (Gardner, 1991). Many schools focus primarily on the tasks that standard tests of achievement measure. This does not allow children to develop other facets of intelligence. Child care personnel can encourage children to develop more than one intelligence by implementing the following suggestions:

- Understand that each child is unique and may be gifted in one area but not in others.
- Let children choose their own methods of learning and work at their own pace (intrapersonal).
- Use cooperative learning that includes feedback from others (intrapersonal).
- Provide a variety of experiences that allows children to use their senses in different ways (kinesthetic).
- Encourage children to use language in word games, crossword puzzles, or debates (linguistic).
- Foster the ability to visualize by providing the opportunity to work puzzles, draw maps, and work mazes (spatial).
- Provide games that require strategy planning or resolving problems (logical-mathematical).
- Help children use music in a variety of activities: writing songs, playing instruments, and creating musical plays (musical).
- Use the outdoors as another classroom by introducing science projects, creating a nature area, or nurturing animals (naturalist).

Language

Middle childhood is a time when the ability to use language to enhance cognitive skills and to manipulate social situations increases rapidly. Children acquire as many as 20 words a day, achieving a vocabulary of 40,000 words by the fifth grade (Anglin, 1993). The list of words they understand and use may include some they have not experienced directly but understand through reading, conversation, television, and computers. They deduce the meaning of a word through knowledge of the context in which it is used.

School-age children define words differently from the way they did as preschoolers. When asked to define a word, preschool children give examples that are based on perceptions. "An orange is something to eat that tastes good." A school-age child will likely be more logical by saying "It's a fruit." Preschoolers also define words by using action-based statements, whereas older children analyze the relationship to other words. A four-year-old will say, "Under something is where I hide my toys from my brother." A nine-year-old might say, "Under is the opposite of over" (Holzman, 1983).

Children practice their language skills by trying to refine grammatical construction. By age 6 most children understand and use grammar correctly, but during middle childhood further improvement takes place. Preschool children acquire new language construc-

What skills can children acquire by using a computer?

tions by adapting what they have previously learned. They discover that "ed" is added to make a verb past tense and therefore say, "He goed." Gradually, school-age children learn the variations of verb forms and use them correctly. Older children may not always use correct grammar even though they know it. In conversation with their peers, for instance, they may say, "Me and my mom had a fight." In school they are able to correctly say, "My mom and I had a fight."

School-age children become adept at pragmatic uses of language. They choose words, modify sentences, or change voice inflections to fit the listener in a particular situation. They may use simpler words and shorter sentences when talking to a younger sibling than they would with their friends. The best example of pragmatic use of language is seen in the jokes told by elementary school children. In order to be successful humorists, they need to recognize what the listener will think is funny and to remember the exact words (Yasilove, 1978).

Further indication that school-age children use language pragmatically is the switch to different forms as the occasion dictates. When making a request of possibly reluctant adults, they are careful to use a polite form of request, "Could I please go to the movie with Rachel?" A more extensive switch in language is called **code-switching** (Holzman, 1983; Yoon, 1992). This means a complete change of form when addressing adults and another

They may use simpler words and shorter sentences when talking to a younger sibling than they would with their friends. The best example of pragmatic use of language is seen in the jokes told by elementary school children. In order to be successful humorists, they need to recognize what the listener will think is funny and to remember the exact words (Yasilove, 1978).

Further indication that school-age children use language pragmatically is the switch to different forms as the occasion dictates. When making a request of possibly reluctant adults, they are careful to use a polite form of request, "Could I please go to the movie with Rachel?" A more extensive switch in language is called code-switching (Holzman, 1983; Yoon, 1992). This means a complete change of form when addressing adults and another when addressing cohorts. They may use elaborated code in the classroom and change to a restricted code when they are on the playground (Bernstein, 1971, 1973). Elaborated code has a more extensive vocabulary, is correct grammatically, and is longer. In contrast, restricted code is more limited and may rely on gestures and voice intonation to communicate meaning. Although they are required to use standard English in the classroom, children also learn the idiosyncrasies of speech specific to their ethnic group or in common usage in their particular region of the country. Some forms differ in minor ways, such as regional accents or colloquialisms in common usage. Certain speech patterns or accents are so distinctive that they can identify the region where a person lives or grew up. A Southern accent is easily distinguished from a Texas drawl. Another variation is Black English, or Ebonics, which uses double negatives: "Nobody couldn't come to the party." Children for whom English is not their primary language face even greater problems. These children are forced to use a language they may barely understand and get behind in school. They may also be mercilessly teased by other children for their accent or misuse of words.

Second Language Development

The influx of refugees and immigrants into the United States has rapidly increased the number of children who are second language learners. They speak a native language at home and are learning English in their out-of-home experiences. Research points out the cognitive, cultural, and economic advantages of bilingualism (Hakuta & Pease-Alverez, 1992). Hence, children who have the opportunity to speak two languages should be encouraged to maintain both. Cognitively, school-age children are able to understand that others may perceive them as different if their language is not that of the majority. They fear they will become the targets of teasing, and this affects their self-concept.

Some basic principles have been drawn from theory and research on second language acquisition (McLaughlin, 1995). The first is that it is rare for both languages to be perfectly balanced. As a child is learning a second language, one language will be predominant. The more the second language is used, the less the native (home) language is used, and hence both languages may appear less proficient. This is a temporary imbalance, and most bilingual children will reach age-level proficiency in their dominant language given adequate opportunities for use.

The second principle is that of the normalcy of code-switching. Young children tend to insert single items from one language into the other (McClure, 1977) primarily to internalize a second language more readily if they are asked to engage in meaningful activities that require using the language. They also need good models for language use and should be given opportunities to experiment with language as they learn correct phrases and intonation.

Implications for Child Care Staff Members

The importance of language in children's development cannot be underestimated. Good language skills are essential for success in school, and children who can communicate their needs and feelings clearly get along better with their peers and adults. Perhaps even more important, good language skills are needed for many of the jobs these youngsters will pursue in the future.

- Provide a wide variety of reading materials: books, magazines, comic books, and newspapers.
- Read to children frequently and encourage them to read alone or with others.
- Plan a variety of activities and experiences that help children expand their vocabularies and their ability to communicate clearly with others. Remember that listening is a part of communicating.
- Model correct English when speaking to children and accept children's forms of speech. Remember that the goal is for the child to communicate, not adhere to rigid rules about language. Do not correct grammar or pronunciation when children are communicating. Respond to the content of communication.
- Use demonstrations, modeling, and role playing to communicate the meaning of language. The more visuals presented to limited English speakers, the more likely they will comprehend what is being presented to them.
- Invite parents of children with different cultural backgrounds to provide activities and information about their culture such as language, food, and special customs.
- Develop buddy and peer groups that will be supportive and provide feedback to the second language learner.
- Provide opportunities for children to use their primary language in ways that enhance their self-esteem. Encourage them to teach useful words or phrases to others. Allow them to use their speech forms in creative ways when writing stories, plays, or poetry.
- Include written or oral language in culturally based activities.

Summary

The thinking processes of school-age children are markedly different from those of preschoolers. Swiss psychologist Piaget was a major contributor to the understanding of how children think and learn. Piaget believed that intelligence is the result of progression through four stages: the sensorimotor period, from birth to 2 years, the preoperational period, from 2 to 7 years, the concrete operations period, from 7 to 11, and the formal operations period, from age 11 to 15. Another general principle of Piaget's theory is that children are active participants in the development of their own intelligence. A third principle is that differences in the rate at which individuals pass through the stages are due to variations in maturation rate.

Behaviorist theory grew out of a need for more precise studies of human development and was proposed early in the twentieth century by Watson. Watson's ideas were based on the classical conditioning of Pavlov and pointed to the connection between a stimulus and response. When a stimulus is followed by a pleasant response, the behavior is likely to be repeated; if the response is unpleasant, the behavior may disappear. Skinner started with Watson's ideas but went a step further. He proposed another type of conditioning, operant conditioning. He observed that children operate on their environment and are reinforced. When the reinforcer is pleasant, the behavior will be repeated, and when unpleasant it is likely not to be repeated. Bandura also agreed with behaviorist ideas but felt that some behaviors could not be explained by simple stimulus and response mechanisms. He saw that some behaviors occur as a result of less direct teaching, through observation of a model and then subsequent imitation of that behavior.

Sociocultural theory, proposed by Vygotsky, has only recently been widely disseminated. Vygotsky assumed that social interaction and children's direct participation in authentic cultural activities is necessary for their optimum development. He pointed to the need to understand cross-cultural variation—the kinds of tools and activities different societies use to help children develop the competencies they will need as adults. Vygotsky believed that children construct themselves, adding to their knowledge and skills, and pointed to the importance of the support system or scaffold in the child's environment. Vygotsky also recognized the importance of language, which forms the basis of social interactions between adult and child. According to Vygotsky, the zone of proximal development is the hypothetical environment in which learning and development take place.

More recent attempts to understand intelligence have brought theories of multiple intelligences. Sternberg delineated three: academic, creative, and practical. Gardner listed eight: body-kinesthetic, spatial, linguistic, logical-mathematical, musical, interpersonal, intrapersonal, and naturalist.

Middle childhood is a time when the ability to use language to enhance cognitive skills and manipulate social situations increases rapidly. Children acquire as many as 20 words a day, achieving a vocabulary of 40,000 words by the fifth grade.

Children practice their language skills by trying to refine grammatical constructions. They are adept at pragmatic uses of language, choosing words, modifying sentences, or changing inflections to suit particular situations. Children also demonstrate their pragmatic use of language when they switch to different forms as an occasion dictates. Code-switching is a complete change of form when addressing adults and another when addressing peers.

Many children speak a non-English primary language in their home and therefore are at various levels of proficiency in using English. Their attempts at learning and using English as well as their primary language should be encouraged. Caregivers should provide an enticing, language-rich environment that supports reading, writing, and speaking English as well as home languages.

Key Terms

centering	code-switching
classical conditioning	concrete operations

elaborated code
formal operations
modeling
operant conditioning
preoperational period

restricted code
scaffold
sensorimotor period
storage strategies
zone of proximal development

Student Activities

1. Observe a group of school-age children. Can you recognize any models the children are using to pattern their own behavior? Are the models real persons (familiar adults or their peers) or characters from television, films, or computer games? Why do you think they have chosen these particular models? In small groups, share your observations with classmates. Discuss the preceding questions.

2. Visit an after-school program serving children from ages 5 to 11. Record the number of times the adults use positive reinforcers. What types of reinforcers seem to be most effective with this age level? Did they encourage repetition of the behavior? What negative reinforcers were also used? Did they discourage the behavior? Share your findings with classmates, and compile a list of responses that seem effective when working with school-age children.

3. In small-group discussions, ask members to relate their own methods of working with children to one of the theories described in this chapter. Do they choose one theory over others? Or do they tend to use each of the theories in an eclectic approach, using several different theories?

4. Plan two activities for a group of nine-year-olds that will help them increase their vocabulary. Share your plans with classmates.

5. Present a demonstration of an activity using only visual gestures and materials to convey your meaning. In small groups, discuss the difficulties of learning concepts and instructions if there is no understanding of the language being spoken. (It would be ideal to have someone who speaks another language, unknown by the majority of the classmates, do this presentation in their native language followed by small-group discussion.)

Review Questions

1. Why did Piaget observe that during the preoperational period children often come to the wrong conclusions?

2. Between ages 7 and 11 children progress to the stage of concrete operations. What new abilities have they acquired?

3. State three applications of Piagetian theory in a school-age child care setting.

4. How does operant conditioning, proposed by Skinner, differ from the social learning theory of Bandura?

5. What are some criticisms of behaviorist theory?

6. How is behaviorist theory used when planning an appropriate environment for school-age children?

7. What is meant by *scaffolding*?

8. What is meant by the *zone of proximal development*?

9. How can child care leaders use Vygotsky's ideas in a multicultural community?
10. State three ways child care leaders can help children increase their language skills.
11. List the eight intelligences delineated by Gardner.
12. Describe the role of the caregiver as it pertains to children who are learning English as a second language. Consider curriculum, peer interaction on behalf of the second language learner, and your own interactions with the child.

Case Study

Angela and Jennine wanted to learn to knit so they could make scarves for their dads. Their group leader, Nancy, promised to show them how since she had been knitting since she was very young. She told them to buy some #6 needles and a ball of yarn in the color they liked.

They came to the after-school program the next day, eager to get started. Nancy cast on the stitches on each of their needles because she felt it would be hard enough for them to learn the stitch without starting with casting on. She demonstrated for each of them, then guided their hands through several stitches. Angela was quickly ready to proceed on her own, but Jennine was having trouble. She would forget which way to wrap the yarn around the needle or how to pull the stitch through. Nancy again guided Jennine's hands, but she still had problems, and Jennine became increasingly frustrated. Then, Nancy remembered that she had a knitting instruction book in the cupboard that showed the step-by-step process. She got it out and propped the page in front of Jennine. Jennine studied it and then cautiously tried each step. Finally, she understood and was exuberant that she was successful at last.

1. Why do you think Angela found the instructions Nancy gave her easy to follow? Why was it difficult for Jennine?
2. How would you describe the methods that Nancy used to teach the girls?
3. What does this tell you about other learning experiences that you provide for the children in your group?

References

Anglin, J. M. (1993). Vocabulary development: A morphological analysis. *Monographs of the Society for Research in Child Development, 58*(10, Serial No. 238).

Bandura, A. (1977). *Social learning theory*. Englewood Cliffs, NJ: Prentice Hall.

Berger, K. S. (2000). *The developing person through childhood and adolescence* (5th ed.). New York: Worth.

Berk, L. E., & Winsler, A. (1995). *Scaffolding children's learning: Vygotsky and early childhood education*. Washington, DC: National Association for the Education of Young Children.

Bernstein, B. (1971, 1973). *Class, codes, and control* (Vols. 1, 2). London: Routledge & Kegan Paul.

Cole, M. (1983). Culture in development.

Gardner, H. (1983). *Frames of mind: The theory of multiple intelligences*. New York: Basic Books.

Gardner, H. (1991). *The unschooled mind: How children think and how schools should teach.* New York: Basic Books.

Gardner, H. (1999). *Intelligence reframed: Multiple intelligences for the 21st century.* New York: Basic Books.

Hakuta, K., & Pease-Alvarez, L. (1992). Enriching our view of bilingualism and bilingual education. *Educational Researcher, 21,* 4–6.

Holzman, M. (1983). *The language of children: Development in home and in school.* Englewood Cliffs, NJ: Prentice Hall.

Locke, J. (1959). *Essay concerning human understanding* (Collated and annotated by A. C. Fraser). New York: Dover.

McClure, E. F. (1977). *Aspects of code-switching in the discourse of bilingual Mexican-American children* (Tech. Rep. No. 44). Cambridge, MA: Berancek & Newman.

McLaughlin, B. (1995). *Fostering second language development in young children: Principles and practices.* Washington, DC: National Center for Research on Cultural Diversity and Second Language Learning.

Pavlov, I. (1960). *Conditioned reflexes: An investigation of the physiological activity of the cerebral cortex* (G. V. Anrep, Ed. & Trans.). New York: Dover.

Philips, S. (1972). Participant structures and communicative competence: Warm Springs children in community and the classroom. In C. B. Cazden, V. P. John, & D. Hymes (Eds.), *Function of language in the classroom* (pp. 370–394). New York: Teachers College Press.

Piaget, J. (1952). *The origins of intelligence in children* (M. Cook, Trans.). New York: International Universities Press.

Rogoff, B. (1990). *Apprenticeship in thinking: Cognitive development in social context.* New York: Oxford University Press.

Skinner, B. F. (1953). *Science and human behavior.* New York: Macmillan.

Sternberg, R. J. (1996). *Successful intelligence.* New York: Simon & Schuster.

Vygotsky, L. S. (1978). *Mind in society: The development of higher psychological processes.* Cambridge, MA: Harvard University Press.

Vygotsky, L. S. (1987). *Thinking and speech* (N. Minick, Trans.). New York: Plenum.

Watson, J. B. (1967). *Behaviorism* (Rev. ed.). Chicago: University of Chicago Press. (Original work published 1924)

Yasilove, D. (1978). The effect of riddle-structure on children's comprehension and appreciation of riddles (Doctoral dissertation, 1978) New York University. *Dissertation Abstracts International, 36,* 6.

Yoon, K. (1992). New perspective on intrasentential code-switching: A study of Korean-English switching. *Applied Psycholinguistics, 13,* 433–449.

Suggested Readings

Moore, T. (1999). Bringing diversity into your center. *Child Care Information Exchange, 126*(Mar/Apr), 35–37.

CHAPTER 6

Development in Middle Childhood: Psychosocial

OBJECTIVES

After studying this chapter, the student should be able to:

- Discuss the major principles of several theories of psychosocial development
- List the concerns expressed by critics of each theory as well as the points of agreement
- Develop strategies that enhance children's psychosocial development

Cheryl is 22 and has lived with her boyfriend for four years. A year ago a female friend and her daughter moved in with them. Cheryl is godmother to the six-year-old girl and has known her since she was born. She is currently working in a privately owned child care center that serves children from 5 to 11 years old. The center is one of five centers operated by the owners.

Cheryl works from 9 AM to 5 PM in a before- and after-school kindergarten group. The children in her group are in the center until their regular classes are in session and return there at the end of the day.

Part of Cheryl's assignment also includes managing two boys who are only four. They are with her all day, at times alone with her and at other times with her in the kindergarten group. These boys had attended one of the other centers that are part of this business, but the teachers could not handle them. Now the two of them spend time alone with Cheryl or with the kindergarten group when she is working there.

She feels the boys have really changed since she has been with them, and she attributes part of her success to the fact that she knows how to talk to them and understands them. "I was hard to handle myself when I was little and got pushed aside." She changed when one teacher really cared about her. Because she wanted to do well for this person, that became a turning point in her life. She thinks all children grow up remembering teachers who made a difference in their lives, and she wants to be one. She thinks that one of the qualities that make her a good teacher is that she can get down to the children's level. She also understands their feelings, particularly when she remembers how she felt when she was a child. Parents also notice that she can remain calm.

Cheryl wants to be an elementary school teacher and is taking classes that will help her eventually reach her goal. When she was 15, she started working to buy her own clothes and help her single-parent mom. Her first jobs in fast-food restaurants and later in retail sales have helped her learn how to relate to and communicate with people.

Theories of Psychosocial Development

The world of children between the ages of 5 and 12 expands as they enter school and begin to experience the environment outside their homes. Increased physical and cognitive skills allow them more independence to explore their neighborhoods, visit friends' homes, and use community facilities such as playgrounds or clubs. In the process, they have many adventures and encounter new people. Parents are often unaware of and have little control over the kinds of challenges their children face as they maneuver in this new territory. How children manage depends a great deal on how they feel about themselves and the kinds of moral values they have learned within their families. Several theories are used to explain how children develop their sense of identity and learn to be successful members of a society.

Psychoanalytic Theory and Sigmund Freud

Freud (1938) was an Austrian doctor and the founder of the psychoanalytic theory of human behavior. While working with persons diagnosed as "hysterics," Freud evolved the theory that irrational behaviors have underlying causes that come from unconscious sexual and aggressive drives that he called *libido*. He saw the psyche as having three parts: the id, the source of pleasure-seeking drives; the ego, or the rational aspect of personality; and the superego, which controls behavior through the development of a conscience. Freud also proposed that the id is present at birth, whereas the ego and superego develop as one progresses through stages of development. In the process, the ego functions as a mediating force between the desire to seek pleasure and the need to yield to the demands of parents and society. Each stage brings with it conflicts that a child must resolve. How well a child is able to do this is determined by the skills and competencies acquired along the way. Freud delineated five stages of development: The first two are the oral period and anal period. Both are concerned with children under the age 3. Freud's third stage begins at age 3 and covers school-age children up to age 6.

Stage 3. Phallic: Three to Six Years.

During the phallic period, the genital areas are the focus of pleasure, and children become aware of physical differences between boys and girls. It is also during this period that children develop attachments to the parent of the opposite sex; boys are attracted to their mothers, and girls to their fathers. Eventually they learn that they must control these feelings and resolve the conflict by identifying with the parent of the same sex. This leads to development of gender identity and sexual orientation, as well as internalization of family moral values.

Stage 4. Latency: Seven to Eleven Years.

The latency period, as the name implies, is a period of latent or quiet feelings. Children's sexual urges are unobtrusive, and energies are directed toward school activities and sports. During this period children develop competencies and refine their self-images.

Stage 5. Adolescence: Twelve Years to Adulthood.

Adolescence brings changes in sexual organs and physical changes in the appearance of both males and females. Strong sexual urges cause the adolescent to struggle with how to satisfy those urges in socially acceptable and safe ways. Moral values incorporated during earlier stages are reexamined and tested against those of their peers, their religion, and society.

Evaluation of Psychoanalytic Theory

Many of Freud's ideas are so widely accepted that they are no longer attributed to psychoanalytic origins (Berger, 1995). There is general agreement that unconscious drives affect some behaviors, although the source of those drives may not be attributed to sexual urges, as Freud proposed. Modified aspects of psychoanalytic theory are evident in research and popular writings about the importance of attachment between mother and infant, gender identity, parental discipline, moral development, and adolescent development.

Some facets of psychosexual theory, however, are no longer considered valid. There is little support for Freud's belief that the way in which conflicts during the oral and anal phases are resolved results in specific personality traits. An even more important criticism of psychoanalytic theory is that it was based on Freud's experiences with white, middle-, or upper-class patients. Present-day developmental theory emphasizes that personality and behavior are affected more by a person's heredity, life events, and the culture in which one lives rather than on conflicts that occur in childhood. There is little support as well for Freud's belief in the struggle between the id and the superego. The strongest criticism of psychoanalytic theory is that it cannot be proven through controlled scientific research. Freudian theory is very much a part of the historical process of understanding human behavior and has affected much of modern thinking about children's development. However, the theory should not be interpreted literally.

Psychosocial Theory and Erik Erikson

Erikson (1963) studied psychoanalytic theory with Anna Freud, the daughter of Sigmund Freud. He later moved to Boston, where he started a psychoanalytic practice. Erikson's work included children from a wide variety of backgrounds. Some were from middle-class, professional families, others from poor families, and some were delinquent children. At first he found it difficult to apply psychoanalytic principles to his work with children who were not typically middle class, but eventually he found that all children have some common characteristics. Erikson expanded Freud's stages of development to encompass the entire life span, with each stage characterized by a challenge or developmental crisis.

Erikson's first five stages of childhood are similar to those of Freud. They are (1) trust vs. mistrust; (2) autonomy vs. shame and doubt; (3) initiative vs. guilt; (4) industry vs. inferiority; and (5) identity vs. role confusion. Erikson delineated three additional stages that follow the childhood years and extend into adulthood: intimacy vs. isolation; generativity vs. stagnation; and integrity vs. despair. The significant difference between Freud and Erikson, however, lies in Erikson's emphasis on a person's relationship to the social environment rather than on the body. He called his ideas the psychosocial theory of development. At each stage of development, the resolution of a crisis depends on the interaction between the individual's personality characteristics and the support and guidance provided by the social environment. How successful or unsuccessful a person is in resolving these crises depends a great deal on competencies and the support and guidance that parents and society provide.

The first two stages cover birth to age 3, while Stage 3 includes school-age children.

These girls are best friends.

Stage 3. Initiative vs. Guilt: Three to Six Years.

During this period children want to attempt many tasks they observe their parents or other adults performing. They sometimes attempt activities that are beyond their capabilities or are outside the limits set by their parents. If given support and guidance by their caregivers, the result will be feelings of success and pride in their own initiative. If they are unsuccessful, they will be left with feelings of guilt.

Stage 4. Industry vs. Inferiority: Seven to Eleven Years.

During this middle-childhood period children expend their energies on mastering new skills at home, in school, on the playground, and in their neighborhoods. When they are successful, they acquire the tools they need for important societal tasks such as getting a job and getting along with others. When they are unsuccessful, feelings of inferiority set a pattern for possible failure throughout life.

Stage 5. Identity vs. Role Confusion: Adolescence.

This period is highlighted by adolescents' search for identity as individuals in a society. They must balance a desire to establish their own uniqueness with a need to conform to the standards set by the society or culture in which they live. Rebelliousness may lead to role confusion, and strict conformity to a stifling of individuality.

Writing is an important societal task to be mastered.

Evaluation of Psychosocial Theory

Erikson's perception of human development is more widely accepted than psychoanalytic theory even though it is based on Freud's ideas (Berger, 2000). Erikson's writings are more contemporary, not based on the Victorian culture of Freud's time. Many ideas taken from Erikson are currently applied to issues regarding care of infants, parenting problems, care of children in groups, and training of caregivers.

Implications for Child Care Staff Members

Two themes are present in both Freudian and Eriksonian ideas about how children develop: the significance of childhood stages in the formation of personality and the importance of the manner in which adults respond to children's behavior during each of the stages. These concepts lead to several specific implications for persons working with school-age children:

- Remember that adults are active participants in helping children resolve the conflicts inherent in each of the stages of development. Provide guidance and support so that the conflicts can be resolved in ways that enhance children's self-image.
- Include families in decisions concerning a child's problem behaviors. The behaviors have been formed within the context of family interactions and will be more easily changed with cooperation from family members.

Approximate Age	Freud	Erikson
3–6	• Phallic stage • Oedipal situation • Identification with same-sex parent • Superego, conscience	• Initiative vs. guilt • Attempt adult activities • Gaining independence • Overstep parental limits, feel guilty
7–11	• Latency • Quiet period, less sexual tension • Psychic energy goes into learning skills	• Industry vs. inferiority • Becoming competent is important • Can feel inferior if unsuccessful • Identity vs. role confusion
Adolescence	• Genital • Seeking sexual stimulation and gratification	• Considering own identity • Establishing ethnic and career identities

TABLE 6-1 Comparison of Psychoanalytic Theories

- Support children's need for competence by providing opportunities for them to acquire new social skills and to practice already acquired skills.
- Support their need to be independent by allowing them freedom to make choices and do things without adult intervention. Let them plan and carry out many of their own activities. Also let them make their own rules within limits that do not interfere with others' rights.
- Let children know their competence and responsibility are valued.

Moral Development

The process of acquiring and using moral values and attitudes continues throughout life. At each step of development, children learn that certain behaviors are acceptable, whereas others bring disapproval and rejection. The years of middle childhood are particularly fertile grounds for learning the lessons taught by the family, culture, and society for several reasons. First, peer relationships become extremely important, sometimes taking precedence over family. Children want to be part of a peer group, so they learn to negotiate, compromise, and play "by the rules" in order to be included. Second, they have already acquired cognitive skills that allow them to think logically and even abstractly. They understand concepts of right and wrong and can consider moral issues related to their own behaviors. Finally, their world has expanded beyond the family into the school and the neighborhood. Toward the end of middle childhood, children begin to look at broad moral issues that affect others: human rights, destructiveness of war, ecological devastation, and global hunger.

Jean Piaget

As discussed in Chapter 5, Piaget's (1932) primary concern was the cognitive development of children, but he was also interested in how children begin to understand justice and develop a respect for social order. He believed that children's understanding of rules goes through stages as their thinking processes change. In the earliest stage, the preschool and early school-age years, children believe that rules are created by an all-powerful authority figure and that they are not to be changed. He called this stage *moral realism*, in which justice is whatever the authority decides at a particular time. By age 7 or 8, children reach another level. During this period they interact with their peers differently, often with give-and-take reciprocity. They also change their ideas about authority, recognizing that punishments may be fair or unfair, depending on the transgression committed. As children approach adolescence, around age 11 or 12, a new stage emerges. Piaget called this stage *moral relativism*. At this level, children are able to be more flexible, change rules, and discuss moral issues.

Lawrence Kohlberg

The most complete theory of children's moral development was proposed by Kohlberg, who used Piaget's theories as a starting point for developing his own theory of moral development. Kohlberg (1963) believed that children's moral thinking developed in stages along with the development of cognitive skills. As cognitive processes changed, the ability to consider moral questions also changed. To test his theory, he presented children with a set of hypothetical stories about moral dilemmas that required decisions involving human life, property rights, or human needs. He examined children's responses to these situations and concluded that children proceed through the following three levels of moral reasoning:

Level I. Preconventional: Emphasis on Punishment and Rewards, Ages 4 to 10

Stage 1. Might makes right.   At this level behavior is labeled good or bad based entirely on the consequences of an action. Children obey authority in order to avoid punishment.

"If you do that, you'll get in trouble."

Stage 2. Satisfy your own needs.   People take care of their own needs first and occasionally the needs of others. Children believe that if they are nice to others, others will be nice to them. "I'll invite you to my birthday party if you let me play with you."

Level II. Conventional: Emphasis on Social Rules of the Individual's Family, Group, or Nation, Ages 10 to 13

Stage 3. Interpersonal concordance.   Good behavior is behavior that others approve of and reward. Approval is more important than any other kind of compensation. Children value conformity to stereotyped images of what majority behavior is. A significant change occurs during this stage: Children recognize intent that is attached to behavior. "He didn't really mean to ruin your building. He was just trying to help."

Stage 4. Law and order.   Emphasis is on authority and obedience to the laws set down by those in power in order to maintain social order. Right behavior means doing one's duty, showing respect for authority, and recognizing the need to maintain social order. "It's not right to take things that don't belong to you. Besides, you might get arrested."

Level III. Postconventional: Emphasis on Universal Moral Values and Principles, Age 13 and Older

Stage 5. Social contract.   People understand that laws and rules exist to ensure individual rights. Right action is seen in terms of standards that society has examined and agreed on. Aside from what has been democratically agreed on, right is also a matter of personal values and opinions. Laws might be changed if a consensus can be reached: "I think we should change the rules of this game so the little kids can play."

Stage 6. Universal principles.   People behave according to universal ethical principles. These principles are abstract, like the golden rule, and involve a basic right for everyone to be treated equally and with dignity: "I don't think anybody should be discriminated against. Everyone should be able to live where he wants or go to school where she wants."

Kohlberg found that individuals progress through the moral hierarchy very slowly. He found that most school-age children function at Stage 1 or 2. He believes that children must be at the cognitive level of adolescents to make moral decisions comparable to Stage 3. Only then will they begin to consider another person's intent before judging behavior as right or wrong. Once they reach that level of thinking, they may be able to go on to question authority and laws in terms of faithfulness to maintaining basic human rights. Each stage must be experienced before progressing to the next level, and no level can be skipped.

Some individuals may become fixed at a certain level and never move on to a higher one.

Evaluation of Kohlberg's Theory

Although Kohlberg's stages of moral development were originally praised by developmentalists as a way of understanding moral education, several researchers took a closer look.

Gilligan (1982) pointed to the fact that Kohlberg's scheme was validated on a group of only males, ages 10, 13, and 16. When women were tested, they scored lower than males; women on average were at Stage 3, and men at Stage 4. Moral development at Stage 3 is an interpersonal level, with emphasis on gaining approval for good behavior. Stage 4 is a more objective acceptance of rules. Gilligan argues that girls develop what she calls a morality of caring, whereas boys judge right and wrong in terms of a morality of justice. Because they are socialized to be caring and nurturing, girls are reluctant to judge right and wrong in absolutes. When faced with making choices, boys immediately determine what is right or wrong followed by a clear solution, whereas girls try to find a variety of alternatives.

One researcher tested Gilligan's ideas and came to a different conclusion. Walker (1988) found that during middle childhood, both boys and girls tended to seek justice when faced with a moral dilemma. Older and more mature subjects were more caring.

Turiel (1983; Turiel, Smetana, & Killen, 1991) pointed out the fact that Kohlberg used hypothetical situations, not the daily circumstances children typically confront. When Turiel used real test situations more closely resembling children's own experiences, he

"Me." Nicole, age 7.

found children can reason better about familiar settings. When playing games, for instance, they function at a higher level of moral thinking. Turiel also found that when children have a chance to discuss issues repeatedly, they make wiser decisions.

A further criticism of Kohlberg's theory is that his stages reflect Western values and cannot be applied to other cultures. Reid (1984, 1989), studying Samoan and European families in New Zealand, found that the needs of family members sometimes take precedence over observing moral principles that apply to everyone.

Implications for Child Care Staff Members

Because middle childhood is a period when children are learning to find their way in the world outside their home, it is important to facilitate their ability to live within society's rules and to get along with others. Child care workers can play an important part.

- Provide children with both male and female caregivers.
- Involve children in solving moral dilemmas that occur in their everyday experiences. Give them opportunities to discuss the possible solutions to and the consequences of each decision, allowing them to find new ways of approaching moral dilemmas.
- Provide children with opportunities to interact with children and adults of different age groups, exposing them to higher levels of moral functioning.
- Create an environment in which individual and family value systems are accepted. It is easy to accept value systems that are like one's own, but it takes more practice to accept those that are different.
- Model the kind of behavior expected of children. Behave in ways that are fair and just rather than imposing arbitrary rules that have no relation to values.
- Allow the children to assist in forming the language of the program rules.

Summary

Freud's psychoanalytic theory of development asserts that there are hidden causes of behavior that originate in the unconscious. He also believed that libido, general sexual or sensual energy, is the driving force behind all human behavior. He saw the psyche as having three parts: the id, the ego, and the superego. The mediating force of the ego facilitates the struggle between the pleasure-seeking id and the conscience-driven superego. Individuals go through five stages during this process.

Erikson based his theory on psychoanalytic principles but felt that the resolution of the conflicts between the id and the superego takes place in the context of the social environment.

How successful a person is in resolving the crises of each stage depends on the support and guidance of parents and society. Erikson delineated eight stages from birth to the end of life.

Although many facets of Freud's theory are widely accepted, there are criticisms.

Erikson's theory is more easily accepted because it is not based on the Victorian culture of Freud's time.

The process of developing moral values continues throughout life. Piaget related moral development to the development of cognitive abilities. He wrote of the stage of moral realism during the preschool and early school-age years. By age 7 or 8 children reach another level, moral relativism. At this level children are able to be more flexible, change rules, and discuss moral values.

Kohlberg formulated the most complete theory of children's moral development. He used Piaget's ideas as a starting point and related moral development to the acquisition of cognitive skills. Kohlberg proposed three levels of moral reasoning, with two stages at each level. He found that individuals proceed through the stages slowly and that most school-age children function at the first level.

Criticism of Kolhberg's theory comes from several researchers who noted that his research focused only on preadolescent and adolescent boys. Gilligan argues that girls develop a morality of caring, whereas boys develop a morality of justice. Turiel contends that Kohlberg's test situations were hypothetical, not actual day-to-day dilemmas children actually face and could understand. Further criticism is that his stages reflect Western values and cannot be applied to all cultures.

Key Terms

adolescence	moral realism
anal period	moral relativism
autonomy vs. shame and doubt	morality of caring
conventional	morality of justice
ego	oral period
id	phallic period
identity vs. role confusion	postconventional
industry vs. inferiority	preconventional
initiative vs. guilt	superego
latency period	trust vs. mistrust

Student Activities

1. Ask several school-age children to discuss some moral dilemmas they are likely to face in their everyday life. The following are some possible scenarios, but you can make up your own.
   a. You and your friend go to the store to buy some candy. You notice that your friend puts a candy bar in his pocket but pays for a package of gum. What should you do?
   b. Your friend's little sister wants to play a game with the two of you, but you know that it will be too difficult for her. What will you do?

   Write down the responses the children make and then put them into one of Kohlberg's stages. Share the results with your classmates during your next class.

2. Ask your parents how they handled the following situations when you were growing up:
   a. Questions about gender differences
   b. Sibling rivalry
   c. Adolescent relationships

   Were their methods influenced by psychoanalytic thinking? If so, in what way?

Review Questions

1. Freud saw the psyche as having three parts. List and define each.
2. How is Erikson's theory related to Freud's ideas, and how is it different?
3. Briefly describe children's development according to Erikson during the following stages:
   a. initiative vs. guilt
   b. industry vs. inferiority
   c. identity vs. role confusion
4. State some criticisms of psychoanalytic theory.
5. What are some ways child care leaders can apply Freudian and Eriksonian theory to their work with children and families?
6. Piaget cited two stages in children's development of a sense of justice and respect for social order. What are they?
7. Kohlberg proposed three levels of moral reasoning. He called Level I, age 4 to 10, pre-conventional. State and describe Stages 1 and 2 at this level.
8. Why did Kohlberg believe that school-age children would find it difficult to make moral decisions having to do with a person's intent behind a behavior?
9. What was the basis for Gilligan's criticism of Kohlberg's theory?
10. Another researcher who criticized Kohlberg's findings is Turiel. What were his concerns?

Case Study

Joaquin is a caregiver of a group of eight-year-olds. He would like to change the way some children react when there are problems among the children. Danisha, the youngest boy in the group, never does anything wrong, but when someone else does, he loudly says,

"You're going to get in trouble for that." Emily maintains control over her two friends by threatening, "I won't invite you to my birthday party if you don't do what I want."

1. Why are the children reacting in this way?
2. Joaquin wants to reinforce the importance of rules but also wants to help the children move on to a higher level of morality. What could he say to the children?
3. When you are faced with helping children make decisions about good/bad behavior, what is it you want them to learn?

References

Berger, K., & Thompson, R. (1995). *The developing person through childhood and adolescence* (4th ed.). New York: Worth.

Erikson, E. H. (1963). *Childhood and society* (2nd ed.). New York: Norton.

Freud, S. (1938). *The basic writings of Sigmund Freud* (A. A. Brill, Ed. & Trans.). New York: Modern Library.

Gilligan, C. (1982). *In a different voice: Psychological theory and women's development.* Cambridge, MA: Harvard University Press.

Kohlberg, L. (1963). Development of children's orientation towards a moral order: (I). Sequence in the development of moral thought. *Vita Humana, 6,* 11–36.

Piaget, J. (1932). *The moral judgment of the child* (M. Gabin, Trans.). New York: The Free Press.

Reid, B. V. (1984). An anthropological reinterpretation of Kohlberg's stages of moral development. *Human Development, 27,* 56–74.

Reid, B. V. (1989). Socialization for moral reasoning: Maternal strategies of Samoans and Europeans in New Zealand. In J. Valsiner (Ed.), *Child development in cultural context.* Toronto: Hogrefe & Huber.

Turiel, E. (1983). *The development of social knowledge: Morality and convention.* Cambridge, England: Cambridge University Press.

Turiel, E., Smetana, J., & Killen, M. (1991). Social context in social cognitive development. In W. M. Kurtines & J. L. Gewirtz (Eds.), *Handbook of moral behavior and development: Vol. 2. Research.* Hillsdale, NJ: Erlbaum.

Walker, L. J. (1988). The development of moral reasoning. *Annals of Child Development, 55,* 677–691.

CHAPTER 7

Helping Children Develop Social Competence

Objectives

After studying this chapter, the student should be able to:

- Discuss strategies for helping children make and keep friends
- State the steps used to help children resolve conflicts
- Describe behaviors that create problems for individuals and the group
- Discuss verbal and other strategies for helping children change their behavior

Santos is a 66-year-old male who just began working in a state-funded children's center housed on a public school campus. He is retired from a management job with a large chemical manufacturer. Wanting to do something to contribute to others, he began doing storytelling and reading to Head Start classes. He loved that so much, he studied for and passed the CBEST (California Basic Education Skills Test) test that evaluates fitness for teaching without a credential. He applied to work in child care and has been working regularly as a substitute for six months. Both the children and center directors appreciate his enthusiasm and caring plus the fact that he is a man and looks like everyone's favorite grandpa. He is very much in demand.

His four grandchildren, ranging in age from two months to ten years, have given him an understanding and a love of young children. Holding a bachelor's degree in history, he felt he needed to gain further understanding of child development and program planning, so he is now taking a course in early childhood education at a local community college. He plans to take additional courses in the coming semester. His goal is to complete more courses, get more experience, and then become a center director.

He still struggles to find the best ways to help children learn the things they will need as they move up the academic ladder. He also tries very hard to reach children who do not seem interested in learning and spend much of their day wandering from one activity to another or disturbing other children. He finds these children a challenge and is trying different methods of engaging them.

As a substitute, he has to try to follow the guidelines of the regular teacher even though his own philosophy may be different. He feels that when he has his own class, he will be able to plan and implement a curriculum that reflects his own values and goals.

Social Competence

Making and keeping friends is of major importance to children during middle childhood. Those who lack social skills do not have friends, tend to exhibit aggressive or passive behavior, have difficulties in school, and have emotional problems. On the other hand, children who have good social skills have lots of friends, get better grades, and will probably function more effectively as adults (Hartup, 1991). Middle childhood is an optimum time for helping children develop the skills they need to get along with others. At this age, they have begun to develop empathy and can consider how others think and feel. At times they are willing to give up gratification of their own needs in order to do what a friend wants. They are learning self-control and take responsibility for behaving in ways that do not conflict with others' rights.

In the past, teaching relationship skills was left to the family but is now included more often in the curriculum of schools and child care programs. In fact, some professionals believe it should be the fourth "R" along with reading, writing, and arithmetic. There are several reasons for this change. Many families do not communicate with one another because everyone is so busy and on different schedules. The parents put in long hours at work; the children have school and extracurricular activities or are in after-school care. Families may be separated, or they move frequently, losing neighborhood stability. The models for how to work out long-term relationships are not readily available. Many marriages end in divorce, and grandparents who are still married may live far away. The child care setting is an ideal place to help children learn how to make and keep friends. The atmosphere is less structured and more relaxed than that in the school classroom. There is time for group discussions or individual conversations. Learning activities can be organized into games or other fun things to do.

Strategies

- Coach children to find more effective ways of behaving toward friends. Ask what behavior causes friends to dislike or reject them. Discuss alternative behaviors and urge them to try them.
- Praise children for times they are successful while interacting with others.
- Model good social skills as you interact with colleagues and parents. The children will observe you and want to use you as a model for their own behavior.
- Discuss with children the characteristics that foster friendships. Encourage them to discuss a time they had fun with a friend and what made it enjoyable. How did they and their friend act toward one another?
- Use games and role-playing. The following section provides several suggestions.

Activities

Make a Friend

Purposes: practice interaction skills

demonstrate approaches to other children

Facilitate mini-dramas of role-playing, in which each child plans what he or she would do to make a friend. Play out the scene. At the end of the scene, discuss what happened and how the participants might have felt. Possible scenarios are the following:

- You are playing a game of basketball with your friends, and a kid you do not know stands at the side watching. Your friends think he is too little to play.
- A new girl comes into your classroom. She has just moved into the neighborhood from another part of the city. Your best friend whispers that she is "kinda ugly 'cause she's too fat."

• A new family moves into the house next door to you. You see that they have twins who look about your age. You are a little shy but would like to have somebody next door to play with.

OK, We'll Do It

Purposes: develop negotiation skills

learn to postpone personal gratification

practice making joint decisions

Divide the children into groups of three. Tell them to pretend their group can choose to do one of the following: see a movie, go out for pizza, or buy a new computer game. Ask each to relate reasons for choosing one over the others. They can choose only one so they will have to decide which it will be. When each group has made a choice, ask them to discuss how well their group worked together. What was the most difficult part of the process? How did they finally reach a decision?

Best Friends Are _____

Purposes: identify characteristics of friendships

practice communicating

appreciation for friends

At group time, tell the children that the topic for discussion is "What makes a friend?" You might relate that when you were their age, you had a best friend, and one of the things you liked about that person was ____. Encourage them to tell one thing they like about one of their friends. Write down the characteristics they describe on either a chalkboard or a piece of paper. Encourage each child to add to the discussion while the rest of the group listens. Read the list and ask them to think about how many of the characteristics they have themselves. Conclude the discussion with ways they can become more like the best friend they want for themselves.

Conflict Resolution

Children are growing up in a world where they witness violence almost every day. They learn ways of dealing with conflict by watching the adults they see at home, in their neighborhoods, on TV, and at school. Often adults behave in ways they really do not want children to imitate. Yet, children often "try on" behaviors they observe in others and only gradually learn to resolve conflicts in more effective ways. Preschool children will call on adults to intervene in resolving disputes. School-age children gradually learn to negotiate a compromise, bargain, or use humor to lessen angry feelings. However, at times those strategies do not work, and children resort to fighting. The fighting may escalate, and children are seriously hurt or even killed. According to the Children's Defense Fund (2004), each day eight children and teens die from gunfire. Between 1979 and 2001, gunfire killed nearly 93,000 children and teens.

What do you think is happening between these children?

Violence is a confrontational and harmful way of settling disputes. The act can be physical, verbal, or emotional. These methods of settling disputes are counterproductive. Violence often escalates until serious injury or death results. However, violence is only one of the styles people use to resolve conflicts. Avoidance is frequently used. When confronted with a difficult situation, the person turns away, withdraws completely, or is silent. This method does not resolve the conflict but only internalizes the angry feelings. After repeated incidents, the anger may intensify until it erupts in either violent behavior or displays of anger out of proportion to the particular situation. The most effective way of dealing with conflicts is problem solving, yet many people, both adults and children, find it difficult to do. Child care leaders can help children go through the steps necessary to resolve their conflicts so that each feels validated and empowered. All parties should be satisfied that they have been heard, that their feelings have been considered, and that the solution is mutually agreeable. When all parties are gathered, the adult can facilitate a discussion that takes the children through the following steps:

1. *Decide to resolve the conflict.* All the children involved in the dispute must agree to solve the problem. "I am willing to try to settle this argument." Set some ground rules:
   a. Each is committed to solving the problem.
   b. Name calling and put-downs are not permitted.
   c. Each will be truthful.
   d. An option is for each child to have a cooling-down period at the peace table where they draw pictures of the participants in the conflict and what happened.

2. *Each child tells what happened.*
   a. Use "I" messages. "I get mad when you . . . " "I am unhappy when . . . " "I feel sad when . . . "
   b. Describe exactly what happened.
   c. Relate how each felt about the incident.
   d. Listen to what the other person has to say.

Example "I was waiting for my turn at the tape player, but she grabbed it. I got mad because she does that all the time." "I had been waiting a long time, and I didn't know she was, too. I was surprised she got so mad at me."

3. *Each child states what he or she needs to resolve the conflict.*
   a. Be specific; use "I" messages.
   b. Listen to the other person's needs.

Example "I just want to have a turn so that I can play the music I like." "I don't always want to hear what she likes."

4. *Explore possible ways of solving the conflict.*
   a. Brainstorm options.
   b. Evaluate the suggestions.
   c. Decide which will be satisfactory to both parties.

Example "Let's think of ways to solve this problem." "Will that solution satisfy both of you?"

5. *After an interval, get the children together to determine whether the solution is working or whether a new approach should be considered.*

Example "How has it been working to have a sign-up sheet and a timer for using the tape player?" The adults in an after-school program can be powerful motivators to help children change their behavior so they can become part of a group, feel good about themselves, and achieve their personal goals. The process may be difficult along the way, but it helps to remember that change takes time and effort.

Strategies

Reading nonverbal cues, seeing another person's point of view, and practicing conflict negotiation are additional skills that children can learn in addition to the steps for conflict resolution. Adults can use various strategies, such as the following, to help children learn these additional skills.

- Increase children's ability to read nonverbal cues from others. Sometimes a look or gesture is misinterpreted, and an argument ensues. When an altercation takes place, encourage the participants to discuss what they saw and what they thought it meant. If there has been a misunderstanding, help them to clarify their meaning. Does ignoring an invitation to play just mean "I didn't hear you," or does it mean "I don't want to play right now. Go away"? Does an angry look mean, "He's mad at me about something" or just that he had a bad day at school?
- Help children to see that others may have a different view. Use discussions to let all children express their own perspectives or state their own needs. One way to accomplish

this is to involve children in planning parts of the program. They may all have good ideas based on their own interests or what is most important to them. Each contribution should be accepted and valued even though it may not be put into action.

- Provide many opportunities for children to learn by trial and error. They have to practice conflict negotiation and ways to cooperate with one another.
- Encourage children who are having frequent conflict difficulties to draft a conflict plan. The plan might include a description of the kinds of conflicts, their usual behavior, and ways they might change their behavior. The plan's final statement should include a future date to evaluate how it is working. A conflict plan might look like the following drawn up by John. "I sometimes get mad when other kids won't let me play. When that happens, I start calling them names. Next time I will try to remember to either suggest how I can be a part of their play or find someone else to be with. I will try these methods then look at how successful they've been in two weeks."

Activities

Silent Stories

Purposes: practice in reading nonverbal cues

increase understanding that others have different points of view

Have children work in pairs. Tell them to use nonverbal ways to tell their partner something about themselves. For instance, they can use gestures to tell their age or things they are interested in. Facial expressions can be used to indicate something that makes them mad or sad. Set a time limit of 5 or 10 minutes. At the end of that time, each child tries to relate to the other what has been learned. Have them clarify any misinformation and discuss another way they might have conveyed the information.

Cultural Scenes

Purposes: practice observational skills

understand the similarities and differences in the ways families carry out familiar routines

appreciate the similarities and differences in cultures

Ask three or four children from the same culture to enact a typical scene from their culture. Allow them time by themselves to talk about what they will do. Examples might be a dinnertime routine, a visit from grandparents, or a birthday celebration.

The remainder of the group observes the enactment, paying attention to procedures and the things people say. When the enactment is finished, allow them time to ask questions of the participants.

Lead a discussion of their observations, focusing on how some of the audience saw things the others did not and how actions or words were interpreted differently.

Shopping Trip

Purposes: practice in working together as a group

develop decision-making skills

resolve conflicts effectively

Divide your class into groups of three. Give each group a catalog. Tell them they have $100 to spend buying presents for a boy and girl who are both nine years old. Explain that they all must agree on what to buy. Set a time limit. When they make their decision, they can cut out the pictures and paste them on a sheet of paper.

Have each group share their choices. Ask children about the problems they encountered and how they resolved them. Why did they make the choices they did?

Build a Tower

Purposes: cultivate creativity

develop leadership qualities

encourage verbal and nonverbal communication

Divide your class into groups of three or four. Pass out 20 pieces of heavy paper and a roll of tape to each group. Tell them they are to construct a tower using only these supplies.

(You can add another dimension by telling them they cannot talk while working on the project.) Set a time limit of 10 or 15 minutes.

Let each group show their tower. Discuss how they managed to complete their tower. Was one person the leader? Did anyone feel excluded? What kinds of nonverbal communications did they use? Is it easy or difficult to understand nonverbal messages?

Brainstorming

Purposes: foster divergent thinking skills

strengthen ability to negotiate conflicts

amplify group cohesiveness

Tell children that many great inventions are the result of a group of people getting together to create something new. You might remind them that it takes numerous scientists and engineers to design and build space vehicles. Divide them into groups of four. Tell them they are going to invent a new bicycle. Give each group a piece of paper, and tell them to designate one member to write down ideas. When they have several designs, ask them to choose one that should be built. Set a time limit of 10 minutes.

Let each group relate their ideas to the entire group. Discuss the value or difficulties of creating as a group. How did they decide on the design that should be built?

Picture Problems

Purposes: increase ability to understand (decode) nonverbal communications in pictures

recognize and accept others' points of view

practice in group decision making

Glue pictures of people in a problem situation onto the front of a large manila envelope. You can find pictures in magazines, coloring books, discarded books, and posters. Have children work in groups of three. Give each group a picture and some paper. Ask them to reach an agreement about the problem portrayed in the picture, then write it down. Tell them to put their paper into the envelope and then pass it on to the next group until all groups have looked at all the pictures. Allow three minutes for each picture.

Collect the envelopes. Read each of the descriptions. Discuss how different groups saw the problem differently.

Fighting Fair

Purposes: practice resolving conflicts effectively

foster independence

expand self-esteem

When two children start to fight or argue, send them to a quiet corner of the room. Tell them they are to have a three-minute time-out. During that time they are to work out a solution to their conflict. Set a three-minute timer. When the timer goes off, ask them to tell you their solution and then implement it. Praise them for success.

Role-Playing

Purposes: resolve conflicts

develop understanding of others' feelings

evaluate solutions to conflicts

Set the stage by describing a situation that creates conflicts. The problem may be between two boys or two girls, a male and a female, or child and adult. Assign children to the roles. Tell them to act out the situation, then reverse their roles. The male takes the female part, the child takes the adult part.

Stop the play before a resolution is reached and ask the rest of the children to suggest a solution. Continue the play as the actors find a solution, possibly using one suggested by the audience. Ask the actors to discuss their feelings while the action was taking place. Talk about the play after it is finished, discussing whether the problem could have been prevented or whether the solution was satisfactory to both parties.

Self-Image

Self-image has two components: our perceptions of ourselves and the perceptions conveyed to us by others. Throughout a lifetime, self-image changes as physical abilities evolve, as cognitive functions change, and as interactions with others are refined. During middle childhood, self-image is tied closely to feelings of competence. Children compare themselves to their contemporaries in terms of physical abilities, academic success, ability to manage behavior, physical appearance, or popularity with their peers. Their evaluations of themselves are sometimes realistic and at other times radically unrealistic. In addition, adult attitudes and behaviors play a significant role in how children feel about themselves. When adults react positively to them, children feel they are valued and therefore have self-worth.

How children feel about themselves has a direct effect on their behavior. If they like themselves and see that others react positively to them, they behave in ways that gain further approval. If children have negative perceptions of themselves, they may use unpopular tactics to gain attention or to satisfy their needs. This solidifies their perception of

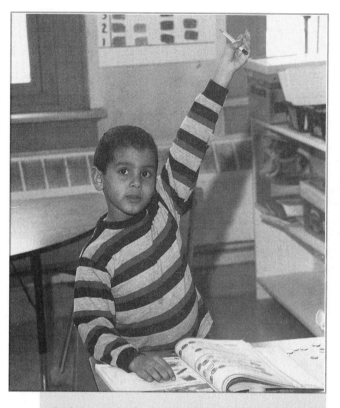

Children who have a good self-image behave in acceptable ways.

themselves as someone who is unlikable or who cannot succeed. Therefore, it is essential that anyone who works with children conveys attitudes that help, rather than hinder, children in the development of their identity and self-esteem.

Strategies

- Develop a genuine interest in every child. Find opportunities to spend time with children individually. Get to know them, listen to them, and try to understand their concerns. Offer help when needed, but also support their ability to find their own solutions to problems.
- Recognize every child's unique qualities and respect their differences. Eliminate prejudice or bias in your own thinking or in the behaviors of the children. Ensure that all activities are nonracist and nonbiased.
- Support self-esteem by involving children in intrinsically meaningful activities. Plan challenging projects in which children and adults work together and in which children develop skills, and gain knowledge. As they acquire skills and feel more competent, children's belief in their own self-worth increases.

- Conduct group meetings that allow all children to ask questions, express concerns, discuss problems, or make plans. During group meetings, there should be a free exchange with no put-downs. Each contribution should be shown respect and consideration, and children should learn to consider all sides of an issue.
- Provide many ways for children to be successful. Offer a variety of activities appropriate for children at different developmental levels. In that way, all children will be able to choose, according to their needs, some activities that are easy for them and others that offer a challenge. Writing and illustrating a simple story is a fairly easy task for nine- or ten-year-olds. Older children might tackle the more difficult task of writing a play complete with dialogue.

Activities

Greetings

Purposes: foster respect and recognition of each child's unique qualities

   develop a feeling of belonging to a group

Welcome each child who comes into your group. Every day, when children enter your room, greet them and spend a minute or so chatting. If any children enter during a group time, stop, greet them, and then help them find a place in the group. Tell them what the group has been doing. Continue the contacts when children are ill. Telephone them at home to find out how they are feeling and when they will return.

Interior Decoration

Purposes: cultivate feelings of responsibility for and control over their environment

   strengthen ability to negotiate differences in ideas, needs, and preferences

In a group meeting, discuss plans for making the room their own. Ask for ideas about what they want to have in "their room." Write down all the ideas on either a chalkboard or a large piece of paper. If needed, suggest some additional ideas they might like to add: a class mural, a rearrangement of the furniture, a room sign or logo, or decorative containers for storage. Ask for discussion of the most important or the most feasible ideas, then vote on the ones to implement. Tell them that they will reevaluate the plan at a specific time in the future.

Getting to Know You

Purposes: develop friendship skills

   increase awareness of similarities and differences between people

Encourage children to get to know others in the classroom. Make a class roster with children's names and pictures. Or make a class book with a page for each child. Information on the page can include a picture, the names of family members, the child's birthday, the child's likes and dislikes, or whatever she chooses to say about herself. Leave the book in a place where classmates and parents can look through it.

   For a more extensive project, have the children make an individual book all about themselves. The purpose of this book is to provide helpful information for the adults who work with these children. (See Appendix A for reproducible pages that can be used for this purpose.)

Puppet Talk

Purposes: foster development of language skills

increase organizational skills

provide an outlet for the expression of ideas and feelings

explore fairy tales and stories from other cultures

Set up a puppet stage. Provide books of fairy tales, fables, or stories from other cultures. Assist children in writing scripts using the stories from the books as the framework or a story of their own devising. Make available materials and instructions for making puppets.
Chapter 11 has some suggestions for making puppets.

TV Talk

Purposes: foster development of language skills

increase each child's feelings of self-worth

Provide a setting where children can interview their classmates. Secure a microphone. Or make one, using a piece of wooden dowel for the handle. Make two slits in the form of a cross on a tennis ball. Slip the ball over the end of the dowel. If you wish, you can spray it with black paint. When the "microphone" is ready, help the children structure an interview. Suggest a few questions they can ask, then allow them to devise their own format. It may also help if you suggest they watch television interviews. If a tape recorder is available, have them tape the interview, then play it back. Ask them to evaluate the interview. What did they find out about the person being interviewed? What other questions might have been asked?

Silhouettes

Purposes: strengthen their ability to work together

develop appreciation for similarities and differences

increase feelings of self-esteem

Have children work in pairs. Tape large pieces of paper onto a wall. Darken the room and provide a bright light. (A strong, steadily held flashlight or a high-intensity lamp will work.) Ask one person to sit sideways in front of the paper while the partner outlines a facial silhouette. Children can sign and color their silhouette. Display the portraits.

Getting to Know Me

Purposes: increase self-esteem

understand how people are alike and different

communicate each person's uniqueness to others

develop appreciation for others' individual traits

"My dad." Vince, age 7.

Ask children to bring things from home that are special to them and that represent who they are. These may be things they like to collect, photos of special people, or mementos of special occasions in their life. The objects must be small enough to fit into a shoe box.

Provide each child with a box, and distribute materials they can use to decorate their box. Wallpaper pieces, wrapping paper, construction paper, collage materials, paint, marking pens, and pictures from magazines are examples.

Allow time at group meetings to have each child show the items from his box and explain why they have special meaning to him.

Family Tree

Purposes: increase self-esteem

            develop appreciation for family differences

            increase communication with family members

            develop pride in one's family

Instruct children to gather as much information as possible about their family. Who are their parents' parents? How about their grandparents' parents? How many aunts, uncles, and cousins can they discover? Help them to draw up a family tree. They can include names or pictures of the people.

Older children can use the computer software program listed at the end of this chapter to gather family information. Caregivers should be sensitive to the fact that some children may live with foster parents. If so, this is not an appropriate activity for the group.

Cooperation

Cooperation with others does not come easily to children. As infants, toddlers, and young preschoolers, they are intensely egocentric. During those years their main concern is satisfying their own needs and achieving their own goals with little focus on the needs of others.

Gradually, during middle childhood, cognitive development enables children to see others more clearly, and they begin to understand that others have needs, too. When others' needs conflict with their own, they learn to compromise and cooperate in order to have friends. They also find they can achieve common goals by working together. Key factors in helping children to learn cooperative behaviors are supportive parents and well-qualified staff members in child care.

Strategies

- One of the most powerful strategies adults can use for teaching children to be more cooperative is modeling, or what parents call "setting a good example." When children see adults helping others, being kind or compassionate, and assisting others to achieve their goals, they see how it can be done. They have a model to follow when confronted with situations in their own daily activities. Conversely, children also imitate selfishness, cruelty, and uncooperative behaviors they observe in adults.
- Another important strategy is emphasizing cooperation rather than competition. During middle childhood, children are striving to succeed at whatever they attempt and constantly compare themselves to others. They want to be the "best, the first, or the fastest." Some competitiveness is inevitable because many of the sports that are popular among youngsters are based on someone winning and someone losing. It cannot be avoided, but it can be minimized by child care staff members. Each child can be recognized for his or her participation during the game, rather than praising only the winner. In addition, there should also be games that do not involve someone emerging as the winner. Several of the games described in Chapter 10 require cooperation and there is no real victor.
- Space for school-age child care should be designed to accommodate groups of varying sizes. When children play in proximity to others, they are forced to compromise or to engage in negotiations concerning the use of space or materials. Space should not be so limited, however, that children feel crowded, for that causes tension and squabbling. Within the work space, materials should be close at hand, adequate in number for all to share, and stored in an uncluttered manner. In this way, children can work comfortably and with fewer conflicts.
- Staff members can help children develop more cooperative behavior by leading discussions about sharing, fairness, taking turns, and negotiating when working together. They can use examples from daily occurrences or hypothetical situations. As an example, fairness is an important issue for school-age children, and conflicts occur frequently. A

Are these children copying the way in which adults communicate?

sensitive child care leader uses these situations to discuss what happened, why a situation may have seemed unfair, or what they can do differently next time. It is also important to help children become aware of the fact that sometimes one child or another has needs that may seem to take precedence over her own. Equity does not always mean fairness but implies that each child's needs are met to the greatest extent possible. Equity should be part of the philosophical approach to school-age care.

In child care groups where children are of different age levels or have special needs, there are many opportunities to help children be more cooperative.

Capable children can be encouraged to take on responsibilities commensurate with their abilities for helping younger or special-needs children with activities, games, projects, or even homework. Both children and adults gain from this arrangement.

- Include activities that require children to work cooperatively toward a common goal. A good example is the production of a play. An entire group could work on this kind of project with some children writing the script, others making costumes, taking roles, designing stage sets, or directing the final presentation. Another example is producing a newsletter. Children have to work together to gather news, write articles, decide on format, print, and distribute the paper. Both of these projects require a great deal of discussion, negotiation, and compromise and can be effective techniques for helping children to develop those skills.

Activities

Sculpture

Purposes: provide opportunity for sharing ideas

increase ability to work under time pressure

strengthen problem-solving skills

Divide the class into groups of three. Give each a pile of toothpicks, some glue, a piece of Styrofoam, and some small corks. Tell them they are to make a single sculpture. The ground rules are that they each get to help decide what to make and to participate in the construction. Set a time limit. (You can also use other objects: clay, Tinkertoys, beads, recycled materials, etc.) Have each group share their sculpture.

Discuss how they decided what to make. What were the problems they encountered? How did they resolve the problems?

Storytelling

Purposes: develop language skills, both talking and listening

create a group fantasy with a beginning, a middle, and an end

Tell the children they are going to write a story together. Use a tape recorder to record it. Designate one child to start the story with a few sentences, then point to another child to continue. Allow any child to pass if he or she chooses not to add to the story. Set a time limit for bringing the story to an end.

Rewind the tape and listen to the story. Ask the children what they thought of their tale. Would it have been different if just one person had told it? If so, how? Transcribe the story, ask the children to do some illustrations to accompany the printed pages, then put it together in book form. Place it in the reading area so children can read the story themselves.

Y'All Come Up

Purposes: increase awareness of others' feelings

foster group cohesiveness

practice problem solving

This game is the opposite of "King of the Hill." One child stands at the top of a hill, then one by one asks others to join. The object is to get everyone onto the hill without anyone falling off. (If no hill is available, use a very low table.)

Discuss what they had to do to keep everyone together at the top of the hill. How did it make them feel to be included? How did it make them feel if they fell off and could not be included?

Class Caring Project

Purposes: increase cooperative behavior

foster feelings of empathy for others

Involve the entire class in planning and implementing a caring project. It can be raising money for a worthy cause, getting involved in a community cleanup drive, or visiting a retirement home. Allow them to research community needs, then choose a project. Have them plan ways to implement their ideas. Encourage them to assign tasks and coordinate ways to follow through. When the project is completed, evaluate what they learned and what they might have done differently.

These are some of the ways you can encourage children to feel better about themselves and learn to function effectively in a group. However, in spite of all your efforts, you may find that some children are still troublesome to themselves and their peers. These children may need extra thought and care.

Changing Children's Behavior

Helping children reverse recurring cycles of behavior that interfere with reaching the goals they set for themselves is one of the most important tasks for teachers in before- and after-school programs. The task is twofold: to stop harmful or destructive behaviors and to encourage children to act in ways that others approve of, thus enhancing their self-esteem.

Stopping destructive behavior begins with a clear understanding by both children and adults about which behaviors are acceptable and which are not. Adults must state their demands clearly, including what the child can do and cannot do, when, and how often. "You may never hit. Use words to tell him how you feel or what you want." Another example is "I expect you to put away your materials where they belong each time you use them. Do not leave anything on the floor to get stepped on or broken." A parent might say, "I want you to take out the trash and put it in the outside can without spilling any. Do it every Friday before it gets dark." Avoid cliché statements of expectations. "Shape up," "Try harder," and "Get a life" are examples of clichés that have no real meaning to children. How do they shape up? What can they do to try harder? How can they get a life?

Making an unspecific demand is a similar mistake adults frequently make. "I want you all to behave when we go to the museum." Children may have concepts of what behaving means that are very different from those of the adult who made the statement. It is more helpful if adults state exactly what kinds of behavior they expect. "I want you all to stay together with the group so that no one gets lost."

Expectations may also be stated in the form of rules. Both families and child care programs have rules that they expect children to abide by. There are three kinds of rules. First, there are the things that are **nonnegotiable**, not open for discussion or negotiation. Mandatory rules apply to actions that can be harmful to others or destructive to property. An example might be "No hitting." Second, there are **negotiable rules** that offer choices. The child is given the option of choosing one of a limited number of alternatives. "You can choose to do your homework now or as soon as we finish dinner and before any TV." When using this strategy, it is important to be sure the child is mature enough to make the decision. One teacher configured negotiable and nonnegotiable rules differently. She defined a line of acceptable and unacceptable behaviors. Acceptable was above the line and unacceptable below. Acceptable behaviors could allow children choices, while unacceptable behaviors were forbidden. If necessary, the adult can offer help in considering the possible consequences of each choice. A discussion with a child who uses unacceptable behavior will help him to make better choices in the future. Finally, **optional rules** are the things that children can reasonably control themselves. An example might be that the parent wants the child to

Hitting or hurting another person is never an acceptable response to anger.

finish her homework before dinner, but the child wants to rest first and do homework later. If the child has shown responsibility in other situations, she should be allowed to choose the time for doing homework as long as it gets done before she goes to bed.

Every infraction must be dealt with every time the behavior occurs if it is to be effective. When misbehavior occurs, restate the rule or expectation firmly and in a way that shows that you mean it. "The rule is no hitting when you are mad at somebody. I expect you to use words to tell him how you feel." Sometimes it is tempting to ignore infractions because of fatigue or discouragement. However, ignoring misbehavior sends the wrong message to a child. Behaviorist theory teaches that intermittent response to misbehavior is a positive reinforcement, increasing the possibility that the behavior will increase, or at least it will not decrease.

A *time-out* is a frequent response to children who exhibit unacceptable behavior, such as aggression, toward another child. The child is removed from an activity area and expected to sit by himself for a specified period of time. He is allowed to cool off and told to think about what he did. The advantage to this method is that the child is prevented from further harming another child and does not get attention for his behavior, thus reinforcing it. The disadvantage of this method is that the child is left alone while he is experiencing strong emotions and may become more resentful toward both adults and other children. Time-outs alone do nothing to help the child learn to express his emotions more effectively, resolve conflicts, or build relationship skills.

To be effective, a time-out has to be followed by a discussion with an adult. The child should be asked to describe what started her behavior and to explore what she was feeling at the time. Further discussion can help her to find alternative ways of either preventing similar situations in the future or reacting to them differently should they occur.

Another method of changing children's behavior is to follow misbehavior with a logical consequence. This does not mean punishment. A logical consequence is intended to help the child learn, whereas punishment is a forceful way to stop behavior. To be an effective tool for changing behavior, this method has to be related to the specific misbehavior. If a child deliberately makes a mess while painting, it is logical to expect him to clean it up. The consequence for misbehavior should be stated in a calm but firm way that emphasizes the child's ability to be responsible for his own actions. "I expect you to clean up all that paint you have just poured onto the floor. You can get a bucket of water and a sponge in the kitchen. You might bring some paper towels, too, in case you need them."

Reinforcing positive behavior is another method of changing children's behavior. This method is based on behaviorist theory, which says that when behaviors are followed by a pleasant response, the behavior is likely to be repeated. Therefore, when children are observed behaving in ways that are expected by adults, they should be rewarded. The rewards can be extrinsic, coming from the environment in the form of a treat, better grades, or a special privilege. Verbal praise and positive feedback are even more effective because they enhance children's intrinsic interest. When the praise and feedback are later removed, children continue to show interest in work (Cameron & Pierce, 1994). Intrinsic rewards come from within the individual and include feeling good about oneself or feeling capable of achieving a goal.

"Me, when I'm mad." Ricky, age 9.

Positive reinforcers are most effective when children are first trying out new ways of functioning. The reinforcer should immediately follow the desired behavior every time the action is observed. When the behavior seems to be fairly well established, rewards can be applied less frequently. Eventually, the reward will not be needed. An example frequently used by both parents and teachers is "I appreciate the way you helped with the cleanup today. It really helps me to get it done more quickly."

Strategies

Children want to behave in acceptable ways but often find their conflicting emotions or lack of experience cause them to act in ways that elicit negative responses from others. If they do not learn another way of behaving, they may be labeled as "bad, naughty, or mean." They may even take on that label themselves and wear it as a badge of importance. "I can be the baddest of the bad." Adults reverse this process by trying to understand why a child is acting in a particular way and then finding ways to help her use more acceptable ways to get what she wants or needs. Child care staff members can:

- try to understand the motivation behind troubling behavior. Is the child trying to get attention? Is he feeling insecure? Is he attempting to boost his self-esteem? Once the behavior is understood, appropriate measures can be taken to bring about changes. Find ways to give attention, offer support to an insecure child, and find acceptable ways to boost self-esteem.
- help children develop an honest sense of their own competence. Point out their special abilities and help them to accept the things they may not do so well.
- help children learn to praise themselves. "You should feel proud of yourself for telling Kevin how you felt when he ruined your block building instead of hitting him."
- allow children to express their feelings in ways that are not hurtful to others. Some children may not be able to put their feelings into words. A discussion with a caring adult sometimes helps them to find acceptable ways to relieve the feelings. Some children may need active ways to relieve feelings, particularly anger. Provide them with pillows to pound or a place to run.
- model acceptable behavior toward other adults and toward children. Adults who are sensitive to others' needs show children how to behave in similar circumstances. Caregivers who help coworkers or express empathy when another is having difficulty demonstrate ways to interact and the positive results that follow.
- help children devise additional ways to act on their feelings of empathy by discussing possible ways to behave. Their own limited experiences may not be enough for them to know what to do, and fear of failing may prevent them from acting. "Let's think of some ways to help a friend who is having a difficult day."
- encourage children to put their feelings into words. They may not have acquired the vocabulary to describe feelings or have not been encouraged to express emotions with words. "Tell her it makes you feel really bad when she calls you names."
- create a nonaggressive environment. Physically, provide plenty of spaces to play and enough age-appropriate materials so that children can engage in activities with minimal conflict. Socially, adults and children should focus on supporting and respecting others, offering encouragement when needed. Wherever possible, make it clear that aggressive behavior gets negative results.

- be consistent. Staff members need to communicate with each other on how behaviors are to be handled.

Communications That Help Change Behavior

The ways in which adults respond verbally to children's behavior can either increase the likelihood of repetitions or bring about changes in behavior. It is normal to become exasperated with children's behavior, particularly at the end of a difficult day. The tendency is then to respond with anger, generalizations, or labeling. At one time or another most adults have made comments such as, "Jason, why are you always getting into fights?" or "Rachel, you're such a loudmouth." These kinds of verbal responses may momentarily relieve the adult's angry feelings, but they do nothing to help the child change. In fact, they may bring about the opposite, a tendency for the child to repeat the behavior. The child knows how to irritate the adult and takes pleasure in doing it again or may feel the negative label gives him status with his peers. Child care leaders can learn to respond in ways that are appropriate to the situation and that will help children gradually change their behavior.

Acknowledge Children's Feelings

Often adults respond to children's expressions of their feelings by denying their existence or trying to change the feelings. Constant denial of feelings or a rush to change them makes children distrust their own inner senses.

Example   Jennifer has been lying on the book area pillows since getting off the bus from school. Her child care leader wants her to get involved and asks why she does not find something to do. Jennifer answers by saying: "Can't you see I'm tired?"

Inappropriate response:

Adult: "How can you be tired when you haven't done anything yet?"

An appropriate response might be:

Adult: "Yes, I know some days at school are tiring. You decide when you're rested and ready to do something."

Describe the Situation

Children are sometimes unaware of all aspects of a situation. They are concentrating on achieving their own goals and are oblivious to anything else.

Example   It is cleanup time before a field trip, and there are still materials that have not been put away.

Inappropriate response:

Adult: "You guys haven't finished cleaning up, so maybe you won't be ready to go on the trip. Why are you always such slobs?"

An appropriate response might be:

Adult: "I can still see some puzzles on the table and some paints that need to go into the sink. The bus will be here in five minutes, so let's all be ready."

Can you tell if these girls are fighting or playing?

Help Children Recognize How Their Behavior Affects Others

Until children reach a stage of maturity at which they are less egocentric, they often fail to understand that what they do affects others.

Example   Two girls are beginning to dress up with some costumes that are kept in a large trunk. Shari pulls out a white dress and says that she wants to be a princess and wear it. Leanne looks at her and tells her she can't be a princess because she is too fat.

Inappropriate response:

Adult: "Hey, you girls. No name calling."

An appropriate response might be:

Adult: "Shari, how did it make you feel when Leanne said you couldn't be a princess because you're too fat?"

Another appropriate response:

Adult: "Leanne, when you call Shari fat it really hurts her feelings. Did you notice how she quickly put away the dress and looked like she was about to cry?"

Behaviors That Create Problems for the Individual or the Group

Even with knowledge of child development and good intentions, child care staff members often find they are baffled by the behavior of one or more children in their group.

These are the children who exhibit similar behaviors to other children, but what they do has increased intensity and is therefore potentially harmful. There may be a child who is not just aggressive when the situation warrants it but who bullies other children seemingly for no reason at all. Another child may spend a good portion of her time alone and resist any attempts to be included in group activities. Still another may be in a perpetual whirl of motion, hardly stopping long enough to have contact with either adults or children. Each of these children desperately needs, and probably wants, help to become a part of the group and to be accepted by others.

The Overly Aggressive Child

Nearly every group has at least one child who seems to be angry all the time and who dislikes both children and adults. Although he often complains that others are picking on him, in reality he is usually teasing other children. At times he may resort to outbursts of physical aggression or verbal attacks. This may be a child who has experienced many failures. He may be feeling powerless and feels good only when he is bullying others. He may also come from a family background that is harsh and punitive and that provides very little nurturing.

"I am mad when my mom spanks me." Kevin, age 5.

Child care leaders can become the significant adults in this child's life, helping him to change his behavior. They can:

* win his trust by showing him they care about him.
* make sure he understands the rules and standards for behavior in the child care setting.
* be consistent with disciplinary actions. Always follow unacceptable behavior with an appropriate action such as a time-out or removal of a privilege.
* try to anticipate situations that are likely to cause his outbursts. Suggest alternative actions, activities, or situations.
* praise and reinforce acceptable behavior whenever possible. Do not overdo, but when praise is warranted, give it. Include a description of the behavior to be repeated. "I'm happy to see that you were able to wait your turn without pushing."
* encourage intrinsic motivation for appropriate behavior. "You should feel proud of yourself for solving your problem with Juan by listening to what he had to say and working out a solution."

The Quiet Child

The quiet or withdrawn child is often overlooked in a group because she is hardly noticed. She does not create problems, does what she is told, but stays by herself. Sometimes she may appear to be depressed or anxious. Behind this behavior the child may just be shy or may feel she is not competent to do the things others do. She may also be afraid of rejection by other children. Child care staff members can:

* capitalize on her interests, initially allowing her to pursue them in seclusion. Gradually encourage her to talk about her interests with one other child, then with two children. From there, it may be possible to move her into related activities in a small group of children.
* involve her in puppetry either alone or with a small group. She may be able to participate behind the stage or by acting through the puppet.
* practice pretend telephone conversations. Start by engaging her in a conversation with you. Choose a topic that is likely to interest her. "I know you have a dog at home named George. I certainly like that name. Tell me about him." Encourage further conversation by additional prompting. "What are some of your favorite things you and George do together?" Encourage her to practice with another child. Suggest topics for the conversation, such as telling one another about favorite things they do on weekends or their favorite movie.
* plan activities that will allow this child to be successful. Acknowledge her achievements by describing the behavior that allowed her to succeed. "You were really creative when you figured out how to make a curtain for the puppet theater. That was good thinking!"
* make specific suggestions about things to say to other children or things she can do to enter into group activities. Praise her efforts when she is successful, pointing out what she did that worked.

The Overly Active Child

The overly active child creates a lot of problems for teachers and caregivers. During group times, he fidgets, talks loudly, or pokes whoever sits next to him. He never settles down to an activity but moves randomly from one to another. His path through the room may be marked by a trail of destruction. When asked to wait his turn for a snack or during games, he gets very angry. He has a hard time making or keeping friends because he is often argumentative or manipulative. This may be acting-out behavior due to stress factors in his life, such as a disrupted family life or not enough attention from his parents.

Some of these children may be classified as suffering from attention deficit hyperactive disorder (ADHD). When attempts to moderate the behavior are unsuccessful, it is important to encourage the parents to get a professional evaluation. Before referring an overly active child, however, some behavior changes can help him control his own behavior. Child care staff members can:

- be consistent about rules. Make sure the child understands the rules, then enforce them after every misbehavior.
- anticipate unstructured times that are likely to create problems. Examples of these times are when the group moves from indoors to outdoors or in the transition between an activity-oriented period to snacks. Give plenty of warning that one period is ending and another will begin. Assign this child a specific task during the time; have him help prepare the snack, then pass it out or let him hold the door while the other children go outside.
- give this child plenty of support. Seat him nearby at group times, accompany him to an activity, and help him get started.
- help him acquire social skills. Suggest ways he might enter into others' play. Remind him of expected behavior while with other children.
- praise him for times he is able to exercise impulse control. "I saw that you were able to stop yourself that time. You must be proud of yourself for that."
- avoid using negative statements whenever possible. Say "You can build your buildings over here" rather than "Don't knock down Sean's block building."
- encourage physical exercise to use up excess energy. Physical activity also helps to stimulate beneficial hormones that bring about greater calmness.
- simplify your environment. Consider whether there are ways you can eliminate clutter and disorder in the classroom. Are materials easily accessible without having to pull out other materials? Do materials get put back in their place so they are available the next time they are needed?

Attention Deficit Hyperactive Disorder (ADHD)

Children with true hyperactive disorders display many of the same behaviors as children who are classified as merely overactive. The difference may lie in the intensity or frequency of the behaviors. Although many times the diagnosis is based primarily on observation of the child's behavior, a more reliable method is now available. Brain scans measure the number of dopamine transporters in the brain. Dopamine transporters send signals from one brain cell to another by releasing dopamine. A group of researchers at Harvard Medical School have found that ADHD sufferers have 70 percent more dopamine transporters than their normal counterparts (Fischman et al., 1999). It still is not certain, however, whether the increased number of dopamine transporters is a cause or an effect of the disorder.

In addition to brain scans, observation and evaluation of a child's behavior are still necessary to make an accurate diagnosis. The behaviors most frequently seen in ADHD children are the following: distractibility, impatience, impulsivity, and a short attention span. They may also perform acts without an awareness of the consequences or risks.

ADHD is diagnosed six times more often in boys than in girls (Arcia & Connors, 1998; Safer & Krager, 1994). This is partly due to the fact that ADHD girls daydream whereas boys act up or talk loudly during class. Girls just don't interrupt class routines the ways boys do.

The most frequent treatment is the use of several drugs, most often Ritalin. Dexedrine and Cylert are also used. These medications increase the production of the neurotransmitters dopamine and norepinephrine, which results in increased attention and less restlessness. It may also be effective to decrease the amount of food additives in children's diets. Some diagnosticians also recommend the addition of vitamin B1 and magnesium. The suggestions made for managing the behavior of overly active children given in the previous section apply as well to the ADHD child and are not repeated here. In addition, child care staff members can:

- refer the family to reliable sources for testing and diagnosis.
- if medication is prescribed as a treatment, make sure the child takes it as recommended.
- maintain close and supportive contact with the family to continue to evaluate the child's progress and condition.
- give positive reinforcement for the child's attempts to control behavior.

The Child with Special Needs

Child care leaders may encounter a wide range of special needs when working with children. Certainly a child who comes to the before- and after-school program after a night of intense parent fighting at home, has had no breakfast, or is temporarily on crutches for a sprained ankle has special needs. This discussion about children with special needs refers, however, to the child who has a diagnosed disability that interferes significantly with his or her development. Some children have learning disabilities that impact their ability to be successful in the school setting when doing reading, writing, or math activities. Others may have a physical problem such as cerebral palsy, which forces them to walk with a limp, wear a brace, or even walk with a walker. There are many diagnosed disabilities, far too many to mention in this textbook. This discussion will be more of a general nature on how to work with children with disabilities. It may be necessary for a caregiver to receive specialized knowledge and training about specific disabilities when children with disabilities are enrolled in the child care program.

The child care leader should realize that each child is unique, including those with disabilities. For example, children with autism may share some common characteristics. However, for each child there is some uniqueness. The severity of the disability and how he manages the challenge of it varies from one child to the next.

Historically children with disabilities were not given an education in the traditional school setting and consequently were not a part of the traditional before- and after-school child care program. In recent years, children with disabilities are fully included in regular classrooms whenever possible. Consequently, these children are being more fully included in child care programs. Inclusion refers to placing children with diagnosed disabilities in settings with same-age peers. Sometimes children who are fully included in the school setting are given supports through the use of classroom assistants. Often these same supports do not exist for the child in the nonacademic setting. Consequently this may pose additional challenges for child care leaders.

An effective child care leader learns about each individual child. He learns about the child's interests, about the child's basic temperament, and how to work with the child. The same basic skills of learning about and working with typically developing children, that is, children without disabilities, also apply to working with children with special needs. Therefore, the first skill for the child care leader in working with children with special needs is to develop a positive attitude about the child. The leader must think of this child as if she or he were any other child in the child care program. Think of the child first, then the disability.

When adults model openness and acceptance of children with disabilities, they have a positive influence on the attitudes of other children in the child care program. School-age children may be blunt and ultimately hurtful with their comments as they notice physical differences in children who look or act in a way that differs from the majority. Children may exclude the child with disabilities and may even taunt or tease the child. There should be a zero tolerance attitude on teasing. Caregivers can help children gain understanding and acceptance of children who are different from them in a variety of ways. Leaders can teach children that different does not mean bad and that it is okay to be curious but not to be mean. The strategies described earlier for helping children develop their identity and self-esteem are also effective for children with special needs. In addition, caregivers can use the strategies listed for helping children learn cooperative behaviors.

A second skill used by an effective child care leader is that of establishing a working relationship with the parents and to be a part of the parent-teacher-caregiver team that supports the child. Assure parents of confidentiality regarding the information they share about their child's disability. Consider the following questions to discuss with parents about a child's abilities and needs:

- What are the child's current abilities related to movement, cognition, communication, and social interaction?
- What motivates the child to explore his environment and interact with others?
- What children in the program have similar interests to the child and could play in cooperative learning groups?
- What tends to overstimulate or even frighten the child?
- What barriers currently exist that impede the child's access to materials, equipment, and peers?
- What are the parents' current goals for the child in the before- and after-school program? (Flynn & Kieff, 2002)

This information will be helpful to the child care leader when planning activities and in thinking about the specific accommodations to make in order to take care of the child and help the child feel successful. Children with identified special needs will have an Individualized Education Program (IEP) with specific goals and objectives. The goals represent what a team of professionals and the parents think the child can accomplish in his areas of disability in a year's time. Objectives are more specific, measurable tasks that show the child's progress toward the goal. The IEP is developed for the child in the educational setting but many of these objectives may apply to the child care setting. A goal may be for the child to give eye contact when someone is talking to him. Another goal might be to follow through 80 percent of the time when being given verbal instructions. A social goal may be to take a role in cooperative play situations.

Accommodations are the modifications that are made to activities and routines in order to meet the needs and goals of the child with special needs. These accommodations may be related to the child's IEP goals. A child with autism may not be able to pick up on instructions given to the entire group or nonverbal cues that it is time to transition to another activity. An accommodation would be to have cue cards that can be handed to the child to read or to enlist the help of a peer to guide the child in transition. A child with a physical impairment may not be able to run while playing a game of soccer with the other teammates. An accommodation would be to involve the child in keeping score or perhaps she is the person who throws the ball back onto the field when it goes out of bounds. Once children get to know the strengths and challenges of the child with disabilities, they can be involved in developing accommodations. They may decide to change how the game of soccer is played so that all people can be included. The leader may have to start this problem solving. "Sylvia really is interested in playing soccer. How can we change the game so she can use her walker on the field and still play?"

It will be important to determine whether the child's needs match the program goals and objectives. Under the Individuals with Disabilities Education Act (1997), a child with disabilities must be included in your program unless:

- A child's condition poses a direct threat to the other children, or your staff, and the direct threat cannot be eliminated through reasonable accommodations.
- A child's condition would require architectural changes that cannot readily be achieved.
- A child's requirement for special equipment or services would impose an undue burden or would fundamentally alter the nature of the program and there was no reasonable alternative.
- A child's condition would require changes in policies, practices, or procedures that would fundamentally alter the nature of the program.

A third skill for leaders to be effective when working with children with disabilities is consistency. Most children, typical and atypical, do best when the daily routine is consistent. Routines give structure and stability to children who may not be very adaptable or who struggle with self-regulation and need to know what to expect. Create consistency by learning how challenges or difficult behaviors are handled at home and in school.

The Child with Autism

One of the disabilities that caregivers of school-age children may encounter in a before- and after-school program is autism. Autism is a complex set of disorders that affect about one-half million people in the United States today. About 2 to 10 out of every 10,000 people, depending on the diagnosis criteria used, will be diagnosed with the disease. Boys are four times more likely to be affected than girls are. The term *autism* is sometimes used to describe several related disorders that are included under the heading of pervasive developmental disorder (PDD). The term is also used to refer to a child who cannot be specifically diagnosed but has severe impairment in behaviors. The standard reference *Diagnostic and Statistical Manual (DSM)* (American Psychiatric Association, 2000) lists the following categories:

Autistic Disorder

Limited social interaction, language, and imaginative play observed in children usually before the age of three. There may also be stereotyped interests and repetitive behaviors.

Asperger's Disorder

Impaired social interactions, restricted interests and activities. No significant general delay in language. Test in the average or above-average intelligence.

Childhood Disintegrative Disorder

Normal development in the first two years, then loss of previously acquired skills. Children who fall within the general spectrum of pervasive developmental disorders may seem relatively normal for the first two years or so, then parents or caretakers notice changes that may include a delay in speech or inappropriate use of words. As an example, many of these children refer to themselves by their name, rather than "I." Or they may repeat the words of TV commercials without seeming to attach any significance to them. Often these children do not want to be held or cuddled and avoid eye contact with others. They seem incapable of spontaneous play and do not initiate pretend games. Their behavior ranges from overactive to very passive and may include aggression toward others or themselves. Changes in routine often bring on temper tantrums.

However, children with autism can be widely different with their own unique characteristics and personality. Some may be only mildly affected, for they make eye contact, display a variety of emotions, and have the ability to communicate. Their abilities to learn may fluctuate from day to day, depending on external stimuli and the level of anxiety the child is feeling. These children may also process information in unique ways, perhaps using mental images rather than words to process and remember information. They may have above-average verbal or memory skills but have great difficulty engaging in any imaginative activities with others. As autistic children grow older, some learn to compensate for and cope with their disability, becoming productive adults who can earn college degrees, obtain meaningful work, and establish families.

Caregivers can help children with autism and their families if they:

* refer parents to programs that can provide evaluation and intervention measures. There is evidence that early intervention (during the preschool years) is the most effective, but even later intervention can help children learn to live with their disability. Some children with autism need to be in a small, specially designed program, whereas others benefit from inclusion in regular programs.

- provide a structured environment for children with pervasive developmental disorder. They need to know what to expect in terms of routines and be given time to manage transitions.
- understand and make use of each child's unique way of learning. Design learning activities that allow each individual to process information in his own way. For instance, use pictures as well as words to describe a process to be followed for an activity.
- use positive reinforcement. This helps children understand what they are doing that is right and increases their self-esteem.
- are flexible and willing to change approaches. Evaluate what you are doing on a regular basis, and find an alternative approach if one is needed to achieve the desired results.
- use good communication skills yourself, and encourage children to use words. Sometimes helping a child to use even a single word to express a need or emotion can lead to greater ability.
- support parents. Living with a child who has autism can be extremely stressful, and parents need to be able to talk to others about their concerns. Be willing to listen without being judgmental. Parents also may need help in finding more effective ways to manage their child at home through educational services or support groups.

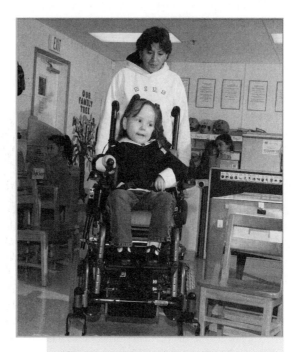

What are some possible physical accommodations to fully include this child?

Summary

During middle childhood, children want to have friends. Those who lack social skills have a difficult time and may be either aggressive or passive, perform poorly academically, and have emotional problems. Those who have good social skills will have lots of friends, get better grades, and probably function effectively as adults.

Children learn to resolve conflicts by observing adults at home, in their neighborhoods, in movies, on TV, and at school. They witness others' violent ways and imitate their actions until they acquire more effective methods. The most effective way of dealing with conflicts is problem solving, yet many adults and children find it difficult. Child care leaders can help children resolve conflicts in ways that allow each party to feel validated.

Role-playing is a way to help children resolve conflicts, develop understanding of others' feelings, and evaluate solutions to conflicts.

Self-image has two parts: our perceptions of ourselves and the perceptions conveyed to us by others. Throughout a lifetime, self-image changes as physical abilities evolve, as cognitive functions change, and as interactions with others are refined. How children feel about themselves has a direct effect on behavior. Adults can strengthen children's self-esteem by a variety of methods.

Cooperation with others does not come easily to children. Gradually, during middle childhood, they learn that others have needs and that they must compromise and cooperate in order to have friends. Children's behavior can be changed when adults state their expectations clearly, including what children can and cannot do. Expectations may also be stated as rules. Misbehavior should result in time-outs or logical consequences. Positive reinforcers also help to change behavior.

The ways adults respond verbally to children's behavior can either increase or decrease the likelihood of repetitions and bring about changes in behavior. Some children exhibit behaviors that are similar to those of other children but are more intense or potentially harmful to the individual or the group. Both the overly aggressive child and the quiet or withdrawn child can be helped. The overly active child may be suffering from ADHD and should be evaluated. Children with special needs are sometimes fully included in before- and after-school programs. Caregivers in a full inclusion program should learn about the child first to learn about his interests and personality. Then, the caregiver can look at the challenges and rewards of the disability. The leader should have an attitude of openness and understanding. He should develop a relationship with the parent and learn how to best care for the child so the child can be successful in the inclusive setting. Caregivers can employ many of the same strategies that they would use to help any child develop abilities to cooperate, to be accepted by others, and to build positive self-esteem. The Americans with Disabilities Act gives child care centers parameters for determining if they are legally required to take care of children with special needs.

Autism is one of the disabilities child care leaders may encounter in children in the before- and after-school child care program. The term *autism* covers a complex set of disorders, sometimes also called pervasive developmental disorders. Symptoms include limited social interaction and imaginative play plus limited language and communication skills.

Key Terms

accommodations   nonnegotiable rules
inclusion   optional rules
Individualized Education Plan (IEP)   self-image
logical consequence   typically developing
negotiable rules

Student Activities

1. In class, practice problem solving using the steps listed in this chapter. Work in pairs, with each member of the pair assuming one side of a controversy. Choose one of the following situations or describe one from your own experience.
   a. Two caregivers share a room. One never cleans up thoroughly when an activity is finished, so at the end of the day, the room is in chaos.
   b. On the playground, one caregiver spends a lot of time with individual children rather than supervising the group. The other adult is left to intervene when altercations occur, stimulate additional activities, and generally manage a large group of children. Share the results with classmates. Was the process easy or difficult? Were you able to use "I" messages when telling what happened? Did each of the partners feel satisfied with the resolution?
2. Work with one of your classmates to determine whether your perception of yourself is the same as or different from how others see you. First, write down five words that describe your partner. Next, write five words that describe you. Compare your partner's list with your own. Did each of you agree when describing the other? How close was your self-evaluation to the way your partner described you? How does this activity contribute to your understanding of the complexity of self-image in children?
3. Interview a caregiver. What methods does he or she use to promote children's ability to cooperate with one another?
4. Imagine that you have just enrolled a first-grade child with autism in your program. Develop a plan for learning about the child and his disability. What strategies will you use to make sure the child is included in small-group activities and is accepted and respected by the other children?

Review Questions

1. State four reasons why professionals advocate teaching children how to relate to others.
2. List and explain the steps in problem solving.
3. State three strategies for helping children learn to resolve conflicts effectively.
4. List five things an adult can do to help children increase their self-esteem.
5. What are some causes of overaggressive behavior in children?
6. Describe the behavior of an overly active child. What might be the cause of this behavior?
7. This chapter suggests that reinforcing positive behavior is effective for changing how children relate to others. Describe this method.

8. One of the strategies for helping children increase their self-esteem is to involve them in projects where children and adults can work together. How does this affect how they feel about themselves?

9. Why is it important to help children increase their ability to read nonverbal cues?

10. Describe one activity that you could use to foster social competence.

11. What are three things that are important to learn about a child with disabilities entering the program?

12. What is the difference between learning about the child with disabilities and learning about the disability?

Case Study

The room where Rowan's child care group meets has only one computer, which is much sought after by all the children. This afternoon Mei wants to e-mail her friend in China and is eager to get started. Three other children are clamoring to get online as well. They each have urgent things they want to do. Emily has a homework assignment, Gregory wants to finish a game he started the day before, and Xavier just wants to explore some information about stars, his newest interest. They all begin squabbling, each declaring he or she should be first. Rowan is so tired of the fighting over the one computer that she would like to just get rid of it but knows the children benefit by using it. Her assistant thinks they should all be told that no one can use the computer until they learn to share.

1. Do you agree with the assistant's advice that none of them should be allowed to use the computer until they learn to share? If you disagree, why?

2. If you were Rowan, what would be the first thing you would do to resolve the problem?

3. Can you think of a plan that would prevent problems like this in the future?

References

American Psychiatric Association. (2000). *DMS-V-TR 2000: Diagnostic and statistical manual of mental disorders* (4th ed.). Washington, DC: Author.

Arcia, E., & Conners, C. K. (1998). Gender differences in ADHD? *Journal of Developmental and Behavioral Pediatrics, 19*(2),77–83.

Cameron, J., & Pierce, W. (1994). Reinforcement, reward, and intrinsic motivation: A meta-analysis. *Review of Educational Research, Fall 1994, 6*(43), 363–423.

Children's Defense Fund. (2004). *The state of America's children, 2004*. Washington, DC: Author.

Fischman, A. J., Daugherty, D. D., Bonab, A. A., Spencer, T. J., Rauch, S. L., & Madras, B. K. (1999). Dopamine transporter density in patients with attention deficit hyperactivity disorder. *Lancet, 34,* 91–96.

Flynn, L. L., & Kieff, J. (2002). Including everyone in outdoor play. *Young Children, 57*(3), 20–26.

Hartup, W. W. (1991). Having friends, making friends, and keeping friends: Relationships as educational contexts. In *Early report*. Minneapolis: Center for Early Education and Development, University of Minnesota.

Safer, D. J., & Krager, J. M. (1994). The increased rate of stimulant treatment for hyper-active/inattentive students in secondary schools. *Pediatrics, 94,* 462–464.

Suggested Readings

Akin, T., Cowan, D., Dunne, G., Palomares, S., Schilling, D., & Schuster, S. (1990). *The best self-esteem activities for the elementary grades.* Torrance, CA: Innerchoice.

Coloroso, B. (2003). *The bully, the bullied, and the bystander.* New York: HarperCollins.

Crary, E. (1990). Pick your socks and other skills growing children need. Seattle: Parenting Press.

Faber, A., & Mazlish, E. (1980). How to talk so kids will listen and listen so kids will talk. New York: Avon.

Frankel, E. B. (2004). Supporting inclusive care and education for young children with special needs and their families: An international perspective. *Childhood Education, 80*(6), 310–316.

Honig, A. S., & Wittmer, D. S. (1996). Helping children become more prosocial: Ideas for classrooms, families, and communities. *Young Children, 51*(2), 62–70.

Pirtle, S. (1998). *Linking up.* Cambridge, MA: Educators for Social Responsibility.

Rohnke, K., & Butler, S. (1995). *Quicksilver.* Dubuque, IA: Kendall/Hunt.

Wittmer, D. S., & Honig, A. S. (1994). Encouraging positive social development in young children. *Young Children, 49*(5), 4–12.

Computer Software

Family Tree Maker 2005 : Broderbund/Banner Blue Advanced.

Web Resources

Americans with Disabilities Act of 1990 (ADA)
http://www.usdoj.gov Click on "Disabilities"
Autism Society of America
http://www.autismsociety.org
Multiple links to information for helping children with autism.
National Alliance for Autism Research
http://www.naar.org

The Background

CHAPTER 8

Program Planning

Objectives

After studying this chapter, the student should be able to:

- Describe developmentally appropriate practice
- Discuss reasons for planning
- List the components of an effective program
- Plan a program

C A R E G I V E R   P R O F I L E

Erik, 26, has been working with school-age children since he was 16 and in high school. At his first job as a camp counselor, he discovered that he liked working with children. He likes being outdoors and enjoys games and sports. When he entered college, he studied physical education, thinking he might like to be a recreational leader. But finances prevented him from finishing his education, and he began to have doubts about his career direction. He took time off and decided to do what he knew he liked—working with school-age children. He took a job as the site supervisor of an on-site before- and after-school program. He has a team of six: four women and two college-age men who work part-time. Together they provide programming for children before school and for kindergarten-age children during the morning and early afternoon hours; they also provide after-school care for children through the sixth grade.

Erik is conscientious about the safety, both physical and emotional, of his children. On one occasion he received a panicky early morning phone call from a child that hadn't yet been picked up by the bus. The child was sure the bus had forgotten him, yet Erik skillfully calmed the child and then made appropriate phone calls to be certain the child received his needed ride to school.

Erik is sure that he wants to work with school-age children as a career. He continues to take classes at a nearby university to learn more about children at this age level.

Developmentally Appropriate Practice

Bredekamp and Copple (1997) first outlined the components of developmentally appropriate practice in educational programs serving children from birth through age 8 for the NAEYC. Albrecht and Plantz (1993) expanded those components in Project Home Safe. Their intent was to develop guidelines specifically for school-age child care programs. Because research on school-age care is still limited, Albrecht and Plantz sought input from school-age child care experts. They also reviewed research studies on the development of school-age children.

Developmental research leads to the conclusion that the most successful programs for young children are based on the premise that an active child in an active environment constitutes the optimum conditions for bringing about developmental changes. Studies done by both Piaget (1952) and Vygotsky (1978) pointed to the importance of children's interactions with their environment and the impact of the social environment on development. Piaget stressed the predictable stages of qualitative changes in a child's thinking that allow him to construct knowledge through interactions with his environment. Vygotsky believed that thinking changes as a result of instruction or support (scaffolding) from the environment and as language skills increase. Therefore, according to Albrecht and Plantz (1993), developmentally appropriate school-age child care programs should be tailored to the developmental characteristics and needs of the children they serve. Quality programs must address the fact that children change tremendously in middle childhood and there are great variations in the rate and type of change in all developmental areas. Even within an individual child there is great variation from one stage to another or within a stage of development. Bredekamp and Copple (1997) wrote of two dimensions of developmental appropriateness: age appropriateness and individual appropriateness.

Age appropriateness means that programs are planned according to a knowledge of the universal, predictable growth and changes that occur in children. As an example, during middle childhood children have increased gross-motor coordination but may still have difficulty with fine-motor skills. Therefore, it is important to provide them with opportunities to further refine their motor skills, while not expecting them to be equally competent at both gross- and fine-motor coordination. Middle childhood is also a period in which children are becoming independent of parents and increasingly want to be accepted by their peers. Program planners need to provide opportunities for children to develop friendships, learn social skills, and function cooperatively in a group.

Individual appropriateness refers to each child's unique pattern and timing of growth. Although every child goes through predictable stages, each does so at different rates. Two children who are the same age may vary tremendously in their abilities, appearance, language, and thinking processes. Child care programs must recognize individual differences and provide opportunities for all children to develop at their own pace and according to their own needs. As an example, one child may be tall for her age, have well-developed gross-motor skills, but find it difficult to carry out logical processes when resolving problems. She certainly should be allowed to practice her physical aptitudes but should also have supportive guidance to think through solutions to problems.

The guidelines listed for Project Home Safe address all areas of an effective before- and after-school program for school-age children beginning with the role of staff. Qualifications of child care leaders have been discussed in a previous chapter, but we should emphasize here that child care leaders should play a supportive role to children. As young people strive for independence from their parents, they look to other adults to guide them through the process of adjusting to the outside world. Albrecht and Plantz (1993) also discuss the importance of adjusting interactions with children according to their age and stage of development. The needs of children who are five to seven years of age differ from those who are approaching adolescence. The youngest children may need more direction and motivators. The oldest children want more autonomy and adultlike responsibilities. The guidelines also indicate the importance of peer relationships as children move toward independence.

Friendships with one or two others and a sense of belonging to a group are essential to children's self-esteem. Adults can facilitate peer relationships by supporting children's developing social skills. Staff members can also initiate activities that encourage children to discuss the causes of conflicts and ways to resolve them. Additionally, developmentally appropriate child care programs use both mixed-age and same-age grouping to help children develop relationships with their peers according to their own developmental needs. Staff members should use positive guidance strategies to help children achieve inner control and self-discipline. Adults need to encourage children to resolve their own differences,

Project HOME SAFE

A Program of the American Home Economics Association

Principles of Developmentally Appropriate Practice in School-Age Child Care Programs

Developmentally appropriate school-age child care programs are tailored to the developmental characteristics and needs of the children they serve. Programs are mindful that children and youth change greatly during the school-age years and that the rate and nature of change vary considerably, both among children and youth and across developmental areas within the same child or youth. Programs approach these developmental realities as opportunities, rather than as problems.

1. Developmentally appropriate school-age child care programs provide resourceful, caring staff who understand the changing role adults play in school-agers' lives.

2. Developmentally appropriate school-age child care programs recognize the increasing importance of peers to school-age children and youth.

3. In developmentally appropriate school-age child care programs, both mixed-age grouping and same-age grouping are used to facilitate the development of peer relations and social skills.

4. Self-selection, rather than staff selection, of activities and experiences predominates in developmentally appropriate school-age child care programs

5. Developmentally appropriate school-age child care programs. Schedules allow great flexibility for children and youth. Required participation in activities and experiences is limited.

6. Environments in developmentally appropriate school-age child care programs are arranged to accommodate children and youth individually, in small groups, and in large groups, and to facilitate a wide variety of activities and experiences.

7. Activities and experiences offered in developmentally appropriate school-age child care programs contribute to all aspects of a school-ager's development.

    a. Activities and experiences foster positive self-concept and a sense of independence.

    b. Activities and experiences encourage children and youth to think, reason, question, and experiment.

    c. Activities and experiences enhance physical development and cooperation and promote a healthy view of competition.

    d. Activities and experiences encourage sound health, safety, and nutritional practices, and the wise use of leisure time.

    e. Activities and experiences encourage awareness of and involvement in the community at large.

Project Home Safe Guidelines
From "Principles of Developmentally Appropriate Practice in School-Age Child Care Programs" by Kay M. Albrecht and Margaret C. Plantz in *Developmentally Appropriate Practice in School-Age Child Care Programs*, 1993. Courtesy of American Association of Family and Consumer Services.

and listen to children and encourage them to verbalize their feelings. Positive guidance also means that staff help children behave productively by describing problem situations and encouraging group problem solving.

Developmentally appropriate programs include space for a wide variety of activities for individual children or small and large groups. The program should include more self-selected activities than staff-selected activities in order to provide a balance to the child's after-school time, which follows the more structured content of their school day.

The last items on the list address the need to plan activities and experiences that meet children's desire to be competent in all aspects of their development: psychosocial, cognitive, and physical. A developmentally appropriate program provides activities and experiences that help children develop their self-concept and need for independence. Children want to feel successful and gain control over their own actions. This sense of success can be achieved by allowing children to direct their own activities and having supportive staff who allow independence but offer guidance as needed.

Children should also be challenged to increase their cognitive abilities. Caregivers should provide varied and interesting activities that are neither too easy nor too difficult for their developmental level. Those planning developmentally appropriate programs should not overlook the importance of physical competence and well-being. Children should have a wide variety of activities in which they can practice skills requiring both large- and small-muscle coordination. A developmentally appropriate program encourages children to develop sound attitudes and practices to ensure their own health and safety.

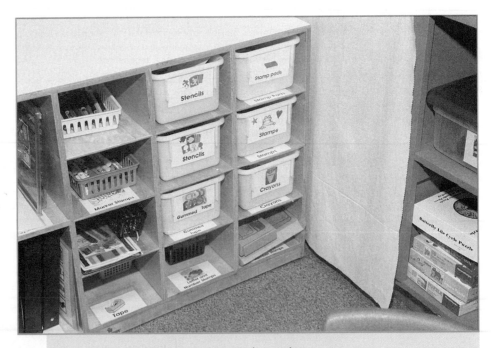

Children should have opportunities to choose their own activities.

Children should have opportunities to learn what constitutes fitness, how to maintain health, and what to include in a healthy diet.

The last item on Albrecht and Plantz's list is a statement concerning children's awareness of and involvement in their neighborhood or community, the world beyond their families, and even beyond the child care setting. As children become more aware of others and less egocentric, they are ready to explore their community and to grapple with societal issues. This is also an opportunity to understand diversity and develop attitudes that respect differences. The youngest children can read books and experience the arts from different cultures. The oldest children may be ready to discuss global issues such as ecological conservation or social ills such as discriminatory practices. They may even become involved in activities to resolve some of these problems.

Holistic versus Academic Approach

A current debate among early childhood professionals asks the question "Which is better, an academic or a holistic approach?" An academic approach to programming involves determining outcomes that can be measured and then planning a program to help children reach those goals. A holistic approach allows the curriculum to evolve based on children's individual and group abilities and interests. This approach does not mean that the curriculum is unplanned, but that it includes a basic structure from which many possible variations can emerge, also called an emergent curriculum. The structure is formed through the knowledge caregivers have of children's abilities and interests, through having a wide variety of materials and activities available for use as needed, and through encouraging children to be involved in planning. We believe that after-school time should be different from in-school time even though some school districts are pressuring their child care centers to use their time to bring test scores up to an expected level. An academic approach may be suitable for a school environment, but a holistic approach should be used in child care.

One of the best ways to design a curriculum is to gather together everyone who has a stake in program outcomes. These stakeholders may be staff members, parents, community agency personnel, and school personnel. Organize a dialogue around the question "What do children need to learn in this setting?" The conclusion will probably include opportunities for children to explore cultural and gender issues, get assistance with homework, acquire social competence skills, pursue their own interests, and learn to appreciate good nutrition and fitness. Other questions might ask whether any of these goals are being met in other environments such as the home, school, church, temple, or community. Participants in this discussion should also decide which goals should take priority and whether the child care center has the resources to meet the goals. Finally, pursue the question of how the goals can complement what is going on in other places in the children's lives or how they can compensate for what is *not* happening. The National Institute on Out-of-School Time (Loosi, 2000) has listed the following components to consider when planning a balanced program:

- the importance of developing genuine relationships with children
- different learning styles of different children: how to work these into an integrated program

- the strengths of arts-based programming
- the importance of culturally relevant programming
- gender-based needs, especially for adolescents
- ways to help children build literacy skills
- homework time and support
- ways to help children develop social competence
- nutritious snacks, exercise, and time for breaks
- opportunities to pursue interests in science, math, and technology
- links with families
- knowledge of limits: linking with community experts and seeking outside help
- the importance of service projects

Additionally, the institute suggests that caregivers use "teachable moments" to develop curriculum ideas or projects. These moments come when children's excitement over something they have learned or experienced suggests the possibility of planning a new activity or project. If a wide variety of materials is available, caregivers can help children explore these ideas. The emphasis is on developing and broadening the children's expressed interests. For example, at group time you might include a discussion about seeing a news broadcast of the effects of a hurricane on a small island off the Florida coast. Then, possible learning experiences that caregivers could develop from this topic are the following:

- using weather instruments to predict weather locally
- researching careers in which knowledge of weather is important: meteorologists, pilots, firefighters, mariners, postal employees, forest rangers
- charting weather data and calculating differences in temperatures and rainfall
- reading literature in which weather is an important factor
- reading weather reports and predictions in the local newspaper, then calculating the rate of accuracy
- logging on to the National Weather Service Internet site to see how weather is charted through satellites at this Web site: http://www.nws.noaa.gov

The preceding ideas are only a few of the possibilities for using teachable moments to create a curriculum. Each center and group of children will have different needs or interests. If you can learn to use this method for planning a curriculum, you will encounter few problems keeping children interested and involved.

Planning for Cultural and Linguistic Diversity

In addition to recognizing that each child is unique and has an individual pattern of growth, remember also that children come from varied backgrounds and cultures. Children's sense of self-worth stems partly from their experiences within the family and their community and their ability to master the skills expected of them in those settings. They will learn best if the expectations and values of their school or child care are congruent with those of the family and community. As an example, children who can communicate well with their family or neighborhood friends in a language other than English may find it difficult to be understood or to learn in other environments. To this end, the NAEYC has published a position statement entitled "Responding to linguistic and cultural diversity—Recommendations for effective early childhood education" (1996). It states that developmentally appropriate programs should recognize that all children are cognitively, linguistically, and emotionally connected to the language and culture of their home.

In "Developmentally Appropriate Practice in Early Childhood Programs" (Bredekamp & Copple, 1997), statements about diversity have been broadened to recommend that programs develop a positive climate for learning within a democratic community.

Examples of how caregivers can create this climate includes knowing each child well and taking into account individual differences and developmental level. It also means bringing each child's culture and language into the school setting so children can feel they belong. Children learn through reading books about other cultures, reading about current events relating to other cultures, and discussing cultural values. Teachers can also group children flexibly in small cooperative groups to work on projects so they can learn through discussions in which they share information or expertise. A democratic community also means that children with disabilities are included as members of the group.

Another aspect of cultural and linguistic diversity is embodied in the 1996 NAEYC statement:

> Acknowledge that children can demonstrate their knowledge and capabilities in many ways.

This statement recognizes that children have acquired many cognitive skills and knowledge before entering school or child care. They should be able to demonstrate those skills using their own language and then begin to build on that base while learning a second language.

> Understand that without comprehensive input, second-language learning can be difficult.

Children may be able to learn a second language, but learning more complex cognitive skills requires an integrated approach. They need a learning environment in which to build on the skills they acquired in their first language while gaining new skills in the second. Children learn more easily when they are given instruction in their primary language.

Additional recommendations focus on families. NAEYC suggests that parents be actively involved in the early learning program, that teachers help parents become knowledgeable about the cognitive value of knowing more than one language, and that programs support the family's cultural values.

Recommendations for programs and practice in these guidelines recognize the importance of respecting and supporting children's home language.

> Recognize that children can and will acquire English even when their home language is used and respected.

Children should be able to build on cognitive skills they have already acquired using their home language. When children have lots of opportunities to read and be read to in their home or in a group setting, they will develop literacy in a second language more easily (Krashen, 1992).

The recommendations also suggest supporting and preserving children's home language. This can be done by an adult speaking the language and also by providing many

How can caregivers support the diversity of children's home language?

examples of the language within the environment. Books, bulletin boards, tape recordings, labels on materials, and signs are all ways to incorporate the home language into the environment. If the caregivers do not speak the child's language, in addition to creating an environment, they can learn words and phrases from that language. If several languages are spoken by children in a group, the task may seem overwhelming. In addition to designing the environment to reflect different languages, children who speak the same language can be grouped together at times to work on specific projects. However, it is important to ensure that these children do not become isolated and are incorporated into other groups as well.

Antibias Curriculum

(a) **Antibias curriculum** incorporates the positive intent of multicultural curriculum and uses some similar activities, while seeking to avoid the tourist approach. At the same time, antibias curriculum provides a more inclusive education: It addresses more than cultural diversity by including gender and differences in

physical abilities; (b) it is based on children's developmental tasks as they construct identity and attitudes; and (c) directly addresses the impact of stereotyping,
bias, and discriminatory behavior in young children's development and interactions. (Derman-Sparks, 1989, pp. 7–8; boldface added.)

The preceding is a quotation from "Anti-bias Curriculum, Tools for Empowering Young
Children" by Derman-Sparks. The "tourist approach" teaches children about diversity
through holiday celebrations, ethnic art activities, and cooking ethnic foods. In contrast, an
antibias approach takes into account children's developmental levels, their interests, and
their concerns. At an early age children become aware of differences among people. Four-
year-olds notice and begin to ask about the differences between boys and girls, why one
child has dark skin, why another speaks with an accent, or why another cannot walk and
has to be in a wheelchair. By the time they reach middle childhood, they may stop asking
the questions because adults are embarrassed or do not know how to answer them. The
result can be the development of prejudices or stereotypes. In a bias-free environment,
Derman-Sparks says, "children should be free to ask questions about any subject, to use
their own ideas in problem-solving, to engage in real dialogue with adults, to make
choices, and to have some say in their daily school life" (p. 8).

To create an antibias curriculum, start with the child care environment by including
things such as:

- photos of children and families that reflect the racial and ethnic makeup of the group
- images of both men and women doing a variety of jobs, not just those that are typically associated with a gender
- images of people with disabilities doing jobs or interacting with others in recreational
  settings
- toys and materials in an antibias classroom should include books that reflect diversity
  of gender roles and ethnic differences as well as people with disabilities; books that
  include different languages, through either stories or alphabets; dramatic play materials that encourage children to engage in common everyday tasks without concern for
  gender roles; implements and tools used by different ethnic groups such as cooking
  equipment, holiday decorations, clothes, or personal objects; art materials that can be
  used to depict people of different skin tones or are representative of different cultures;
  small toys and manipulatives that depict racial diversity
- opportunities for children to see or hear different languages through signs, labels,
  story tapes, or songs
- music activities that include music from other cultures

The Importance of Planning

If you think of yourself as a spontaneous and flexible person, you may wonder whether
you really need to plan. Nevertheless, when you work with children, looking ahead is
absolutely essential. Without it, a day can lead to chaos, unhappy children, and irritable
adults.

Planning ensures you can provide a variety of play opportunities that will attract and
stimulate children and enhance their development. Curriculum is a plan of activities that
accomplishes the goals of a program. Caregivers should provide a balance between old and

new activities. Some should be familiar things children like to do over and over again. Others should be new things to spark their interest.

Planning ahead allows you to gather the materials needed to carry out an activity. Knowing a day or week in advance what you will need gives you time to find, purchase, or prepare whatever you will require. When children have to wait while you collect supplies, they get restless. Then, when you are ready, they may not still be receptive.

Planning lessens the number of conflicts between children. A group of children can engage in free play for periods of time, but eventually differences arise. During the three hours or so that children are in after-school care, some free play, along with planned activities, keeps children busy and involved. Petty arguments and irritability will decrease.

Plans allow staff members to divide responsibilities. Everyone should know specifically what they will be required to do during a period of time. Some may have responsibility for playground supervision and others for setting up activities in the classrooms. Every step of the day, including transitions, activities, snack, and free play, should be planned ahead of time.

The most important function of program planning is to ensure that both the short- and long-term goals of the program are met. Short-term goals are those that can be achieved during a single day, a week, or even, perhaps, a month. Long-term goals are those that will not be achieved until a fairly long period of time has passed. This span may cover several

Children are usually eager to try new activities.

months or even a school year. Children need to feel successful through the completion of short projects or at the end of a single activity. But they also should be learning to carry through activities that will not bring rewards until a considerable period of time has passed.

Planning also helps staff members to apply the guidelines for developmentally appropriate practices. As each day's activities are decided, they can be measured against the guidelines. Will they allow children to develop their physical skills? Are there opportunities for creative expression? Is there a balance between staff-initiated activities and time for child-initiated ones? Are there activities at different levels of difficulty so that children at diverse developmental levels can participate and feel successful?

Plans allow you to keep parents and the school administration informed of program activities. Make written plans so this information is readily accessible. Post your plans on a bulletin board for parents. Provide copies for the administrative person at your school or center.

Integrated Curriculum

Planning an integrated curriculum is one approach to meeting the goals of a school-age child care program. An integrated curriculum is the linking of two or more subject areas such as literacy and math, or linking an academic subject to the community or vocations. This is accomplished by providing meaningful experiences that allow children to develop a variety of skills and knowledge that lead to the understanding of the relationships and how things fit together. A school-age program is an ideal place to provide children with such meaningful experiences because it can allow for the necessary time for integration. An integrated curriculum activity has two or more primary goals. For example, an art activity could have a goal of teaching children painting techniques. Another goal would be to link the activity with someone in the community who paints pictures. The artist could visit the classroom and paint alongside the children. This activity can be further integrated with a literacy goal of doing research about the techniques of a specific artist such as Jackson Pollock or Vincent Van Gogh. Often it requires more than one child care leader to implement an integrated curriculum. In this example, one caregiver might be responsible for the art activity and finding an artist while a second caregiver could plan the artist research activity. (One resource for research would be http://www.gettingtoknow.com.) A key component to integrated curriculum is that children make connections between one subject and another. In this example, literacy, art, and the community are connected. Children can experience how research, personal techniques and creativity, and local and historical artists are connected.

What Should Be Included in a Program?

Start with the routine things you and the children do every day. Plan who will pick up children at their schools, and know what the children will do when they first arrive at day care. Decide who will take roll, when you will have the snack, who will supervise the playground, and what activities will be ready. These activities may seem trivial, but they are not. Children enjoy a predictable environment. Carefully planning your schedule makes the day run more smoothly for both adults and children.

Capitalize on children's interests.   Some children may want to continue themes they are working on at school, whereas others may have some current interests unrelated to school.

Holidays, too, create excitement that can generate ideas. Television or movies may also pique interests you can use. Sometimes one child has a special interest that can be shared with others. Use this child to generate enthusiasm in other children as they work together on projects.

Increase children's awareness of and respect for cultural diversity.   Plan activities to help children embrace that they live in a society that includes peoples of many races, colors, and religions. This philosophy can be conveyed through books, holiday celebrations, art activities, toys, building projects, games, and festivals. Make these topics an integral part of your program, not just something you do on special occasions. Ask parents for help. Use the children as resources for customs that are representative of their culture.

Include opportunities for language-minority children to share their language with others. An example might be to have one child read or tell a story with another translating as the tale progresses. Learn and use words from the minority language during the day's activities.

Foster children's desire to become competent.   Let them help with daily routine tasks that allow them to use real tools. Teach them to cut up fruit for snack time. Let them answer the telephone and take messages. Include them in the maintenance of your environment.

Plan projects that use tools. Show them how to use a saw, hammer, and drill for woodworking projects. Let them measure with a T square, a tape measure, or a yardstick.

Encourage children's natural play interests.   Keep a store of props that inspire music, drama, and dancing. Help them also to be more competent with fads that sweep through groups of children. Yo-yos, roller skates, and skateboards are not just "time wasters" but allow children to develop their skills. Use these interests to foster their physical development and greater self-esteem.

Plan a balance of activities.   Include both group and individual activities. Have quiet times interspersed with active play. Allow times for activities the children themselves initiate and conduct as well as those you choose and direct.

Have enough choices so all children can find something to do.   Variety will allow for different interests and levels of capability.

Include some activities that will re-create everyday experiences.   Remember that children who spend after-school hours in child care will miss these kinds of experiences. Take children with you to do the shopping for snacks or for a special art project. Arrange trips to local businesses. Take walks around your community.

Allow time to meet the special needs of school-age children.   Let them be alone or give them time to do what they want. Provide opportunities for them to make new friends or spend time with existing friends. Some children may even need time to rest or just do nothing.

Plan how transitions will be accomplished.   Transitions are those times when all or part of the group change places or activities. The morning arrival and end-of-the-day departure

Most school-age children have the skills needed for soccer.

are also transitions. Each of these transitions should be thoughtfully planned in order to prevent chaos and to help children develop self-control and self-direction. Plan ahead by having curriculum areas set up so the next activity is ready as soon as the children move. For instance, when going from group time to individual activities, tell the children what is available and have them choose what they are going to do before they leave the group area. In that way, they can move directly to an activity. Minimize waiting time or times when children have nothing to do. Provide books, videos, or tapes for those times when children have to wait for others to be ready to move to the next activity or when a parent is late for pickup. Alert the children that a change will be taking place, allowing them time to finish whatever activity or task they have been engaged in. "You have five minutes to finish up your project, then it will be time for cleanup."

Involve the children in cleanup. Assign areas to be responsible for and give them guidelines of what needs to be done. "Put all the blocks back on the shelf, matching the sizes and shapes." "The leftover snacks can go into the refrigerator, wipe off the tables, and throw away the paper cups and napkins."

Suggest an activity to avoid boredom on long trips. Sing songs, play games, or provide a snack. Children will find the time less stressful when they are occupied.

Additional guidelines for planning.   Be sure that all activities are developmentally appropriate. Know what children are capable of doing. Plan activities that allow success but also offer a challenge.

Vary the settings for activities. Try painting outdoors or put on a play under a tree.

Be flexible. If your plans are not working, change them. Or allow children to decide they want to do something different from what you had planned.

Encourage adult/child and child/child interactions. Sometimes set up activities so you can be involved with children. At other times, encourage children to work together.

Help children change their attitudes about male/female stereotyping. Beware of falling into the trap of unconsciously planning different activities for boys and for girls. Encourage them instead to try all activities.

Organizing the Program

There are several approaches to organizing the program for your after-school group. The following are types that have proved successful in different situations. No one is more effective than the other. The appropriateness of each depends on many factors: your goals, the children involved, the physical layout, the materials available to you, and the ratio of children to adults. You may even use several types for greater variety, so try what works for you.

Independent Projects

Many children have abundant ideas about what they want to do. Their own enthusiasms lead them to be involved in reading, making maps, constructing models, or collecting. These children will work diligently by themselves. Some children want to continue alone on a project they began with a group. They may follow a group project to grow crystals with a study of how crystals are used in tools, industrial equipment, or even jewelry.

Often you will initiate an idea for a project based on the interests or needs of a particular child. A child may talk about a visit to a local planetarium with her grandparents. You can suggest a variety of activities about stars and the solar system. Another child may need encouragement to use language. Begin with making simple puppets, then a puppet theater. Few children will be able to resist staging their own plays.

It is important to allow as much freedom to pursue individual interests as possible. Children should feel they can still do the kinds of things they might do if they were home. All you have to do is allow enough time, provide the materials, and offer guidance when needed.

Group Activities

In order to foster group unity, at times you want all the children to engage in the same activity. A group may work on a single project that has many parts. Each part will be completed by small groups of children. An example might be preparation for a drama to present at a parent meeting. Some children can write the script, some make costumes, some the scenery. Then, new groups can be formed to delegate acting parts, rehearse, change scenes, and arrange lighting. This is a typical example of a long-term project that might be many months in the making.

Sometimes limitations on space or equipment may dictate your decision to have all children doing the same thing at the same time. If you have limited space indoors for

"Me doing a magic trick." Vince, age 7.

extensive projects, you may have to divide your group with some children on the playground while others work in the classroom. Some child care facilities have one room set aside for a specific activity such as arts and crafts. In this case, children may have to sign up to use the room or groups are scheduled for designated times.

Groups may have a variety of configurations. Some may consist of children who are close to one another in age or abilities. Others may have a mixture of ages and proficiencies. When there are wide differences in ages such as from 5- to 12-year-olds in a class, plan some things for the younger children and others for those approaching adolescence. Each age level has different developmental needs and interests. At other times, a mixed group allows opportunities for the older children to help the younger ones. This can add to the older children's self-esteem and to the competence of the younger ones.

Whatever the reason for grouping children together for an activity, make sure these activities build on previous skills or interests. Also make certain these experiences further the goals of your program.

Interest Centers

An interest center is a space carefully arranged to accommodate the activity for which it will be used. A variety of interest centers throughout the room allows children to move freely from one to another. This encourages exploration in different areas of the curriculum. Typical interest centers found in child care environments are block building, science, art, reading, music, cooking, computers, dramatic play, and games. Within each of these areas, basic materials are always available to the children. Some materials are changed from time to time to add new interest and stimulation. A block area might contain a selection of standard wooden blocks, animals, cars, or signs. At times you might add people, trees, boats, airplanes, or colored blocks. Styrofoam sheets, flat wood pieces, or metal forms also invite new kinds of play. Stock an art area with paper, crayons, marking pens, scissors, and paste. For variety, add different colors, sizes, or shapes of paper. Consider using paper punches, staplers, and templates.

Field Trips

Field trips can be a simple walk around the block or an all-day trip to the beach. Both should be planned carefully, although obviously a walk takes less planning than an all-day excursion. Start by deciding the purpose of the trip. A walk can reinforce a project to map your neighborhood or collect material for a nature collage. A trip to the beach can include collecting shells or studying wave patterns as the tide changes. As with all other activities, fit this into the overall pattern of activities.

Plan each detail so both you and the children know what to expect. Obtain permission slips from parents for car or bus trips. Arrange for lunch and transportation. Make sure there are enough adults to properly supervise the children. Discuss the arrangements with your administrator and other staff members. Tell the children where they are going, what they will do, and what the rules will be. (Make sure you visit the site ahead of time so you will know what to expect and can plan appropriately.) Have the children wear recognizable clothing such as a special t-shirt or a large name tag with program information.

Plan further with the children so they will get maximum benefit from the trip. For instance, if they are going to the beach to gather shells for a collection, prepare ahead. Read books, look at pictures, and talk about different kinds of shells they might find. If you are fortunate to have a video camera, take it along to record interesting finds and to document where the shells were found or what the children saw in tide pools.

Do a follow-up when you return to the center or on the following day. Ask children to share what they collected and tell about what they saw. They should also be encouraged to relate what they learned from the trip, what they liked best, and perhaps even how would they change the trip if they went again. You can then create a book documenting the field trip by having each child draw a picture and briefly write about the trip.

Clubs

Clubs are ongoing groups organized around common interests of the participants. When they belong to a club, children have an opportunity to pursue a topic or an interest in depth. They learn to set goals for themselves, solve problems, and cooperate with others on common goals. Some club activities may require them to do extensive research and then to communicate their findings to others, thus developing skills that are part of scientific endeavors. Typical topics are photography, calligraphy, cooking, magic, collecting (shells, rocks, or stamps), stitchery, space, drama, or sports. Within any group of children, there are likely to be other ideas as well. A leader for the group is appointed, either a staff member or an outside volunteer. Sometimes you can find a parent, community resident, or senior citizen with a special interest who will be willing to share information with the club. Decide how many the group can accommodate, and ask the children to sign up.

Clubs can provide children with the experience of making a long-term commitment. When they sign up for a club, they state they are willing to spend a specified period of time with the group. This may be as short as one month or as long as four to six months.

Clubs also give children the chance to be a part of a small unit within the larger day care group. This can foster friendships built on a mutual interest. In addition, club participation helps children learn to govern themselves as they set rules and elect officers for their organization. This is particularly important to the older children, the 12- to 14-year-olds.

At the end of the period, encourage children to share what they have learned with others. This can be in the form of an exhibit, a presentation, or a demonstration. Whenever possible, invite parents to participate in these events. Schedule a presentation for a parent meeting. Draw their attention to a display when they come to pick up their children. The children can also write about the club's activities for your center's newsletter.

Spontaneous Activities

You should have a store of activities ready that can be used for unexpected situations. One of your aides calls in sick, the weather turns cold and rainy, another group stays too long on the playground, or the CD player breaks down. All of these and many other emergencies will happen, so it helps to be well prepared.

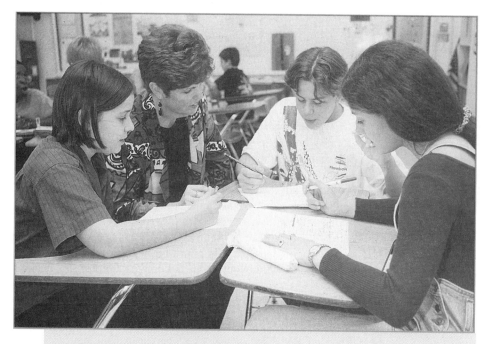

Some children may need help with their homework.

Know some games you can use to keep a group occupied. "Twenty Questions" is an old standby that everyone enjoys. Learn some others as well. Every caregiver should have a store of songs children like to sing. They often want the same ones over and over again, but occasionally introduce a new one. You might consider learning some stories or making up your own. Tell these with appropriate dramatics.

Have some materials you can bring out for rainy or snowy days when you have to be indoors. These materials should be a selection of things you do not put out every day. A new game, special books, or unusual art materials are some of the possibilities. Indoor days could also allow children to spontaneously organize activities such as dramatizing a familiar story or dancing to music.

Some spontaneous activities will be child-initiated. In order for child-initiated activities to occur, adults have to be willing to follow children's lead, and the environment must have a variety of easily accessible materials. This kind of play is most often seen in the dramatic play center, where children engage in elaborate imaginary or real-life scenarios.

A wide selection of costumes and accessories affords children the opportunity to work through troublesome feelings, learn social skills, and increase their ability to communicate clearly. Dramatic play also takes place with blocks and with additions such as animals, human figures, cars, airplanes, and rockets. Children also engage in spontaneous activities outdoors, but here too, they need time and materials to allow them to fully explore their fantasies. The adventure playgrounds seen in some public parks capitalize on this idea by providing boards, boxes, hammers and nails, and pipes. Children can use these to construct objects they need for their play.

Community Involvement

You can use community resources to provide children with a wider range of activities. Instead of duplicating classes or facilities that are available elsewhere, use these to enrich your program. This kind of reaching out also gives children less of a feeling of isolation from the kinds of experiences their school friends might be having.

Some of the possible situations are the following:

A Girl or Boy Scout troop could meet at your site so your children could attend.

A local swimming pool might offer reduced rates for children when they are supervised by their own teachers or caregivers.

A nearby volunteer nature center might offer to sponsor activities your children could attend.

Have resources come to the center. For example, organizations that train dogs for the blind will come and talk and bring a dog.

Your children could attend community classes sponsored by the local school district or recreation department in return for having an extra adult to supervise.

Join other sites within your child care organization for some activities.

Community activities might also include participation in the community in other ways. For instance, your children could get involved in beautifying their neighborhood. They can grow plants from seeds, make them available to residents, and even offer to plant them if needed. Recycling is also a popular cause. Children can set up bins for receiving materials and then take them to a redemption center. A local rest home for elderly patients may appreciate visits from the children. They can collect toys for less fortunate children to be distributed at holiday time. Do not forget the possibility of children lobbying their governmental representatives over issues affecting children. They can write letters, make posters, distribute flyers, or appear at hearings.

Community involvement is a valuable participation experience for children and should not be missed just because they are in child care.

Making a Schedule

A good program is more than just a series of activities. The structure of those activities within the context of the day allows children to enjoy their time in child care. Allow plenty of time for each activity but not so much that children get bored.

From reading the previous pages you know what goes into a typical day with children. Start by writing down the specifics for your program. Include everything you do each day, then add things that have to be done less frequently. Next, estimate how much time to allow for each activity. As you put your schedule into effect, you will probably revise it a few times.

A typical schedule for a before- and after-school program may look like the following:

6:00 A.M.   Children arrive individually. Breakfast is available for children who are hungry. Some children may want to finish homework, others finish a project from a previous day. Still others may want to work quietly at an art center or read. A few may be wide awake and need to run off energy outdoors.

8:15 A.M.   Children complete whatever they are doing and prepare to go to school.

8:30 A.M.   Children board the bus for their elementary schools.

When children return to the center at the end of the day, they may follow this schedule:

3:00 P.M.   Children arrive in a group on the bus. Some may be hungry and need a snack. Others may want to rest a bit before joining activities. Still others may need to spend time with their caregiver to talk about what happened at school.

3:15 P.M.   Most children want to be outdoors after a day of sitting in school. Schedule outdoor free play, exercises, organized games, or sports.

4:00 P.M.   Group time, music, planning, discussions, problem solving.

4:15 P.M.   Indoors for a variety of activities: homework, clubs, individual projects, reading, cooking, or talking with friends.

5:30 P.M.   Finish activities, straighten environment, and collect belongings. Children may read alone or in a group until parents arrive.

Your job as a teacher or child care worker should be enjoyable and exciting. Planning helps to avoid many of the frustrations that make that difficult to achieve.

Summer Programs

Summer brings about a variety of changes in a child care program. Staff members may change, additional people may be needed, or the number of hours they work might be longer. The number and ages of children can also change, particularly if the program has been sharing space with a Head Start program or public school. The weather changes and that affects what happens. In some locales, it is too hot, too rainy, or too smoggy for the children to engage in certain activities. Perhaps the most important change is that there is more time to participate in activities so the schedule can be more relaxed. There should be no need to rush children from one activity to another. Therefore, the summer curriculum should not be a duplicate of the rest of the year, but add new dimensions to the program. The following are some suggestions for an all-day summer program.

Involve Children in Planning

The children may have wonderful ideas about how to use the longer days of summer. They may want to establish clubs, plan weeks around a theme, or suggest an overnight camping trip. Set up a suggestion box so that they can share their ideas about ways to make the program more interesting. Conduct a survey during group time. Print out short questions such as "What is your favorite thing to do?" or "What is one thing you would really like to add to our program?" Allow the children time to think about their answers and reply in writing. Collect the responses, then report back about what they suggested. Choose several to implement during the summer.

Rearrange the Environment

A project to spruce up the environment is a good project for when the weather is too hot to play outdoors. Spend group time discussing ways the children would like to change the room arrangement. Choose a plan, then assign groups of children to work on specific areas. When the children have had time to function in the new surroundings, evaluate the plan. Revise it if necessary.

Long-term Projects

Blocks of time can be set aside for projects that take place over days, weeks, or even the entire summer. A group of children can write a script for a play or adapt an existing story. Some can make costumes, others can design and construct the sets, and some can learn the lines and practice the play. An integrated curriculum approach can be applied to a puppet play from writing the play, constructing the stage, and making puppets. What makes this different for the same activity during the school year is that it can be done at a leisurely pace so that children can enjoy the process at each step.

Sports

If the weather permits, children can have time to practice and refine their skills at a favorite sport. Find a volunteer who can coach them on ways to improve. Schedule games with neighboring child care or summer camp programs. Have children plan and present a sports fair with demonstrations of equipment, accessories, and games. If a pool is available, have them design and produce a water ballet.

Field Trips

Summer is the perfect time for field trips. What better time to spend the whole day at the beach exploring tide pools, making sand castles, or cooling off in the surf. Other suggestions for all-day field trips appeared in previous pages, but the difference in the summer is that more time can be allowed for the visit. A trip to the zoo can include a picnic lunch planned and prepared by some of the children. A trip to the museum may include time to watch a film on a particular artist.

Gardening and Cooking

Plant a garden with summer vegetables and herbs. Some plants, like carrots or radishes, grow fairly quickly, but others can be speeded up by using already sprouted plants from a nursery. Have the children research the growing time for each variety, then choose plants that will have different times for harvesting. When the plants have matured, the children can pick a few at a time, then incorporate them into recipes to be served at lunch or snack time. Provide cookbooks and gardening guides to be used for the necessary research.

Allow Quiet Time

The long stimulating days of a summer program can cause some children to become fatigued. Therefore, it is important to allow time for them to read quietly by themselves, spend time with friends talking, or "hanging out." Make certain the environment has inviting places for these activities: a cozy reading corner or secluded places where several children can be together.

Read Aloud

Choose a long book that all the children will enjoy and read it aloud to the group. Choose a stopping place each day that will create some suspense. Ask the children what they think is going to happen next. At the beginning of the next day's session, ask them to recall what had just happened in the book when the reading ended.

Plan Special Events

Include the children in planning for a special event. This may entail making costumes, decorating the environment, finding equipment, and inviting parents or others to participate. Some ideas for special events are the following: carnival, scavenger hunt day, mystery day requiring detective skills, kite flying, olympics, and backwards day. Each of these can take several days of preparations and should include assessment of the success following the day.

Organize a Fund-Raising Event

Ask the children to decide the kind of event to be planned and how much money they might bring in. When figuring potential profit, they have to consider the cost of any materials they might need. Suggestions for fund-raisers are selling popcorn, cookies, or unused toys or games brought from home. After completing the event, let the children figure out the profit, decide what to purchase, and then take them shopping.

Community Facilities

Take advantage of community facilities to enrich the children's summer program. Many libraries having reading programs. Participating children are encouraged to read a specified number of books and to receive an award for doing so. The library may also have group reading times that the children can attend.

Museums may also have summer discovery programs that children can attend. Some have classes in science, astronomy, archeology, biology, and art where children can have hands-on experiences.

The children may take classes (for additional fees) at local riding stable, dance studios, swimming pools, tennis courts, or art studios.

Summary

Developmentally appropriate practices are those that are tailored to the developmental characteristics and needs of the children and youth they serve. Age appropriateness means that programs are planned according to a knowledge of the universal, predictable growth and changes that occur in children. Individual appropriateness refers to each child's unique pattern and timing of growth.

Guidelines for developmentally appropriate practices address all areas of an effective child care program for school-age children. They include the role of staff members, provision for the development of peer relationships, the use of positive guidance, an environment that accommodates small and large groups, and activities that are geared to the developmental level of the children.

A current debate among early childhood professionals concerns which is better, an academic or a holistic approach to programming. The academic approach is based on predetermined, measurable goals. A holistic approach allows the curriculum to evolve based on children's individual or group abilities and interests. One approach is to provide experiences through an integrated curriculum in which goals of specific content areas are combined into the presentation of one activity.

The NAEYC has made recommendations for working with children whose home language is other than English. Adults should recognize the importance of children's home language and acknowledge that children can demonstrate their knowledge and capabilities in many ways. Learning a second language can be difficult, and children need to be able to build on their cognitive skills using their home language. They will then be able to move on and gain new skills in the second language.

NAEYC recommends that programs support children's home language by providing examples of the language in the environment. Books, bulletin boards, tape recordings, labels on materials, and signs are all ways to incorporate the home language into the child care environment. Adults should also learn some words and phrases from the children's home language. When several languages are spoken by children in a group, it helps if they can work together at times.

An antibias curriculum incorporates the positive intent of multiculturalism and uses similar activities and materials. In addition, it allows children freedom to ask questions about differences, is based on developmental tasks, and directly addresses the impact of stereotyping, bias, and discriminatory behavior.

Planning is essential to a good child care program. It ensures a variety of activities that interest children and needed materials will be ready. Conflicts between children will be less frequent. Staff members can share responsibilities. You can implement both short- and long-term goals. Parents and administrative personnel can be kept informed.

Everyone who is involved should be included in planning: all staff members, children, and parents.

When planning activities for your child care group, capitalize on children's interests. Increase their awareness of cultural differences. Foster children's desire to be competent by teaching them how to do real jobs using real tools. Encourage their play interest and provide enough choices of things for them to do. Try to balance activities between group and individual, quiet and active, child initiated and adult initiated. Include everyday experiences such as a trip to the grocery store or a walk around the block. Allow time to meet each child's needs. Do not forget to plan for transition times.

Transitions, those times when all or part of the group moves from one activity to another, should be planned as carefully as other parts of the curriculum. Minimize waiting time by having the next activity ready; provide books, videos, or tapes to keep children occupied. Alert children before the change is to take place and involve them in cleanup.

There are several ways to present activities: independent projects, group activities, interest centers, field trips, clubs, spontaneous activities, and community projects.

Draw up a schedule by first listing everything you do each day. Allow adequate time for each activity but not so much that children get bored.

Summer programs mean changes in personnel and the number or ages of children. The longer days allow for a variety of activities that may be similar to those during the rest of the year, but have the new dimension of added time.

Key Terms

academic approach
age appropriateness
antibias curriculum
curriculum

emergent curriculum
holistic approach
individual appropriateness
integrated curriculum

Student Activities

1. Talk to a group of school-age children. Find out what they are interested in by asking what they do after school, what they read, or what they watch on television. Is there a difference between boys' interests and girls' interests? Are there age-level differences?
2. Write a short paragraph about what you liked to do when you were between six and ten years old. How did you get started with these interests? Did your parents encourage them? Did your friends?
3. Survey your community to find out what resources are available that might be used by a school-age child care group. Is there a wide variety, or are there limited choices?
4. Set up a schedule for an all-day child care program. Include as many of the suggestions from this chapter as possible.

Review Questions

1. Define developmentally appropriate practice. What is the difference between age appropriateness and individual appropriateness?
2. What is the primary role of staff members in a child care program? How should they adjust their interactions to the youngest children and then to the oldest?

3. State five reasons for careful planning when you work with school-age children.
4. Defend the statement "Staff members should have paid planning time each day."
5. How can you include children in your planning?
6. In what ways can parents help you to plan a good program?
7. Suggest three activities you can include to increase children's desire to become competent.
8. List three approaches to presenting activities.
9. In what ways can field trips be used to enhance a child care program?
10. How can children who attend child care be more involved in their community?

Case Study

François and Marissa have both been assigned to a group of 10- to 12-year-olds in a YMCA after-school program. Marissa had been a preschool teacher and has a degree in early childhood education. François worked for many years as an assistant teacher in a fourth-grade classroom. They have widely differing opinions about how their program should be planned. Marissa believes they should rely to a great extent on what the children want to learn or do and develop the curriculum from there. François has read the curriculum guidelines of the local school district and thinks they should be reinforcing what the schools teach. He points to the fact that at the nearby school many of the children attend, reading and math scores are extremely low. He says it is their job to help the children increase their academic skills so they will be able to go on to the next grade level.

1. How would you describe their different approaches to curriculum planning?
2. How can they resolve their differences so they can work together and the children gain the maximum benefit?
3. Can you think of a way to combine the two approaches?

References

Albrecht, K. M., & Plantz, M. C. (1993). *Developmentally appropriate practice in school age child care programs* (2nd ed.). Dubuque, IA: Kendall/Hunt.

Bredekamp, S., & Copple, C. (Eds.). (1997). *Developmentally appropriate practice in early childhood programs* (Rev. ed.). Washington, DC: National Association for the Education of Young Children.

Derman-Sparks, L. (1989). Anti-bias curriculum: Tool for empowering young children. Washington, DC: NAEYC.

Krashen, S. (1992). *Fundamentals of language education.* Torrance, CA: Laredo.

Loosi, S. E. (2000). *Making an impact on out-of-school time.* Wellesley, MA: National Institute on Out-of-School Time.

NAEYC position statement: Responding to linguistic and cultural diversity—Recommendations for effective early childhood education. (1996). *Young Children, 51*(2), 4–12.

Piaget, J. (1952). *The origin of intelligence in children* (M. Cook, Trans.). New York: International Universities Press.

Vygotsky, L. (1978). *Mind in society: The development of higher psychological processes.* Cambridge, MA: Harvard University Press.

Suggested Readings

Bergstrom, J. M. (1990). *School's out.* Berkeley: Ten Speed.

Boutte, G., Van Scoy, I., & Hendley, S. (1996). Multicultural and nonsexist prop boxes. *Young Children, 52*(1), 34–39.

Cech, M. (1991). Globalchild—Multicultural resources for young children. New York: Addison-Wesley.

Katz, L. G., Evangelou, D., & Hartman, J. A. (1990). *The case for mixed-age grouping in early education.* Washington, DC: National Association for the Education of Young Children.

Lewis, B. (1995). *Kid's guide to service programs.* Minneapolis: Free Spirit.

CHAPTER 9

Creating an Environment

Objectives

After completing this chapter, the student should be able to:

- Describe ways in which the physical environment enhances development
- State general guidelines for planning indoor and outdoor space
- Draw a plan for a child care room with an adjoining playground
- Discuss ways to adapt the environment when space must be shared

Teresa, age 18, had just started her first classes at a community college. The instructor in her human development class announced that the local school district ran a before- and after-school child care program and needed aides for the coming year. This sounded like the perfect opportunity for Teresa. She needed a part-time job that would let her take classes in the morning, and she knew she didn't want to work retail, fast food, or sit behind a desk. She was immensely enjoying her human development class and was excited about the opportunity to relate what she was learning in the class to working with children. Teresa applied at the local school district. Fortunately, the program offered some additional training, so she felt a bit more at ease about her ability to be successful in her job. She was hired to work each afternoon from the time the children got out of school until the center closed at 6:00.

At first Teresa performed tasks such as preparing snacks, playing board games with children, or helping them with homework. In her training she learned how to encourage children's cooperation and how to lead them in recreational activities. Consequently, she was soon able to lead children in large-group activities. However, it didn't take long for Teresa to realize she needed more formal education, so she is carefully planning her next semester of classes at the college. She has found that there is a class about programs for school-age child care as well as classes that will help her learn about curriculum subjects such as science, art, and music. She was also thrilled to discover that there is a class to help her learn more about families and parents.

How the Environment Enhances Development

The physical environment is the basic component of a child care program—the foundation for everything that happens there. The very best program activities, materials, or equipment are less effective if the physical setting does not meet the needs of the children for whom it is designed. The physical setting should be developmentally appropriate, supporting and enhancing all areas of children's development: physical, cognitive, emotional, and social. The environment should encourage children to participate in activities that will further their development, not discourage them.

Earlier chapters indicated that children's physical development is proceeding rapidly during middle childhood, although fine-motor control lags slightly behind gross-motor control. Indoor areas can be planned to provide children opportunities to increase both these skills. To develop fine-motor control, they need space where they can work puzzles, do art projects, build with small blocks, or construct models. There should also be space for dancing or active games that will increase gross-motor control and eye-hand coordination. Outdoor areas provide many opportunities for gross-motor activities such as running, jumping, and throwing. Child care leaders should provide a variety of activities that progressively enhance physical development. As children become more adept at using their large muscles, they should have a place where they can play hopscotch, baseball, or soccer and swim, bike, or skate. Space can also be provided for activities that increase small-muscle control. Planting seeds in a garden bed, doing nature collages, and modeling with clay are some examples.

A developmentally appropriate child care environment provides many places where children can enhance their cognitive abilities. In Chapter 5, you read that Piaget and Vygotsky believed that children need to be active participants in the development of their own intelligence. In order to do that, the environment must invite participation and offer a wide variety of choices. Children must be free to explore and discover, to hypothesize and experiment, in order to increase their knowledge about the world around them. Each area must include space for children to work comfortably and to have their materials close at hand.

You need storage space to keep ongoing projects safe or to display their work. Social skills and language are also components of cognitive development. Work areas should be conducive to verbal interactions among the children. Round tables for some activities and enclosed spaces for others encourage children to talk to one another. Comfortable places for reading also encourage children to increase language skills.

During middle childhood, peer relationships and a sense of belonging to a group become extremely important. Children will usually find places where they can get together, but an effective child care environment will structure places that foster both a group rapport and friendships between children. The setting needs to have a space where all of the children can gather at one time for activities or discussions. The environment should also include places where two friends can just hang out and talk. Spaces for clubs also allow children to form relationships and share interests within a small group.

Developing the Plan

The originators of child care centers seldom have the luxury of choosing or building a facility that fits the program they envision. Most often after-school programs are housed in extra classrooms, multipurpose rooms, cafeterias, or gyms. However, within any physical space, it is possible to create an environment that welcomes children and makes them feel safe and secure and enhances their development. It just takes more thought and ingenuity in some situations than in others.

If you are not sure where to start, get a feel for how children play. Watch them playing in your neighborhood, at a park, or on a school playground. Note how the children group themselves. Do they all play in one large group or do two or three children do something together? You probably will see that the groups are small and that children tend to stake out their own territory. They meet in specific places each day, and then continue play activities together. Watch, also, how they change their space whenever they can. Many will use boxes for forts, some will build tree houses from scrap lumber, while others pitch tents so they can be alone. Some children add materials to already existing structures to suit their own needs. They place a wide board on the jungle gym to make a platform for their space ship or enclose a climbing structure with large packing boxes for a clubhouse.

Consider the characteristics of your particular group of children. Their diversity should be reflected in your environment. Look at their age level. Are they all about the same age or do ages vary? What skills and abilities do they have in common? What are their interests? Is there a predominant ethnic group? Do some children have special needs? Each of these factors should be considered when planning your environment.

Next, think of the goals of your program. Your space should allow children to do the things stated in your goals. If you want children to be able to work independently, you have to provide a place where they can do that. If you want to encourage a group feeling, you need space where the whole group can gather or do things together. If your goal is for children to develop their physical skills, you must provide space and equipment where that can happen.

This reading area is partially enclosed by book racks.

When you have followed the preceding suggestions, you should have a fairly good idea of your constituents—the children who will use your environment. In addition, your goals tell you what you want these children to be able to do. It is up to you to set the stage where children and activities can mesh. The following general considerations will guide you in planning both indoor and outdoor space.

Overall Design of Indoor Space

Make the indoor space attractive and homelike. Add color. Place flowers on a shelf or table and hang artwork done by the children on the walls. Paint some of the furniture an interesting color. Put a colorful rug in a corner to set off that space with a touch of brightness. Try changing the lighting. A harsh light is somewhat jarring and distracting. A softer light might create a more relaxed atmosphere.

Set up boundaries for activities. A corner of the room invites privacy. Make it more secluded with a free-standing rack for books. A table and shelves can define space where individual projects are to take place. A rug tells children this is a place for floor activities. A large space that is left open can accommodate group meetings.

Areas should be used consistently for the same purpose. The block area should be used for block building, not active games; the quiet area for reading or quiet talking, not loud music activities. That is not to say these can never be changed. Change them when the need arises. If a space is not working as planned, discuss it with the children, then be open to their suggestions as to how the area can be rearranged.

Well-planned indoor space allows for both individual and group activities.

Leave pathways for easy access to all activities and to entrances and exits. Look at the most likely traffic patterns children might use to move around the room or from indoors to outdoors. Arrange work areas so they are undisturbed by children tramping through them.

Make each area readily identifiable by children, staff members, and parents. The kinds of materials you place there, the furniture, or the arrangement should inform everyone of the purpose. Some programs go so far as to place signs at these areas. A good idea, perhaps, but purpose can be conveyed just as effectively by the materials and equipment.

Remember that some activities go well together and can be placed next to one another. Others clash and diminish the usefulness of each. Dramatic play may be incorporated into block building; these two activity areas can be in proximity. On the other hand, children trying to read quietly in a corner will be disturbed by noisy construction projects. These two areas should be some distance from one another.

Minimize crowding in activity areas by allowing enough space for large-group functions and limiting the number of children who can work comfortably at other areas. An open area where the entire group can meet should be spacious enough so that children are not pushing right up next to one another. In the activity areas, avoid crowding by making it clear that only a specified number can participate at an activity at any one time. Four chairs at a table indicate that four people can sit there. The children may attempt to add chairs but can be reminded of the limitation, then directed to another area.

What Should Be Included?

There should be enough space so children can move about safely. Check the licensing regulations in your state to determine the number of square feet per child you will need.

Add enough tables, chairs, shelves, and cabinets to accommodate your program. Leave enough room so children do not bump into furniture or trip on equipment.

Include places where children can work on individual or group projects. They will probably need a table, some chairs, and a place to keep their work until it is completed.

This area may also include a place where they can display their completed work.

Have a place where the children can keep their belongings. Children will be coming to you from school carrying backpacks, lunch pails, and jackets. Everyone should have a cubby, shelf, or box in which to deposit these articles until they are ready to go home.

Make room for messy activities near a water supply. Many art projects such as clay, painting, or papier-mâché will require a ready supply of water. Cooking projects, too, tend to be messy. These two areas can be right next to each other and share a sink for water.

Set aside an area for quiet reading, resting, or just talking with friends. An enclosed corner as just described will serve this purpose. Furnish it with a low sofa, beanbag chairs, large pillows, and a soft rug. Add books and magazines.

Leave an open area where your whole group can be together at times. Many schools leave the center of a room for this purpose. This space can also be used for large-muscle activities indoors when you cannot go outside. You can dance or do exercises or gymnastics when the space is unobstructed.

What makes this display of books inviting to children?

Remember to arrange a place where children can complete their homework.   Have computers and printers available for homework. Provide access to the Internet. A table and chairs in a quiet area of the room are needed. Make sure the lighting is adequate so children can see well. Some children will be able to work together at one table, whereas others may need their own work place. You may have to set up a small individual table for the child who needs to work alone.

If you can, provide high spaces and low spaces.   Many centers with limited floor space resort to a double-decker approach. Imagine a climbing structure that could serve as a dramatic play area in the upper level with a quiet hideaway underneath. The upper level might even become a stage for dramatic productions.

Designate places to hang artwork, display photographs, or feature news items.   This area can be a bulletin board near the entrance so parents can also enjoy it. If you do not have a bulletin board, use picture gum or masking tape to attach items to the wall.

Provide adequate storage.   This area should include both closed cupboards and some that are accessible to the children. Use closed cupboards for the things you do not use all the time.

Examples are special art or project supplies, games, table activities, or books. Some materials should be on open shelves or cupboards so children can use them as they wish. Always keep a basic assortment of art materials readily available. Change these periodically with those you have stored away.

If your curriculum includes club activities, arrange a place for children to meet. Let the children decorate the space and add a sign with the club name. Furnish the club area with whatever is needed for their particular activity. A collectors club will need a table and chairs. A drama club could use a stage and a place to store props.

If your group includes some older children (children between the ages of 10 and 13) design a special place for them. A separate room would be best, but if you cannot provide that, set up a corner for them. Make it their special place in which younger children are not allowed. The equipment might include a tape recorder/radio, model kits and games, beanbag chairs, or large pillows. If the room size permits, add a Ping-Pong, an air hockey, or a pool table.

Do not forget the adults when you design your indoor space. Arrange a place where you can prepare materials and keep any records that are required by the program administrators.

In addition, you will need a cupboard or drawer where you can keep your personal belongings.

Parents, too, must be considered. Provide a place for sign-in/sign-out sheets and mailboxes for notes to individual families. In addition, you might install a bulletin board where you can post schedules, pictures of the children, reminders of upcoming events, or any other items of interest to all the parents. Designate a space for lost-and-found articles.

Now that you know what must be included, you can conceptualize the placement of activity areas. Try using a scale drawing of your room. Mark the doors and windows, then designate areas. Check that you have included an area for each activity in your program plan. Try to imagine yourself and the children living in the space. When you actually place furniture and storage cabinets in the environment, walk through it again, thinking about how it will function. If you are satisfied, try it with your group of children. After a period of time, evaluate your arrangement and get input from the children. Do not be afraid to change it, however. As long as everything is movable and not built-in, you can reorganize it. Be flexible.

When You Have to Share Indoor Space

You may not have the luxury of a space that can be set up and left intact at the end of each day. It can be overwhelming to have to arrange your environment at the beginning of each day, but with a bit of preplanning and some imagination, it can be done. If you use adaptable materials and have movable cabinets, your task can be managed. The following are some suggestions that have worked for other programs, but each space may require you to devise your own strategies.

Set up interest centers each day. This process will be easier if you plan ahead by having all the materials you will need in a basket, a large box, ice-cream cartons, or shoe boxes. Carry them to the table or area where children will use them. Install large casters or wheels on cupboards, bulletin boards, or dividers used to designate areas. Sometimes it helps to label these to specify their use. Put locks on the cupboards.

Design furniture that can be taken apart when it must be put away at the end of the day. Buy or construct modular furniture made from sturdy, lightweight building material such as tri-wall. Add large vinyl pillows and vinyl beanbag chairs to be used in reading or listening areas.

A large pegboard on wheels is adaptable for many uses. It can be a convenient place to hang woodworking tools or art supplies. It can also divide one work area from another. (You can divide spaces with folding screens, sheets, or blankets, as well.) Have some shelves that are also equipped with casters. Use these for art materials, games, block accessories, and science materials.

Use plastic stackable containers for the children's belongings.

Carpet squares can define an activity area if there is no rug. This will make the floor more comfortable as well as designate a space. Carpet pieces can often be obtained inexpensively from carpet stores or carpet installers. Allow children to rearrange the indoor environment. They may be able to see possibilities that adults have not considered. Before starting, however, discuss with them the kinds of activities that must be provided for, then have them offer suggestions. Compile their suggestions, then let them vote on the ones to be implemented. Draw up a plan and execute the changes. Evaluate how the plan is working after a trial period.

Work together with other occupants of your space so that everyone has an understanding of what can be done and what cannot. Meet with the principal or building administrator on a regular basis to reinforce mutual commitments to serving children and their families and to resolve any problems that arise. Maintain contact with teachers to determine ways in which the goals of the child care center can complement those of the school. Set up an agreement with school secretaries about use of office equipment and the telephone. Have an explicit understanding with the janitors about who is responsible for cleaning and taking out the trash and who will clean up when others use the space.

Overall Design of Outdoor Space

It is rare that child care staff members are able to design a new playground. Most have to adapt an existing facility to suit the needs of their program and the children they serve. Whether starting from scratch or adapting an existing playground, it helps to visit other child care centers, parks, or schools to see how others have planned play spaces for children. Note how the children use both the open spaces and any permanent equipment. Are some not used at all? What kinds of equipment attract the greatest number of children or hold their interest the longest? What kinds of play occur? What do children do in the open spaces? This valuable information will be useful when planning child care outdoor areas.

The next step is to take an inventory of everything in the outdoor space that will be available to the center. Map out areas that cannot be changed, and indicate the places that are open. Brainstorm ideas for the space with other staff members. If children are already enrolled in the center, get their input. They may have wonderful suggestions for what they would like to have. Make a priority list of what will be needed, and figure the cost of each

This structure can be used for many kinds of play activities and is therefore considered multipurpose.

item. If financial resources are limited, plan to purchase first items that are likely to be used the most or that have the greatest capability for multiple uses. Are there things that staff members or parents can build or install, thus decreasing the cost?

Clarify program goals that will be supported by the outdoor environment. What is it you want children to be able to do as a result of using the space? Remember that outdoor space is not just for helping children to develop physical skills but can help them grow cognitively and socially as well. Outdoor play can involve problem solving, investigating, observing, listening, matching/naming objects, and predicting, to name just a few cognitive skills. Socially, outdoor play can help children learn to cooperate, share, develop friendships, engage in group fantasy play, and foster a group cohesiveness.

A playground should be based on a knowledge of child development. Review the chapters on development at the beginning of this textbook to remind you of what school-age children are like. They are extremely active and like to have lots of space to run, jump, and throw. They want to be competent at any activities that require physical agility and need places where they can practice their skills. They want to have places where they can be with their peers, either one-on-one or with a group.

"Me on the bars." Mariah, age 10.

Design your space with children's special needs in mind. If the group includes children with physical limitations, include spaces to which they will have access. Some possibilities are to include paved pathways that are wide enough for a wheelchair, a raised sandbox or a sand table, wheelchair-accessible areas for throwing balls, and climbing equipment with a transfer station, allowing a child to go from chair to climber. Many playground equipment companies will offer advice on how to adapt their pieces to fit the needs of children with disabilities.

Safety

Children's safety is a top priority for all child care centers and is therefore treated here as a separate subject to consider when planning or renovating outdoor play areas. The process should begin with a survey of the area to be used. Do a safety audit of existing structures by comparing them to standards, guidelines, and laws set by federal and state agencies. Information can be obtained from the following sources:

United States Consumer Product Safety Commission: *Handbook for Public Playground Safety* (1988)
4330 East-West Highway
Bethesda, MD 20814-4408
Phone: 301-504-6816
Fax 301-504-0124 or 301-504-0025
http://www.cpsc.gov E-mail: info@cpsc.com

National Program for Playground Safety
University of Northern Iowa
Cedar Falls, IA 50614-0614
Phone: 800-544-PLAY or 319-273-2416
Fax 319-273-7308

E-mail: playground-safety@uni.edu
Pamphlets and videos and can answer questions.

Americans with Disabilities Act of 1990 (ADA)—the *Americans with Disabilities Act Accessibility Guidelines* (ADAAG) http://www.ada.gov
Phone: 800-514-1301 (voice)
800-514-0383 (TTY)

American Alliance for Health, Physical Education, Recreation and Dance (AALR)
1900 Association Drive
Reston, VA 22091-1598
Phone: 800-213-7193
http://www.aahperd.org

American Society for Testing & Materials (ATSM)
100 Barr Harbor Drive
West Conshohocken, PA 19428-2959
Phone: 610-832-9585
Fax 610-832-9555
http://www.astm.org
Information on playground site and surfacing-testing materials.

Check also with your state licensing bureau for regulations affecting playground space and equipment. Your state may also have laws pertaining to playground safety. California, Michigan, Texas, North Carolina, New Jersey, and Connecticut all have such laws. Others have proposals in process. Familiarize yourself with these laws before making a final playground audit. Information about laws can be obtained from your state attorney general's office.

Additional guidelines you can use for planning a safe outdoor environment for children follow:

1. Make sure the equipment is appropriate for the age of the children who will be using it. Your knowledge of developmental stages and abilities should help to determine whether equipment is too easy or too difficult.
2. Do a daily environmental inspection, looking for bottles, cans, animal waste, standing water, or anything else that may create a hazard. Include a survey of equipment, looking for rust, splintering wood, or exposed bolts.
3. Choose cushioned surfaces for beneath equipment as a fall zone. Asphalt, black top, grass, packed dirt, and concrete should not be used. Choose pea gravel, sand, or hardwood fiber/mulch. The height of the equipment will determine the depth of the material used. Usually 12 inches of loose fill will be adequate for equipment up to 8 feet in height. If synthetic material is used, the manufacturer will recommend the depth.
4. Make sure all climbing equipment meets consumer safety standards. Steps on ladders should be in good condition, and handrails should have appropriate grip sizes. Protective barriers should be at least 38 inches high for school-age children.
5. Swings should have soft seats, and only two should be placed in one framework. They should be positioned at least 24 inches apart at the base of the seats and 30 inches from any supports.
6. There should be a cushioned fall zone 20 feet in front and 20 feet in back of the pivot height of the swing. The cushioned zone should also extend 6 feet to each side of the support structure.

7. Slides should be securely anchored. The steps should have firm handrails and provide good traction. Drainage holes in the steps will prevent moisture that makes them slippery. Make sure there is no space between the slide platform and the bed where strings from clothing can catch. If the slides are metal, they should be in a shaded area.

8. Seesaws should be designed with secure handles of a size that school-age children can grip easily. There should be a soft bumper under the seat, and all pivot points should be covered.

9. Merry-go-rounds should be firmly anchored into the ground with handles that children can grasp easily. There should not be enough space beneath the bed so children could slide under. All parts of the gearbox should be covered. A governor should control the maximum speed of the unit.

10. Be sure that all areas with potential hazards are easily supervised and can be seen from various vantage points. Be sure no trees or other structures block your view.

11. Always provide adequate supervision when children are using playground equipment. You must have an adult near who is attending to what the children are doing. That person must be aware of the rules for using the equipment and be capable of enforcing the rules when necessary.

What Should Be Included?

Include both single-purpose and multipurpose equipment.   Most children love the old standbys: swings, jungle gyms, climbing rope, and a sandbox. Swings are single purpose: they can be used only for swinging. A climbing structure can be multipurpose, having many different kinds of play possibilities. A sandbox seems to be single purpose on first glance. You immediately think that it is just for digging, but children can find almost endless ways to incorporate other kinds of play into this area. They will build dams, cook elaborate foods, and search for dinosaur bones, to name just a few.

Add some materials so children can construct their own equipment.   Large blocks, boards, cartons, cable spools, and sawhorses present interesting possibilities. Consider using tires, inner tubes, logs, and sheets of wood or cardboard. These are materials for "adventure playgrounds" that are actually available in some parts of the country. Children can be marvelously inventive in what they can devise.

As needed, bring out equipment to stimulate new play ideas.   Balls, racquets, hoops, hockey sticks, jump ropes, tumbling mats, and horseshoes are just a few choices. (Do not forget a pump for rejuvenating deflated balls.) Chalk for sidewalk games, yo-yos, and batons might be added depending on the interests of the children. In different kinds of weather there are additional items to use. When it is hot, bring out a hose, buckets, sprinklers, a small pool, and boats. For areas that get snow, provide shovels, sleds, and snow saucers.

Include areas where children can have some privacy.   A playhouse, park bench, tree house, or even a secluded corner under a tree can be a place where children can gather to chat with a friend or just be alone.

Allow spaces for special activities, some protected from inclement weather.   Some games need a hard surface, others dirt. Set aside a safe place away from pathways where children can practice skateboarding or roller skating. Use a covered area for art or table activities that can be enjoyed when the sun is hot or even when it rains.

Have a variety of surfaces on your playground. Include grass, dirt, cement or asphalt, sand, or wood chip areas for added interest. In addition to these surfaces, it is nice to leave some planted areas in the yard. Trees, flowers, shrubs, or a garden area add a pleasing touch to any yard.

Provide an opportunity for children to learn about and gain respect for their natural environment. Growing urban areas have almost obliterated any wild and natural places for children to play. As a result, many children today have little contact with the outdoors, and many even express fears of insects, snakes, and plants (Bixler, Carlisle, Hammitt, & Floyd, 1994). The playground of a child care center can allow children to explore the outdoors within a relatively safe setting. Create an area that contains unmanicured grass, bushes, plants, some rocks, a small hill, some trees, and a birdbath and feeder. Add a garden where children can grow vegetables or flowers, plant flowers that will attract butterflies or hummingbirds, and include wild grasses or plants native to the area. In addition, allow children to construct their own play spaces or private hideaways with tree limbs, boards, boxes, and large tires. Children will strengthen their appreciation of the outdoors if they share responsibility for maintaining the area.

Remember to have a water outlet in the yard, both a drinking fountain and hose faucet. Active children get thirsty, and water is needed for many art projects. If hoses are added, children will be able to build dams in the sandbox, learn how water sculptures any area where it runs freely, maintain a garden, or observe how sunlight shining through sprinkler spray makes a rainbow.

The outdoor area of a child care center may be the only opportunity some of today's children have to engage in free, active play. Many live in apartments or areas where they cannot play outside their houses because it is not safe. In addition, many will get home after dark. Therefore, you should put as much thought into the kinds of activities you provide for children outdoors as you do for inside time. Play outdoors is not just a chance to run around and let off steam but also an opportunity for additional learning and the acquisition of skills.

When You Have to Share Outdoor Space

If you have to share outdoor space with other programs or with neighborhood children, you have an additional challenge. You probably will not be able to change the environment, but you can add your own movable play equipment. Bring out easels and painting materials, a box of balls or other sports equipment, digging tools in a crate, or games to play on the grass. You will have to look at the possibilities of the space available and add whatever you can.

Allow your children to mingle with others using the space. It would be difficult if your children felt different from neighborhood youngsters in a park just because they were in child care. Establish clear rules about where they can go and what they can do, but allow as much freedom of movement as you safely can.

Environment affects us all in subtle ways. A good atmosphere will encourage children to be relaxed and engage in productive play. Poor conditions may result in upset children who cannot settle down to sustained activities. Design your child care space with thought, and be willing to change it as needed. You and your children will be glad you did.

Summary

The physical environment is the basic component of a child care program, the foundation for everything that happens there. A developmentally appropriate environment will support and enhance all areas of children's development: physical, cognitive, and social. Few child care staff members have the luxury of designing a facility that exactly fits the program they envision. Most have to adapt space in unused or dual-use spaces within another facility. With thought and ingenuity, it can be done, however.

Some overall guidelines help you plan indoor space. Make it homelike, adding such things as color or soft lighting. Delineate boundaries for activities, and use these spaces consistently for the same purpose. Leave pathways to doorways as well as to all classroom areas. Each area should be easily identifiable as well as exist comfortably with adjacent spaces.

Children's safety should be a top priority for all child care centers. Planners should obtain guidelines, regulations, and laws that govern playgrounds. Make sure the equipment is age appropriate and has cushioned surfaces beneath potential fall areas. Climbing equipment should meet consumer safety standards, swings should have soft seats, and all equipment should be securely anchored into the ground.

Include in your indoor environment the following:

- enough space to meet licensing requirements
- a place for individual or group projects
- a cubby for each child to keep his or her belongings
- a water supply for messy activities
- an area for reading, resting, or talking
- an open area for large gatherings or active games
- a place for children to do homework
- high places and low places
- a bulletin board for art, notices, and parent information
- adequate storage
- a club area
- a special place for older children
- a place for caregivers and parents

When you have to share indoor space, you can organize materials in easy-to-carry boxes or crates, install casters on all furniture, use shelves or pegboards to divide work areas, use carpet pieces to delineate a space, allow children to set up the environment, and work with other occupants to avoid misunderstandings.

Before you begin to draft a design for a playground, visit a variety of places where children play: other child care centers, school playgrounds, or parks. Your playground should reflect what you know about children. All outdoor areas should be safe but also offer some challenges to children. If you have children with special needs in your group, you will have to do additional research to know how to meet their needs.

Include in your playground the following:

- both single-purpose and multipurpose equipment
- some materials children can use to construct their own equipment

- balls, hockey sticks, jump ropes, etc.
- space for special activities
- a variety of surfaces
- a water outlet
- a natural, unstructured space

When you have to share outdoor space with other programs, add movable equipment, allow children to mingle with others using the area, and establish clear rules about what children can and cannot do.

Key Terms

ADA   safety audit
multipurpose equipment   single-purpose equipment

Student Activities

1. Obtain several catalogs from companies that supply playground equipment. Select a climbing apparatus and three other articles for a school-age playground. In class, explain your choice in a group of two other students. Compile the list of choices from each group member, then negotiate and agree on buying only three items.
2. Visit three child care sites that are under different auspices: church, recreation program, school district, community organization, or privately owned. Record the kinds of furniture and equipment available in their indoor space. Share your findings with your classmates.
3. Draw a floor plan of an ideal indoor space for a group of 20 children from ages 6 to 11.
4. Use the list of things to include in an indoor environment discussed in this chapter. How might you have to adapt your plan to accommodate a child in a wheelchair?

Review Questions

1. List five general guidelines to remember when planning indoor space.
2. Indicate which of the following activities can be placed next to one another: block building, music, art, science, cooking, karate club, homework, drama practice, woodworking, wood sculpting, reading, table games.
3. State five things to be included in indoor space.
4. List three possible storage containers for children's belongings. Can you suggest any others?
5. Describe the arrangement of an art area.
6. What are the requirements for a space where children can do their homework?
7. What is meant by single-purpose and multipurpose equipment? Give examples of each.
8. Why is it important to provide wild spaces for children in an outdoor play area?
9. List some equipment you might take outside to stimulate new play ideas.
10. In what ways can you adapt both indoor and outdoor equipment when you have to share space with other programs?

Case Study

Dion and Hazel have been hired to be co-leaders in a new child care center in an upscale urban area. As they start to plan, they realize they have quite different ideas about what should be in the room. In addition, the director tells them she wants the room to convey the high academic standards she believes in. The parents who have already enrolled their children are well educated and want their children to be successful in school.

1. If you were responsible for planning this environment, where would you start?
2. How can you take into consideration the differing ideas of the two caregivers, the concerns of the director, and the demands of the parents?
3. Is there a way to make the environment flexible so that it can be changed if needed?

Reference

Bixler, R. D., Carlisle, C. L., Hammitt, W. E., & Floyd, M. F. (1994). Observed fears and discomforts among urban students on field trips to wildland areas. *Journal of Environmental Education, 26*(1), 24–33.

Suggested Readings

Clemens, J. B. (1996). Gardening with children. *Young Children, 51*(4), 22–27.

Haas-Foletta, K., & Cogley, M. (1990). *School-age ideas and activities for after school programs.* Nashville: School-Age Notes.

Herman, M. L., Passineau, J. F., Schimpf, A. L., & Treuer, P. (1991). *Teaching kids to love the earth.* Duluth: Pfeifer-Hamilton.

Marotz, L. R., Cross, M. Z., & Rush, J. M. (2004). Health, safety, and nutrition for the young child (6th ed.). Clifton Park, NY: Thomson Delmar Learning.

Morris, L., & Schultz, L. (1989). *Creative play activities for children with disabilities: A resources book for teachers and parents.* Champaign: Human Kinetics.

Nabhan, G. P., & Trimble, S. (1994). *The geography of childhood: Why children need wild places.* Boston: Beacon.

Rivkin, M. S. (1995). *The great outdoors, restoring children's right to play outside.* Washington, DC: National Association for the Education of Young Children.

Sutterby J., & Frost, J. (2002). Making playgrounds fit for children and children fit for playgrounds. *Young Children, 57*(3), 36–41.

Wardle, F. (1997a). Outdoor play: Designing, building, and remodeling playgrounds for young children. *Early Childhood News, 9*(2), 36–42.

Wardle, F. (1997b). Playgrounds: Questions to consider when selecting. *Dimensions, 25*(1), 9–15.

Wilson, R. A., Kilmer, S. J., & Knauerhase, V. (1996). Developing an environmental outdoor play space. *Young Children, 51*(6), 56–61.

The Curriculum

CHAPTER 10

Games and Other Fun Things to Do

Objectives

After studying this chapter, the student should be able to:

- Discuss why games should be part of a child care curriculum
- Plan and implement a variety of games for outdoor and indoor play
- List some guidelines for making games fun

Danica worked in the business world for 20 years at a management level. She already had a business degree. Danica enjoyed her job, but the day came when the company was consolidating and downsizing, and they made her an offer she couldn't refuse, so she took an early retirement from the company. She decided to do something she really loved, and that was work with children. She started by volunteering at her church. Within a short time, she was offered a position as a classroom aide. Her job at the church was only in the mornings. One day in a casual conversation with a parent, she was asked why she wasn't a teacher at the elementary school. She said that at this point in her life, she didn't want to go back to college full-time or work full-time, but that she would love to work with school-age children. She was then told about the local school-age child care program. She immediately applied for a job as an assistant child care leader.

Now, two years later, Danica is working exclusively for the school-age program. She has gone back to college, taken some classes in school-age child care, and this year is the cosupervisor for a program serving over 100 children at a local elementary school. She is finding that her work in business management has been helpful with the organizational aspects of the job. She has made friends with site supervisors in other programs, and they continue to support one another with ideas about management, working with parents, effective and positive discipline techniques, and curriculum.

How Games Can Enhance Development

Games offer children a change of pace after a day in school. Their choice of activity in the after-school hours, though, will depend on their energy level and personality. Some have a lot of energy after sitting down all day and need to be active. Others are tired and want to rest. Some children are gregarious and ready for playing in groups. Others want to be by themselves and choose activities they can do alone. Fortunately, games offer a wide variety of options. They can be intensely vigorous or played quietly. Participants can be in large or small groups, or one child can play alone.

Games provide many opportunities for children to practice their physical skills. Although boys and girls have just about equal motor skills, boys have greater forearm strength and girls greater overall flexibility. Their body size, coordination, and inherited talent will also affect their agility. As a result, they often select games at which they can excel; boys often prefer basketball or volleyball, and girls choose gymnastics. Encourage them to try new activities by emphasizing the fun of participating, not the degree to which they are successful.

Children learn to work together when they play games. By middle childhood, most understand that rules are for everyone and that they must abide by the rules to be a part of a group. Typically, they often spend more time discussing and negotiating the rules of a game than they do actually playing. In the process, however, they learn about fairness, how to take turns, and to accept that each person can be a leader or a follower. In addition, they experience the fun of a group effort.

Games reinforce and extend children's cognitive skills. They are using logic when they have to plan the next move in checkers or a series of strategies in chess. "If I do this . . . then next I do that . . . this will happen." Many games involve problem solving as well. A marvelous example is a game called Jenga®. The game begins with a completed tower, 18 levels with three blocks at each level. Each player removes one block and places it on the top of the tower without toppling the structure. It takes a great deal of looking, thinking, and predicting before deciding which block can be safely removed. Trivial Pursuit® encourages children to remember facts. Dice games or Yahtzee® require math skills.

Children can gain an appreciation for their own or other cultures by playing the games of different countries. They learn that games are often played as part of celebrations, for holidays, or to bring groups of people together in a common activity. They will also find that in some cultures, games teach children skills they need for survival. Figure 10-1 on page 184 and Figure 10-2 on page 192 are two examples of ethnic games. *The Multicultural Game Book,* by Orlando (1994), lists many more.

Some children will view games as an opportunity to win or to be the best in order to enhance their self-esteem. You may not be able to entirely eliminate this tendency toward

A computer and a selection of games can help children develop new skills.

competitiveness because it is so much a part of their environment at school, on television, and in the news. However, you can minimize this tendency by including games that are noncompetitive and encourage creativity. Also, reinforce children for their efforts and their skills, rather than being best or first. A poem by Zwerling, published in the January 1991 issue of *Young Children,* addresses the matter of competition. He wrote:

Child's Play

I watched the relay races today,
First grade recess
Filled with teachers' whistles and students' squeals,
with shouts and seeming delight.
The winning team screamed and jumped,
Gave high-fives and handslaps just like on t.v.
One winner clenched his fists and put on a game face,
Almost grim, Will Clark in the Series
Giving high-fists and raising arms in triumph.
The other team slowly walked away;
And I thought this really is the beginning.
Surely, surely, there is a better way.
How can there be losers in children's play?

Games and Safety

A section on planning a safe outdoor environment is found in Chapter 9, but some specifics need to be considered when children are engaged in games or other outdoor activities. School-age children often overestimate their competence and attempt feats that are beyond their capabilities. They also compare themselves with their peers and want to be the best at whatever they do. Watch a group of boys on skateboards and observe the risks they take. The following guidelines will help to prevent serious accidents to the children in your care:

1. Set clear rules for using all equipment, and make sure the children know the rules. Ensure that the rules are vigorously enforced.
2. Never allow children to use equipment in inappropriate or unsafe ways or engage in an activity that is potentially injurious.
3. Before planning any vigorous activity, consider all the ways children might get hurt, and eliminate the most serious hazards. When the activity is introduced, make the children aware of the possible hazards, ask them to suggest ways to prevent injury, and add additional cautionary measures if necessary.
4. Provide appropriate safety equipment with sports activities such as knee and elbow pads, helmets, and catcher's mitts.
5. Have enough adults to supervise the activities and maintain the required ratio of adults to children. Train staff to position themselves where they can see the widest area under their supervision and to be vigilant at all times.
6. Apprise every staff member of the center's policies and procedures for managing accidents. There should be a written statement easily accessible to every classroom that includes procedures for dealing with an accident, telephone numbers for nearby emergency services, and information regarding notification of parents.

7. All staff members should know first-aid procedures. They should be able to treat minor injuries such as scrapes or bruises as well as recognize when an injury requires medical attention.

8. Staff members should carry out a follow-up after an accident, reviewing the causes and making suggestions for preventing a similar mishap in the future.

9. Do a follow-up with the children. Children may be upset by the accident and need to be comforted. They may want to know what happened and why. Make sure the discussions with children are low key but factual and honest, focusing on ways to prevent the same kind of injury in the future. Never tell children the accident would not have happened "if John had only listened to me when I told him to stop." Honestly describe what happened. "John was going too fast around the skateboard area and wasn't able to make the turn."

Outdoor Games

Generations of children have played outdoor games. If you look at pictures painted several centuries ago, you are likely to find children playing some of the same games they still play today. Pieter Bruegel's paintings done in the sixteenth century, for instance, include children playing blindman's buff, hide-and-seek, and drop the handkerchief. The street games played on the sidewalks of New York and other large cities have been passed down from parent to child, with each generation adding its own variations. Most of these games are noncompetitive but are designed to test the player's skills. This section will remind you of some of the old favorites as well as provide you with some new ideas.

Activities

Jump Rope

Purposes: develop physical coordination
              promote cooperation to maintain rhythm
              enhance language development, especially for children learning a second
              language

Jumping rope is often done to a rhythmical song or chant. The beat sets the timing for jumps and counts the number of times the individual jumps before making an error.

In other chants, words direct the individual to perform different motions while continuing to jump.

Cinderella,
dressed in yellow,
Went upstairs to kiss a fellow,
By mistake, she kissed a snake,
How many doctors did it take?
1,2,3, . . .

Teddy bear, teddy bear, touch the ground,
Teddy bear, teddy bear, turn around,
Teddy bear, teddy bear, jump real high,
Teddy bear, teddy bear, pat your thigh.

Hopscotch

Purposes: develop balance and large-muscle strength
          encourage play by traditional rules
          increase eye-hand coordination necessary for aiming

A hopscotch board can be seen on the floor of the forum in Rome, indicating that generations of children have played the game. Paintings by the sixteenth-century artist Pieter Bruegel show children playing hopscotch. In Italy, the game is called "heaven and earth," earth being the starting point, and heaven the finish.

Draw the traditional pattern for hopscotch. Vary the rules by hopping with the stone held on the back of the hand. Or hop without the stone, but with the eyes closed.

Instead of the usual rules for hopscotch, try some variations. Set up a set of six squares, three on each side. Number them from one to six. Have children jump through the squares in sequence with a stone held between their shoes. They must jump with both feet together like a kangaroo. If the stone is dropped, that player's turn is lost.

Hopscotch   Hopscotch Variation

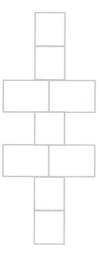

5	6
4	3
1	2

Sock Ball

Purposes: develop eye-hand coordination
          reinforce playing by rules

Push a tennis ball or sponge ball into the toe end of a tube sock. Tie a knot close to the ball. Children can toss this ball back and forth holding the open end. Vary the throws: twirl the sock before throwing, toss it underhand. To make catching more difficult, especially for older children, rule that they can catch the ball only by the tail.

Stalker

Skills: Large motor and listening skills
Ages: 7 and older
Players: 7 or more
Materials: Two scarves for blindfolds; watch or timer

Place of Origin
Botswana

About the Game
The *springbok* is an animal similar to a gazelle, but is found only in southern Africa. Like many games from this region, this one is about a real-life skill: hunting. For centuries children have played this game imitating adult Bushmen stalking a springbok. Through play, children learn the lifelong skills of good hunters: patience, concentration, eye-hand coordination.

Playing the Game
1. Have all the players form a circle. Choose two players to start the game: one will be the HUNTER, the other the SPRINGBOK. Blindfold them both and then spin them around. Have one player announce for the hunt to begin.
2. Moving quietly within the circle, the HUNTER tries to catch the SPRINGBOK, while the SPRINGBOK tries to avoid the HUNTER. Players forming the circle can either remain silent or make animal noises to distract the HUNTER and SPRINGBOK. No one is allowed to touch the HUNTER and SPRINGBOK.

Ending the Game
After a set period of time, if the HUNTER fails to catch the SPRINGBOK, the "animal" wins and a new HUNTER is brought out. If the SPRINGBOK is caught, two new players take over.

FIGURE 10-1   Stalker game

From *The Multicultural Game Book* by Louise Orlando. Copyright © 1994 by Scholastic Inc. Reproduced by permission.

Leapfrog Race

Purposes: foster trust in others and group cohesiveness
develop large-muscle coordination

Have the children line up single file in two separate lines. When the starting signal is given, the first player in each line crouches down on hands and knees. The next player jumps over his back and then becomes a second back. The third player then must leap over two backs before becoming the third back. This continues until all players have had a turn. When the first player has jumped over all his teammates' backs and is at the head of the line again, he stands up. Each player at the end of the line follows the same procedure until all players are standing. The first team to have all players standing is the winner.

Catch the Dragon's Tail

Purposes: promote group cooperation
practice being leaders and followers
increase gross-motor skills

Eight or ten children line up, one behind the other. The last person in the line tucks a handkerchief in the back of his belt. At the start signal, the dragon begins chasing its own tail. The object is for the person at the head of the line to snatch the handkerchief. When the head finally gets the handkerchief, she becomes the tail. The second in line then becomes the new head.

A version of this game is played in China, where the dragon is a symbol of good fortune. The game is often played at Chinese New Year celebrations. In the Chinese version, the children line up, putting their hands on the shoulders of the person in front. The first person is the head and the last one the tail. The tail calls out: "1, 2, 3, dragon." The head leads, running and twisting, trying to catch its tail. If the body of the dragon breaks, the dragon dies. The head then moves to the end of the line and becomes the tail. The game continues with a new head leading until everyone is too tired to play.

Pom-Pom Paddle Ball

Purposes: develop eye-hand coordination
provide practice in pair cooperation

Make paddles using five-inch lengths of broom handle or dowel. Drill a hole in one end of the handle. (Do this with the wood securely held in a vise.) Using wire cutters, cut the hook off a wire coat hanger just below the twisted part. Shape remaining wire into a triangle. Pull a knee-high nylon stocking over the triangle. Secure the end with a bit of tape. Push the two ends of the wire into the handle.

Make a pom-pom by looping yarn around a six-inch piece of cardboard. Use enough yarn to make a small ball. Slip the yarn off the cardboard, then secure the middle with a piece of yarn. Clip all the ends and shape into a ball.

Children can play in pairs, tossing the pom-pom back and forth. Vary the game by having children form into two lines facing each other. A group of six children works best. Have them toss the pom-pom back and forth between one team and the other.

What games could be played with this ball?

Obstacle Course

Purposes: develop gross-motor skills
          foster self-confidence by presenting increasingly difficult tasks

Set up an obstacle course using whatever equipment you have available. Place a sign showing the number at each station so children can proceed in sequence. Start with easy tasks and make them increasingly difficult. However, be sure that all activities are safe and that all the children can complete most of the tasks. Some suggestions are:

- walk through a ladder that is lying flat on the ground
- crawl through a tunnel made of tables or large cardboard cartons
- balance on a balance beam or walk on the edging of a sandbox
- jump in and out of a staggered series of tires lying flat on the ground
- jump from wooden packing boxes of several heights
- swing from a knotted rope
- climb a rope net
- shinny down the fireman's pole of a jungle gym

Snake

This game is played by children in Ghana, where there are many different kinds of snakes.

Purposes: develop coordination
provide practice in cooperating with others
increase gross-motor skills

One person is chosen to be the snake. The snake goes to his home, an area that is large enough to fit several children.

When given a signal (blow a whistle), the snake comes out of his home and tries to tag other players. Anyone who is caught holds hands with the snake and tries to catch others.

The original snake is the head and determines who is to be tagged next. The end person, or "tail," can also tag players.

If the snake's body breaks, the group must return to its home and start again. Free players can try to break the snake's body, forcing the snake to return home.

The game ends when all the players have been caught or when everyone is totally out of breath.

Tug of War

At one time, tug of war was a portrayal of the battle between the forces of good and evil. In Burma, the battle represents the natural occurrences of rain or drought. The custom is to allow rain to win.

In Korea villagers play the game to determine which village will have the best harvest. This version is played in Afghanistan.

Purposes: develop gross-motor skills
increase coordination
provide practice in balancing
increase the ability to plan strategies

Provide the players with a baseball bat or a wooden board about three feet long (sand all edges so they are smooth).

The players draw a line on the ground and stand on opposite sides. Each player clutches the board. The object of the game is to pull the other person across the line.

Active Games That Can Be Played Indoors

You should know a few active indoor games children can play when the weather prohibits outdoor play. Even on warm days, children sometimes need to be moving around while inside. The following are some games that can be played indoors, but you can set them up outdoors if you wish.

Activities

Beanbag Bowling

Purposes: practice in taking turns
cooperation needed to set up pins after each turn

You will need one or two beanbags and four to ten tall, slim cans. Pringles® cans work best, but you can also use tennis ball cans. In addition, you need a smooth, shiny floor or a long piece of plastic carpet cover. Place the cans in one of the configurations shown below. Each child sits at the end of the "alley," then slides the bean bag toward the pins. Children can keep score, adding the number of pins knocked down at each turn.

For a variation of this game, use cylindrical floor blocks for the pins and a soft ball. Players roll the ball, knocking over as many pins as possible.

String Ball Bowling

Purposes: increase eye-hand coordination
increase ability to reproduce a pattern when resetting the pins
increase math skills
develop teamwork and cooperation

A version of this game was played in France many years ago. It was brought to the United States by Dutch settlers and developed into the modern game of bowling.

Use a hollow ball, either a tennis or racquet ball. In addition, you will need duct tape, string, and cans or plastic bottles. Cut a small slit in the ball. Have children knot one end of a six-foot length of string, then push the knot into the slit. Tape the string to the top of a doorway, letting the ball clear the floor by about three inches. Find 10 plastic bottles of the same size. Spray paint them all the same color. Pour 1½ inches of water into each. Replace their caps securely. Set the bottles in a triangle, leaving space on either side of the doorway. Players swing the ball around the pins on either side and hit them from the back.

Beanbag Shuffleboard

Purposes: practice motor skills of throwing, pushing
improve math skills: writing numbers, adding
taking turns, scorekeeper and player

Use masking tape or chalk to mark off a court on an area of smooth floor. The court should be a large triangle, sectioned into six segments. Number each segment, giving the smallest segment the highest score. Children sit on the floor at the large end of the triangle and slide their beanbag along the floor. Each has two turns. Each can keep his or her own score, or a scorekeeper can be appointed. After a set number of turns, the scores are totaled.

Shuffleboard

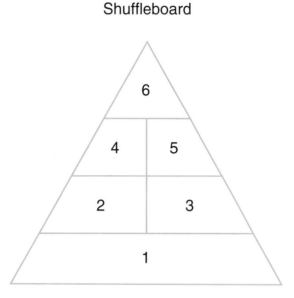

In a variation of this game, a broomstick or long dowel can be used as a shuffleboard stick. Instead of sitting, children stand, then push the beanbag with the stick.

Ping-Pong Jai Alai

Purposes: refine eye-hand coordination
         encourage cooperation when working in pairs

Provide a Ping-Pong ball and tall can for each child. A Pringles® can, tennis ball, or large frozen juice can is suitable. Children drop or toss the ball with one hand, then try to catch it in the can. You can vary the game by suggesting they let the ball bounce twice or three times before catching it.

Children might also work in pairs, with one child releasing the ball while the other catches. The catcher then puts the ball in play for her partner.

Indoor Basketball

Purposes: strengthen eye-hand coordination
         rehearse turn taking

You will need the inner ring of an eight-inch embroidery hoop, heavy tape, and a Nerf® ball. Have children tape the hoop to the wall as high as their arms can reach. To play the game, each player gets three chances per turn to make a basket.

Box Marble Shoot

Purposes: develop small muscles of hand and fingers
         increase math skills: number recognition and addition

For this game you need a shoe box, felt marking pens, scissors, and marbles. Draw five arches on one side of the box. Make one large arch, two medium, and two short. Mark number values above each arch. Cut out the arches. Each player gets three marbles and several turns to complete the game. Players shoot their marbles, trying to get them through the slots. At the end of a set number of turns, each player totals her score.

Kulit K'rang

Children in Indonesia play this game with small shells.

Purposes: develop eye-hand coordination
          increase reaction time
          predict where pieces will fall

The players sit in a circle around a bowl. Each player is given an equal (10–15) number of playing pieces (dried beans, peanuts, pebbles, or seashells). Leave about 20 pieces in the bowl. Each player places his pieces on the floor in front of him.

The first player puts a piece on the back of his hand, then tosses it in the air. He must grab another piece from his pile, then catch the falling piece.

If he has successfully caught the falling piece, he takes one piece from the bowl. If unsuccessful, he must put one piece in the bowl.

Play continues until the bowl is empty or all the players are out of pieces. The player who then has the most pieces wins the game.

Indoor Games

There are many commercial games you can use in child care. Ask the children what they like to play at home. Remember the games you enjoyed when you were a child. Visit toy or game stores to find games that are appropriate for school-age children. In addition to the commercial board games, there are some that you and the children can make. Also, encourage the children to think of their own ideas for games. Once you begin, new ideas will be generated.

Introduce children to simple card games; they are inexpensive because they require only a deck of cards. Some are described here, but you can find others in the books suggested at the end of this chapter.

Activities

Three-dimensional Tic-Tac-Toe

Purposes: develop ability to recognize spatial relationships
          use deduction; predict results when moves are made

Mark off a 9 × 9-inch square on a piece of tagboard. Leave a small border around the edges. Divide the square into nine 3-inch squares. Cut a toilet paper tube into five ¾-inch rings. Cut the heads off 10 wooden matches. Glue or tie pairs of matches together in the shape of an X. Children can use felt markers to color the tube circles one color and the match Xs another. Players take turns, one using the Xs and the other the Os. Each places his token on a square. The purpose is to get three of his tokens in a row down, across, or diagonally.

Memory Game

Purposes: practice the ability to match like symbols

develop the ability to remember placement of objects in space

Find 20 pairs of pictures. You can use playing cards from two decks or secure your own matching pictures. They should all be the same size and with no identifiable marks, patterns, or colors on the back. Two to four children can play this game.

Mix the cards, then place them facedown on a table. Players take turns selecting two cards at a time. The cards are shown to the other players. If the cards are a matching pair, the player keeps them. If not, they are placed back in their original spot. The next player then has a turn. The game ends when all the pictures have been picked up. The player with the most pairs is the winner.

Twenty Pairs

Purpose: practice ability to match like pairs

accept that it is all right to lose

This game can be played by three or more and requires a pack of 52 cards.

Remove one queen from the deck, then deal the remainder to the players. The goal of the game is to get rid of one's cards by getting matched pairs and laying them on the table.

Each player picks up and examines his cards. He can discard any matching pairs by placing them facedown on the table. If he has three cards of the same value, he can discard only two of them.

To begin the game, the player to the left of the dealer fans out his cards and offers them face down to the next player on his left. That player takes one card and incorporates it into his hand. If he now has a pair, he places it facedown on the table. He, in turn, offers his cards to the next player. The procedure continues around the table until all the players have managed to pair and discard their cards. One person is left holding the odd queen.

Rotation Dice

Purposes: practice in taking turns

enhance math skills: set recognition, adding

Two or more players can play the game, and all you need is a pair of dice.

Each player takes turns trying to get a specified number on each throw. There are 11 rounds to the game.

In the first round each player tries for a two. In the second, each tries for a three. In the third round, each tries for a four. Succeeding rounds follow the sequence to the last round when the sum of both dice must be 12.

If a player succeeds in throwing the number she is trying for, she gets that number of points. For instance, if she is trying for a five and succeeds, she can add five points to her score. If she does not succeed in throwing the number she needs, she ends that turn with no points. At the end of the eleventh round, the scores are totaled, and the player with the most points wins.

Nim

PLACE OF ORIGIN
China

Skills: Counting, creative thinking and planning skills
Ages: 8 and older
Players: 2
Materials: 21 toothpicks, beans, or other small markers

About the Game

This is the thousand-year-old Chinese game of nim. It doesn't have any set patterns or rules. Here, however, is one way it might be played.

Playing the Game

1. Players will need 21 toothpicks or other small game pieces. Arrange the sticks in one row as shown in the picture.

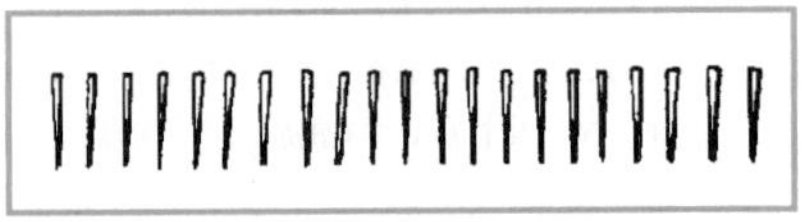

2. Taking turns, the players pick up 1, 2, or 3 sticks at a time.

Winning the Game

The player to pick up the last stick, loses.

FIGURE 10-2 Nim game
From *The Multicultural Game Book* by Louise Orlando. Copyright © 1994 by Scholastic Inc. Reproduced by permission.

Tic-Tac-Toe Dice

Purposes: strengthen math concepts: writing numbers, number recognition, adding

Two or more players can play. You need two dice, a score card, and a pencil for each child. (The score grid can be drawn on a piece of paper or a 3 × 5-inch card.) Have each player make a score grid with 12 squares.

In each of the spaces, write the numbers from 1 to 12. Start with the upper-left square with one proceeding down the first column. Put five at the top of the second column, go down to eight. Write nine at the top of the last column with 12 at the bottom-right corner.

Each player throws the dice only once each turn. On each play players cross out a number or numbers on the score card. They can cross out a total or each of the two numbers. Players also can cross out any combination of numbers that equals the total on the dice. As an example, if a five and a two are thrown, the following combinations can be crossed out: six and one, or five and two, four and three, or one, two, and four. The first person to cross out all the numbers is the winner.

Tic-Tac-Toe

1	5	9
2	6	10
3	7	11
4	8	12

Solitaire

Card games that are played alone in the United States are called "solitaire." In England these games are called "patience."

Purposes: increase ability to concentrate
          reinforce ability to count accurately
          practice recognition of symbols for suits

Shuffle a deck of cards. Deal out seven cards in a line, with the first card faceup and the others facedown. Deal out the line again with the second card faceup and the others facedown. Follow this pattern starting consecutively with the third, fourth, fifth, sixth, and seventh cards.

If an ace is showing, remove it and put it above the line of cards. Turn over the card under it, or if it was the first card, replace it with one from the deck. The object of the game is to fill each of the suits from the ace to the king in a line above the game line.

Remove three cards at a time from the remainder of the deck, looking only at the top card. Play a black card on a red card, sequencing the numbers from largest to smallest. Cards can be removed from one pile to place on another, thus freeing the bottom card. The game ends when all four suits have been filled or no more plays can be made from the remaining deck cards.

Ajaqaq

During the dark winters Canadian Eskimos play a variety of games to pass the time. At one time they believed that playing this game would make the sun return earlier.

Purposes: develop fine-motor skills
            increase eye-hand coordination

Give each player a curtain ring or similar weighted ring about 2 inches in diameter, an 8-inch stick, and 20 inches of string. Tie one end of the string to the ring and the other around the end of the stick. Hold the stick in one hand. Flip the ring in the air, then try to catch it on the end of the stick.

All Ears

Purposes: develop listening skills
            associate sound with familiar objects
            discriminate similar sounds from one another

This is a game for a group of children. All you need are several objects that make a sound.
    Sit where you cannot be seen by the children (behind a shelf or a hanging bedsheet). Make a sound with each of the objects. Players guess what the object is or what action made the sound.
    Some ideas for making a sound:

- shake a rattle
- bounce a ball
- pour water
- cut a piece of paper with scissors
- staple two pieces of paper together
- open a can of soda that has a pull tab
- snap your fingers
- crumple a piece of cellophane
- blow up a balloon until it pops
- rub two pieces of sandpaper together
- saw a piece of wood
- pound a nail into a piece of wood
- bite an apple
- unwrap a candy bar
- rotate a hand eggbeater
- jingle some coins together

At the end of the game, ask the children to think of other objects that can make a sound. Add some of those to your next game.

Guidelines for Having Fun with Games

Before introducing any game to children, play it yourself. Know how the game is started and how the first player is determined. Although you want children to read the rules of a game, you should be familiar with them.

Introduce new games periodically. Although children like to play the same games over and over, they also need to keep extending themselves. Once they master a game, there may be little challenge. Therefore, look for new games. Talk to other caregivers to get ideas.

Encourage children to invent their own games. All games start with an idea of something that would be fun. Let them make their own board games, develop new ways to play outdoor games, and think of new ways to use available materials.

Help children feel competent when they gain new skills. Provide authentic feedback by describing their real accomplishments. Praise their efforts to improve their own performance, for being able to solve a problem, or for being a committed team player.

Encourage children to share their own favorite games with the group. Suggest that they bring games that are part of their cultural background.

Encourage youngsters to try increasingly difficult tasks. Once they have mastered one task, they are often more willing to try harder ones. Encourage them to do so, but do not pressure them. Praise them for their efforts.

Stress cooperation rather than competition. You cannot avoid having a winner and a loser when playing some games. Children need to learn they do not win all the time. Some

Children enjoy the challenge of new games.

of the challenge in playing certain games is to see who can be first or fastest. However, you do not want children to have winning as the primary focus of games. Therefore, do not set up contests or give prizes. Instead, praise all children for their participation, their sportsmanship, and their efforts.

Be flexible about rules. Many games have an accompanying set of rules. However, young children like to change rules or develop their own. Allow them to do so when all the players agree. Enjoy physical activity yourself. Feel the joy children experience when they run, catch balls, or shoot baskets.

Remember the games you especially enjoyed in childhood. Teach the children how to play them. Your enthusiasm will be contagious.

Enjoy the challenge of indoor games. Sit down and play solitaire. Try Trivial Pursuit® with some friends. Try some of the other games described in this chapter. Above all, have fun.

Computers

With the proliferation of computers, child care personnel are asking if they, too, should invest in computers for their centers. They wonder whether children need to learn to use a computer and, if they do not, whether it will affect their ability to be successful as adults. They also question how available the equipment should be—whether children want or on some kind of limited schedule. Bigger questions include where to get the money to buy equipment and who will repair it when there are problems. Finally, who will monitor children's Internet explorations? All of these questions are legitimate ones to ask before deciding to bring computer equipment into a child care center. The answers should come from both child care staff members and parents.

There seems to be support for the use of computers as adjunct learning tools or additional means that are not a part of traditional reading programs. Computer reading programs are particularly effective in helping children learn to read, comprehend what they read, or improve spelling. Some teachers point to the value of allowing children to work individually and at their own pace while using computer software. In the early grades, the most often-used software programs are skill-based games or word processors for writing stories. As children get older, they can begin to use a computer for researching information for school projects or for pursuing their own interests. Many children also enjoy sending e-mail to friends or distant correspondents.

One important reason for including computers in after-school programs is that some children may not have any other access to this technology. In affluent communities computers are likely to be in every classroom, and children may very well have their own computer at home. For children in poorer neighborhoods, the after-school program may be the only source for learning how to use this tool. Even though a school district may have computers, after-school programs might be able to allow children more open-ended computer time than in the classroom. Girls lag significantly behind boys in computer use, and free exploration time could allow them to feel more at ease.

The question of Internet safety should be carefully considered. Curious children who are adept at "surfing the Net" can get into Web sites that give them misinformation or put them in dangerous positions. Software programs can filter Internet access to sites you do not want children to explore. You should also solicit active participation from staff, parents, and children to decide the kinds of access that will be available to children and ways to prevent problems.

Choose software programs carefully, reviewing them before introducing them to the children. So many of the games available for computers either are violent or teach children values you may not want to promote. In a 1996 position statement, NAEYC stated that principles of developmentally appropriate practice should be applied. NAEYC believes that "in any given situation, a professional judgement by the teacher is required to determine if a specific use of technology is age appropriate, individually appropriate, and culturally appropriate" (NAEYC, 1996). You can also find reviews of software and help in choosing appropriate programs on the Internet at the following Web sites:

Superkids™ Educational Software Review
Reviews new software. Includes games to increase vocabulary and increase logic
   and reasoning.
http://www.superkids.com
Science information for upper-elementary children designed by Miami University in
   conjunction with the National Science Teachers Association and the National
   Science Foundation with students at Miami University Center for Human
   Development, Learning, and Teaching at Miami.
http://www.units.muohio.edu/dragonfly
A site designed primarily to provide easy e-mail access to children and includes
   interactive games.
http://www.juniornet.com
Knowledge Adventure© has a wide range of software from different sources as well
   as a special page for educators. Includes product reviews and demonstration
   programs that can be downloaded.
http://www.knowledgeadventure.com

Guidelines for Caregivers

Although this section on computers has been placed in the chapter titled "Games and Other Fun Things to Do," that should not be construed as meaning that computers are not an important tool for learning. Computers can be a vital element of learning if they are integrated into the total curriculum. Teachers and child care personnel often use the term integrated learning to describe the use of interrelated disciplines such as language, math, or science to achieve a goal. This can be seen most often in a project approach where children work on self-initiated projects individually or in a group. The explorations to complete the project may entail the use of a word processor to write letters, stories, poems, or reports. Even children who are just learning to write can be adept at this because they can delete and rewrite easily, without the difficulties that come with laboriously handwriting words. The Internet can be used to research information to include in a report or to follow additional areas of interest.

In order for children to make the most effective use of computers, teachers or caregivers must play several roles depending on the level of competence of the children.

Instructor: When computers are first brought into the program, children will need time to become familiar and comfortable with the hardware (the computer) and software (the programs). At this time teachers must take the most active role, guiding the children through the various steps necessary to explore the new medium.

Coach: As children gain experience, the adult can begin to withdraw active participation, allowing children to work independently or to rely on peers to provide help as needed. The adult becomes a facilitator, providing support when needed or ensuring appropriate behavior.

Model: Children will more likely use computers as an important tool for learning if they see teachers or caregivers using them. The adult can demonstrate the ease with which a story can be recorded on the computer or classroom materials and charts can be produced.

Summary

Children need a change of pace after long hours at school. Some like to be active while others need to rest. Some are ready for socializing, but others want to be alone.

Games allow children to practice motor skills and to work together. Games also reinforce and extend cognitive skills.

Some children will view games as an opportunity to win, but you can minimize this tendency by including noncompetitive games.

Always be aware of safety. Know the laws and guidelines governing child care settings. Set clear rules and enforce them consistently. Have enough adult supervision. Staff members should have first-aid training.

Many popular outdoor games have been played by generations of children.

Active games that can be played indoors allow children to work off energy.

Although there are many commercial games children like to play, there are others you can make.

Games should be fun. Guidelines for enjoying games with the children in your child care center are:

- introduce new games periodically
- help children feel good about themselves when they acquire new skills
- encourage children to try increasingly difficult tasks
- stress cooperation rather than competition
- be flexible about rules
- enjoy physical activity yourself
- remember the games you played as a child, and teach them to the children
- enjoy the challenge of indoor games
- have fun

Computers can be an important addition to the after-school program. Children can work at their own pace writing stories or poems and researching information for school projects. The child care center may be the only place some children will have access to a computer.

Questions of safety of the Internet and appropriateness of software programs must be considered. Adults must take several roles while helping children to become knowledgeable about computer use: an instructor who actively participates, a coach who provides support as children work independently, and a model who demonstrates how to use computers in a variety of ways.

Key Terms

adjunct learning tools
authentic feedback
integrated learning

Student Activities

1. Visit an after-school program. Interview two children on their favorite games. Ask them the following questions:
   - What is your favorite game?
   - What do you like best about that game?
   - What do you dislike about it?

Summarize your findings. Were there any games mentioned by several children? Why do you think those games were popular? Share your findings with the class.

2. Choose one of the indoor or outdoor games listed in this chapter. Teach the game to a group of school-age children. Was it successful? If not, why not?
3. Make one of the games described in this chapter. Try it out with a group of adults and children together. Did both adults and children enjoy the game? How do you think the participants benefited from playing the game?
4. Interview a senior citizen. Ask him or her to describe a favorite childhood game. Why was it a favorite?

Review Questions

1. What are the factors that affect children's choice of active games?
2. What are the best materials to use for cushioning surfaces under a swing?
3. What should be done to ensure the safety of children when they engage in vigorous outdoor play?
4. Name three academic skills that are reinforced when children play table games.
5. List four outdoor games.
6. Name three indoor games that allow children to move around.
7. Briefly describe how twenty pairs is played.
8. List eight guidelines for having fun with games.

Case Study

Ryan, Joel, and Trevor were playing on the outdoor climbing structure. They were pretending they were on a spaceship heading to Mars. They went up and down one of the ladder sections, saying they needed to check on the equipment. Trevor and Joel were rushing to be first down the ladder, pushing and shoving each other. Trevor lost his footing and fell to the ground. Although there was a ground cover of safety mats, Trevor was momentarily unconscious and had a cut on his forehead where he hit something as he fell. The cut was bleeding, but Trevor wasn't crying. Their caregiver, Anthony, knelt over Trevor without moving him and waited for him to recover consciousness. It took only a few seconds, but all the children were standing around looking very anxious. When it was safe to do so, Anthony picked up Trevor and took him to the office so his mother could be called and the director could take care of the cut on his forehead.

1. Is there a way this accident could have been prevented?
2. What would you say to Joel?
3. How would you explain the accident and Trevor's injuries to the children?

References

National Association for the Education of Young Children. (1996, November). NAEYC position statement: Technology and young children—Ages three through eight. *Young Children, 51*(6), 11–16.

Orlando, L. (1994). *The multicultural game book.* New York: Scholastic Professional.

Zwerlling, M. (1991). More food for thought, Child's play. *Young Children, 46*(2), 82.

Suggested Readings

Brandeth, G. (1981). *The world's best indoor games.* New York: Pantheon.

Chipman, G., & Chipman, J. (1983). *Games! Games! Games!* Salt Lake City: Shadow Mountain.

Collis, L. (1989). *Card games for children.* Hauppauge, NY: Barron's Educational Series.

Haugland, S. W. (1999, November). What role should technology play in young children's learning? *Young Children, 54*(6), 26–34.

Johnstone, M. (1988). *Card games.* London: Ward Lock.

Sackson, S. (1992). *A gamut of games.* Mineola, NY: Dover.

Stassevich, V., Stemmler, P., Shotwell, R., & Wirth, M. (1989). *Ready-to-use activities for before and after school programs.* West Nyack, NY: The Center for Applied Research in Education.

Web Resources

Sports Illustrated online magazine for kids. Information about teams and athletes, plus games and activities to increase interest in sports.
http://www.sikids.com

How knowledge of science can increase sports skills. Hands-on activities and answers to frequently asked questions.
http://www.exploratorium.edu/
    Search for "sports".

CHAPTER 11

Imagination and the Arts

Objectives

After studying this chapter, the student should be able to:

- Discuss the importance of art, music, and drama to children
- Plan and implement appropriate activities for art, music, and drama

C A R E G I V E R   P R O F I L E

Julene started working with children about 30 years ago. She taught pre-school for a brief time, but when the youngest of her three children was four, she was hired by the local school district as an elementary classroom aide. She did that for 15 years, but as times changed, the employment demands grew greater, and the school district limited the number of hours she could work. One day she saw an ad in the newspaper for school-age child care in a neighboring community. She answered the ad and was hired. Today Julene is a site supervisor. She plans on staying in her current position until she retires. In her current position, she serves a student population of approximately 125 children on an elementary school site. Nearly 60 of them are kindergarten children with half of them attending the center in the morning and the other half attending in the early afternoon. The remainder of the children attend in the late afternoon hours after school is dismissed.

Currently her goal is to become a better trainer and mentor of others coming into the field. She continues to take college classes and works at keeping current in her field. Recently she completed a mentoring and supervision class and is now in a position to mentor a college student in her community lab experience.

Julene's daughter and granddaughter (age eight) live at home with her. Her daughter has followed her mother's example and works in a school-age program in another school district. Julene is proud that her daughter has committed to working in programs that she had attended since she was an infant.

Role of the Arts in Supporting Development

Watch a group of children as they paint at easels, dance with scarves, or listen to music. Notice their expressions of concentration, joy, or relaxation. You cannot help but conclude that creative activities satisfy children in a way few other experiences can. Children enjoy the arts because everyone can be successful. There is no right or wrong answer or just one way of doing things. They also find it is a way to communicate things they might not be able to put into words. They can use bright colors when they are happy or subdued colors to show sadness. They often feel more relaxed after they pound, roll, or cut clay to release pent-up emotions. They learn what their bodies can do when they dance to music. They relive and remake their own experiences with puppets or in plays.

Art can be shared with others or experienced privately. Painting alone lets a child express feelings or ideas that might not be easy to put into words. Group painting on a mural entails planning, compromise, sharing, and cooperation—all of which are important social skills. Listening to music alone can be a way to release tension and achieve a sense of inner peace, experience emotions vicariously, or just enjoy the sounds and rhythms. Even dancing can be enjoyed alone and offers opportunities to increase physical abilities such as large-muscle control and coordination. Group dancing can be a social activity requiring sensitivity to a partner or to the group. Patterned dances necessitate remembering sequences, an important cognitive skill.

Art, music, and drama can help children from diverse cultural and ethnic backgrounds gain a greater appreciation for their own culture as well as share their heritage with others. Children can view art done by prominent artists from different countries, or they can use the same materials. Some cultures use sand for painting, others paint with brilliant colors, while still others use only black on white paper. Music can tell stories about a people, convey values or ideas, or use a rhythm that can be identified with a way of life. Children can dramatize a folktale, write their own plays, or use puppets from different countries. Through each of these media, children learn how others live their lives. The result should be a greater tolerance for differences and a greater appreciation of similarities from one country to another.

Very young children use art experiences simply to try out materials. In preschool, children use all their senses to investigate the properties of art materials. They want to find out how colors mix together, how a paintbrush works, and how clay feels. They seldom know ahead of time what they are going to create. In kindergarten, children still enjoy just trying out materials for the pleasure of the experience, but they are beginning to realize they can express feelings and past occurrences as well. They sometimes decide to portray something specific, as Ryan did in his drawing shown in Figure 11-1. "I'm going to draw

FIGURE 11-1 "I'm getting in trouble 'cause I'm jumping on my mom's bed." Ryan, age 7.

a picture of me when I get in trouble for jumping on my mom's water bed." By the end of the elementary years, they can set goals for themselves and want recognition for their accomplishments. "I want to learn how to paint with oil paints."

The arts can provide children with a lifelong interest in all creative media. When children view others' creations, they are introduced to new ways to express ideas and feelings. When they study paintings or sculpture, they appreciate how artists use color and form to create something beautiful. While they listen to music, they hear how other people express emotions. When they watch a play, they share in others' experiences.

An important function of the arts is the opportunity to use both sides of the brain. There are two distinct hemispheres of the brain that serve different functions. This division or lateralization is most often associated with adults, but studies of children show that even though there is an early tendency to specialization, children's brains are still malleable (Brooks & Obrzut, 1981). The left side of the brain specializes in language and in logic, uses deductive thinking, and is associated with science and mathematics. The right side of the brain uses an intuitive approach associated with creative processes. Traditional education and even society tends to value left-side thinking, but children should be encouraged to use creative thinking as well. The arts present the perfect opportunity to do just that.

Most important of all, art is a perfect medium for helping children develop divergent thinking and convergent thinking. Divergent thinking is a process of thought or perception that involves considering alternatives, taking a line of thought that is different from the usual. In art there are no right or wrong answers and no single way to accomplish a creative task. So children can ask themselves "What if I used a different kind of paper for my picture?" or "I wonder if this would sound better in a different key or another instrument?" Convergent thinking is just the opposite. It means to narrow down many ideas to a single, focused point. A child may want to express a feeling generated from a past experience. His thinking process will consider the many ways in which this could be done: through a painting, a sculpture, a piece of music, and a dance. Through a process of considering and eliminating, he will decide which will serve his purpose most effectively.

When you plan any creative activities, start first with children's interests. Capitalize on these to formulate your program. Allow them to expand their interests or find new ways to express them. Find out also what they are learning in history or social studies at school. Plan activities that complement these school experiences. For some children, the creative activities they experience in child care will be all they have. Cutbacks in school districts' money or personnel are often felt first in school art programs. For these children, your program will become an even more important part of their lives. Let them enjoy one or more of the arts every single day.

The most effective art program will meet the needs of both the youngest children and the older ones. Younger children want plenty of opportunities to freely explore what they can do with materials. They should have lots of materials available at all times and time to use them in any way they want. The result of their efforts should be less important than the experience. As children get a little older, approaching the end of the elementary years, they become more critical of what they produce. They want to learn how to use real tools to enhance their efforts. They appreciate the opportunity to learn techniques from real artists or people who have special skills.

Visual Arts

There are so many art activities youngsters enjoy that this chapter can give you ideas for just a few. Read the books listed at the end of this chapter, investigate what is available at your local library, and talk to other teachers or caregivers. Attend workshops sponsored by NAEYC or other professional organizations. Look around you at all the possible materials children can use to construct, paint, or draw. Throw nothing away, for it might become part of your art program!

Activities

Clay and Other Kinds of Modeling Media

Purposes: develop fine-motor coordination
enhance understanding of spatial relationships
transform an idea into a three-dimensional object—from symbolic to concrete

Gray or terra cotta clay.   Easy to use, can be dried in a kiln. Provide plastic forks or knives, small combs, garlic presses, and small pieces of sponge for varying the texture of sculptures. Add real sculpting tools for further interest.

Display pictures of Native American pottery. Tell children pottery bowls can be made using long coils of clay. Demonstrate how to roll the clay into a long coil, then start winding a tight circle for the bottom. Continue winding, building on the base circle. Keep the bowl shape. When the desired height has been reached, the outside of the bowl can be smoothed with a sponge dipped in water. Allow the bowls to dry, then provide glazes so the children can paint on designs. Fire the bowls. Display the bowls.

Polymer clay.   Readily available but tends to be difficult to soften and work with. It comes in a variety of colors. Will not harden for a permanent sculpture.

Dough.   Fairly inexpensive, you can vary the texture. (See Figure 11-2 for recipes.)

Papier-mâché.   Paper strips or pieces plus liquid starch. Use a balloon for a base. Dip the paper in the starch, and then lay it on the surface of the balloon. Overlap the pieces and make at least two layers. Let it dry thoroughly, and then prick the balloon. You should have a fairly solid round sphere. (Finished product can become the head or body of an animal. Use paper towel tubes as the legs and neck. This can also be used as a puppet head.)

For added interest, bring a Mexican piñata to class. Show the children that it has been made of a papier-mâché sphere similar to the ones they have made. Encourage them to make their own piñatas with balloons and papier-mâché. When the papier-mâché is dry, prick the balloon. Help the children cut a slit at the top of the sphere so that the piñata can be filled with candy if desired. Pull out the balloon. Provide tissue paper in a variety of colors, scissors, a small brush, and liquid glue. Show the children how to cut fringed strips from the tissue paper. Brush the sphere with the glue. Tell them to lay the strips evenly on the sphere, each strip slightly overlapping the previous one. Remember to leave the slit visible if the piñata is to be filled.

Flour and Salt

4 cups flour
1 cup salt
Food coloring
Water to moisten
Mix the dry ingredients together. Add food coloring to water. Add water to dry mixture to achieve the desired texture. This dough will dry hard in the air and then can be painted. If a reusable dough is desired, add two tablespoons of cooking oil.

Sawdust Dough

2 cups sawdust
Liquid starch
1 cup flour or wheat paste
1 tablespoon glue (if flour is used)
Mix until the dough has a pliable consistency. Can be air dried and then painted.

Cornstarch Clay

1 cup cornstarch
1/3 cup vegetable oil
2/3 cup flour
Put cornstarch in a bowl and add oil. Mix well until starch has been absorbed. Gradually add flour until the mixture is thick and the desired consistency. Knead well for several minutes. Store in an airtight container.

Cooked Dough

1 cup flour
1/2 cup salt
2 teaspoons cream of tartar
1 cup water
1 tablespoon oil
1 teaspoon food coloring
Combine dry ingredients in a saucepan. Mix liquids and gradually add to dry ingredients. Cook over medium heat, stirring constantly until a ball forms. Remove from the heat and knead until the dough is smooth. (This is a very pliable dough that lasts for a long time.)

FIGURE 11-2   Variations of play dough

Construction

Purposes: reinforce divergent thinking through exploring possibilities in found objects
          enhance understanding of spatial relationships
          develop fine-motor coordination

Styrofoam and pipe cleaners. Use Styrofoam meat trays or packing pieces, heavy cardboard, or cork board as a base. Cut pipe cleaners into different lengths. Add additional peanut-shaped, round, or square Styrofoam package fillers for further interest.

Toothpicks, natural or colored. Combine with small corks, drinking straws cut in different lengths, or small wooden beads. Lengths of copper or colored wire can be added. This sculpture can be freestanding or pushed into a base of Styrofoam.

Wood. Use a flat piece of wood or heavy cardboard as a base. Add lumber scraps cut into interesting shapes, wooden beads, wooden buttons, tongue depressors, wood stir sticks, wood lathe scraps. (Many interesting shapes can be obtained from a furniture manufacturer or a high school woodworking class.) Furnish white glue. For a variation, add pieces of tree bark, small twigs, or seed pods.

Recyclable cans. Create "can creatures" using clean soda or juice cans. Provide construction paper in assorted colors, fluorescent paper, markers, scissors, white glue, and assorted objects (yarn, buttons, beads, feathers, etc.). Encourage children to imagine a "creature" with the can as the body. They can cut out feet or arms from the paper. Make hair from fringed pieces of paper or yarn. Buttons or beads can become eyes or clothing decorations. Display the "creatures" when they are finished.

A variation of this type of construction uses chopsticks. Explain to the children that people in Asia use chopsticks instead of forks. (This activity might follow preparation of a Chinese or Japanese meal.) Give each child a chopstick and a piece of polymer clay for a base. Provide feathers, yarn, construction paper, scraps of fabric, small movable plastic eyes, felt-tipped markers, scissors, and white glue. Encourage the children to use their imaginations to create interesting "people."

Sand casting. Use a flat cardboard box filled with slightly damp sand for a mold. Mix a batch of plaster of Paris in a bucket. Children can make a free-form depression in the sand.

Pour in plaster of Paris and let it set. For a variation, let them press shells or other objects into the sand. Remove the objects to leave an imprint before pouring the plaster.

Collage

Purposes: increase appreciation of the natural environment
          enhance sensitivity to differences in color, texture, and appearance of different
             materials
          develop fine-motor skills

Nature collage. Have children collect natural objects outdoors or on a walk: leaves, twigs, bark, dried grass, seed pods, acorns, pinecones, feathers, rocks. Give each child a base of heavy paper, tagboard, Styrofoam, or wood. Provide white glue.

Paper collage. Small pieces of paper: wallpaper, gift wrap, greeting cards, paper doilies, construction paper, aluminum foil, or cellophane. Give each child a base of cardboard, heavy textured paper, or thin box top (from stationery or shoe box). Provide white glue.

Fabric. Small pieces of fabric: felt, lace, ribbon, yarn, buttons, colored beads, small silk flowers, and dried or paper flowers. Give each child a base of colored tagboard, construction paper, or a thin box top. Provide white glue.

Shapes. Provide children with a piece of drawing paper on which has been drawn one of the following shapes: squares, triangles, rectangles, circles, ovals parallelograms cut from construction or other kinds of paper. Challenge the children to create a picture with the shape as the base. Provide marking pens, paints, an assortment of paper and fabric pieces, scissors, and white glue.

Seeds.   Provide an assortment of seeds in different colors and shapes. Give each child a piece of heavy paper, cardboard, tagboard, or wood for a base. Provide white glue and a small brush. Encourage them to create a picture using the seeds.

To stimulate interest in seed collage, display pictures of the New Year's Day parade floats in Pasadena, California. Explain that many of the colors that are seen on the floats are made from millions of seeds that are glued on to the base.

African Kente Cloth

Kente cloth is used for shirts, ties, and hats in many African countries. Display pictures of the cloth or obtain samples. Point out that the cloth is made up of simple geometric patterns on square or rectangular shapes.

Supplies needed: construction paper of assorted colors, rulers, scissors, crayons, or marking pens. Display the cloths when they are finished along with pictures of Kente cloth.

Large Masks

Masks have been used for ceremonies to bring power and spiritual forces to the people who wear them. They often have intricate designs or carvings. Display pictures of ceremonial masks, or visit a museum that displays them.

Supplies needed: large pieces of tree bark or palm frond bases (large pieces of corrugated cardboard can also be used), scissors, white glue, construction paper in assorted colors, found objects. Remind the children they can build up parts of their masks with construction paper pieces or add found objects to make the masks scarier.

Painting and Drawing

Purposes: increase language—new words relating to artistic endeavors
      provide opportunity to move from one intellectual level to another in a
        nonthreatening environment (scaffolding)
      increase awareness of cultural differences and similarities through appreciation
        for ethnic art

Crayon rubbings.   Use any thin white paper over flat stones, leaves, sandpaper, corrugated paper, cardboard shapes. Use the flat side of a crayon to cover the entire sheet of paper, picking up the design underneath.

Chalk painting.   Cover a sheet of paper with a thin layer of liquid starch. Provide several colors of chalk, either sharpened to a point for a thin line or blunted for a thick line. Use a rag, piece of paper towel, or fingers to mute or brush colors together.

Melted crayons.   Use pieces of crayons without paper coverings. Allow children to smash crayons in a heavy bag with a mallet. They can then sprinkle crayon bits onto a piece of paper, cover it with a second sheet. Let them press the paper with a warm iron. Peel off the top sheet. A variation can be achieved by sprinkling crayon bits on paper, then setting it in the hot sun to melt.

Notice the organization and presentation of these art materials. How do they encourage creativity?

Tempera paint.   Provide a variety of colors so children can choose their own palette. Give them a choice of brushes: thin, fat, stiff, or soft. Provide a variety of textures of paper: rice paper, grocery bags, parchment, newsprint, or wallpaper. Try changing the shape of paper: long, thin rectangle; large or small oval; large or small square; triangle, hexagon. For added interest, let them paint outdoors, on the floor, at table easels.

Textile paint.   Provide a variety of colors of textile paint (obtain from a fabric store). Give children a choice of fabrics of different colors, textures, and sizes.

Crepe paper paint.   Use paper with a slick finish (finger paint or butcher paper). Provide each child with lengths of crepe-paper streamers. Give each a squirt bottle of water. They can tear the crepe paper, lay it on the paper, then spray it with water. The colors will fade onto the paper, running together. If the paper is tilted, the colors will run down the paper.

Paint with different tools.   Provide toothbrushes, feathers, roll-on deodorant bottles, small sponges, cotton balls, sponge-top bottles, cotton swabs, foam swabs (used for cleaning audio and video equipment), flexible spreaders (used in cake decorating), or squeeze bottles.

Oil-like paint.   Mix one part powdered tempera with two parts liquid dishwashing detergent. Mix well until the mixture becomes thick and creamy. Use a small palette knife or craft stick to spread the paint on paper.

Field trip.   Visit an artist's studio. Ask the artist to demonstrate some techniques to the children. Point out the safety precautions the artist uses.

Museum visit.   Visit a museum. Request a tour with a docent who can tell the children about the exhibits. Children will enjoy seeing how artists painted people, landscapes, or abstract designs. As a variation, visit an art gallery to see special exhibits.

Display ethnic and cultural arts.   Obtain paintings, sculptures, folk art, and illustrated books from different cultures. In conjunction with the displays, provide children with art materials that use the same colors or materials. Encourage them to produce their own ethnic art.

Example 1: Display Asian landscape paintings. Provide the children with long sheets of white paper and the subtle colors typical of these paintings: pale greens, tans, black, creamy beige, white, and orange or red for accents. Supply brushes with slim bristles. Encourage children to make their own landscapes of an imaginary view or of a place they have been to. (To add interest to this activity, play some Asian music while the children paint.) When they are finished, mount the pictures with a piece of bamboo at the top. Tie a black string to the bamboo and display the pictures.

Example 2: Display pictures of Native American sand paintings. Tell children to look at the designs that were used. Supply them with square pieces of cardboard, colored sand (obtain from pet stores or make your own by mixing powdered tempera with the sand), white glue, and small brushes. Instruct the children to draw a design on the paper, then paint glue on a part of the design that will be one color. Sprinkle the sand on that portion, and let it dry briefly before painting another section. Continue in this manner until the painting is complete. Display the paintings when they are completely dry.

"Prince, ballerina, and the kids. They're at a dance." Stephanie, age 5.

Example 3: Show children paintings done by Mexican artists. Tell them to observe the vibrant colors and color mixes that these artists used. Provide some bright paint: orange, red, yellow, pink, purple, black. Tell children to create their own picture, perhaps portraying an experience from their own lives. Display the pictures.

Equipment to Have Available

- aprons or old shirts
- brushes—various sizes and shapes
- boards for clay—Masonite, plastic, or wood
- drying racks
- easels—floor and table
- matting knife
- paper cutters—for single sheets and for large rolls of paper
- craft sticks, palette knives
- rags and towels for cleanup
- reproductions of fine art
- rulers, measuring tape
- scissors—assorted sizes, left- and right-handed
- sculpting tools, garlic press
- sponges—large and small, natural and manufactured
- staplers

Discussion

Enhance children's experience by helping them learn more about art. Discuss the following topics with them:

- how things look: light, texture, color, position
- effect of using contrasting colors: light and dark, bright and dull
- two-dimensional surfaces: forms, variations in size and shape
- drawing techniques: line drawings, imaginative and decorative styles
- painting techniques: dry or wet brush, stippling, finger painting, color mixing
- new words: colors—ivory, crimson, burnt sienna, hot or cold, primary
- professions: painter, sculptor, ceramist, illustrator, cartoonist, designer, museum director

Music and Movement

When children enter kindergarten, most are able to sing simple songs, although they may not always be on pitch. They have favorite songs and seem especially attuned to music with a pronounced rhythm. Given a few simple instruments, they will imitate rhythms they have heard or create their own. They also like to move to music, using their whole bodies or just their hands or feet. By the end of elementary school, most children have developed a good sense of rhythm and beat. They can remember and sing a large selection of songs and have added the new skill of being able to sing in harmony. Some are able to play instruments, and a few will be able to write down simple musical patterns or songs.

"Me dancing." Rachel, age 5.

Music should be a part of every day. It does not have to be a formal music time but can be integrated into the daily routine. Start the day with a few songs, then have instruments available for children to use when they wish.

Take instruments outdoors on occasion so children can play or dance in a different environment. Occasionally play records or tapes during activity times.

Activities

Purposes: increase physical coordination
        develop listening skills
        provide an outlet for expression of feelings
        enhance appreciation of ethnic contributions to the arts

Musical styles.   Play different kinds of music: classical, lullaby, folk music, marches, gospel, rock, or jazz. Have the children identify each style, then ask them to compare two styles. How are they alike or different? Provide many opportunities to hear music, encouraging the children to really listen to how the music is formed. Place tapes or CDs in a listening corner for children to enjoy at leisure.

As an added interest, play selections of music from different countries and cultures. Select reggae from Jamaica, opera from Italy, a mariachi band from Mexico, sitar music from India, balalaika music from Russia, flute music from the Andes, or Native American drum music. Ask the children to compare the sounds of the music. Why do they think the music is representative of the country?

Paint to music.   Play different kinds of music as children paint. Suggest they paint what they hear. Include ethnic music.

Children can make their own music with an electronic keyboard.

Dancing with props.   Add props to enhance movement: scarves, balloons, hoops, colored rope, streamers, or dress-up clothes.

Mirroring.   Provide a scarf for each child. Group them in pairs. Have one child act as leader, making movements using the scarf. A second child mirrors those movements. After a short period, change places.

Instruments.   Provide a variety of simple instruments: autoharp, drums, rhythm sticks, shakers, castanets, tambourines, bells. Allow children to experiment with the sounds.

Provide the materials for children to make their own instruments. [See Anders, *Making Musical Instruments* (1975), listed at the end of this chapter.]

Listening corner.   Set up a listening corner with a tape recorder or CD player and earphones.

Provide a selection of tapes. Change them periodically.

Musical statues.   Play a tape or CD while children dance. Instruct them to "freeze" in whatever position they are in when the music stops. Stop and start the music several times.

Shadow dancing.   On a sunny day, take the tape or CD player outdoors. Encourage children to dance, watching their own shadows as they move.

Video.   Let children view a video of dance segments. (Check your library or watch for television shows you can tape.) Discuss the kind of dance portrayed, then encourage children to dance to the video.

Visitor.   Invite a musician to your center to demonstrate techniques. If possible, allow children to try out the instrument. Include musicians who play instruments that are typical of a particular ethnic group or are representative of a country.

Equipment to Have Available

- autoharp(s)
- banjo
- blank tapes for recording
- books—song, poetry
- dance props—tap shoes, tutus, scarves, streamers, canes, hoops, ropes
- earphones for listening center
- ethnic musical instruments—maracas, bongo drums, Chinese temple blocks
- guitar
- piano
- tape or CD player—assortment of tapes or CDs; select all kinds of music including ethnic and holiday pieces
- recorders
- selection of percussion instruments—drums, rhythm sticks, shakers, castanets, tambourines, bells
- television monitor and videotape player

Children can follow a story with a taped recording.

Discussion

Some concepts to discuss with children to enhance their learning:

- musical terms: tempo, pitch, dynamics (loud/soft)
- movement: walking, running, swaying, balance
- dance forms: ballet, folk, tap, interpretive, jazz
- instruments: names, how they produce sound, care of instruments
- listening: differentiating sounds, following musical directions or beat

Drama

From a very early age children engage in dramatic play. Toddlers charm their parents by imitating actions or situations they observe around them. Preschoolers use dramatic play to try out what it feels like to be a grown-up. They play at being mom or dad, doctors, fire-fighters, or teachers. As they get a little older, dramatic play becomes a way to conquer feelings of being scared or helpless. Four-year-olds and young "school-agers" play at being monsters, Superman, or the current popular TV figure. During the middle childhood years, youngsters use dramatic play to consolidate and understand what they are learning in school and at home.

What scripts and stage plays could this costume be used for?

Although they may still dress up and act out situations, they also use small toys, blocks, or other materials to replay a trip to the fire station or other community facilities. They may also reenact what they see happening on television news or familiar shows. Older children take a more organized approach to dramatic play. They want to write their own scripts, assign parts, make costumes, and stage plays. This activity provides a variety of opportunities to practice skills that youngsters are trying to develop during this period of their childhood. Writing a script entails listening to how people talk during conversations, writing words, and organizing a story line. Negotiations and compromise are necessary to be certain that all participants have an opportunity to contribute according to their own skills or interests.

The best kinds of dramatic play occur when children can play whatever they wish. Allow children many different opportunities to use their imaginations in both spontaneous and organized activities. Make materials available as their interests dictate.

Activities

Purposes: provide practice in negotiating and compromising during a group effort
enhance the ability to set long-term goals and to postpone gratification
increase the ability to portray ideas, feelings, and experiences through drama
or using blocks

Puppets.   Design and make different kinds of puppets. Try shadow, finger, stick, papier mâché, or sock puppets. Read about how puppets are constructed and used in other countries. (See Figure 11-3 for ideas.)

Puppet theater.   Permanent or impromptu. Older children can make a permanent theater using carpentry tools and plywood. Make a theater from a large-appliance box. An impromptu stage can also be as simple as a table covered with a blanket or a wall of large blocks.

Produce a puppet play.   Have children write a simple script or use a favorite story. Let them make the puppets, plan the production.

Drama kits.   Collect a variety of props children can use for dramatic play. Store them in related sets for different jobs: beautician, doctor, mechanic, or astronaut. (Listen for children's interests, then provide additional props for play.)

Makeup.   Provide makeup (theatrical makeup, if possible) and mirrors. Allow children to try out ways to use makeup. Have tissues and cold cream for cleaning up when they are finished.

Blocks.   Provide both small and large blocks. Add accessories as children's interests dictate: cars, airplanes, boats, people, animals, trees, signs. Add additional materials: cardboard packing forms, Styrofoam pieces, plywood, or cardboard tubes.

Play.   Have children write and produce a play. They can also adapt a book or use a published play. (Check the library for suitable plays.)

Tell stories.   Encourage the children to tell their own stories that have a beginning, a middle, and an end. During group time, have one child start a story with a few sentences. The next child takes up the story line and continues with a few more sentences. Each child must listen to all the previous storytellers in order to remember the gist of the story before continuing.

The last child has the most difficult part because she must bring closure to the story. As a variation, tape the story as the children tell it. Place the tape in the listening corner so that children can hear it again.

Read folktales.   Folktales are stories that once were told by parents, grandparents, or community storytellers. Originally they were not written down but passed on from generation to generation. Read folktales at group times or encourage small groups or pairs of children to read to one another.

Papier-mâché Puppet
   Materials needed:
      dried papier-mâché sphere made on a balloon
      length of cardboard tubing from paper towel roll
      felt and cloth scraps
      yarn, ribbons, buttons
      marking pens
      tempera or acrylic paint, small brushes
      scissors, glue
   Directions:
      Cut a small opening in one side of the sphere. Gently push the cardboard tubing into the opening. Paint the face with flesh tones. Let the face dry overnight before adding features. Use yarn for making hair. Cut fabric or felt scraps for clothing, making it large enough to cover the child's hand. Decorate clothing with ribbons or buttons.

Sock Puppet
   Materials needed:
      clean sock, can be white or colored
      buttons
      eyes (you will find these in a hobby shop)
      felt, fabric scraps
      yarn, pipe cleaners, ribbons
      scissors, glue
   Directions:
      Show children how to fit the sock over their hand and then make a moving mouth with thumb and fingers. Let them glue scrap materials onto puppet to create a face.

Shadow Puppets
   Materials needed:
      cardboard strips or craft sticks
      construction paper
      scissors
      marking pens
      staple gun
   Directions:
      Have children draw a figure on the construction paper, then cut it out. Staple the figure to the cardboard strip or craft stick.

FIGURE 11-3 Puppets

Invite an adult storyteller to visit.   Ask the adult to tell the children a story that was a favorite when he or she was a child. Encourage stories that have been part of a family tradition or culture.

Field trip.   View a puppet play or children's drama. Look for professional performances at theaters or amateur performances at schools, community centers, or libraries.

Equipment to Have Available

- blocks—wooden floor blocks, large hollow blocks, small colored blocks
- block accessories—cars, boats, airplanes, people, animals, trees, signs
- boxes, shelves, racks for storing props
- carpentry tools—saw, measuring tape, yardstick, hammer, sander, nails
- dress-up clothes—skirts, dresses, capes, shoes, hats, wigs, scarves
- floor lights—standing lamps, spotlights
- mirrors—individual makeup mirrors, full-length mirrors
- puppet theater or materials for construction
- sewing tools—needles, thread, pins, scissors
- tape recorder
- window shade or curtains

Discussion

Some concepts to discuss with children:
- imagination: new ways to tell a story or express feelings
- props: how to make props and costumes for their productions
- scripts: books, poems, films, TV shows
- skills: skills needed to produce a drama
- puppets or marionettes: which one fits a particular character
- manipulating puppets to create a story

Not all children are going to grow up to be painters, sculptors, actors, musicians, or playwrights. However, you want them to learn that when they go out into the sometimes harried world of adulthood, the arts will provide continuing pleasure and relaxation. By having a variety of art activities available, all children can find one that suits their own individual needs and abilities. So, make art of all kinds an integral part of your day. Both you and the children will reap boundless benefits.

Summary

Creative activities satisfy children in a way no other experiences can. This is because they all can be successful. They can communicate nonverbally and release emotions. They learn about themselves and can relive or remake their own experiences.

An additional bonus is that art can be shared with others or experienced alone.

Creative activities should be based on children's interests. Some form of art activity should be part of every day.

Very young children use all their senses to explore the properties of art materials. By kindergarten age, they learn that their feelings and experiences can be portrayed symbolically. Art activities provide the media for doing so. By the end of middle child-hood, children set goals for themselves and want recognition for their accomplishments.

The most effective art program will meet the needs of both the youngest children and the older ones.

Kindergarten children can sing simple songs and like to imitate rhythms they have heard or create their own. By the end of elementary school, most children have a good sense of rhythm and beat. They can remember many songs and even sing in harmony. Some can play instruments or compose music.

From an early age, children engage in dramatic play. Toddlers imitate what they see.

Preschoolers try out adult roles. During middle childhood, youngsters use dramatic play to consolidate learning. Older children want to write their own scripts and produce their own plays.

The arts will provide continuing pleasure for children into their adult years. Art of all kinds should be an integral part of the child care day.

Key Terms

convergent thinking
divergent thinking
lateralization

Student Activities

1. Visit a library, museum, community center, and theater in your community. Ask about programs or resources they might have that would interest school-age children. Prepare a list to share with your classmates.
2. Plan and implement one of the activities suggested in this chapter. Write an evaluation of the experience. Were there things you could have done differently? If so, how?
3. Talk to teachers and caregivers in three different child care groups. Ask which creative activities their children most enjoy. Find out why they think those activities are so popular.

Review Questions

1. This chapter stated that "creative experiences satisfy children in a way few other experiences can." Give three reasons why that statement was made.
2. In what way does a preschooler's use of art materials differ from that of a child approaching adolescence?
3. Give five examples of art activities appropriate for school-age children.
4. List three musical concepts to discuss with children in order to enhance their learning.
5. You want to encourage children in your child care group to enjoy more music. What kinds of equipment should you have available?
6. Relate the developmental steps in children's dramatic play from toddlers to older middle children.
7. List some accessories children might use with blocks for dramatic play.

Case Study

Hannah is a lively six-year-old. Her favorite activity is using whatever art materials are available each day, and she spends most of her inside time there. However, she constantly wants reassurance and praise for her efforts. She will finish an interesting collage, then run to Susan wanting her to look at it. She will ask, "Do you like my picture? Do you think those colors go together?"

1. How would you respond to Hannah's "Do you like my picture"? Explain why you would answer in that way.
2. How would you react to her "Do these colors go together"?
3. Hannah spends most of her time at this one activity. Would you do anything to broaden her interests? If so, what?

References

Anders, R. (1975). *Making musical instruments*. Minneapolis: Lerner.

Brooks, R. L., & Obrzut, J. E. (1981). Brain lateralization: Implications for infant stimulation and development. *Young Children, 36*(3), 9–16.

Suggested Readings

Bernstein, B., & Blair, L. (1982). *Native American crafts workshop*. Belmont, CA: David S. Lake.

Bruchac, J. (1991). *Native American stories*. Golden, CO: Fulcrum.

Carlson, L. (1993). *EcoArt*. Charlotte, VT: Williamson.

Carlson, L. (1990). *Kids create!* Charlotte, VT: Williamson.

Cherry, C. (1990). *Creative art for the developing child* (2nd ed.). Belmont, CA: David S. Lake.

Corwin, J. (1990). *African crafts*. New York: Franklin Watts.

Gomez, A. (1992). *Crafts of many cultures*. New York: Scholastic Professional.

Gutwirth, V. (1997). A multicultural family study project for primary. *Young Children, 52*(2), 72–78.

Haas, C., & Friedman, A. (1990) *My own fun—Activities for kids ages 7–12*. Chicago: Chicago Review Press. (Available from School-Age Notes, Nashville)

Kohl, M., & Potter, J. (1993). *Science arts: Discovering science through art experiences*. Bellingham, WA: Bright Ring.

Milford, S. (1990). *Adventures in art, art and craft experiences for 7- to 14-year-olds*. Charlotte, VT: Williamson.

Ringenberg, S. (2003). Music as a teaching tool: Creating story songs. *Young Children, 58*(5), 76–79.

Ryder, W. (1995). *Celebrating diversity with art, thematic projects for every month of the year*. Glenview, IL: Scott Foresman.

Sierra, J. (1991). *Fantastic theater, puppets and plays for young performers and young audiences*. New York: H. W. Wilson.

Computer Software/Video

Children's Songs Around the World (Laserdic VHS). Baldwin, NY: Education Activities. Primary.

China: Home of the Dragon (Mac Windows CD-ROM). Orange Cherry/New Media Schoolhouse. Intermediate, Advanced.

Let's Visit Mexico (Mac IBM CD-ROM). Fairfield, CT: Queue. Advanced.

Meiko: A Story of Japanese Culture (MPC CD-ROM). Novato: CA: Broderbund/Digital Productions.

Thinkin' Things Collection 1 (Mac IBM Windows MPC CD-ROM). Redmond, WA: Edmark. Primary, Intermediate.

Thinkin' Things Collection 2 (Mac IBM Windows MPC CD-ROM). Redmond WA: Edmark. Primary, Intermediate, Advanced.

Thinkin' Things Collection 3 (Mac MPC CD-ROM). Redmond, WA: Edmark. Intermediate, Advanced.

Web Resources

Best children's music: list of best children's music, musical books, links to music education Web sites.

http://www.bestchildrensmusic.com

Smithsonian Museum site for educational resource guides, lesson plans, programs, and other resources.

http://www.si.edu

Museum of Modern Art in New York has several click-on related sites. Education site offers programs and publications for children, their families, and their schools.

http://www.moma.org

Kennedy Center in New York supports art education for grades K–12. Includes ideas and lesson plans.

http://www.artsedge.kennedy-center.org

Getty Museum in Los Angeles has a variety of programs for teachers and children including guided visits to the center.

http://www.getty.edu

Puzzles and activities to increase reading and comprehension skills.

http://www.eduplace.com Click on "edugames"

On-line exhibits and films that explore the science of music.

http://www.exploratorium.edu Click on "Science of Music"

Book titles from the "Children's Book Awards" and "Year's Best Books."

http://www.acs.ucalgary.ca Search for CLWG: children's literature Web guide

CHAPTER 12

Science and Math

Objectives

After studying this chapter, the student should be able to:

- Discuss how investigative science and math activities enhance cognitive development
- Plan and implement appropriate science and math activities using the process approach
- Recognize the science and mathematics processes children use
- Discuss the leader's role in supporting children's cognitive development through facilitation of science and math activities

Dmitry is the youngest of four boys. He has many fond family memories of growing up with older siblings. He also has great memories of being with other children in an after-school program. As he reflects on them, he realizes that those childhood experiences prepared him for what he does today as a child care leader. He understands the concept of "the society of children" and recognizes that school-age children like to form clubs and make up their own rules.

Dmitry recalls a club, the Skydivers, that he and a group of friends formed. They were very interested in space adventures, and the child care leaders helped them pursue those interests. He and his friends made pretend space helmets from milk jugs and used recycled keyboards and electronic equipment to form their space commands. The leaders encouraged them to write to the Jet Propulsion Lab for science materials and helped them plan a parent night to look through telescopes. Dmitry remembers those exciting adventures and tries to follow the interests of the children he now works with at the child care center.

Currently his primary group of children is also expressing an interest in space. Dmitry's excitement about space is rekindled, and he is able to lead the children in pursuing knowledge via the Internet. Some of the children have the NASA channel on their televisions at home and are making reports back to the group. The children are gathering information about the planets.

Saturn seems to be their favorite, so Dmitry has challenged them to find out what they would need to survive on Saturn once their pretend spaceship lands. The children play with walkie-talkies in dramatic play. At the art center they are creating a model of Saturn. They have chalked off an area on the ground outside for their spaceship to take off from and land on. The children have learned that they can come to Dmitry when they have ideas or need materials. He has acquired skills in encouraging critical thinking by asking questions such as "What do you think you would need to live on Saturn? How could we find out what the atmosphere is like there?"

Role of Science and Math in Development

Children in school-age child care come to their care-giving situation with the daily learning experiences of the math and science curriculum during their regular school day. One aspect of care giving is to support the educational experiences of children. Learning does not happen only during the school hours. The before- and after-school program is an ideal place for children to expand their understanding of what they learn in school through exploration and practice. Over the last 10 years the American Association for the Advancement of Science, the National Council of Teachers of Mathematics, and the National Academy of Sciences have been working collaboratively with educators to establish a set of standards in mathematics and science. They believe that teaching and learning math and science is not solely the responsibility of teachers and schools. Science and math have relevance in everyday life, and members of these organizations contend that it is time to stop the stereotype of the crazy genius working in isolation in a laboratory. An overall goal is for children to become scientifically literate (National Science Board, 1999). The scientific literacy standards are an attempt at that goal as they are educational outcomes that define what it is that children should know and be able to do.

Children as Natural Scientists

Children are often exposed to the traditional careers of firefighter, teacher, doctor, and so on, but rarely are they introduced to the idea of being a scientist or mathematician. Some children may have thoughts about these potential career choices. And children, by their very nature, are already actively engaging in those roles and use the skills scientists and mathematicians employ.

What do scientists do? They explore, investigate, observe, record data, make hypotheses, develop theories, and draw conclusions. Scientists use mathematics as they measure, make quantitative and qualitative comparisons, classify information, and make charts and graphs of their findings. From very early ages, children naturally explore and investigate, observe, ask questions (hypothesize), and draw conclusions. They try to make sense out of what they see and to solve the problems they encounter. They develop their own theories of how the world works. According to Piaget, this is known as constructing knowledge. They come to know concepts (construct knowledge) as a result of their own experiences and their own thinking about those experiences.

During middle childhood, children's ability to develop more logical theories increases as they shift from preoperational thinking into more concrete thinking where they see cause-and-effect relationships more realistically. The five-year-old sees relationships and draws conclusions but has difficulty grasping concepts such as reversibility or recognizing that quantities of matter remain unchanged. As children's cognitive abilities mature, they realize that things can change physical form and be transformed again, such as water becoming ice and again becoming water.

Children's construction of knowledge is greatly enhanced by what Vygotsky refers to as scaffolding. Recall from Chapter 5 (sociocultural theory) that children can experience cognitive development when they are supported by a skilled peer or adult who has the abilities to scaffold their experiences. Dmitry was able to draw on his own knowledge and experiences to scaffold the children's learning about Saturn as he encouraged their critical thinking. Scaffolding may be through specific questioning that provokes thinking or guided participation that in turn helps the learner through the steps of a process and encourages the learner to think. Consider the activity, "Is it liquid or solid?" When left to their own devices and thinking a child may only explore the sensory aspects of the materials and may never explore the substance from the perspective of thinking about it being liquid or solid. Through the scaffolding process, a knowledgeable peer or adult can discuss the characteristics of solids and liquids and guide the science participants to more in-depth exploration and subsequent understanding.

Is it liquid or solid? (Messy but easy to clean up!)
Mix equal parts water and cornstarch on small trays. Encourage the children to investigate with their fingers. Be prepared to provide utensils, such as spoons, plastic knives, or spatulas, for further investigation. Discuss with the children the characteristics of a solid (holds its own shape) and characteristics of a liquid (pourable, wet, takes the shape of its container). Encourage children to hypothesize and form theories about the mixture.
Hint: It is both. The cornstarch remains a solid. It does not dissolve in the water, but its particles are suspended in the water.

Seven- or eight-year-olds are able to understand that something can change from one form to another, and they enjoy the process of doing so. They seem to investigate the world by asking, "How can I make it change?" or "How can I make it move?" As they actively engage with materials, they hone their observation and investigative skills. They continue to construct, test, and refine their theories. They are, in Piagetian terms, "constructing their own knowledge." Constructing personal knowledge about the world continues at all ages (even throughout adulthood). Child care leaders will construct their own knowledge about how children use scientific inquiry skills as they provide opportunities for children to make investigations.

Science activities allow children freedom to explore materials and carry out experiments in a nonthreatening atmosphere. Not only do they increase their scientific inquiry skills, but they also gain confidence in seeking solutions to problems. This investigative environment allows children the opportunity to take risks. They try new things, make mistakes, learn from their mistakes, and continue trying out new ideas.

Science activities also allow children to work together as they discover concepts of physics, chemistry, and biology. They share ideas. They each bring their personal experiences and knowledge to the investigative process and thereby help one another as they brainstorm to develop theories, hypotheses, and strategies for experimentation and exploration.

Children As Natural Mathematicians

Children are naturally provided with opportunities to use mathematics on a daily basis. Spontaneous activities occur such as when children need to add scores when playing games or when they have to figure out how to divide a set of materials so everyone has an equal share. Preoperational children are found counting everything in sight once they learn how to count. They don't yet understand that the quantity of a set of objects stays the same when the objects are moved. According to Piaget this is a lack of conservation of number. Yet children enjoy the task of counting. Children between the ages of 5 and 7 are in transition from preoperational thinking to concrete operations. Children in concrete operations are better able to conserve number if they are given ample opportunity to work with materials and count. Through scaffolding children can be given guidance in counting correctly.

How many are there? (A test of number conservation)

Make a collection of 30 items that may be of interest to children, such as a jar of marbles or coins. The objects should all be the same size. The child care leader can put the objects in two rows of fifteen so that each row takes up the same amount of space.

⊕ ⊕ ⊕ ⊕ ⊕ ⊕ ⊕ ⊕ ⊕ ⊕ ⊕ ⊕ ⊕ ⊕ ⊕

⊕ ⊕ ⊕ ⊕ ⊕ ⊕ ⊕ ⊕ ⊕ ⊕ ⊕ ⊕ ⊕ ⊕ ⊕

Ask a five- or six-year-old how many objects are in each row. Then, invite the child to move the objects in one of the rows outward. Again ask the child how many are in each row. The child who can conserve number (knows that the quantity of objects stays the same even though their arrangement may change) will merely say there are 15 in each row. The nonconserving child will recount the objects.

Life presents many opportunities for children to note physical characteristics, also known as attributes. Children use the attributes to sort the objects into categories. According to Piaget, this sorting is called classification. At home it is seen when children put all the socks together in one place in a dresser drawer or sort the silverware into the appropriate places when helping parents put away clean dishes. In classrooms it may be identifying the various shapes and sizes of blocks and reshelving them in their appropriate place, or putting all the markers together, pencils in their own place, and scissors in another. Children may group together objects when investigating science. For example, they may group together objects that sink and others that float in a sink-and-float activity.

Children in preoperational thinking (nonconservers) can manipulate small quantities of objects and solve problems. If a child is allowed to have five crackers for snack and has taken only four, the child can figure out how many more crackers he would need. Children in concrete operations can think about numbers and manipulate them to solve problems. When given a large group of items to count, they may group them in piles of tens and then count by tens to determine the total number of objects. Children given the task of setting the tables for snack can now recognize that there is a relationship between the number of tables, the number of chairs per table, and the total number of children. How many children are here for snack today? How many tables will we need to set up? We have eight tables with six chairs at each table; is that enough? How can we find out? Using advanced mathematics, they can further think about how to solve the problem if snack is served in shifts of three groups of children.

Math and Science Are Related

Science, by its very nature, provides a rich opportunity for children to use their developing math and problem-solving skills. They use basic math skills such as comparing, classifying, and measuring while engaged in exploratory science activities. Children use these skills to help organize and further their science discoveries. They may compare the sizes of earthworms, categorize animals according to their habitats, or measure ingredients when exploring the reaction of mixing vinegar and baking soda. Children use the language of math to communicate their ideas and discoveries to each other. Key vocabulary such as *more, bigger, heavier, faster,* and *longer* can be heard from children engaged in discovering the world around them. Think again about the activity, "Is it liquid or solid?" Children can be given the opportunity to measure their own ingredients. They can calculate how much cornstarch and water will be needed for the entire group. Once given the materials, they will have conversations that can't help but include mathematical language as they investigate and compare their cornstarch goop to that of others. They may want to experiment with what happens if they add another teaspoon of water or cornstarch. Child care leaders can guide children in organizing their discoveries in the form of charts, tables, and graphs. The mathematical skills of counting, noting attributes, and classifying can be integrated in nearly every science activity.

The Process and Content of Science

Children are incredibly curious about the world around them. Some children verbalize their thinking, whereas others simply act on their thoughts by experimenting as they search for answers. The *process* of science involves inquiry, experimentation, observation, and hypothesis testing. What if we raise the pendulum higher to try to knock down the block? How can we make the cars turn when they get to the end of the ramp? How can we make a river in the sandbox? Can we dig to China? What kind of magnet is the strongest? Why do some things float and others sink? What would happen if we mix all these colors of paint together? As children work to formulate answers to their questions, they are discovering the *content* of science—the scientific facts. These discoveries by children can be enhanced with the encouragement of the use of mathematics. How high is the pendulum? What is the elevation of the ramp? Does it make a difference in how far a car will travel? Is there a difference in the weight of the things this magnet attracts compared to this other magnet? How could we make a chart to record the discoveries of what happens when we mix paint? Recall that learners must construct their own knowledge about the world (Chapter 5, principles of Piagetian theory). School-age children are concrete learners. This requires them to be active participants in the process. They are thinking of questions and manipulating materials to gain understanding of scientific principles. Although children can memorize those facts, they do not gain a true understanding without having an actual hands-on experience.

Are you ready to absorb?
Provide the children with a tray lined with a piece of wax paper. Using eyedroppers, drop droplets of colored water onto the wax paper. (Color water with food coloring. Use the three primary colors: red, blue, and yellow.) Encourage them to count the number of droplets of each color. Older children can measure the diameter of the droplet. When the children have finished experimenting with dropping the colors, ask "Are you ready to absorb?" Have the children lay an absorbent paper towel onto the droplets. Children can measure the diameter of the absorbed liquid and note changes. Provide children with different types of absorbent materials. Listen to what the children say and watch as they investigate the materials. What are the processes that the children are engaged in? What is the science content they are learning as a result of their actions? What do you think they would have learned if you had demonstrated the process and not given them the materials to manipulate? Questions to scaffold learning could include "Do you remember how many drops of liquid you used to get that color of green? I notice that this area of absorbed liquid is larger than the other one. Why do you think that happened?" Scientists write their discoveries in some form of journal so the information can be shared with others. Encourage children to write in their science journal.

The Science and Math Environment

Science can be a part of outdoor play, a field trip, a guided small- or whole-group time, an interactive display often known as an interest center, or a specific science and math area of the classroom. Ideally, science and math materials are always available for children to explore as they work to expand their knowledge. An interest center can house the many treasures children bring to share, be it an insect, a special rock or shell, or the acorns that fell from their neighbor's tree. Often children will find something such as a praying mantis or walking stick on the playground and want to share it with other children.

When the child care facility has a center devoted to science and math, then science experiments, observations, recording of science findings, and other science and math activities can be a part of the daily choices. An area designated for science and math gives children and parents the message that science and math are important, integral parts of the curriculum. Plants, pets, and books add a visual, inviting appeal to such a center. Have standard math and science tools readily available to encourage children's spontaneous investigations. Rulers, meter sticks, measuring tapes, balances or scales, stop watches, magnifying glasses, and insect containers are a few items that should be included in the center. Children's science journals and materials to record information on are other standard materials for the science center. The materials in the center can change from time to time to provide different learning opportunities. It is not necessary to spend large amounts of money on science and math equipment. You can use a variety of recycled materials. For example, disposable plastic containers can be used for collecting insects, and small water bottles with the bottom cut off make great funnels. Save old jars, wires, clocks, cardboard tubes, plastic bubble wrapping, and so on. In fact, anything that is called junk may be of use in an experiment. You might also ask parents if they have any of these materials they would be willing to donate to your program. As you read about the various areas of science that follow, you will find that the activities suggested present many opportunities for children to investigate and that the materials used are minimal in cost.

Role of the Leader in the Science Activity

The most important component of the science environment is the child care leader. An adult who takes an interest in the children's science discoveries and explorations validates what they are learning. The leader can ask divergent questions. These are questions that have no specific answer and require the child to think critically. For example, in a pendulum activity, a tennis ball is attached to the end of a hanging rope. The children experiment with placement of boxes and try to knock them down. Some divergent questions might be: "How can you stack these boxes so the ball can knock them down?" "What do you think would happen if you stacked them in a different way?" "What would happen if you put them in a different place?" This type of questioning encourages the children to think critically, to act on their thinking, to form their own questions, to problem solve, and ultimately to construct knowledge and develop theories and conclusions. The leader can also ask questions that encourage children to integrate mathematical thinking with their science discoveries. An extension of the pendulum activity would be to measure the distance of the pendulum from the floor and the height of the objects to be knocked over. Children can measure and record their measurement, then experiment. As they change the placement of objects, they can measure again. The leader can ask children to predict what they think will happen. Having completed an activity, children can be encouraged to write down what they have discovered in their science journals. Recall from Chapter 5 (sociocultural theory by Vygotsky) that children acquire new skills and knowledge via scaffolding and interactions with more-skilled peers or adults. This interaction may be verbal prodding to encourage thinking. It may be actual modeling how to measure a distance, or providing assistance in completing a task such as creating a graph to record information. Leaders must be careful not to take the lead in the discoveries, but rather to follow the lead of the children. Let children do the thinking and experimenting. When the adults take an interest in the activities and interests of the children, the children get the message that what they are doing is worthwhile. Remember that the children are in the Eriksonian stage of industry versus inferiority (see Chapter 6). They are forming opinions about themselves. They are forming an opinion about themselves as learners, as critical thinkers, as scientists, and as mathematicians.

   When planning a science activity, the child care leader should have some ideas about the knowledge possibilities of the activity. Piaget identifies three types of knowledge: social, physical, and logicomathematical. Social knowledge is the information children cannot construct for themselves. What is its name? (e.g., magnet, iron) What are the scientific terms? (magnetism, repel, attract) Physical knowledge refers to how objects behave as a result of their characteristics. This is information that the children learn as they explore. What does it do? How does it change? What does it feel or sound like? Logico-mathematical knowledge refers to how objects compare to one another. This is also knowledge that children must construct as they discover similarities and differences, noting attributes. How are these objects alike? This knowledge enables children to classify and categorize information.

The science leader should have access to background information about an activity to guide children's thinking. Internet access can give some immediate information in the child care setting. When searching Web sites, look for links such as education, educators, kids, or activities. See the Helpful Web Sites at the end of this chapter. Books from the library can also be made available. Often parents can be a resource for background information, or they may be willing to get involved in the information-discovery process through their own Internet search or exploration.

The science leader must also be a careful observer. By carefully observing children's interactions with their world, the adult can facilitate children's further learning by presenting additional materials and information. For example, a child working with a pendulum trying to knock down blocks may be unsuccessful because she consistently stacks the blocks out of the reach of the pendulum. The child tries many techniques in releasing the pendulum but with no success. When told, "I wonder if there is another place to stack the blocks," the child will most likely rethink the situation and make changes in the blocks.

A final step to facilitating children's science experiences is for the leader to help them record their findings. True scientists record their findings, draw diagrams, and write about their experiments so they can share the information with others. In a school-age program, children can be encouraged to draw pictures and write (or dictate) what they have learned. They can write about their strategies, observations, and new theories and hypotheses. These discoveries can be posted on a bulletin board so parents, other children, and guests will be able to see what children are learning. Drawings and written accounts can also be collected and made into a book for display. Incorporating reading and writing, along with science, takes the child care program another step beyond just baby-sitting. Documentation makes learning visible so that parents and others know what is going on at the center. So often the only thing a parent has to judge what happens in the program is the piece of paper (artwork) that comes home in the child's hand. They do not see the vast effort put into a block structure or the trial and error of a science activity. This also gives parents something to talk to their child about. Rather than, "What did you do today?" the parent might say, "I see that you are experimenting with . . . Tell me about it."

There are additional ways to document children's experiences. You can use a large piece of easel paper to write comments the children made during the exploration process or when working in a small group. This is modeling the process of gathering information and documenting it. This documentation can be posted for parents to see. Children can have personal science journals that they draw and write in. Science activities can be reported in a monthly newsletter.

Physical Science: How Can I Make It Move?

On an adult level, physics is defined as "the science of dealing with the properties, changes, and interactions of matter and energy." Children construct knowledge of physics by acting on the principle, "How can I make it move?" For example, a group of first graders could use a variety of balls for rolling and objects such as empty cans, milk cartons, or plastic bottles to knock down. The children can learn about the distance from the objects or weight of the ball being rolled and of the objects being knocked over. They can experiment with placement of the objects. Math tools of a scale and a meter stick will be valuable in making the connection between the science and related math concepts. To learn physics principles, they use actions such as pushing, sliding, rolling, tilting, pounding, and throwing and materials such as sand, pendulums, magnets, balls, wheels, pulleys, marbles, paint, and water. Their manipulations cause immediate action that is visible and comprehensible. As children create movement, they can observe the results of their actions, continue the action so as to gain mastery, formulate theories, make changes in actions, and refine their original theory or formulate additional theories. These activities give children an opportunity to apply math through measurement of length or distance, speed, and weight. Physical science activities tend to hold children's interest the longest and have a vast amount of learning possibilities. Children are actively involved with the materials and can vary the actions, and the results of those actions are immediate.

Activities

Physical Science

Purposes: develop the scientific skills of observing, experimenting, and theorizing

predict outcomes and formulate conclusions

interact with materials and develop theories about physical phenomena

develop a personal confidence as a scientist

Experiment with pendulums.   Suspend a cotton clothesline rope from the ceiling, a doorway, or a swing set with a ball attached to the end of it. Children can stack plastic cups, cardboard boxes, or blocks and try to knock them down by swinging the pendulum. They will naturally experiment with placement of the blocks and the positioning of the pendulum. Various sizes and weights of balls can be provided for additional exploration. They may discover the relationship between the length of the pendulum swing and its ultimate force as it collides (or fails to collide) with the blocks.

A variation on the pendulum would be to attach other things to the end of the rope. Try attaching a paintbrush. Place a large piece of cardboard under the pendulum, and discover what happens when the pendulum swings. Hang an empty half-gallon plastic milk bottle upside down from the pendulum (remove the bottom). Fill the bottle with sand. Remove the cap and let the pendulum swing. (Great to do outdoors!)

Explore inclined planes.   Rain gutters cut into lengths of 3', 5', or left at 10' make great ramps for balls, marbles, water, and toy cars. Provide other materials for children to discover concepts about things that slide and roll. Incorporate Legos® for children to build cars. Have a scale available for children to weigh the load of the cargo of their cars and a meter stick for measuring the height and length of the incline as well as the distance the various objects travel. Children can discover the relationships between the height of the incline, its length, and the weight of the objects traveling down the plane.

Additional things may be used for inclined planes. Cove molding can be found in the wood trims and molding department of your local home improvement store. Cut it into various lengths and add it to the block center, or use it as an outdoor activity to provide children ample opportunity for ongoing exploration of incline planes. Cardboard tubes from wrapping paper or mailing tubes can also be used as inclined planes. Large durable ones can be obtained from businesses that lay carpeting. (Carpet is rolled up on them.)

Discover propelled objects (target practice).   Provide balls of different kinds and sizes and materials for the target such as cardboard blocks, milk cartons, cardboard cylinders from paper rolls, and large juice cans. Children work indoors or outdoors as they discover the relationship between the placement of target objects, the kind and size of ball used, and the physical force with which it is propelled. Keep in mind that science discoveries are related to math concepts so be sure to also have measuring tools and paper and pencils for children to write down the outcomes of their experimenting.

Additional discoveries can be made with Ping-Pong balls with Velcro® attached and a fabric target such as felt. Children learn best when they can clearly see when their propelled ball has landed.

Try a floor target with beanbags to toss on it.

Simple catapults can provide additional discoveries. Make them with a plastic spoon and a wooden ruler. Attach the handle of the spoon firmly to the end of the ruler by wrapping a rubber band tightly around it. Small pom-pom balls placed in the bowl of the spoon can be propelled to a target. Children will use them by pulling back on the bowl of the spoon with one hand, holding the ruler with the other hand, and releasing the spoon.

Explore magnetic force.   Magnets can be another staple for your science center. Wand and horseshoe magnets can be purchased from toy stores. Small, inexpensive (but not very durable) circular magnets are available at stores that sell electronic equipment. Strong internal magnets can be purchased from a store that sells products for large farm-animal care. (Internal magnets are used inside a cow to collect pieces of metal that the cow may ingest.) Children can work with a variety of magnets and incorporate measurement as they notice and record the distance between the magnets when they visibly repel or attract each other. Additional activities could include encouraging children to use the magnets to drag through the sand looking for particles of iron, to investigate a variety of metal-looking objects to determine which contain iron, or to use around the classroom, looking for metal with iron. Develop a collection of small items such as bolts and paper clips that are attracted to a magnet. Use this collection with the large magnets that are found on the inside of stereo speakers to build temporary sculptures that are held together by magnetism.

Another way to use magnets is for moving objects. Place magnet wands, or internal magnets under the table or under a piece of Plexiglas®. Place lightweight objects such as paper clips on top of the table or Plexiglas. Use the magnet to move the objects. Encourage children to see what happens when they place magnets on top of the table and move magnets underneath.

Additional Physical Science Activities

Other physical science activities could focus on:

- spatial awareness (fitting objects in, out, through, under, etc.)
- air (fans, blow-dryers, homemade fans)
- construction (wood with hammers, nails, saws, screws, screwdrivers, and hand drills)
- pulleys and wheels
- kitchen tools (scoops, basting bulbs, sifters, beaters, gadgets)
- opticals (binocular, magnifying glasses, kaleidoscopes)
- making, listening to, and identifying sounds
- light and shadows

Chemistry: How Can I Make It Change?

Chemistry deals with the properties, composition, and transformation of substances. Many chemical experiments require skills, equipment, and knowledge too advanced for the school-age child. Yet, chemical exploration opportunities can be provided that are age appropriate and enable children to learn concepts of chemistry and further their scientific skills of theorizing, observing, and experimenting.

Keep in mind that school-age children are concrete learners (see Chapter 5, Piaget) and therefore must be able to act on their environment and see the results of their actions. Observations of the physical characteristics of substances and explorations that create transformations are very appropriate chemistry for this age group of children. For example, children can explore transformation by mixing substances such as vinegar and baking soda, baking cookies or biscuits, or adding water to sand. The child's natural tendencies are to respond to the internal question, "How can I make it change?"

Activities

Chemistry

Purposes: further develop scientific skills of observation and theorizing

observe physical characteristics of substances and phenomena that change those characteristics

acquire awareness of chemistry in our everyday lives

Exploration of nature's tie-dyeing.   Provide various substances that can be combined with water to make a medium for dyeing fabrics. The spice turmeric makes a yellow-orange, coffee and tea make browns, and cabbage or beets cooked in water create a reddish color. Children can also draw from their experiences of things that stain their clothing such as mustard, chocolate, and grape juice. Give the children various containers to explore substances that could dye fabrics. Provide strips of muslin or some white, cotton fabric such as old T-shirts.

An extension of this activity would be to try various types of fabrics. (Be sure to provide the children with smocks to protect their clothing when doing this investigation!)

Experience the effects of heat on food.   Cooking projects provide a great opportunity for children to experience transformations. Children can wash, cut, and prepare vegetables such as carrots, potatoes, or green beans. With adult supervision, they can cook them, noting the effect of heat on the taste, consistency, texture, and color of the vegetables. Children can use a timer to measure specific amounts of cooking time and notice what happens. Measure after one minute of cooking time, three minutes of cooking time, five minutes, and so on. These discoveries can be written in a chart format and later shared with parents or posted in the classroom. Other cooking activities might include melting cheese for nachos or in grilled cheese sandwiches or cooking eggs in a variety of styles (scrambled, poached, hard-boiled, over-easy).

Investigate substances that make foods rise.   Making things such as bread, biscuits, cookies, and pancakes gives children the opportunity to experience the effect of using

Marble Rollways

Brief description: Children will work in teams to create a structure that they can roll marbles through.

Science concepts explored: Children will learn about the relationship between the slope of a surface and the velocity of a rolling object. They will discover where a rolling object is propelled to.

Materials:
- thin cardboard in pieces of various sizes
- paper cups
- paper towel and/or toilet-tissue cardboard tubes
- paper
- masking tape
- yarn or string
- berry baskets, juice cans, or small plastic containers
- marbles
- other recycled materials as available
- scissors, rulers, pencils, markers

Procedure: Materials are displayed on a table. Entice the children by asking a divergent question, "How could you use these materials to create a structure that will let the marbles flow through it?" Divide children into teams to create their structure. (Hint: Create teams with a variety of ages. The older child can be a leader for the younger ones.)

Role of the leader:
- Set up the work environment.
- Give children adequate time (30 minutes or more).
- Provide children with a space to display their finished product.
- Make comments about what you see, and encourage children to verbalize what they are doing. "I notice that you decided to put this tube here. What do you think will happen?"
- Encourage further exploration by asking divergent questions or making comments. "How far do you think the marble will roll after it drops through the tube?" Be sure to have tape measures or meter sticks available.
- Guide children in writing and drawing about their structure and their discoveries.

Guide children in creating a note to parents telling about the work they are doing.

Learn about inclines and velocity.

Create a Worm Environment

Brief description: Children will create a temporary worm environment to learn about their tunneling behaviors.

Science concepts explored: Characteristics of worms such as their bodies, their habitat, and their diet.

Materials:
- tall, thin jar (preferably no more than 5 inches in diameter)
- sand, soil, and water
- ruler
- magnifying glasses
- worms (can be obtained from a bait shop)
- ½ an apple
- ½ an onion
- knife and cutting board
- two containers for mixing
- factual books about worms such as *It Could Still Be a Worm* by Fowler (see Suggested Readings)

Procedure: Place soil in container and mix with enough water to make the soil damp. In another container mix sand with water, making the sand damp enough to clump together. Layer the soil and sand in the tall thin jar in 1-inch layers. Place the worms on top of the top layer. Watch what the worms do. Cut onion and apple in ½-inch pieces. Put on top of the soil. Place the container in a box, making sure no light can enter the box. Leave for four days. During that time, read about worms and predict what they will do while they are in the box. After four days, take the container out of the box and examine the tunnels. Use magnifying glasses before or after the activity to examine the structure of the worms. Be sure to keep the work space moist. Worms don't like to be in the light, so examinations will have to be brief. Return worms to a safe place in a garden when finished with examination.

Divergent questions: What do you think the worms will do when you put them on top of the soil? What will they do while they are in the jar in the box? What do you think worms like to eat? How could we find out?

Role of the leader:
- Set up the work environment. Be sure to have ample literature available for children to further their investigations.
- Use a search engine on the Internet to find information about worms.
- Investigate with the children.
- Encourage the children to draw and write about their experiment and findings. With the children create a display for parents.

Watch worms at work.

substances such as yeast, baking soda, or baking powder. Additional benefits to cooking activities are the math and reading experiences that they provide as children read recipes and measure ingredients. Investigate heat as a means of transformation. The sun is a natural way to use heat and see its effects. Guide children in an experiment melting leftover stubs of crayons. They can discover what time of day the sun is most effective in melting or what location in their play yard is the warmest. They can further investigate by putting crayons in various containers that would reflect heat, limit air circulation, or contain heat. The effects can also be seen on discarded videos, CDs, and cassette tapes.

Other chemistry transformations to explore:

- condensation and evaporation (breathing on cold glass, investigating a puddle over time, or melting ice over time)
- effects of freezing various liquids (ice cubes made of various substances, salted water)
- absorption (materials that do and do not absorb water)
- dissolving (substances that do and do not dissolve in water)
- color mixing

Biological and Earth Science: How Do I Fit In and What Is My Role?

Environmental science and biology involve the study of plants and animals. Earth science studies elements of the earth. Because all of these are intertwined, it is impossible to study one without investigating the others at least on some level. They may include an aspect of chemistry or physical science. When learning about plant life, it is also necessary to investigate soil, the sun, and water. Earth science investigations involve phenomena such as shadows, the heat of the sun, properties of water, weather, and composition of rocks. You may recall that the effects of heat were considered in an activity in the chemistry section of this chapter. An investigation of shadows may more appropriately fall under the physical science section because it addresses the question, "How can I make it move?" An investigation of weather that is interesting for children would require that the children be actively involved in learning how the weather affects them; they would discover the role they can take in understanding the weather and adapting to its impact on them. The key to successful earth and biological activities is to develop them in such a way as to provide children opportunities to act on the materials, observe characteristics, make predictions, and develop theories.

Learning about the care of plants, animals, and the environment should not encourage experimentation that would cause harm to something living. A goal would be for children to develop a knowledge base about environmental issues and an understanding about their role in the care of living creatures and their life-support systems. Learning about the human body and its functions and care, including nutrition, is also included in this aspect of science (see Chapter 14). Children have a natural sense of wonder about the world. Biology and some earth science discoveries are focused on answering the question, "How do I fit in and what is my role?"

Ideally, science materials are always available for children to explore.

Activities

Biological Science

Purposes: develop an understanding of the natural environment

acquire the ability to nurture and care for living creatures

observe the life cycles of plants and animals

cultivate awareness of endangered species and the need to preserve them

Let children care for live animals.   A bird, gerbil, guinea pig, hamster, rabbit, snake, fish, salamander, lizard, or tortoise are common choices. Ask children to help choose the animal to be added to their classroom. Before introducing the animal, have children research what the animal eats or drinks, what kind of environment it needs, and how to care for the animal. Consult with a local pet store and check with a veterinarian. Guide children in Internet searches to further their knowledge. Construct a habitat appropriate for that animal.

To stimulate scientific inquiry, encourage children to observe the animal. For instance, a hamster can generate questions about what kinds of vegetables the animal will eat. Let them predict, then test out various choices by offering a selection of lettuce, carrots, celery, and spinach. Note which the hamster prefers. Which will it not eat?

Older children can add to this activity by creating imaginary animals. Stimulate their imaginations by reading aloud Dr. Seuss's *If I Ran the Zoo* (1950) (see Suggested Readings). Set up a display of the animals when they are finished.

Oil and Water Rolling

Brief description: Children try to combine oil and colored water in an attempt to make them mix.

Science concepts explored: Children can discover that oil and water do not mix and that paper absorbs oil differently than water.

Materials:
- small container of vegetable or corn oil
- small container of water colored with a small amount of tempera paint (preferably a color such as blue that contrasts with the yellow of the oil)
- spoons (one for each container)
- construction paper, wax paper, foil
- tray to hold construction paper
- spoons for mixing

Procedure: Children should first predict what they think is going to happen when they put the two liquids together. Place the paper, foil, or wax paper on a tray. Drop a spoonful of oil and one of colored water onto the paper. Notice how each liquid stands out on the paper. Tip the tray, causing the liquids to run toward each other on the paper, and try to get them to mix. After exploration, encourage the children to think of something they can use to mix the liquids. Allow the children to mix. Encourage them to wait and see what happens.

Divergent questions: What do you think will happen when the two liquids meet each other? How could you make them mix without using a spoon? What do you think would happen if you used a different kind of paper for the liquids?

Role of the leader:
- Set up the work environment. Be sure to test the liquids before presenting them to children to be sure the water isn't too thick with the added paint.
- Ask divergent questions, and be prepared to have materials ready to allow children to further explore to test their ideas.
- Do the activity with the children, showing your enthusiasm for discovery.

Can you mix oil and water?

Let children observe the life cycle of frogs.   Get some frog eggs or tadpoles from a stream, pond, or lake. Put them in an aquarium with plenty of pond water and a few pond plants. Feed the tadpoles extra food: boiled spinach or other leafy green vegetables. Observe the growth.

Encourage children to predict how long it will take the tadpoles to turn into frogs. Let them chart the growth, noting the decrease in size of the tadpoles' tails and the appearance of legs. How close were they in their predictions?

Cultivate a garden outdoors.   Involve the children in a discussion of whether they want a vegetable or flower garden. Provide seed catalogs, books on plants, or magazines that have a gardening section. Take a trip to a local nursery.

A globe can help children understand world weather changes.

Have children measure the amount of space that can be allotted to the garden, and research the types of plants that can be grown at different seasons of the year. Have them draw a plot plan, spacing the various plants according to what they have learned about plant requirements. Plant the garden.

Invite further inquiry by asking the children to keep track of which plants come up first. If they have planted vegetables, which are ready for harvesting the earliest?

Play Twenty Questions to encourage children to use their senses in identifying fruits, vegetables, or parts of aromatic plants. Choose five or more examples that have distinctive odors. Punch holes in the sides of a corresponding number of paper bags. Place each item in a separate bag and fasten it shut. Code each bag with a number on the outside. Prepare a card with the code numbers and a space for naming the contents. Allow each child to smell the bags and write down what they think it is. When every child has had a turn, open the bags and let them check their answers.

Keep potted plants in the classroom.   Include a variety of plants: those grown from seeds, from cuttings of mature plants, and from pits or tubers (avocado pits or sweet potatoes). Research plant requirements for growth. How much water do different kinds of plants need?

What kind of food do plants require? Why do some plants grow better in shade than in bright sunlight? Ask children to prepare a bulletin board showing different plants that grow in the shade and those that require a lot of sunshine. Suggest that they draw pictures of the plants, use seed packets, or cut out pictures from magazines to show the plants.

To further encourage scientific inquiry, tell the students they can perform an experiment to determine how much sunlight a plant needs. Have them plant a bean seed in each of 10 plastic cups filled with sterile potting soil. Place half of the cups at various distances from a window light source but not in direct sunlight. Cover the other cups or place them in complete darkness. Keep the soil in all the containers wet, but be careful not to overwater. Compare the growth of the two sets of plants once a week and chart their progress. Record the height and condition of the plants in each container. As a conclusion to the experiment, discuss what they have learned about plant requirements for sunlight.

Growing mold.   Pour a thin layer of canned soup into a flat dish. Have children place bits of dirt, bread crumbs, or floor dust onto the soup. Cover with a plastic wrap and put in a warm place. Within a few days mold spores will begin to grow. Provide a magnifying glass or microscope so children can examine the different "plants."

To stimulate further inquiry, do a second experiment to observe molds growing on other materials. Rub a piece of bread on the kitchen floor, sprinkle it with a little water, and place it in a sealed jar. Place a piece of cheese in another jar and a fruit peel in a third jar. Seal the jars and place all three in a dark location. Observe the changes periodically, noting the different times it takes molds to grow on the three media. Provide a microscope or magnifying glass so children can see the molds. Are the molds that grow on bread, cheese, and fruit peels the same as or different from those on the soup?

Learn about endangered species and what can be done to prevent total extinction of these plants and animals.   Contact National Geographic, the National Wildlife Federation, or the Sierra Club to find out if they have videotapes, magazines, speakers, or other sources of information about endangered species. *The Sierra Club Guide to Planet Care and Repair,* by McVey (1993), published by the Sierra Club of San Francisco, is listed in the Suggested Readings section under Biological Science. Children can also obtain additional information from:

The Nature Conservancy
Worldwide Office
4245 North Fairfax Drive, Suite 100
Arlington, VA 22203-1606
Phone: 800-629-6860
http://nature.org

National Wildlife Federation
11100 Wildlife Center Drive
Reston, VA 20190-5362
Phone: 800-822-9919
http://www.nwf.org

The Sierra Club National Headquarters
85 2nd Street, Second Floor
San Francisco, CA 94105
Phone: 415-977-5500
Fax: 415-977-5799
http://www.sierraclub.org

If there is a wildlife preservation area in your vicinity, schedule a field trip. Observe and record the plants and animals found at the preserve. Follow the visit with a discussion of why it is important to save these plants and animals from extinction.

Older children can explore what is happening to the rain forests throughout the world.

They can write to:

Rainforest Action Network
321 Pine Street, Suite 500
San Francisco, CA 94104
Phone: 415-398-4404
Fax: 415-398-2732
http://www.ran.org

Provide books for children to read on their own. Some excellent sources are *At Home in the Rain Forest* by Willow and Jacques (1992); *The Rainforest* by Goodman (1991); and *What's in the Rainforest?* by Ross (1991). See the Suggested Readings section for more information. Place the books in the reading corner, and allow time during the day for the children to read. Place a map of the world on a bulletin board, and ask children to color in rain forest areas as they discover them in their reading.

Activities

Earth Science

Purposes: cultivate curiosity about the Earth and the solar system

encourage scientific inquiry

provide practice in predicting outcomes

increase knowledge of the principles of earth sciences

Explore the solar system.   Obtain posters or photos taken during space explorations. The National Aeronautics and Space Administration (NASA) has views of Earth taken from outer space, pictures of astronauts at work, and photos from space probes of Mars, Venus, Mercury, and Jupiter. The Jet Propulsion Laboratory in Pasadena, California, and the Smithsonian Air and Space Museum in Washington, DC, are also sources of materials. Your local library may have books, cassette tapes, or videos as well. Set up a bulletin board display. Obtain books on space that children can read or browse through in the book corner. Provide a tape recorder or CD player and earphones if tapes or CDs are available. To stimulate children's interest in space and space travel, ask them to draw or paint a picture of what they would find if they were actually on one of the other planets. They might do another picture of things they would take with them on their trip to the planet. Display the pictures, and ask children to discuss their choices and explain why certain items would be necessary or desired.

Help students understand the principle that allows a rocket ship to enter space by explaining that it is based on Isaac Newton's third law of motion (for every action there is an opposite and equal reaction). Provide each child with a balloon. Tell them to blow up the balloon and hold their fingers tightly around the neck to keep air from escaping. Let the children release their balloons, one at a time. Do they know what happens? How does Newton's law apply? (The balloon pushes air backward as it is released through the neck.

The escaping air pushes the balloon forward.) The children can also consider which balloons went the farthest and why. Is there any way they might control where the balloon rocket goes?

Visit a planetarium, if possible. Your community may have one, but also find out if a nearby college or university has one.

Chart the weather for a month.   Provide a calendar form for each child or a large one for a bulletin board. Obtain a thermometer that records both temperature and barometer readings that can be placed outdoors. Have children record daily temperatures, barometer readings, and weather conditions. Ask them to bring weather reports and predictions from daily newspapers. Have them keep track of how many times the predictions are correct. Can they predict the weather based on a given day for the following day?

Have children write for more information about weather predicting and tracking. Good sources are:

American Meteorological Society Headquarters
45 Beacon Street
Boston, MA 02108-3693
Phone: 617-742-2425
Fax: 617-742-8918

U.S. Dept. of Commerce National Oceanic and Atmospheric Administration
Phone: 202-482-6090
Fax: 202-482-3154
http://noaa.gov

There is also a bimonthly magazine:

Weatherwise
Heldref Publications
1319 18th Street NW
Washington, DC 20036
Phone: 800-296-6207
http://weather-wise.org

Have children make a rain gauge.   You will need a clear plastic tube that is sealed at one end (jewelry beads often come in this kind of tube), a ruler, masking tape, a pencil, and a piece of clay. Attach the tape along the entire length of the tube. Calibrate by placing the ruler against the tape, then (starting from the bottom) mark off 1 inch, 2 inches, and so on, to the top of the tube. Set the tube into the clay, making sure it stands straight. Place the gauge outdoors where it will collect rain. Add rainfall records to the weather charts.

Tell children they can make "lightning." Provide each child with a balloon. Inflate the balloons, then darken the room. Tell children to rub their balloon on the carpet or on their wool clothing. Have pairs of children hold their balloons end to end, almost touching. If the room is dark enough, they will see an electrical spark jump between the balloons.

Equipment to Have Available

- animal habitats, an incubator for hatching eggs
- ant farm with a supply of ants
- aquarium with books on tropical fish

What are these children discovering?

- binoculars and bird identification books
- insect house, insect-capturing containers, butterfly net
- calculators, computers, software programs
- collections of shells, rocks, and fossils
- flashlights
- hair-dryer, small vacuum, bicycle pump
- household scales or simple balance with weights
- levers, incline planes, pulleys, wheels
- magnets: bar and horseshoe, assorted sizes
- magnifying glasses, insect collections
- measuring cups
- microscope with prepared and blank slides
- mirrors, plain and ground
- prisms, eyeglasses, gyroscopes, color wheels
- PVC pipe lengths, rain gutters, wood planks, wood blocks
- rock-polishing equipment, jewelry tools
- rulers, meter stick, T squares, tapes, protractor
- tripod
- sun-sensitive papers and outlines

Scientists draw pictures and write about what they have learned.

- telescope, books on astronomy, a globe, compass
- terrarium, seeds, potting soil, small pots
- indoor and outdoor thermometers
- computer
- VCR, selected cassettes or CDs, tape or CD player, earphones

Math in Child Care

Keep in mind that a primary function of a school-age program is to support children as they gain tools for living. Math is one of those tools. Recall earlier in Children as Natural Mathematicians, that there are everyday, real-life problems that provide the opportunity for children to experience and understand math concepts. When children manipulate, count, and measure real objects, they develop concepts that they can eventually relate to numerals and equations. They need to hold objects in their hands, weigh, or count them so that the concepts of size and number are evident. The caregiver of school-age children will most likely be able to recall some of the math concepts he or she learned in school. Basic number computations of addition, subtraction, multiplication, and division, as well as concepts related to money, time, temperature, geometry, and measurement of lengths, volume, and weight are generally the concepts that will most likely to come to mind. Real-life situations provide opportunities to problem solve by using math computations, including working with fractions and percentages. Children develop strategies for solving these problems. Additionally, children are taught to organize their math thinking and to communicate in the language of math to express their ideas. It is noteworthy to point out that appropriate math in before- and after-school child care programs is not about the mechanics of the pencil-and-paper math practiced in school. It is about incorporating math in everyday life and giving children an opportunity to construct their own knowledge about mathematical concepts while supported by the child care leader.

Cracker Division

Brief description: Children will use math strategies to figure out how to divide up a plate of food at the snack table. Children should work in groups of three or four.

Math concepts explored: Children will use the problem-solving strategies and math communication abilities to count, divide, create equal quantities, and notice possible remainders as a result of the division process.

Materials:
- *The Doorbell Rang* by Hutchins (1989) (see Suggested Readings)
- counters (small objects such as beans or buttons that can represent crackers, a minimum of the same number of crackers)
- crackers (enough for the group of children to count and divide)
- tongs (for moving crackers)
- napkins (one for each child)

Procedure: Read *The Doorbell Rang*. Give children an opportunity to discuss the problem in the story and their ideas about how the problem was solved. Then, pose the problem of having a plate of crackers and not knowing how to divide it so every child has an equal amount. "What ideas do you have about how we could divide these crackers?" Give children counters to simulate crackers to count and move around as they explore the division process. Once children have figured out a solution to the problem, they can use their strategy to divide up the plate of crackers. How many will each one receive? As children become proficient at this, provide an unequal amount of food that would require them to have remainders.

Let them problem solve what to do with the remainders.

Divergent questions: Is there another way you can divide up the crackers? What would happen if there was one more person in your group?

Role of the leader:
- Set up the environment.
- Be sure to have ample counters and crackers available for children to experience the division process.
- Listen to the children's ideas and facilitate each child having a turn to express and work with his or her ideas.

Activities

Number Concepts and Computation

Purposes: strengthen ability to count and carry out mathematical calculations

increase ability to use math concepts in new situations

organize quantities according to common attributes

recognize how we use math in everyday life

Games that involve math.   A quality school-age program should include a variety of age-appropriate math and reasoning games of varying difficulties. In addition, the more experienced children should be encouraged to teach others new games (Harms, Jacobs, & White, 1996). Monopoly® comes in a version for children from age 9 and up; Monopoly Junior® is for ages 5 to 8. Yahtzee®, ages 9 and up, involves counting, addition, and the exploration of probability. Scrabble® for ages 8 and up requires addition and multiplication in the score-keeping process. Battleship® is a two-person game that teaches children about coordinates and is for ages 7 and up. Visit your local toy stores for games that involve math concepts of counting and keeping score. When children have to keep score they are given opportunities to use addition and subtraction.

Eat a fraction snack.   Involve children in the preparation of sandwiches or foods that involve fractions. Cut the food into halves and fourths. Discuss these fractions and notice that the fractional parts come together to make the whole sandwich. Encourage children to notice such things as how many whole sandwiches can be made from eight fourths (8/4). Cut apples, oranges, celery, and carrots into sections. When eating snacks, children can be given half of an apple. Have them cut it again in half (½ divided by 2). Talk about the fractions they are using. Write them for the children to see. Encourage them to write their own fractions.

Dividing up a plate of food.   Children can be involved in the daily division of food for snack. Create a "Math Team" to count the available items and figure out how many can be given to each child. Another approach would be to have the team calculate how many of an item will be needed for the entire class. For example, if there are 35 children and each one can have 4 crackers, how many crackers will be needed all together?

Classify objects according to common characteristics. Collect a variety of objects and scraps that are made of either natural or synthetic materials. Include cotton balls and synthetic sponges, wool and synthetic fabrics, wood and vinyl flooring materials, plastic and wood toys, paper and plastic office supplies, newspaper, and cellophane. Tell children to decide what each material is made of, and sort into piles for natural or synthetic. Once the objects are grouped, children can count and compare the quantities of the various sets of objects.

In autumn, collect an assortment of leaves to be sorted according to colors and shape. Provide an assortment of small objects with a variety of tools to pick them up. Include beads, buttons, seeds, small animals, miniature cars, and so on. Have children use tweezers, tongs, strawberry hullers, or needle-nose pliers to pick up the objects and place them in small boxes, egg cartons, or partitioned boxes. Let children develop their own rules for sorting. They may match the objects according to color, size, or category of the objects. Can some objects be placed in more than one category?

Construct a Hopscotch

Brief description: Children will use measuring tools to make a hopscotch board on the playground. (See Chapter 10, Games and Other Fun Things to Do.)

Math concepts explored: Children will explore the concepts of length and width, and the attributes of squares and develop skills in linear measurement.

Materials:
- Rulers, meter sticks, tape measure (ones used in construction)
- Protractor (to measure 90-degree angles)
- Pencils and paper for recording information
- Clipboards for holding papers
- Sidewalk chalk

Procedure: Show children a drawing of the hopscotch game board. Put the children into teams of two to four to decide how they can make one. Children will need to practice jumping and measuring the distance of their jumps. They can use that information to determine what size squares they will need to draw. Children can record their measurements on paper then use those measurements to make a drawing of their hopscotch.

Role of the leader:
- Learn the steps before presenting the project to children by practicing making squares with a protractor and something with a large straight edge.
- Scaffold drawing squares by using a protractor to make 90-degree angles.
- Model how to use measuring tools.
- Be with the children to scaffold the process when needed, but be sure to let children make discoveries, including mistakes, on their own.

Activities

Measurement

Purposes: increase vocabulary and understanding of concepts related to measurement

practice using various tools of measurement

increase ability to see how measurement is used in everyday life

Weigh a variety of objects.   Set up a center with different types of scales: balance, electronic, and spring. Include many different objects the children can weigh or balance. Ask children to weigh the objects and record their weights. Are the weights the same on different scales? Which objects are the heaviest? Are the heaviest objects also the largest?

Encourage them to experiment with the balance. How many objects of one kind on one side of the balance does it take to counterweight objects on the other side? After a few experiments with this activity, provide different objects and ask the children to estimate their weight before putting the object on the scale. How accurate were they?

Provide a bathroom scale so children can weigh themselves. Include a basket of large stones. After determining their own weight, how many stones does it take to equal that amount? Make a wall chart of children's weights and the equivalent number of stones. Ask children to sort objects according to their weight. Let children weigh a collection of rocks, then sort the rocks into groups. To simplify the activity, tell them to put together those that weigh one pound or less, then between two and three pounds, and so on.

Measure in feet and inches.   Secure a measuring tape to the floor or use two yardsticks, end to end. Tell children to look at the divisions on the tape, pointing out the inch and feet marks. Have children lie down next to the tape. Ask one child to record each child's height in feet and inches.

The youngest children can reinforce the concepts of feet and inches by making a string showing their own height. Use colored yarn, Cheerios for the inches, and colored beads to signify feet markings. Older children could make a chart of all the group members to add to the weight chart just described.

Tell children they can measure a friend with a different kind of "feet." Supply each child with a piece of white construction paper, and ask each one to trace a friend's foot. Cut out the foot shape. Have children take turns lying down while another child uses the foot pattern to measure how many it takes. Show them how to turn the pattern end over end each time so that they start from the correct place each time the foot is moved. Record the number of "feet" it takes to go from foot to head.

Measuring time.   Stopwatches, digital clocks and clocks with hour and minute hands, and calendars are some of the tools used every day to measure time. Involve children in the daily monitoring of the schedule. Use a clock or stopwatch to measure how much time for such things as outdoor time, for taking turns while playing games, or for measuring how long until time for snacks. Children can record the time of day along with the number of children present. Remember to have clipboards, paper, and pencils readily available so children can record the information. Involve children whenever possible in using the calendar. If children are given jobs, they can be recorded on a calendar. Let the children post special events on the calendar. Make a large calendar each month out of poster board for the children to use.

Older children can make these monthly calendars. The leader should be only a guide in the process, letting the children do all the work. The children can be encouraged to use the calendar to find out how many days until the guest speaker is to arrive or how long until the field trip. Talk every day about the days of the week. Make certain that the use of the calendar revolves around how it is used in our everyday lives. Children will learn these concepts when they see that they are relevant to everyday life. There is no need to have a boring calendar time as a part of a whole-group time where children recite, "Today is Monday, June 6, 2005."

Measuring temperature.   Children can use a large outdoor thermometer such as found in a gardening store to measure temperature. Use different colors of masking tape to place on the edge of each 10-degree section of the thermometer. For instance, the 40s might have blue tape, the 50s green, the 60s yellow, the 70s orange, and the 80s red. Young children can read the thermometer by noting which color the needle points to. They can use a calendar or other chart format to record the temperature at different times of the day. The measurement of temperature can be combined with measuring time by recording the temperatures at different times of the day. As the children progress in their skills, the tape can be removed and children can be taught about the increments between each of the sections on the thermometer.

Measuring volume.   Children use measuring cups and spoons of a variety of sizes when they are involved in food preparation (see recipes in Chapter 14) or in making the various doughs described in Chapter 11. These measuring implements can be used in play as children work with materials such as bird seed, sand, or water in the water table.

Activities

Working with Money

Purposes: strengthen ability to count money

experience real-life applications of the planning for the use of money

increase vocabulary and understanding of concepts related to money

Creating snack menus.   Provide them with the USDA guidelines for nutrition (see Chapter 14). Give the children paper to chart their daily food intake so they can match it with the guidelines. With adult guidance, children can be given the responsibility of developing the snack menus along with the shopping lists and an approximate budget and cost per child.

Work with money in dramatic play.   Children will often create their own grocery stores, pet stores, or restaurants. These play scenarios are a perfect setting for children to work with concepts of money. They can price items, purchase items, use cash registers, count money, and give change. Make menus, coupons, and grocery ads to also incorporate literacy.

More Math Activities

Prepare a snack that requires math skills.   To help children practice the skill of recreating a pattern, have them prepare kabobs. Older children can use serrated knives to cut fruits and cheese into equal-sized chunks. (Younger children may require help from an adult, or an adult can do this part.) Supply one bamboo skewer per child. The adult makes a pattern using alternating pieces of different fruits interspersed with cheese. Ask the children to form like kabobs for themselves.

Provide several large pizza shells. (These can be found in the frozen-food section of the market.) Supply the necessary toppings: mozzarella cheese, parmesan cheese, pepperoni, sliced mushrooms, and so on. When the pizzas have been baked, ask the children to count the number of children in the group and decide how many pieces to cut each pizza into.

Estimate numbers by guessing how many objects are in a jar. Obtain a large (16 oz.) clear glass or plastic jar. Fill the jar with pretzels, crackers, jelly beans, or other small snack items. Place the jar in front of a chart labeled "Weekly Food Estimates." Provide small cards or slips of paper near the jar and a marking pen. Ask children to write down their name and an estimate of how many objects there are in the jar. Use push pins to attach the cards to a bulletin board. At the end of the week, ask a "Math Team" of several children to open the jar and count the items. (Remember to use health practices of washing hands and using food-handling gloves.) A next math step would be to have a team decide how to divide the snack among the entire group of children. You can also have the group count the items together. Who guessed the closest to the actual number? Have the children write the actual count on their own card. Place the cards in an envelope and save them. After repeating this activity over several weeks, are they getting better at estimating?

Equipment to Have Available

- baskets, boxes, egg cartons
- collections of small objects: beads, buttons, seeds, animals, cooking equipment
- rulers, meter sticks, tape measures, calculators
- scales: balance, spring, electronic
- table games
- tweezers, tongs, needle-nose pliers
- thermometers
- pretend money
- stopwatches, timers, traditional and digital clocks

Guidelines for Child Care Staff Members

There are some guidelines to help child care leaders plan activities that allow children the maximum opportunity for learning. They are:

- Give children many chances to explore and experiment on their own. Set up learning centers or have materials easily available for children to use when they wish.
- Provide enticing materials that will encourage them to participate. Listen to the children to find out what they are interested in, and then supply them with the means to pursue those interests. In addition, stimulate them to explore new interests.
- Do not give answers too readily. Ask questions that stimulate children to hypothesize, predict, or think of other possibilities. "What would happen if you . . . ?" "What can you do differently next time?"
- Listen to the children to find out what they already know or what they are thinking. Help them to correct any misinformation or add to the knowledge they already have. Design appropriate activities that will lead them to a higher level of understanding.
- Make a special effort to encourage girls to enjoy science. Many young women believed at an early age that science was not for them. Girls need to hear about successful female scientists such as Madame Curie, Rachel Carson, Lt. Col. Eileen Collins (the first woman space shuttle commander), Dian Fossey, and Dr. Myra Logan (first woman to perform open-heart surgery). Girls also need to experience the joy of discovery themselves.
- Maintain a questioning attitude and a sense of wonder yourself. Be alert to any possibilities for exploration, and you will probably learn along with the children.
- Document children's work and learning. By making learning visible, administrators, parents, and the children themselves can readily see that the activities children engage in cause them to think critically and develop cognitively.

Summary

Children are incredibly curious about the world around them and consequently are natural scientists and mathematicians. They use scientific skills of observing, investigating, predicting, drawing conclusions, and developing theories about everything they encounter. Many of children's discoveries require the use of the mathematical skills of comparing, measuring, and classifying. They must use the vocabulary of math to explain their discoveries to others. The goal of a science and math program is to provide opportunities for children to develop these skills. Because they are concrete learners, school-age children need to have active involvement with materials. By directly working with materials, formulating their own questions, and developing their own ideas, they are "constructing their own knowledge." It is this process of science and math that enhances cognitive development.

The science and math environment and an interested leader provide a setting for children to investigate their world. The adult leader, providing additional information and materials when needed, has a role in providing children with divergent questions to encourage children's critical thinking. Suggested activities focus on the children's natural inclinations as they ask, "How can I make it move? How can I make it change? How do I fit in and what is my role?" Adult sciences of physics, chemistry, earth science, environmental science, and biology fall into these three more simplistic categories that recognize how children work in the environment to construct knowledge.

A before- and after-school program can provide children with many opportunities to use and reinforce math concepts they are learning in school and to experience the use of math in everyday life. This can be done with both spontaneous and planned activities. Spontaneous activities occur when children play games or prepare snacks. Planned activities can be designed so children manipulate, count, and measure real objects. In this way, children can further their sense of the number system and how it works.

Guidelines for staff members to help in planning activities that allow children maximum opportunities for learning are:

- Give children lots of opportunities to explore freely.
- Provide enticing materials.
- Do not give answers too readily, but encourage children to find answers to their questions.
- Listen to children to find out what they already know, then help them to correct any misconceptions.
- Maintain a questioning attitude and a sense of wonder yourself.

Key Terms

constructing knowledge   physical knowledge
divergent questions   scientific literacy
logicomathematical knowledge   social knowledge

Student Activities

1. Plan one of the activities described in this chapter, and implement it with a group of school-age children. Record your observations of the children as they participate in the activity: What did they do and say? Bring the materials and your observations to class and share them with your fellow students.
2. Plan a field trip for a group of schoolchildren to a local site of scientific interest. The power-generating station, the beach, an observatory, a nature reserve, a museum, and

a radio or television station all provide insights into how science is basic to civilization. Follow up the trip with discussions about what the children learned. Describe the trip to your classmates. Were there things you would do differently next time?

3. Visit your local library to find some background information about an aspect of science. (Hint: Books written for juveniles are easily understood by the science novice and can also be taken back to the child care facility as a resource for the children.) Find at least two books on a subject, and develop an age-appropriate, exploratory activity for school-age children. Bring the books and an activity plan outlining an activity that you can share in class.

4. Plan a snack menu for a week for a group of 35 school-age children. Develop a grocery list and cost of the food per child. Design a plan to implement involving children in this process and share your project with the class.

5. Visit at least three of the Web sites listed at the end of this chapter and give a presentation to the class as to their usefulness to the school-age child care leader.

Review Questions

1. Children are natural scientists and mathematicians. Explain that statement.
2. What are the skills necessary for scientific inquiries?
3. Explain how science and math are related.
4. Explain what it means to construct one's own knowledge.
5. Explain the difference between the *process of science* and the *content of science.*
6. Explain why the child care leader is considered the most important component of the science environment.
7. Briefly describe three physical science activities.
8. What kinds of activities can children engage in that help them answer the question, "How can I make it change?"
9. Explain how you can structure biological science activities to actively involve children.
10. List five inexpensive items or pieces of equipment that can be used for science experiments.
11. Name three unplanned or spontaneous situations in which children must use math.
12. Planned math activities can be designed to help children progress to the stage that Piaget called concrete operations. Explain what this means.
13. List five pieces of equipment that can be used for math exploration.
14. Describe two math activities.
15. The text presents guidelines for staff members when planning and implementing math activities. What are they?

Case Study

Olivia and Juanita, both age 8, have been watching two slightly older boys work with a combination of rain gutters and blocks to create a raceway for their cars. The boys abandoned their work to play a game with some other friends. Nicole, the child care leader, noticed that the girls appeared interested in the boys' exploration.

1. What questions could Nicole ask that would cause the girls to think about the inclined-plane exploration and ultimately entice the girls to explore the gutters?

2. What science and math concepts could the girls learn from working with gutters and cars?

3. How could the girls document the scientific concepts they learned? How could Nicole document their work?

References

Harms, T., Jacobs, E. V., & White, D. R. (1996). *School-age environment rating scale.* New York: Teacher's College Press.

National Science Board. (1999). *Preparing our children: Math and science education in the national interest.* Arlington, VA: National Sciences Foundation.

Suggested Readings

General Science Books

Blaw, L. (1994). *Super science.* Bellevue, WA: One from the Heart Educational Research.

Churchill, E. R. (1991). *Amazing science experiments with everyday materials.* New York: Sterling.

Friedhoffer, R. (1990). *Magic tricks, science facts.* New York: Franklin Watts.

Kim, H. (1994). *Showy science.* Glenview, IL: GoodYear.

Lind, K. K. (2000). *Exploring science in early childhood education.* Clifton Park, NY: Thomson Delmar Learning.

Moomaw, S., & Hieronymus, G. (1997). *More than magnets.* Beltsville, MD: Gryphon House.

Tolman, M. N. (2002). *Hands-on science activities for grades K-2.* Indianapolis, IN: Jossey-Bass.

Van Cleave, J. (1996). *202 oozing, bubbling, dripping and bouncing experiments.* New York: John Wiley & Sons.

Wheeler, R. (1997). *Creative resources for elementary classrooms and school-age programs.* Clifton Park, NY: Thomson Delmar Learning.

Biological Science

Alan, G. (1992). *Jack and the beanstalk.* New York: Doubleday Books for Young Readers.

Challand, H. J. (1986). *Plants without seeds.* Chicago: Children's Press.

Dr. Seuss. (1950). *If I ran the zoo.* New York: Random House.

Fowler, A. (1997). *It could still be a worm.* New York: Children's Press.

Goldenberg, J. (1994). *Weird things you can grow.* New York: Random House.

Goodman, B. (1991). *The rainforest.* New York: Tern Enterprise.

McVey, V. (1993). *Sierra Club guide to planet care and repair.* San Francisco: Sierra Club.

Ross, S. (1991). *What's in the rainforest? 106 answers from a to z.* Los Angeles: Enchanted Rainforest Press.

Tolman, M. N. & Morton, J. O. (2002). *Hands-on life science for grades K–8.* Indianapolis, IN: Jossey-Bass.

Unwin, E., & Edom, H. (1993). *Science with plants.* Danbury, CT: Scholastic Library.

Willow, D., & Jacques, L. (1992). *At home in the rain forest.* Watertown, MA: Charlesbridge.

Zike, D. (1993). *The earth science book, activities for kids.* New York: John Wiley & Sons.

Chemistry

Hauser, J. F. (1999). *Super science concoctions: 50 mysterious mixtures for fabulous fun.* Charlotte, VT: Williamson.

Johnstone, L., & Levine, S. (2003) *Kitchen science.* New York: Sterling.

Physical Science

All About Science I (Mac IBM CD-ROM). Fairfield, CT: Queue.

Adley, N. (1991). *The science book of electricity.* Orlando: Harcourt.

Hauser, J. F., & Kline, M. (1999). *Gizmos & gadgets: Creating science contraptions that work (& knowing why).* Charlotte, VT: Williamson.

New A+ Science (Mac IBM Windows). Oklahoma City: American Education Corporations.

Tolman, M. N., & Morton, J. O. (2002) *Hands-on physical science activities for grades K–8.* Indianapolis, IN: Jossey-Bass.

Earth Science

Everything Weather (Mac MPC CD-ROM). Princeton, NJ: Bureau of Electronic Publishing (Thynx).

Exploring Our Solar System (Mac Windows CD-ROM). Chatsworth, CA: AIMS.

Tolman, M. N., & Morton, J. O. (2002). *Hands-on earth science activities for grades K–8.* Indianapolis, IN: Jossey-Bass.

Space Shuttle (Mac MPC CD-ROM). Novato, CA: Mindscape Educational Software.

Stars and Planets (GS IBM). Mill Valley, CA: Advanced Ideas.

Weather: Air in Action Series (Mac Windows CD-ROM). Chatsworth, CA: AIMS.

Math

Baroody, A. J. (1987). *Children's mathematical thinking: A developmental framework for preschool, primary, and special education.* New York: Teacher's College Press.

Briziula, B. (2004). *Mathematical development in young children: Exploring notions.* New York: Teacher's College Press.

Hands-On Math (Apple II Mac IBM). Grover Beach, CA: Ventura Education Systems.

Hutchins, P. (1989). *The doorbell rang.* New York: William Morrow.

Kamii, C. & Housman, L. B. (2000). *Young children reinvent arithmetic: Implications of Piaget's theory* (2nd ed.). New York: Teacher's College Press.

Millie's Math House (Mac IBM Windows CD-ROM). Redmond, WA: Edmark.

Web Resources

Source of information on science and nature
http://smithsonianeducation.org
Information from the Endeavor space shuttle on a mission to map the Earth
http://spaceplace.nasa.gov/en/kids/
Link to NASA information
http://www.jpl.nasa.gov
Information about the 2004 Mars exploration
http://mars.jpl.nasa.gov
National Weather Service provides forecasts, data, and maps. Links to regional offices and general meteorological information

http://www.noaa.gov

A database of earth, life, and physical hands-on science activities for all ages and abilities

http://www.letstalkscience.uwo.ca/

Sample activities from AIMS (Activities Integrating Mathematics and Science)

http://www.aimsedu.org

Activities from PEACHES (Primary Explorations for Children and Educators in Science) from the Lawrence Hall of Science

http://www.lawrencehallofscience.org/gems/peaches.html

Science U includes interactive models and activities using geometric formulas and facts, online simulations, graphic software, and a library of reference materials.

http://www.ScienceU.com

Ask Dr. Math provides a forum for answering children's math questions. It also includes searchable archives for additional information.

http://mathforum.org

Click on "Ask Dr. Math"

Activities for students and teachers using math and aeronautics

http://www.planemath.com

Click on "Geometry Center (Science)"

Science and math lesson plans from the Educator's Reference Desk

http://www.eduref.org

Interactive, age appropriate math activities from The National Council of Teachers of Mathematics

http://www.nctm.org

CHAPTER 13

Planning for the Future

Objectives

After studying this chapter, the student should be able to:

- Explain the importance of preparing children for future adult roles
- List skills future workers will need
- Plan and implement experiences that help children explore a variety of jobs and workplaces

Leana had known since she was a little girl that she wanted to be a teacher. Growing up, she played teacher with her dolls and friends. But her thoughts about teaching changed when she was in high school looking for a job. She noticed that the local parks and recreation center was looking for camp counselors. She was intrigued and applied for the job. That was the summer that changed her life. She found out just how much she loved being with children. She enjoyed the physical activities and the time to pursue things like cooking and crafts. She was surprised to find how intently the children would listen each day as she read from chapter books. But the thing that stood out for her most was that she was doing a job that provided a great service to families and an incredible amount of self-satisfaction.

Leana discovered that there were many children who were in child care from the early morning hours until nearly dinnertime. There were single parents as well as dual working parents struggling to support themselves on two incomes. There were also professional parents whose career demands required them to work long hours. She learned that these same parents really cared about their children and wanted quality care for them. These parents needed caregivers like Leana, caregivers who would be a role model to their children and provide them with opportunities to learn about life and to enjoy those activities with them. Leana had found her niche.

Leana also recognized quite quickly that the task of providing quality care was far greater than she had ever imagined. She realized she needed guidance in providing stimulating activities that would promote children's development. She yearned for more positive discipline techniques that fostered responsible actions and self-esteem in children. Leana realized she needed college classes to help further her abilities to do what some people said she was a natural at doing, that is, providing quality care to children.

Today, Leana is working full-time in a before-and-after-school care program. She is nearly finished with her associate degree in child development. When asked what she wants to do when she graduates, she says, "I want to keep doing what I am doing. I just want to be the best that I can be at caring for these kids."

Importance of Preparing Children for the Future

There is a revolution taking place in the workplace, says Toffler (1990) in his book *Powershift: Knowledge, Wealth, and Violence on the Edge of the 21st Century*. Most people accept Toffler's premise that tomorrow's workers will have to master new techniques in order to manage complex technology. In addition, Toffler says the whole character of the workplace will have to change in order to take advantage of the new tools. Workers will be expected to take a more active role in decision making. They will need to resolve problems and challenge preconceived assumptions. He predicted there would be few places for uneducated people or those without the required characteristics and skills.

High school or college is too late to begin preparing young people for their future employment. It is a process that begins in early childhood and continues throughout the school years. While it is impossible to know what kinds of jobs will be developed in the future, we do know, however, that many future career opportunities will involve literate, educated workers. In order to help children be prepared, children must be encouraged to be motivated learners who retain and use what they have studied. They must have meaning-based experiences that emphasize thinking, cooperative problem solving, decision making, and an opportunity to challenge preconceived ideas. Many of the activities throughout this book stress just those skills.

In addition to acquiring skills for the future, children should have an opportunity to experience the real world of work. At each stage of development, children differ in their ability to think about the future and their own role as adults. As they grow and have more experience, their ideas change. Tai, whose drawing is shown in Figure 13-1 on page 259, wants to be a baby-sitter. At age 7, being grown up may mean being a teenager who can take care of younger children as her sister does. Ten-year-old Elizabeth, whose drawing appears in Figure 13-2 on page 272, already knows she is going to be a zoologist. She has developed an engrossing interest in animals and has a large collection of pets. She may very well continue this focus, but she could also branch out into other areas as she learns more about the adult world.

The school-age period is a good time to introduce children to adult jobs and workplaces. Although you may not have the equipment or resources to introduce children to advanced technology, you can help them experience a variety of jobs. Start with their interests. Listen to their conversations, watch their play, and observe what they draw. Implement their ideas through the use of theme units or special-interest clubs. Plan visits to local workplaces.

Exploring the Options

The following activities are only a small sample of areas that might interest children. Use them as a starting point from which to develop experiences that will spark the enthusiasm of your particular group of youngsters. Have children work in small groups and share their results.

Activities

Map Maker (Cartographer)

Purposes: provide practice in portraying concrete objects as symbols on a map

encourage cooperative problem solving

FIGURE 13-1   "When I grow up I want to be a babysitter." Tai, age 7.

increase awareness of spatial relationships

reinforce math concepts of area, distance

Set up an interest center with a globe, an atlas, and maps of the area surrounding your school. Prepare activity cards asking the children to find specific places on the globe or map. Sample directions might include:

- Find the country we live in.
- Outline the state where our city is situated.
- Find our school on the map.
- Find your street on the map.
- Mark a route from your home to school.
- How many blocks is it from your house to school? How many miles?
- How long does it take to drive from home to school? How long would it take if you were to walk?
- Where do your grandparents live? How many miles?
- How long would it take to get to your grandparents' house in a car? By airplane?

Map your neighborhood. Provide children with notepads and pencils. Take them on a walk around the school neighborhood. Instruct them to write down distances in blocks. Tell them to note where buildings are located. When you return to school, have the children draw a map of your neighborhood on a large piece of paper.

Construct models of the buildings in your neighborhood to place on the map.

Equipment to Have Available

- atlas, maps
- cardboard
- compass
- glue
- map maker software program
- marking pens
- paper, variety of sizes
- pencils
- rulers, measuring tape
- scissors
- T square
- tape

Place the neighborhood map in the block area. Encourage children to use blocks to construct the buildings.

Obtain a plot plan of the area around your center. (Call the planning office at your city hall.) Discuss the kinds of information shown on the print and how it is used.

Provide map puzzles. There are wooden and jigsaw puzzles of the United States. Look for them in toy stores or contact your local history museum.

Construction Worker

Purposes: increase vocabulary to include words related to construction projects

practice ability to translate an idea into a concrete object

strengthen decision-making skills

provide opportunities to work together cooperatively

learn to use a variety of tools safely

Let children plan and organize a workshop area. Discuss common tools needed to construct objects from wood. Supply the suggested tools, and then demonstrate how each is used. Stress the safety precautions to observe. Ask the children to draft a set of rules for the care and use of tools.

Build an object from wood. Provide different kinds of wood: soft pine, balsa, plywood, doweling. Encourage the children to develop their own ideas about what to construct. Show them how to plan a project by making a drawing of the finished product. Provide rulers to make exact measurements, emphasizing how important it is to understand mathematical concepts in order to have a good finished product. Have them list the materials they will need, and then let them implement their project. Some possibilities are boxes for

A woodworking center can let children explore tools and tasks related to carpentry or construction.

storing small items, a puppet theater, games. They might also build boats, trucks, cars, airplanes, and a diorama setting for their models. Coordinate a woodworking project with map making by building a model of your neighborhood with wooden stores and houses.

Make a replica of a construction project.   Discuss different kinds of construction projects: home building, office complexes, freeway construction. Collect and display pictures of construction projects in progress and of finished buildings. Provide toy replicas of equipment needed to construct areas of a city: earth movers, trucks, cement mixers. Encourage children to create a city in progress in the sandbox using houses from their woodworking projects.

Invite a carpenter to visit your class.   Ask him or her to bring special tools used on construction projects. Discuss the use of each of the tools. Allow children to ask questions. They might ask: What are the qualifications for the job? What do you have to know to be able to do the job? What do you like about your job? What do you do each day?

Equipment to Have Available

- assorted nails and screws
- awl
- C clamps
- hammers (11 to 13 ounces)
- level

- miter box, miter saw
- planes
- pliers
- rasp
- rulers, measuring tape, T square
- safety glasses
- sand paper, assorted grades
- sawhorses
- saws (coping, crosscut, rip)
- screwdrivers (slot and Phillips)
- vise
- wood pieces, assorted sizes and shapes
- wood glue
- workbench

Chef's Club

Purposes: provide opportunities to explore career options

work cooperatively to prepare and serve a snack for the group

strengthen group decision-making skills

practice measuring using fractions and whole numbers

Develop a bulletin board of people cooking at home and in restaurants.   Ask children to contribute pictures of their family cooking together or pictures that they have found in magazines. Encourage them to discuss what is needed to prepare a meal for a family or for the patrons of a restaurant.

Visit a restaurant.   Talk to the chefs. Tell children to observe the process for preparing meals. What is done ahead of time? What are the kinds of things that have to be done just before serving a meal? Ask the chefs how or where they learned to cook. What do they have to know to be a chef? What are the qualifications for the job? What is the hardest part of their work? What do they like best?

Visit a bakery or factory that produces large quantities of a food product.   Tell children to notice the kinds of equipment needed to automate food production. Find out if computers are used to program the machinery. Interview a worker or supervisor. What are the qualifications for the job?

Prepare pizza for a snack.   Set up an assembly line to prepare the pizzas. Use frozen bread dough, canned biscuits, English muffins, or bagels for the crust. At station one, the bread dough or canned biscuits are rolled into rounds and placed on a cookie sheet. At station two, seasoned tomato sauce is spread on the rounds. (There are several kinds of pizza sauce available at any supermarket.) Station three, grate the cheese and sprinkle it over the tomato sauce. Station four can add additional toppings such as olives, mushrooms, pepperoni, or cooked sausage. Station five is responsible for putting the pizzas in the oven and watching them until done.

A Chef's Club can prepare snacks for the entire group.

If large rounds of bread dough were used as the crust, the final station, six, must figure how many pieces to cut each pizza into in order to serve the group.

Prepare a snack from a recipe that requires measuring.   In Chapter 14, Figure 14-2 is a recipe for Navajo fry bread. Also, look for cookbooks with simple recipes. The NAEYC book *More Than Graham Crackers* listed at the end of Chapter 14 has many recipes that are designed for children.

Set up a restaurant and kitchen.   Have children arrange an area of the room with a table and chairs plus a kitchen area where food can be prepared. They can create signs for the restaurant, decorate the table with flowers, and write a menu. Supply them with aprons and chef's hats. Add tableware and some cookware. Some children can role-play being the chef while others can be the waitstaff and the patrons.

Equipment to Have Available

- aprons, chef's hats
- baking pans
- blender
- chopping boards
- electric frying pan
- ice-cream maker

- knives (serrated)
- measuring cups and spoons
- mixer, food processor
- mixing bowls
- oven
- pictures of food and food products
- popcorn popper
- pot holders
- recipe books
- rolling pins
- sponges, buckets for cleanup
- spoons
- spatulas
- tableware
- trays
- vegetable scrapers

Space Travel and Communication

Purposes: foster curiosity about the solar system

increase knowledge about the U.S. space program

challenge preconceived ideas about outer space

strengthen the ability to think creatively

Design a space alien. Research which planets have conditions that might support life. As an example: Venus has an atmosphere that is brownish yellow and is made up primarily of carbon dioxide gas with clouds of sulfuric acid. The temperature is around 880° Fahrenheit (470° Celsius). Design a space alien who could live in those conditions. Either draw a picture of the alien or construct one from papier mâché or other materials.

Explore communication between astronauts and the ground. Have children research the technology used to make Earth-to-space communication possible. Sources where children can write for information are cited in Chapter 12. Obtain pictures of a communication room at Cape Canaveral. Provide used circuit boards, computer equipment, and telephones. Encourage children to set up a communication center where they can role-play interactions between Earth and a spaceship.

Build a space shuttle or spaceship. Provide children with large pieces of cardboard or large packing boxes. Encourage them to design and build a spaceship. They can paint the outside and equip the inside with places for the astronauts to work. Place the spaceship near the communication center so the children can talk back and forth.

Brainstorm space travel in the future. Ask children to imagine what space travel will be like in the future. Will people go into space as easily as they fly across the country? Will spaceships land and stay for a period of time on other planets? What part would they like to play in space travel of the future? Ask them to write down their thoughts or draw a picture. Display the various responses.

Equipment to Have Available

- aluminum foil
- balloons
- books, posters, photos from NASA
- cardboard pieces
- colored marking pens, crayons, art paper
- duct tape
- glue
- old computers, keyboards
- packing boxes
- paint and brushes (black, silver, white)
- papier mâché
- plastic tubing
- ruler, yard stick, tape measure
- telephone, microphones
- wires

Environmental Conservationists

Purposes: develop awareness of environmental issues

strengthen ability to plan and carry through a long-term project

practice cooperative problem solving

increase ability to communicate ideas

Create a bulletin board showing environmental issues.   Examples are images of burning rain forests, soil erosion because of logging, and polluted streams or lakes. In conjunction with a study of weather, investigate how these practices affect not only the immediate environment but also the global environment. Ask children to brainstorm alternatives to these harmful practices. Write down their responses, and include that information on the bulletin board.

Increase pollution awareness.   Have children write to companies that have the potential for polluting their communities. What are they currently doing to eliminate pollution? Are there additional plans as information becomes available and technology advances? What would the children do when they are adults to prevent environmental pollution?

Start an ecology club.   Let the children choose interest areas concerning the environment: ozone layer, smog, greenhouse effect, nuclear waste, solar energy, lasers, and sound waves. Have them research what these elements might be doing to the environment and what is being done to prevent further damage.

Compile a scrapbook.   Have children collect newspaper or magazine articles on the destruction or preservation of natural resources: rivers, forests, lakes, wilderness areas, animal habitats. Classify the information according to the kind of resource. Compile a large scrapbook of the articles, and leave it in the reading corner for children to browse at leisure.

Analyze food packaging for potential harm to the environment.   Examples are candy wrappings that contain a plastic wrap inside a cardboard box. All sorts of foods are sold or packaged in Styrofoam, which does not biodegrade. When the Styrofoam breaks up, it can be eaten by wildlife. Plastic rings that hold six packs of drinks can strangle birds and fish. Have children write to companies that make the products or publish an article in the child care center newspaper.

Concerned Consumers

Purposes: increase ability to infer results based on previous information

think creatively when finding new uses for household objects

communicate information and ideas to others

Survey packaging materials that are biodegradable or nonbiodegradable.   Explain to the children the meaning of the words *biodegradable* and *nonbiodegradable.* Biodegradable refers to those objects that will disintegrate over time such as paper, food scraps, and garden clippings. Nonbiodegradable refers to objects that will not disintegrate such as plastic, metal, and Styrofoam. Ask the children to think of things they have at home that fit the two categories. Group them in twos or threes and tell them that each group will survey an aisle in the grocery store. Take a trip to a nearby store. (Get permission from the store manager before planning this trip.) Provide children with paper, pencils, and clipboards or a book to write on. Assign each group an aisle of the store. Tell them to go slowly through the items on the shelves, noting things that are packaged in biodegradable and nonbiodegradable packaging. Discuss the information they have gathered when they are back at the center. Can they think of better ways to avoid filling the environment with trash that will still be there many years into the future?

Sort items into biodegradable and nonbiodegradable.   Collect items and ask children to bring in empty boxes, bags, or other materials that were used to package goods. Have them sort them into piles according to their degradability.

Survey the trash at the child care center.   Have children collect the contents of the classroom wastebaskets into plastic bags. Sort the contents according to those that could be reused and those that can be sent to a recycling center. Ask for their suggestions on how to decrease the amount of trash. Have them prepare a list of suggestions to distribute to the school.

Test the biodegradability of several items.   Have children dig one hole for each item in an unused part of the playground. Pour some water in the hole and let it soak into the ground. Place one object in each hole, then cover it with dirt. Mark the places with small signs to show what is buried there. Some suggestions for items to bury are newspaper, egg carton, tin can, plastic food carton, and paper bag. Have them predict which items will deteriorate. Dig up the objects at the end of 30 days. How accurate were their predictions? Would some of the items degrade if left longer?

Recycle household objects.   Ask children to bring one object from home that would have been thrown away. Place all the objects on a table, and ask children to think of things that could be done with each. Provide any additional materials they need to make useful items from the objects. Some things children might make are sand shovels from plastic bottles, a paint applicator from roll-on deodorant bottles, a rocket from an oatmeal box, and towers from painted cans of all sizes to add interest to block buildings. A large variety of objects can also be used to create sculptures or other art projects.

Equipment to Have Available

- bulletin board
- computer
- cups, bowls
- glue
- newspapers, magazines
- paper, pencils
- scale, balance or digital
- scissors
- scrapbooks
- shovels, buckets
- tape: masking, duct, cellophane
- tape recorder
- typewriter

Advertising

Purposes: develop critical thinking skills

evaluate and challenge preconceived ideas

increase ability to observe objectively

communicate information to others

Develop children's awareness of how television shapes our buying habits. Ask children to think about commercials they remember from their television viewing. Talk about the claims made by the ads. Discuss the purpose of the ads. Did the ads make them want to buy the product?

To further children's awareness, tape a half-hour children's television show, then view it with the children. Have them keep track of the number of commercials and the amount of time devoted to them. Discuss their reactions to the commercials. Do they want to buy the product? Why or why not? Do they believe the claims? Are there distortions in the way the product is shown? Discuss how television creates illusions when showing products.

Ask children to bring from home something they bought or had their parents buy after seeing a television ad. Ask them to write an ad that is honest but would make people want to buy the product. Have them read their ads, then post them on a bulletin board.

Set up a product-testing lab. Bring in several products that would be found in most households. Allow children to test and compare different brands of the product. For example, test two brands of paper towels, each claiming to absorb more water and to be the strongest. Ask children to decide how they can test those claims. (Pour the same amount of water on each and pull the edges.) Which held up without tearing? Another example: Certain cereals claim to contain more raisins per serving. Select two brands and pour out the contents into two large bowls. Have children count the number of raisins in each. Yet another example: two brands of chocolate chip cookies claim to have more chips per cookie. Ask the children how they can test that claim. (Dissolve the cookie in water, then extract the chips for counting.) Ask the children for other possibilities for testing, then implement those ideas.

Taste-test products children are familiar with through advertising.   Select one product to compare such as crackers, cola, or canned fruit. Choose several brands of the product. Cover the outside of each of the items so they cannot be identified. Label each with a number or letter. Provide children with a cup, bowl, and a spoon. You will also need a serving spoon for fruit or other products that need to be spooned. Ask the children to take small portions of each item, then rate each product. Use a numerical scale or Best, OK, Not Good to show their assessment of each. Did they all agree which one was best, or were there differences?

Solicit ads for newspaper publication.   Ask children to survey other adults at the center or their parents to see if they want to place an ad in the center's newspaper. Have the children write the ad copy and include any appropriate artwork. If a computer is available, there is a lot of clip art that can be used for this purpose. They can also cut and paste pictures on their ads for later photocopying.

Equipment to Have Available

- computer, word-processing program, clip art
- bowls, spoons
- paper
- pens, pencils
- typewriter
- videotape player, television

Newspaper Publication

Purposes: work cooperatively on a common task

   increase decision-making skills

   plan and organize a series of tasks

   increase writing and communication skills

Write, edit, and publish a newspaper.   Have the children plan the various tasks: reporter, editor, photographer, illustrator, cartoonists, and production staff. Discuss the length of the paper and when it will be published. Have them set a schedule for completing tasks. They can interview adults in the center, obtain interesting stories from other children, gather information from their parents, or write an editorial on a topic pertinent to the center. Produce the paper and distribute it to other classrooms.

Plan a trip to a local newspaper office.   Arrange to visit a newspaper office, and schedule interviews with several employees. Prepare children by asking them to think of questions they would like to have answered. They might want to know how someone becomes a reporter or what the most exciting parts of the job are. How are other jobs they see being performed important to the final product? What are the best and most difficult parts of any of the job categories? Follow up the visit with a discussion of the complex process of producing a newspaper and what kinds of jobs they might like to prepare for.

Equipment to Have Available

- camera
- colored marking pens
- computer, word-processing program, printer, scanner
- newspapers
- paper (printer and drawing)
  tape recorder

Scientist

Purposes: increase awareness of the different fields of scientific study

develop familiarity with research devices

provide experience in using a variety of scientific tools

stimulate curiosity about the sciences

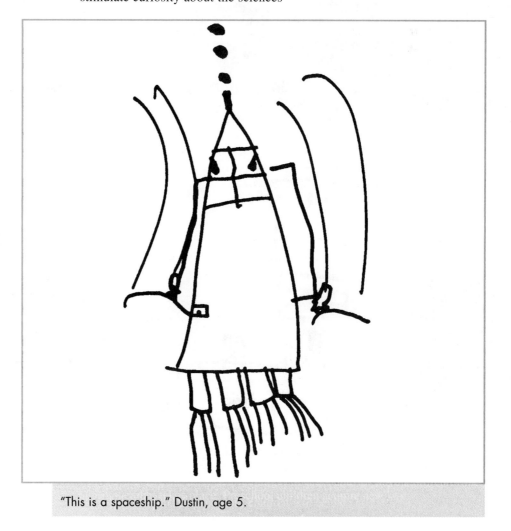

"This is a spaceship." Dustin, age 5.

Perhaps this child will have a career in acting.

"When I grow up I want to be a teacher." Rachel, age 6.

Scientist for a day.   Provide a variety of tools that scientists use, such as a microscope and prepared slides, telescope, metal detector, compass, barometer, or rain gauge. Teach the children how to use the devices, then allow them to experiment freely. Ask them to imagine the kind of scientists who would use the devices and what kinds of information they may be able to find.

Visit a site where scientific devices are used.   Examples are a weather station, a university research lab, a water-treatment plant, a company that has a research component, or any other appropriate site in your community. Arrange to have an employee at the site tell the children how the devices fit into the overall purposes of the facility and the qualifications for workers.

Equipment to Have Available

- barometer
- compass
- metal detector
- microscope, prepared and blank slides
- telescope

Guidelines for Child Care Staff Members

Encourage children to practice their skills as they participate in curriculum activities. Focus on the characteristics and skills referred to by Toffler. He said workers of the future will need to take an active role in decision making, resolve problems, and challenge preconceived assumptions. The following list includes Toffler's suggestions as well as some additional ones.

Future workers will probably need to be able to:

- solve problems
- work cooperatively
- make decisions
- understand spatial relationships
- think creatively
- read and speak fluently
- practice safety procedures
- plan for use of time and materials
- operate complex and technological equipment
- use a variety of tools
- be accurate and precise
- be able to be retrained for a new career
- evaluate and challenge preconceived ideas
- have a college degree or advanced specialty training

Plan ahead when you invite speakers to visit your center. Prepare the speaker by suggesting topics that are of special interest to the children. Set a time limit. Ask the

FIGURE 13-2 "Feeding my bird." Elizabeth, age 10.

presenter to bring visual materials whenever possible: pictures, videos, tools, or instruments are some examples. Ask the children to think of questions they might want answered.

Plan just as carefully for visits to community workplaces. Visit the site yourself, and determine what will be of interest to your group. Talk to the person in charge to plan exactly what the children will see. Prepare the children by describing what will happen on the visit. Follow up with a discussion when you are back at your center.

One of the exciting aspects of working with school-age children is that they are such avid learners. They want to explore the world outside of their own families, schools, or neighborhoods. They are eager to be competent and will work diligently to accomplish difficult tasks. You can capitalize on these characteristics when you plan your curriculum. In addition, you are helping to prepare these young people for their future as adult workers in a complex global society.

Summary

Future workers will have to manage complex technology. In addition, they will need skills that allow them to take an active role in what happens at their work site. They will need to be able to solve problems, work cooperatively, make decisions, understand spatial relationships, practice safety procedures, plan for use of time and materials, operate complex equipment, use a variety of tools, be accurate and precise, and challenge preconceived ideas. Practice in these skills can be built into the activities in a child care center.

The theoretical concepts of industrial technology can best be presented to the school-age child through relatively simple activities.

Lists of equipment and materials that support these activities are presented.

Invite speakers to visit your center to talk about their jobs. Prepare ahead of time by suggesting topics, limiting time, and asking children to think of questions to be answered.

Arrange field trips to community workplaces. Visit the site yourself, and plan what the children will see. Prepare the group by telling them what will happen. Follow up the visit with a discussion.

Key Terms

biodegradable
meaning-based experiences
nonbiodegradable

Student Activities

1. Survey your child care group concerning what they want to be when they grow up. Are their interests similar to or different from those discussed in this chapter?
2. Visit your community library. List available resources you could use in planning this curriculum area. Besides books, do they have videos, films, or recordings?
3. Plan a field trip to a work site in your community. Choose a company that uses computers to automate their production.
4. Discuss with your parents and grandparents any changes they have seen during their lifetime in regard to modes of travel and communication or advances in science or medicine. Find out what their lives were like without these technological advances. Share this information with a group of children.

Review Questions

1. Why is it important to expose children to a variety of adult work roles?
2. When do children begin developing ideas about what they will be when they grow up?
3. List several activities that are related to map making.
4. Describe how to set up a production line for the preparation of pizza for a snack.
5. Name two activities that will help children be aware of decreasing the amount of trash they accumulate.
6. List five characteristics future workers will need.
7. Do you agree with Toffler's premise that future workers will have to take a more active role? Write several sentences supporting your answer.
8. List guidelines for planning and implementing a field trip to a community workplace.

Case Study

During group time, the children in Vera and John's room were discussing what they wanted to be when they grew up. Amy declared she wanted to be a nurse. Seth said he wanted to be a gardener and take care of people's yards like his dad did. Evan loudly declared that those were "dumb" jobs and that he was going to be a doctor so he could make a lot of money.

1. Would you respond in any way to Evan's choice of a job based on the amount of money he could make? If so, what would you say?
2. What could you say to Amy and Seth?
3. How could you help each of these children to broaden their thinking about their future?

References

Toffler, A. (1990). *Powershift: Knowledge, wealth, and violence on the edge of the 21st century.* New York: Bantam.

Suggested Readings

Blaw, L. (1994). *Super science.* Bellevue, WA: One from the Heart Educational Research.

D'Amico, J., & Drummond, K. (1996). *The science chef travels around the world—Fun food experiments and recipes for kids.* New York: Wiley.

Doan, D. (1983). *Teaching problem-solving strategies.* Menlo Park, CA: Addison Wesley.

Douglas, F. (1991) *A carpenter.* New York: Greenwillow. Primary.

Douglas, F. (1992) *A chef.* New York: Greenwillow. Primary.

Gardner, R. (1994). *Science projects about chemistry.* Springfield, NJ: Enslow.

Horenstein, H. (1994). *My mom's a vet.* Cambridge, MA: Candlewick. Advanced.

Kalman, B. (1991). *Reducing, reusing, and recycling.* Toronto, Canada: Crabtree.

Kenda, M., & Williams, P. (1992). *Science wizardry for kids.* Hauppauge, NY: Barron's Educational Series.

McVey, V. (1993). *Sierra Club kids' guide to planet care and repair.* San Francisco: Sierra Club.

Vitkus-Weeks, J. (1994). *Television.* Parsippany, NJ: Crestwood House, Silver Burdett. Advanced.

Computer Software

Career-O-Rama (Mac MPC CD-ROM). Brunswick, ME: Wintergreen/Orchard House. Intermediate, Advanced.

Job City Series (Mac IBM Laserdisk). Altamonte Springs, FL: Techware Corp. Intermediate, Advanced.

Jobs for Me! (Mac IBM). Ontario: Logicus. Advanced.

CHAPTER 14

Getting Fit, Staying Fit

Objectives

After studying this chapter, the student should be able to:

- Discuss the physical health of children in the United States
- Plan and implement age-appropriate nutritional activities
- Plan and implement age-appropriate fitness experiences
- State suggestions for caregivers when implementing a fitness program

Takeshi was 17 and was ready for a summer job. He knew that he didn't want to work in fast food or in a store. Mowing yards and construction work had no appeal to him, either. People had told him he was good with children and he was a people person. He had a great deal of common sense. But what could he do with that? The answer came one day when a friend invited him to apply at a local YMCA to be a camp counselor. Takeshi felt guilty being paid for something he enjoyed so thoroughly. He was a natural leader and the youngsters adored him. He quickly learned how to facilitate group games and guide children toward solving their problems with one another. By the end of the summer, Takeshi was offered a position as an aide at the local YMCA before-and-after-school program. Once he turns 18, he can be promoted and in time move up to site supervisor.

Takeshi discovered that working at the child care program is different from summer camp. The group becomes like one huge family. There the focus is on teaching children life skills. At camp there were fun crafts, games, swimming, and lots of field trips. Those things are still here, but now the curriculum includes much more to help children's development. The children are involved in the planning and preparation of snacks. The leaders have weekly meetings to talk about the kids and their needs. The leaders communicate with the elementary teachers about behavior, homework needs, and ways to expand on what kids are learning in school.

Although Takeshi had fun in the summer, he enjoys his job as an aide even more. He has come to realize how great an influence he can be on children and how much he is needed in their lives. He is looking ahead to college now and thinks he will take some psychology or child development classes.

How Healthy Are Our Children?

Health-care providers, teachers, and child care workers frequently see children who are obviously in poor health or who do not get needed medical treatment. These children are often listless and cannot concentrate. Some are thin, whereas others are overweight. Many cannot keep up with their peers during active play or games. These professionals know that good health and overall fitness are essential to children's development and achievement. Yet many children are not healthy! Let's look at some of the facts about the status of children in the United States.

In Chapter 4 you read that 15.6 percent of American children between the ages of 12 and 19 are obese. Overwieght children are at higher risk for a variety of health problems: increased blood pressure and blood cholesterol levels. These children may also have orthopedic or respiratory problems.

The Children's Defense Fund (2004) has published some shocking statistics about children's oral health. Their information indicates that more than half of all children ages 6 to 8 and 78 percent of all 17-year-olds have untreated dental problems. Dental problems should be taken seriously because they can progress into infections and abscesses. Some children fail to consume adequate diets because their teeth hurt.

As you read in Chapter 3, approximately 14 million children live in families with incomes below the poverty level. Many of these children have no health insurance coverage and consequently suffer from a variety of conditions (Children's Defense Fund, 2004). In 2002 one in eight children in the United States had no health insurance. Many have inadequate nutrition, have poor academic performance, and suffer from chronic physical conditions.

Asthma is a chronic health condition that affects almost five million children (Children's Defense Fund, 2004). This illness can be mild or life-threatening, ranging from mild shortness of breath to chest pain and inability to breathe requiring a visit to an emergency room. In addition to asthma, many children suffer from respiratory allergies and repeated ear infections. Although these seem mild, the fact that they are recurring interferes with children's total health and their ability to progress in school. Other health concerns in young children include communicable diseases, hearing and vision limitations, and ambulatory limitations. Among teenagers, early sexual behavior that leads to pregnancy has decreased. The Centers for Disease Control (www.cdc.gov) reported that the

Children can chart changes in their height to measure growth.

number of births in the period between 1999 and 2000 the number of births in women 15-19 decreased from 48.8 per 1,000 to 47.7 per 1,000. The National Institute on Drug Abuse (www. nida.nih.gov) reported that between 2001 and 2004 there has been a 17 percent decline in drug abuse among teens. However, that same report indicates an increased use of inhalants that are easily accessible in the form of glue, shoe polish, and gasoline.

You can do little about some of these problems other than advocating more and better health-care resources in your community. However, you can have an impact on the small group of children in your child care group. Provide them with experiences that foster attitudes and practices that will improve their well-being. You can also give them knowledge that will enable them to continue these throughout their lifetimes.

Because snack time is already a part of every session in after-school child care, it is a good place to start. Teach children what their bodies need to stay healthy.

Help children plan to make changes in their food habits. Ask them to decide on one change, making it as specific as possible. They may decide to change the kinds of snacks they consume rather than eliminating all snacks. Take responsibility for providing nutritious snacks each day that are not high in fat or sugar. This may involve being creative at times but will be worth the effort. Fruits, vegetables, whole-grain breads, cottage cheese or yogurt, whole-grain cereals, and nuts or nut butters can all make flavorful and nutritious snacks.

Activities

Good Food, Good Health

Purposes: increase ability to make informed decisions about food choices

expand knowledge of nutritional requirements

encourage participation in planning food for snacks

Teach children what their bodies need to stay healthy. Prepare a bulletin board that shows the food guide pyramid, which is the latest recommendation by the U.S. Department of Agriculture. Encourage the children to consider their own diet. How many food groups did they have for breakfast? How many are in today's snack? What are some things they could have for a snack that would be nutritious? The food guide pyramid is shown in Figure 14-1.

Navajo Fry Bread

Purposes: increase cultural awareness

practice math concepts by measuring ingredients

foster cooperation

Prepare a snack of Navajo fry bread. This is a snack that is representative of a culture and can be prepared fairly quickly by hungry children. Assign two or three children to do the initial measuring and mixing. Divide the dough in half, allowing two more children to roll it out and cut it. Two more children can be assigned to fry the finished squares.

CAUTION: Be sure to set up the preparation area to allow maximum safety. Place the electric frying pan on a table. Extend the cord from the pan to a convenient wall outlet, then push the table against the wall. The cord will be out of the way, and children will not trip on it. Caution the children not to touch the hot pan and to use long-handled tongs to turn the bread. Supervise carefully when frying is taking place. See Figure 14-2 for the recipe.

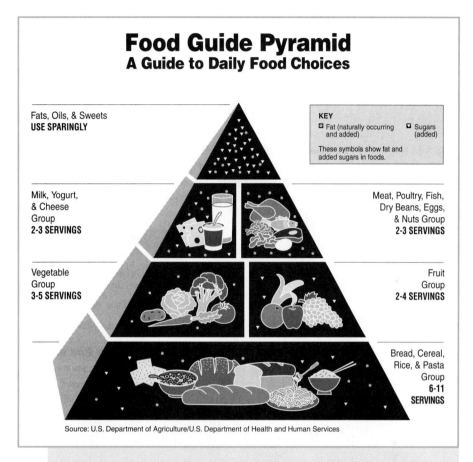

Food Guide Pyramid
A Guide to Daily Food Choices

Fats, Oils, & Sweets
USE SPARINGLY

KEY
◻ Fat (naturally occurring and added)   ▽ Sugars (added)

These symbols show fat and added sugars in foods.

Milk, Yogurt, & Cheese Group
2-3 SERVINGS

Meat, Poultry, Fish, Dry Beans, Eggs, & Nuts Group
2-3 SERVINGS

Vegetable Group
3-5 SERVINGS

Fruit Group
2-4 SERVINGS

Bread, Cereal, Rice, & Pasta Group
6-11 SERVINGS

Source: U.S. Department of Agriculture/U.S. Department of Health and Human Services

FIGURE 14-1   The U.S. Department of Agriculture Food Guide Pyramid

1 cup whole wheat flour
1 teaspoon baking powder
1/2 teaspoon salt
1/2 cup lukewarm water
8 to 10 tablespoons salad oil for frying
Sift the flour, baking powder, and salt together into a bowl. Stir in the water, then use your fingers to finish the mixing. Knead the dough with the heel of your hand, dusting it with flour if it gets sticky.
Roll out the dough to 1/4 inch thickness. Cut it into squares.
Pour the oil into an electric skillet. (Use just enough to coat the bottom of the pan.) When it is hot, but not smoking, quickly fry the squares of dough a few at a time. Using a long-handled slotted spoon, brown one side, then turn them over and brown the other. When browned and puffed up, remove from the pan and place them on a paper towel. Serve them with honey or jam.
The recipe makes about 24 fry bread squares.

FIGURE 14-2   Navajo fry bread recipe

Fancy Five Sandwiches

Purposes: reinforce knowledge of foods from the food guide pyramid

expand experiences with different foods

communicate information about choices to others

Provide the following foods from the food guide pyramid:

Bread: whole-wheat bread, wheat pita bread, whole-wheat tortillas
Fruits and vegetables: cucumbers, tomatoes, bananas, raisins, apples, sprouts
Meats and meat substitutes: peanut butter, hard-cooked eggs, sliced turkey
Milk: low-fat Swiss cheese, low-fat cheddar cheese, low-fat cottage cheese
Fats: low-fat mayonnaise or margarine.

Group the foods on trays labeled with their group name. Allow each child to make a sandwich using as many of the food groups as possible. During snack time have each child describe his or her sandwich and name the groups.

Taste Trip

Purposes: increase cultural awareness and appreciation

expand food preferences

Select foods from several different countries. Set them out on trays with labels indicating where they are from. Encourage children to taste several items, and then write their reactions. The following are some suggested foods, but visit your local supermarket to find others.

- From Haiti: mango; peel, slice, and add to fruit cups
- From Central and South America: burro banana; add to salads or fruit cups
- From Hawaii: papaya; cut in half, seed, peel, and slice
- From Japan: Asian pear; eat raw or bake
- From Mexico: cactus pears; peel and eat or add to salads
- From New Zealand: feijoa, also called pineapple guava; peel and slice
- From New Zealand: kiwi fruit; serve in thin slices peeled or unpeeled
- From New Zealand: passion fruit; scoop out pulp and serve over yogurt
- From China: lichee fruit; buy in cans at most supermarkets
- From Mexico: jicama; peel and slice, serve with a seasoned cottage-cheese dip
- From East Indies or Mexico: mango; peel and slice
- From South America or Hawaii: pineapple; peel, core, and cut into chunks

Menu Planning

Purposes: expand ability to make cooperative decisions

practice mathematical calculations when determining how much to buy

use food pyramid to make food choices

Plan snacks for a week. Appoint a committee to plan nutritious snacks for a week. Instruct them to include items from at least two food groups. When they have completed their

A bulletin board about milk focuses on one of the
food groups.

menu, ask them to make a shopping list of required ingredients. They may have to consult
cookbooks or ask someone to help them determine quantities. If you have a cook at your
center, he or she would be a good resource person. Schedule a trip to the supermarket to
purchase the food. See the reading list at the end of this chapter for books that contain
recipes. Also, a list of scrumptious snacks can be found in Figure 14-3.

Ice Cream in a Bucket

Purposes: observe the physical changes that take place when the mixture freezes

               participate in a group effort to achieve a goal

Make ice cream in a bucket. Most children have never had the opportunity to make homemade ice cream, and this is a unique experience. The recipe shown in Figure 14-4 gives
the directions.

    As a variation to this method, use one of the ice-cream makers that are on the mar-
ket. Several types are electric and one operates with a handle that must be turned. The

Apple slices, peanut butter, raisins
Assorted raw vegetables with seasoned cottage-cheese dip
Banana slices-dip in honey, roll in nuts
Celery stuffed with peanut butter or cheese spread
Cheese balls—form balls with softened cheese, roll in chopped nuts
Cottage cheese with fruit
Deviled eggs—add yogurt, mustard, salt and pepper to the yolk
Fresh fruit gelatin—any fruit in season; do not use kiwi or fresh pineapple
Fruit kabobs—banana wheels, pineapple chunks, cherries, strawberries, orange wedges
Fruit shakes—blend fruit and nonfat dry milk in blender with a few ice cubes
Graham crackers, peanut butter, and applesauce
Granola or Grape-nuts® sprinkled on yogurt
Ice cream with fruit—in milk shakes or in make-your-own sundaes
Nachos—tortilla wedges, refried beans, cheddar cheese. Heat in microwave oven until cheese melts
Nut bread with cheese spread
Peanut butter on whole wheat bread with raisins, dates, apples, banana, applesauce, chopped celery, shredded carrots
Pizza—use pizza dough or English muffins, add pizza sauce, cooked ground meat, cheese, tomatoes, mushrooms, chopped bell peppers, olives
Tacos or burritos—fill with cheese, leftover meat, sliced tomatoes
Tiny meatballs made with ground meat, rice, and seasoning
Wheat toast with tuna salad or cheese, broiled to melt
Yogurt with fruit

FIGURE 14-3 Scrumptious snacks

hand-operated freezer is ideal for making frozen yogurt. Merely mix crushed fresh fruit with plain yogurt. Add a small amount of sugar or honey, then pour into the container. Freeze according to the machine's directions.

Parent Demonstration

Purposes: increase awareness of cultural meanings of food preferences

expand food experiences to include those from other countries

Invite a parent to cook a favorite recipe that is representative of his or her culture. Demonstrate how the food is prepared and cooked. Let children taste the final product. Note: discuss the food with the parent before the presentation. Remind the person that it has to be something simple and that can be quickly prepared. Hungry children will not want to wait too long before tasting. Consider also the constraints of your facility. Where will the food be prepared? Will it be safe? Do you have an oven, a frying pan, or whatever else will be required? Ask the parent to choose a food that is enjoyed by children. For added interest, ask a parent to demonstrate a dish that is specific to his or her culture. Have the parent

You need:
a large plastic bucket
a one-pound coffee can with a plastic lid
2 cups of rock salt
Beat together in the coffee can:
1 egg
1/4 cup honey
Add 1 cup milk
1/2 cup cream
1 teaspoon vanilla
dash of salt
Be sure the coffee can is only half-full or the ice cream will spill over the sides as you freeze it.
Put a layer of ice in the bottom of the pail. Crushed ice freezes faster, but cubes will work also. Sprinkle the ice with part of the salt. Put the lid on the coffee can and set the can on top of the ice. Pack more salt and ice in the pail around the sides of the can. Sprinkle layers of ice with salt as you fill the bucket. When the ice is almost to the top of the can, take off the plastic lid.
Stir the ice-cream mixture around and around with a big wooden spoon, letting the can turn too. Keep on stirring and watching. Let the children take turns with stirring because it will take from 15 to 30 minutes for the ice cream to freeze to mush. You will probably want to eat it right away while it is soft. If you want to wait until it hardens, put more ice and salt around the can and let it sit for an hour or two.
This recipe will serve four to five children. You will probably want to make more than one batch. Also if you are concerned about possible salmonella bacteria in the raw egg, you can coddle it. Heat water to 140 degrees. Pour enough water into a cup to completely cover the egg. Let it stand for one minute. Any bacteria will be killed and the egg will not cook.

FIGURE 14-4   Ice cream in a bucket

explain whether this is a dish the family might eat frequently or if it is served on special occasions. Some possibilities are:

An Asian stir-fry dish. Provide chopsticks and ask the parent to demonstrate to the children how to use them.
Mexican burritos with homemade salsa
Japanese noodles and vegetables
Jewish potato latkes or cheese blintzes
Indian puri
Spanish sopapillas

Cookbook

Purposes: cooperative effort to achieve a goal

increase reading and writing skills

plan and carry out a long-term project

Compile a book of the children's favorite recipes. The children may have to consult a cookbook or ask their parents for help with this. Use a computer or typewriter to type the recipes. Make copies for each of the children in your group. Let each of them make a cover for their book.

Cook, Cook, Cook

Purposes: reinforce knowledge of nutritional requirements for health and fitness

practice in decision-making skills

experience foods from different cultures

Involve children in cooking projects often. Each experience is an opportunity to reinforce good nutrition and the importance of making appropriate food choices. It is also an opportunity for children to broaden their tastes and to experience foods from different cultures.

Japanese Rice Balls

1 cup short-grain white rice
1 1/2 cups water
salt

Put rice in a saucepan and add water. Soak for 30 minutes, then cook until all the water is absorbed. Let the rice cool with the pan covered for about 5 minutes or until it is cool enough to handle (already cooked, cold rice can be used if no stove is available). Tell children to wet their hands, then take a scoop of rice. Form the rice into a ball and make a hole in the middle. Place a pickled Japanese plum in the hole. If desired, the ball can be wrapped with a piece of nori (seaweed).

Flour Tortillas

4 cups whole wheat flour
1 teaspoon salt
1/3 cup vegetable oil
approximately 1 cup warm water

Mix the flour and salt: add oil, mix together with fingers. Stir in enough water to make a firm ball. Knead the dough until it is smooth, then let it rest for 20 minutes. Pinch off a golf-ball-size piece of the dough. Roll it out on a floured board until it is 4 inches in diameter. Cook on an unoiled griddle for about 2 minutes on each side.

Equipment to Have Available

You will need some equipment for food preparation or cooking. If your center has a kitchen, most items will be available there. If not, accumulate the basics, then add to them as your children become more involved in their culinary projects. The number of each item that you require will depend on the size of your group of children.

- bottle and can opener
- bowls, several sizes for mixing ingredients

- cake pans, both sheet pans and layer pans, muffin tins
- colander, strainer, flour sifter
- cookie cutter, cookie sheets
- cutting boards, plastic or wooden, large boards and individual size
- eggbeaters, scrapers
- fork, tongs, both long-handled
- gelatin molds, both single and individual
- grater, four-sided is best for children to hold
- hot plate
- knives, serrated for greater safety (if ends are pointed, round them with a tool grinder)
- measuring spoons, liquid and dry measuring cups
- pancake turner, spatula, wooden and slotted spoons
- pastry brushes
- potato masher
- rolling pin (you can also use pieces of dowel)
- saucepans
- skillet (electric)
- timer
- vegetable peeler, apple corer

When you can, add the following:

- corn popper
- electric blender and mixer
- electric food processor
- ice-cream freezer
- portable bake oven

Getting Fit, Staying Fit

The kinds of outdoor play experiences children have today are vastly different from the past. Many children live in urban areas in apartments where there is no space to play. Even in residential areas where there are yards, many children do not go outdoors because of fear for their safety or because they would rather sit indoors watching television. Even when children are outdoors, studies show they are not active enough to raise their heart rates for very long periods of time (Gilliam et al., 1981, 1982). Increased heart rate is one indicator of fitness.

Although an after-school child care program provides a safe place where children can play outdoors, there is still a need to institute an exercise regimen. The fitness statistics described at the beginning of this chapter indicate that children are far from fit. Many children do not conform to the standard of fitness described by the American Alliance for Health, Physical Education, Recreation, and Dance (AAHPERD) (1995). They describe fitness as a physical state of well-being that allows people to:

1. perform daily activities with vigor
2. reduce their risk of health problems related to lack of exercise
3. establish a fitness base for participation in a variety of physical activities

Their standards address several components: aerobic endurance, body composition (proportion of fat and lean), muscular strength, and flexibility. A good fitness program will address all of these. In addition, exercise can also relieve some of the tensions children feel because of the pressures of school or family problems.

Schedule exercise sessions before snack time. Always begin with warm-up activities. Warm-up serves two purposes: It limbers up the muscles in preparation for exercise and prevents possible injuries or strains. In each of the following lists of exercises, the first ones are the easiest. Start with a few from each category. Gradually add others or move on to more difficult exercises when the children have increased their fitness. Above all, make the sessions fun. Adding music at times helps to keep the pace going and increases the enjoyment. Finally, end the session with stretching exercises.

In all of the exercises, an adult leads the exercise and models the proper movements.

Activities

Warm-up

Purposes: prepare for exercise in order to prevent injuries or strain

foster a sense of well-being that will increase the likelihood of continuing a fitness regimen

Start exercises with a warm-up. Do the following:

1. Head tilt. Stand with feet apart, hands on sides. Drop head forward, then arch head back as far as possible.
2. Head tilt, side to side. Stand with feet apart, hands at sides. Keeping shoulders stationary, drop head to one side then the other. Touch ear to shoulder.
3. Head turn. Stand with feet apart, hands at sides. Turn head to right as far as possible, then to the left.
4. Shoulder shrugs. Stand with feet apart, arms at sides. Tighten abdominal muscles while raising shoulders up to ears. Lower them and repeat.
5. Knee bends. Stand with feet apart and arms outstretched at shoulder height. Tighten abdominal muscles. Bend right knee while keeping the other leg straight out to the side. Reverse, bending left knee.
6. Torso bend. Stand with feet apart, hands at side. Keep legs straight while leaning to one side, then the other. Let hand slide down thigh. Stand straight, then repeat.

Arm and Hand Exercises

Purposes: increase strength in arms and hands

develop awareness of muscle action

Stand with legs together. Bring left arm forward and up. Swing right arm back. Reverse process.

Stand with legs apart. Hold both arms together. Swing them down, then up, in a semicircle.

Go from left to right, then from right to left.

Stand with legs apart, arms stretched out at shoulder level. Rotate arms in circles, first in one direction, then the other.

Stand with legs apart. Grasp a yardstick or three-foot-long piece of dowel at each end. Keep the legs straight while swinging arms from side to side.

Extend one arm from the elbow, keeping upper arm close to the body. Place a small - rubber ball in the extended hand. Squeeze as hard as possible while counting to four. Change to other hand and repeat. As strength increases, continue the count up to eight.

Leg Exercises

Purposes: increase strength in leg muscles

cooperate with a partner

develop group cohesiveness

Squat with feet flat and palms touching the floor. Push one leg straight back. Hold for a few seconds, then reverse.

Run in place, raising knees as far off the floor as possible. Vary this exercise by telling the children to jump, then land in a squat when they hear you clap. Another clap is a signal to jump and continue running in place.

Stand with feet together, hands extended to the front at shoulder height. Raise one leg at a time, trying to touch each hand.

Sit on the floor. Grasp one foot with both hands and pull it up to the nose. Repeat with other foot.

Lie on the floor on one side. Rest on the elbow and forearm with legs outstretched. Lift and lower one leg, keeping toes pointed straight. Turn to other side and repeat.

Lie on right side, body propped up by right elbow. Put left hand on the floor in front of body. Lift left leg a few inches, then swing it forward. Repeat several times. Turn to other side and repeat.

Squat on floor, with hands flat on the floor. Jump with both legs, extending feet straight out back. Return to a squatting position.

Sit on floor with legs straight and apart. Point toes toward floor while clasping left knee with both hands. Push body forward toward knee as far as possible. Push several times, then straighten to sitting position again. Repeat with other leg.

Form children into pairs for this exercise. Each player places a ball on the ground or floor behind her. Partners join hands. One player in each pair sits on her ball while the other remains standing. As the seated player stands up, the partner lowers herself onto her ball. Alternate sitting several times.

A group of five or more children can participate in this exercise. Players stand in a circle, all facing in the same direction. The first player passes a ball over his head to the player behind him. The second player has to reach up for the ball, then pass it through his legs to the next player. Continue this alternation several times around the circle. You can also use two balls so each player has more turns to reach or bend.

Torso Exercises

Purposes: increase torso flexibility and strength

work with a partner to achieve a goal

Lie on the stomach with hands outstretched to the side. At the same time, raise legs and hands while arching back. Hold for a few seconds, then lie flat again. Repeat.

What are some other individual outdoors activities that can help children stay physically fit?

Two children can work together on this one. One child lies on floor with hands clasped behind the head. Raise the knees, but keep feet flat on the floor. The second child holds her partner's feet firmly on the floor. The partner tightens her abdominal muscles and pulls to a sitting position. Hold for a count of five, then slowly lower to a prone position again. They then change places.

Stand with feet apart. Stretch arms out to the side. Bend over and touch right foot with left hand. Keep right arm stretched up in the air. Return to standing position, then repeat with the other arm.

Equipment to Have Available

In addition to exercises, there are some simple pieces of equipment that will encourage children to participate in physical activities. They are not expensive and in fact may already be in your school.

- Jump ropes. Have several so more than one child can jump at a time. Have at least one that is long enough for two children to hold while others jump.
- Beach balls, gigantic balls. Children can throw or roll on balls.

Healthy children have lots of energy.

- Nerf® balls. Use with paddles described in Chapter 10 (Pom-Pom Paddle Ball). Imagine a volleyball game played with a Nerf® ball and nylon paddles!
- Hoops. Children can jump in and out. They can be laid in patterns on the floor so that children have to hop or jump from one to the other.
- Frisbees®. Can be played by two or more children.
- Balance beam. You can find a low beam in many school equipment catalogs. They are also simple to make. Children can walk across with eyes open or closed. Have them try to walk across holding a plastic or wooden egg in a spoon.

Guidelines for Child Care Staff Members

Remember that cooking and eating food should be fun. Do not pressure children to taste unfamiliar foods. If you keep offering interesting varieties, their curiosity will probably get the better of them. Also, they will see that others try out those strange things you bring to class, and they may want to get involved.

Set up a cooking environment with maximum safety in mind. Position the cooking table against a wall, with the electrical cord behind the table and out of the way. Teach children the rules and how to accomplish the tasks safely. They are quite capable of cutting up vegetables without getting hurt and using an electric frying pan without getting burned. (We, the authors, have used both knives and frying pans with preschoolers without mishap.) Supervise closely and never leave an area where children are cooking.

Try not to impose your own food likes and dislikes on children. If you really hate a particular food, then do not include it. You may think you will be able to hide your dislike from the children, but they will sense it.

Be a good role model. Do everything you can to be healthy yourself. Demonstrate good eating habits by bringing only healthful foods to school.

Provide a variety of activities and materials that encourage active play. Tag games, ball games, jump rope, follow-the-leader, and obstacle courses are all possible physical activities that can be incorporated into the daily program.

Allow children to choose an activity according to their developmental capabilities or fitness level. A vertical ladder leading to a high piece of climbing equipment may be too difficult or intimidating to the youngest children. They might be able to master a short ladder leading to a low platform. Young children can hit a ball on a support, while older children may be ready to try hitting a ball when it is pitched to them.

Set up active play stations indoors and outdoors. Chapter 10 includes suggestions for active games to be played indoors. Begin with those and then add others of your own design. Install basketball hoops outdoors at different heights; provide places to toss balls at a target, a place to jump from, or cement areas for skating.

Allow ample opportunities for children to practice skills. This means having more than one ball or that group activities should be organized for a small number of children. Only one ball or large-team games entail waiting idly for a turn with little chance to participate and practice.

Enjoy exercising yourself and children will enjoy it. Avoid any comparisons or competition.

This is not a time to see who can do the most sit-ups or jump the highest. Be careful not to use phrases such as "Let's see who can keep the ball in the air the longest." Simply say "Keep the ball in the air as long as possible."

Encourage parents to use health-care resources for themselves and their children. Find out what is available in your community, then share this information with parents.

Be an advocate for good health programs and policies for children. Join professional organizations that will lobby for health programs. Speak or write to local government officials about the need to protect children.

Volunteer for health-related events in your community. Include your child care group when you can. Health fairs, running, or bicycling events are some examples.

The health of children is too important to be overlooked.

Summary

Health-care providers, teachers, and child care workers all see children who are in poor health or need medical treatment. Many children are overweight and are at higher risk for increased blood pressure and cholesterol levels. Chronic health conditions include asthma, allergies, and ear infections. The rate of pregnancies and drug abuse among teeenagers has decreased, but there has been an increase in the use of easily accessible inhalants such as glue, shoe polish, and gasoline. One-quarter of children have decayed or missing teeth.

As a child care worker, you can provide children with experiences that foster attitudes and practices to improve their health. You can also give them knowledge that will enable them to continue to be healthy throughout their lives.

One way to develop health consciousness is to begin with the foods children eat. Introduce them to the food guide pyramid, and help them plan and prepare nutritious snacks. Expose them to new foods and different methods of cooking.

Although children who are in child care spend time each day playing outdoors, there is still a need to focus on fitness. The AAHPERD definition of fitness includes performing daily activity with vigor, reducing the risk of health problems related to lack of exercise, and establishing a fitness base for participation in physical activities. In order to achieve this degree of fitness, children and adults need to exercise.

A variety of exercises for specific parts of the body are described. In addition, there are some simple pieces of equipment that encourage children to engage in physical activity.

There are some suggestions for caregivers as you institute a good food program. Cooking and eating should be fun, so do not pressure children. Keep maximum safety in mind. Do not impose your own food likes or dislikes on children. Be a good role model by eating only healthful foods.

There are some additional guidelines for helping children to achieve fitness. Enjoy exercising yourself. Encourage parents to use health-care resources for themselves and their children. Be an advocate for good health programs in your community. Participate in health-related community events.

Key Terms

AAHPERD
chronic health condition
food guide pyramid

Student Activities

1. Make either Navajo fry bread or ice cream in a bucket at home. Invite your family or friends to taste-test the results. Did they like the food? If not, why not? Were there any difficulties you encountered that were not provided for in the recipe? How can you change the procedure to eliminate the problem?
2. Make a list of your own favorite foods. How many are healthful and how many might be considered junk foods?
3. Buy or borrow one of the pieces of equipment listed in this chapter. Try it out. How many activities can you think of to do with this equipment?

Review Questions

1. Name two agencies that have done studies on fitness of American children. What were their conclusions?

2. Name the food groups in the food pyramid. State the recommended daily servings of each.
3. Describe an activity a parent might conduct in a child care center.
4. Describe two activities that encourage children to try new foods.
5. Name 10 pieces of equipment that you need for food preparation.
6. Define fitness.
7. Describe three exercises that strengthen leg muscles.
8. List four pieces of equipment that will encourage children to be active.

Case Study

Holly and Louisa are 11 years old and are beginning to look and act like teenagers. They sit together for long periods of time looking at teen magazines that Holly brings in her school backpack. They talk about the clothes, the models, and the film stars that are featured in the magazines. At snack time, they often refuse the food, saying that it will make them fat. An assistant caregiver in their group thinks the magazines should be banned from the program.

1. Do you agree or disagree with the position of the assistant? Explain your reasoning.
2. What would you say to the girls?
3. Can you think of some activities to include in your program that might help them to have a more realistic image of young girls and women than is portrayed in teen publications?

References

American Alliance for Health, Physical Education, Recreation, and Dance. (1995). *Moving into the future, national physical education standards.* Reston, VA: Author.

Children's Defense Fund. (2004). *The state of America's children.* Washington, DC: Author.

Gilliam, T. B., Freedson, P. S., Greenen, D. L., & Shahraray, B. (1981). Physical activity patterns determined by heart rate monitoring in six-to-seven-year-old children. *Medicine and Science in Sport, 13*(1), 65–67.

Gilliam, T. B., MacConnie, S. E., Greenen, D. L., Pels, A. F., & Freedson, P. S. (1982). Exercise programs for children: A way to prevent heart disease? *The Physician and Sports Medicine, 10*(9), 96–108.

Newacheck, P., & Taylor, W. (1992). Childhood chronic illness: Prevention, severity, and impact. *American Journal of Public Health, 82*(3), 364–371.

Suggested Readings

Gianciolo, S., with R. Trueblood-Noll & P. Allingham. (2004) Health consultations in early childhood setting. *Young Children, 59*(2), 56–61.

Cook, D. (1995). *Kids' multicultural cookbook.* Charlotte, VT: Williamson.

Harrison, J. (1993). *Hooked on fitness—Physical conditioning games and activities for grades K–8.* West Nyack, NY: Parker.

Rowland, T. W. (1990). *Exercise and children's health.* Champaign, IL: Human Kinetics.

Wanamaker, N., Hearn, K., & Richarz, S. (1979). *More than graham crackers.* Washington, DC: National Association for the Education of Young Children.

Warren, J. (1992). *Super snacks.* Everett, WA: Warren. (Available from School Age Notes)

Web Resources

U.S. Department of Agriculture. http://www.usda.gov   Click on "Food and Nutrition"

Center for Science in the Public Interest. http://www.cspinet.org

American Dietetic Association. http://www.eatright.org

Children's Health Information. http://www.kidshealth.org

SECTION V

Resources and Regulations

CHAPTER 15

Using Community Resources

Objectives

After studying this chapter, the student should be able to:

- Discuss the advantages and disadvantages of using community resources
- Describe a variety of activities appropriate for seniors and children
- List activities for which teen volunteers are suited
- Describe ways to use resources outside the child care center
- State ways to make a volunteer program effective

Aleisha needed a job. She had just started classes at a community college. She had applied for financial aid and was able to receive some money for tuition, and she was fortunate enough to still be living at home with her parents and her two little brothers. But Aleisha wanted more than just a paycheck. She wanted a job that would give her skills and training toward a career. The catch was that Aleisha didn't have any idea what she wanted for a career. She had had a job working at a shoe store when she was in high school and found out that her favorite customers were the children. So, she was thinking that something related to children would be nice. She wasn't even sure what she wanted to study in college. When she was trying to decide what classes to take, she found one called human development. It sounded interesting, much more interesting than history! Little did she know that that class would help her find a direction in her career journey.

The human development instructor announced that an employment opportunities board was posted outside the child development center. Aleisha checked it out. The only job posted that would work in her schedule was one for a nearby school-age program. Aleisha applied the next day and started immediately as an aide. She quickly found she could apply what she was learning in class to her observations of the children and families she worked with. She noticed the developmental differences in children. In class, she learned about how children think, develop language, and socialize. She was able to apply what she was learning to her work.

Aleisha now has an educational plan and a career path. Because she sees that her job with the school child care program offers opportunities for her to advance, she now knows she needs a degree. Her goal is to become a director of multiple sites and to get at least her associate degree in child development. Who knows? She may even go on and get a bachelor's or master's degree.

How Community Resources Can Support School-Age Programs

Teachers and caregivers sometimes greet the idea of using community resources to enrich their curriculum with mixed reactions. Some cite the general hassle involved in recruiting and training volunteers. Others say they cannot get students out into the community because of transportation problems. Some point to the fact that except for summers, the time children spend at the center is too limited. Some caregivers say it is difficult because of the wide age differences of the children they serve. All these are valid reasons but should not deter you.

The problems can be resolved. You may find the benefits to the children will be well worth the effort.

School-age children are ready and eager to learn about the world outside their immediate environment. When they go to kindergarten, they take that first step away from their home and out into the community. Most find it a fascinating place and are eager to find their own place out in the world. Developmentally they are ready. They have good muscular control and want to try out their skills in new ways. Cognitively, they have a good memory and a much longer interest span. Coupled with this, they can postpone rewards, allowing them to work on projects that take a long time to complete. They are ready to consider different ways of thinking or doing things. They find that not everyone lives or thinks as they do. When presented with alternatives, they like to consider the options. In addition to all these characteristics, school-age children have a high energy level. They need lots to do and challenges to meet.

One of the ways to involve children in the community is to invite residents or representatives from agencies and organizations to participate in activities at your center. This method has a distinct advantage in that it eliminates transportation problems and does not entail travel time. An added advantage is that the school becomes known and this may be helpful when fund-raising is necessary. What is most important, however, is that both children and outside adults benefit from this relationship.

Intergenerational Programs

Intergenerational programs are one way to bring the community into the child care center. These programs use older persons and young adults or teenagers as volunteers. Older persons especially are often looking for meaningful ways to share their energies. At the same time, some children either do not know or do not live close to grandparents. Both can benefit from the relationship. The adults will feel they can still make a difference in someone else's life. The children will enjoy increased self-esteem because there is someone who listens to and cares about them. Both can learn to appreciate the similarities and differences that exist between the generations.

Child care centers can use the talents of older adults who come from a variety of jobs and professions. Artists, teachers, musicians, scientists, gardeners, veterinarians, and cooks are just a few who have knowledge and skills that can be shared with children. These people can do what grandparents do: plan special activities, demonstrate how to do things, go on outings together, and celebrate holidays and special occasions.

Recruit older persons through the following:

- active living centers
- community centers
- groups for active seniors
- parks and recreation departments
- senior centers
- retirement communities
- churches
- special-interest groups: hobby clubs or computer users
- subsidized housing complexes for persons over 55

- senior citizens service agencies (county or city)
- notices in volunteer information columns of newspapers

You can also write to organizations for seniors to find groups in your community. Try:

American Association of Retired Persons
909 K Street NW
Washington, DC 20049

Gray Panthers
215 South Juniper Street, Suite 601
Philadelphia, PA 19107

Activities for Seniors and Children

The following is a list of just a few things older adults can do with children. You can develop others based on the needs of your particular center or the talents of the adults available to you.

Tutoring

Assist individual children with math, English, or homework.

Many retired teachers want to maintain contact with children but do not want the structure of a classroom setting. They might find helping in a child care center to their liking. Children will appreciate help with schoolwork and someone who will listen while they practice conversing in English.

Science Experiences

Demonstrate scientific phenomena: electricity, chemistry, weather.

Plan and conduct hands-on science activities for the children. Schedule hands-on activities to follow a demonstration. Any of the activities described in Chapter 12 or contained in the books on the reading list for that chapter would be suitable.

Share an interest in exotic plants (orchids, cacti, tropical plants, etc.).

Work with children to make exhibits for a school science fair. Invite other school groups and parents to see the results.

Cultural Awareness

Demonstrate musical instruments specific to a culture. Let children play them.

Cook and taste ethnic foods. Use traditional cooking pots and implements.

Teach dances of native peoples. Make costumes and plan a performance of dances.

Display toys and games used by children in different cultures. Tell how they are used. Let children try them out.

Read children's books from different countries in the native language, then translate. Discuss how the stories reflect life in that country.

Show children folk arts or crafts. Teach children how to create some typical folk objects.

Share with children the ways holidays and special occasions are celebrated in their native country.

Develop a network of pen pals from different countries. Help children write letters to a pen pal.

Encourage children to use the Internet to find pen pals in other countries (http://www.epals.com).

Collections

Share special collections: rocks, shells, fossils, insects, stamps. Work with children to classify and organize their own collection.

Act as an adviser to a club based on collections.

Chess, Checkers

Teach children how to play and organize tournaments. Be an adviser for a club.

Plan and conduct a tournament. Consider a tournament between adults and children.

Cooking

Prepare a variety of foods with children: bread, ice cream, muffins.

Share favorite recipes or recipes passed down from family members. Prepare holiday specialties.

A game of chess with a volunteer sharpens the ability to analyze problems and plan strategies.

Help children put together a book of recipes for foods they and their families especially enjoy.

Reading

Read stories to children. Children love hearing stories read to them in groups or one on one.

Listen while children read. Discuss the story or ask questions about the story. "What happened when . . . ?" or "What if . . . ?"

Take individual children on a trip to the library. Browse together, then choose books to take back to the center.

Puppet Making

Help children make puppets and then put on a puppet show. This can be a long-range project beginning with writing a script, making the puppets, planning the production, and then performing.

Life Stories

Older adults can tell children about their own childhood. Many children cannot conceive of a world without the modern conveniences they take for granted. A good storyteller can paint a picture of life in "the old days."

Share photo albums of their own childhood with children. Show themselves as babies, as "school-agers," and as teens.

Help children compile their own life story. Older children will be able to write theirs.

Younger children can portray their history through photographs and drawings or collages.

Art Projects

Work on special art projects. Teach children new techniques for creating art: airbrush painting, mold making, using charcoal for drawing. Accompany children on a tour of the studio of an artist who uses one of these techniques.

Help children plan and paint a mural. This can be either a child-only project or a joint project between adults and children. Each could contribute something to the finished product.

Field Trips

Accompany children on trips to museums, plays, or factories. Extra adults provide better supervision and can share their knowledge with children as well.

Woodworking

Teach children proper use of power tools and hand tools. Supervise woodworking projects.

Accompany children to a furniture-manufacturing site.

Computer Assistance

Help children use the computer in new ways. Work with them to set up an e-mail newsletter to their parents. Discuss the kinds of topics they think their parents would want to know about. Help them set up the format that can be used each month as they update the information. Guide them in writing articles and inputting them into the computer. They will also have to obtain an e-mail address from the parents so they can set up an address list.

Play computer games with the children. Be sure to check the content before introducing them to a new game since so many have content that would not be appropriate for children.

Help children develop a pen pal network with children in other child care settings or even in other countries. See the Internet site http://www.epals.com or type pen pals in the search engine of the computer to choose other pen pals options.

Gardening

Teach children the basic needs of plants. Help them to prepare, plant, and maintain a garden.

Plant a vegetable garden and harvest vegetables. Prepare vegetables for a snack: raw vegetables and a dip or zucchini bread.

Bicycle Maintenance

Teach children how to repair and maintain their own bikes.

Teach safety rules to observe when riding a bike.

Photography

Teach children the basics of using a camera. If possible, help children to develop their own pictures.

Help children put together an exhibit of their photographs for a parent bulletin board.

Needlework

Teach children how to knit or crochet. Help them create simple garments: a scarf, hat, small blanket.

Teach children embroidery stitches. Help them to create a pillow cover, place mat, wall hanging.

Help children make a simple hand loom. Teach them how to weave place mats, wall hangings, pot holders.

Accompany children to needlework shops to see the variety of materials available. Purchase materials needed for a project.

Activities Using High School and College Students

Although many young people can do the things suggested for older persons, they may have a different approach. They may also be better suited for some activities. The following are some activities young people may be especially suited for.

"Me being a black belt." Ricky, age 9.

Sports

Teach children proper techniques for playing popular sports: tennis, basketball, baseball, soccer, golf, swimming, or gymnastics. Practice with individual children who need help in perfecting their skills.

Organize a game with another child care center, possibly at a nearby park.

How can volunteers assist in a school-age program?

Drama

Work with children to write, produce, and perform a play. Children can make their own costumes, design and construct scenery, or set up proper lighting.

Dance

Teach children how to dance ballet, tap, clogging, or current popular dances.
Help children choreograph a dance. Perform for other children or parents.

Conversation

Talk with and listen to children. Teens may be able to help children express their worries or fears or discuss their problems.

Field Trips

Accompany children on active field trips: park, zoo, beach, nature walk.

Exercise

Teach children some basic exercises such as those suggested in Chapter 14.

Cultural Awareness

High school exchange students from other countries can tell about life in their homeland: their play activities, school, their family.

Games

Play table or language games with children. Children and teens enjoy Monopoly®, Clue®, Trivial Pursuit®, Scrabble®, Life®, or card games. Teens will contribute their own enthusiasms for language games such as telephone, taking a trip, 20 questions, or charades.

Community Agencies, Organizations, and Businesses

You may decide you do not want volunteers who come to your school but would rather schedule periodic activities that use facilities in your community. Nearly every area will have some resources that would interest children. Check your neighborhood, call government offices, and talk to other caregivers. If you have lived in the area for a long time, where did your parents take you when you were a child?

Museums

Natural history museums are an excellent source of persons to do presentations or conduct tours of the museum. Consider presentations on local history, plants, or animals indigenous to the area.

Children's discovery museums are marvelous places for a field trip. These are places where children can touch, manipulate, and participate in a variety of activities.

Art museums may conduct tours, specially designed for children. Most large museums have a docents program, volunteers who know a great deal about the art in the galleries. Sometimes a tour is followed by a session in which the children can create their own art.

Library

Many libraries have a children's librarian who will help children choose books. They may also have reading incentive programs: a reward for children who read a specified number of books.

Libraries often have film series or other activities that are suitable for young children.

Ask whether the library can supply or recommend storytellers. Ask the storyteller to visit the program to tell about the art of storytelling and then tell a story.

Businesses

Some businesspeople may be willing to conduct a tour of their facility and then answer questions or tell children how to prepare themselves for that line of work. A newspaper office, dairy, radio station, or a computerized office might interest children.

Fire Station

Take a tour of the facility. Discuss requirements for becoming a firefighter.

Some departments have fire-prevention programs featuring Smokey the Bear and could do a presentation.

Police Station

Take a tour of the facility. Discuss requirements for qualifying to be a member of law enforcement.

Some departments have drug prevention programs and could do a presentation.

Wildlife Refuge

A few communities have areas set aside for endangered animal species or plants. Some conduct nature walks. Others may have plant propagation workshops where children help plant seeds or transplant native plants or trees.

Community Facilities

Find out whether your children can use a local riding stable, swimming pool, or public tennis courts.

All of these activities will enhance your child care curriculum immeasurably. However, you may still be thinking that it is all too much trouble. There are some ways to resolve problems that schools and child care centers have found helpful.

Guidelines for Using Volunteers

It is important to have an organized method of managing those persons from your community who participate in your program—your volunteer corps. They should see themselves as an integral part of what you are trying to achieve. To begin with, they will be more valuable if they know what they are expected to do, if they are trained and supported as they work with you, and if they know they are appreciated. Time and effort spent in setting up this kind of program will pay off in the long run. Your volunteers are more likely to stay with you longer. They will contribute to your curriculum rather than be an additional burden.

Prepare a booklet of information that clearly states expectations for volunteers. Spell out what their job is and what their hours will be. Let them know who will be supervising them and to whom they can go when problems arise.

Check your local licensing requirement regarding fingerprinting volunteers. If necessary, tell volunteers where it can be done.

Assign volunteers to simple, specific tasks at first. Start with having them work with one child alone at an activity. As you learn more about each person's abilities and strengths, you can gradually allow greater responsibility.

Plan and conduct an orientation for each volunteer. Develop a program that gives a general overview of your center and its goals and philosophy. Suggest ways of interacting with children. State rules that apply to the children and to themselves.

Ask for a specific time commitment from each volunteer. Because a lot of effort goes into making a volunteer program successful, it is important to avoid constant change in its members. Have each volunteer say how much time and for how long a period they can commit themselves to your program.

Provide ongoing supervision and training. Additional training as volunteers become more familiar with your program will enhance their self-esteem and make them more committed.

Evaluate and provide feedback periodically. Remember that volunteers are not getting paid for their time. To make it worthwhile, they must feel they are appreciated and that they are learning.

Have realistic expectations for your volunteers. Remember that they may not always be available when you need them. Older persons sometimes have health problems, and young people have many other demands on their time.

You may have to make some adaptations to your environment in order to foster an effective intergenerational program. Consider the following changes to accommodate both older adults and teenagers in your setting.

Place small sofas or wide armchairs in a quiet corner. This will invite an adult or teen and one or two children to sit together to read or talk.

Install an extra-wide swing in the playground. The favorite place for many children of past generations was in the porch swing with grandpa or grandma. Not many have that experience today, but a wide swing can bring a little of that atmosphere to your playground. Children will also enjoy swinging with a teenager who may be a little daring and swing them fast.

Provide at least one table high enough for an adult or a teenager. Let children sit on stools so they can work with the adult at this table on art projects, science experiments, writing, or whatever they wish.

Provide a place where children can leave a message for the adult or teenager. Most volunteers are not there on a daily basis, but children may want to write them a note about something that happened or just leave a special drawing. This can be an important avenue for developing a relationship.

Provide a place where the adults or teens can keep their own belongings.

Plan a means for thanking volunteers. Write a letter at the end of a specified period of time or give an award. You can also have a special meeting or dinner to recognize the contribution that volunteers have made to your program.

Removing Barriers to Community Participation

At the beginning of this chapter, we indicated that many caregivers have mixed reactions to the use of community resources. They cite a variety of reasons. Here are some solutions that other programs have found successful:

- Walk to places that are close to the child care center.
- Rent or use donated buses and vans from churches (these are usually not used by the church during the week).
- Take small groups at a time, using public transportation or private cars.
- Divide groups according to age levels of children and take trips to different sites.
- Use senior volunteers to take small groups or individual children for a walk into the community.
- Have parents pick up their children at the place being visited—park, swimming pool, library.

REMINDER: Before you take any children on trips outside your child care facility, you must obtain written permission from their parents. You should also check with your insurance agent to be certain that the form of transportation you will use is covered by your policy.

Intergenerational contact is not a new concept. In past generations young children were often cared for by older brothers and sisters, aunts, uncles, and grandparents. Each age level contributed to the child's knowledge of what growing up means. Each age level was a model children could imitate. Today's children who live in nuclear and mobile families may miss that experience. Using volunteers can re-create that kind of environment. It is well worth the effort in terms of benefits to the children and to the volunteers themselves.

Summary

Teachers and caregivers are sometimes reluctant to use community resources. They say the problems are difficulty in recruiting and training volunteers, transportation problems, the short time children spend at the center, and the fact that children are at such different age levels.

One way to involve children in the community is to invite individuals or representatives of agencies to visit the center. Using older persons as volunteers is one method that has been successful in some programs. A variety of activities for seniors and children is possible depending on the talents and interests of the volunteers.

Teenage volunteers can do many of the same things older persons can, but there may be some for which they are better suited. Teens can participate in more active experiences such as sports, dance, and exercise.

Community agencies, organizations, and businesses may have resources for activities that will interest children. Museums, libraries, police, and fire departments may have programs.

Businesses might be willing to conduct tours of their facilities.

An organized method of managing volunteers will make the program more effective.

Prepare a manual of information, and start volunteers doing simple, specific tasks with children. Have an orientation, provide ongoing supervision, and give volunteers feedback about performance. It is also important to have realistic expectations for your volunteers.

You may have to alter your physical environment to make the most effective use of volunteers. Have places where an adult and child can sit together and a high table that is comfortable for an adult. Provide a place where children can leave messages for volunteers and where adults can keep their belongings.

Remove barriers to community participation by using public transportation or walking to nearby sites. Rent church-owned vehicles that are unused during the week. Take small groups at a time. Use senior volunteers to take individual children into the community. Have parents pick up children at the place being visited.

Key Terms

intergenerational program
volunteer corps

Student Activities

1. Talk to an older person in your family about his or her childhood. How different was it from your own growing years? In what ways might this information help you to understand that older person better?
2. Visit a senior center in your community. Find out whether they have any volunteer programs. If they do, ask what seniors hope to get out of participating in their community. If the center does not have a volunteer program, ask why.
3. Plan one activity either a teenager or older person could do with a group of nine-year-olds. List the materials that they would need and describe any special procedures.

Review Questions

1. Caregivers are often reluctant to use community resources. List the reasons discussed in this chapter.
2. State five places to recruit senior volunteers.
3. Describe five activities in which seniors can share their cultural heritage with children.
4. Name two activities that are especially suited to teens and school-age children.
5. State the resources that are often available through museums.
6. This chapter listed seven things you can do to make a volunteer program more effective. What are they?

7. In what ways can you change the environment of a child care center to make it easier for volunteers to interact with the children?

8. This chapter stated seven ways to remove barriers to community participation. What are they?

Case Study

Bob Wolf is 67 and retired two years ago from a computer software company. He has seven grandchildren whom he loves to be with and decided he wanted to volunteer to work with young children. He found that the director and caregivers at a local business-sponsored program welcomed him with open arms. He came twice a week to the center, taught the children woodworking techniques, and spent a lot of time showing them how to use the computer. Most of the children looked forward to his days, but three boys never participated in the activities he organized. When he was not there, they sometimes imitated the way he walked and made fun of the fact that he was almost bald.

1. What should be done about the attitude of the three boys toward Bob?

2. Is there something Bob could do to help the boys feel more comfortable with him?

3. Can you think of an activity that will help children to be more accepting of older people?

Suggested Readings

Horsfall, J. (1999). Welcoming volunteers to your child care center. *Young Children 54*(6), 35–36.

Kaplan, M., Duerr, L., Whitesell, W., Merchant, L., Davis, D., & Larkin, E. (2003). *Developing an intergenerational program in your early childhood care and education center.* State College: Pennsylvania State University.

Kazemek, F., & Logas, B. (2000). Spiders, kid curlers, and white shoes. Telling and writing stories across generations. *The Reading Teacher, 53*(6), 446–451.

Lierman, H. W., & Mosher-Ashley, P. M. (2002). Strategies to expand a pen pal program from simple letters into a full intergenerational experience. *Educational Gerontology, 28,* 337–345.

Seefeldt, C., Warman, B., Jantz, R., & Galper, A. (1990). *Young and old together.* Washington, DC: National Association for the Education of Young Children.

Smith, B. J., & Yeager, A. (1999) Intergenerational communities: Where learning and interaction go hand-in-hand. *Child & Youth Services, 20*(1/2), 25–32.

CHAPTER 16

Quality and Standards

Objectives

After studying this chapter, the student should be able to:

- Discuss changes in the goals for school-age child care
- State the methods used to upgrade the quality of programs
- Relate the progress that has been made toward developing a credential
- Discuss evaluation of programs

Ellie knew from the time she was a little girl she wanted to be a teacher or an actress. That all changed when she was in high school and was in a car accident that paralyzed her from the waist down. She would be in a wheelchair for life. How could she do either of those? Because of her disability, she was able to receive physical and financial assistance at the university, so she decided to at least pursue her dream of learning about children and study child development.

Ellie had a variety of classes to choose from: preschool and kindergarten classes and an after-school enrichment program for school-age children. One of Ellie's classes also required that she participate in the university laboratory program with children. At first Ellie worked with the preschoolers. She was tenacious in her desire to succeed, and before long it became apparent to the school's director that Ellie didn't let her disability limit her. She found a way to do almost everything. When the course ended, the director hired Ellie as a teacher's assistant. Eventually Ellie moved to the kindergarten and the school-age enrichment program. She continued to flourish.

Ellie has now been in the enrichment program for two years. She says that she loves it the most. She likes being able to have more in-depth conversations with children. She is able to be more creative and complex with the curriculum she presents. She also believes by the example of her life she is able to model trying and succeeding, even when it may be difficult.

The children adore Ellie, and she is good at what she does. The center doesn't have a wheelchair ramp by one of the doors, so the children love helping Ellie get inside the classroom. Sometimes she can be found with a child on her lap zooming around the playground. Other times she may be on the basketball court throwing baskets or wheeling herself along in relay races with the children. She leads the children in movement and dance and organizes them in theatrical performances.

Someday Ellie may finish her degree and move on to be an elementary teacher. Someday she may pursue an acting career. But, for now, Ellie is happy and successful.

Changes in the Goals for Child Care

Five years ago, school-age child care was seldom included as a topic for workshops and presentations at many conferences organized by the professionals in early childhood education. Now it is frequently discussed at professional gatherings. According to the Web site www.childstats.gov, in 2002 in 78 percent of families with children under age 18, both parents worked outside the home. The need has brought about a rapid proliferation of programs. However, the increase in numbers must be accompanied by attention to quality.

Research studies show that children who attend quality programs benefit in other aspects of their life. A survey by the California Department of Education (1996) found that children in quality programs were less likely to be retained in a grade or placed in special education programs and were also less likely to have behavior problems or become involved in vandalism around their school.

Public perception of school-age child care has also changed. Early generations of after-school programs were found in settlement houses, with the purpose of caring for the children of poor or indigent families. Some were set up to offer a safe haven for children who lived in high-crime neighborhoods, to foster self-esteem, or to overcome academic deficits (Halpern, 1992). The adults were seen as supervisors or baby-sitters and little training was required or encouraged.

Early models for the curriculum were the traditional day camp or recreational prototype. During World War II, centers were set up to provide care for children of families who were working in the war industries. The centers were seen as a safe, exciting place led by activity directors and supervisors of play. Questions were being asked about what constituted quality in child care, and some workshops and technical school classes were available. Often space had to be shared with other facilities for children. At present, school-age care is recognized as an important part of services for children. It is now seen as a place for growth, nurture, and life skills. The role of the adult is as a facilitator of positive development through healthy interactions. Questions about quality focus on the kinds of adult-child interactions that promote growth. Degree and credential programs are available for training, and child care staff members are working collaboratively with school personnel.

A critical need—if quality is to be promoted and maintained—is the involvement of all those who are concerned with the education and care of children in a community. Involving such a wide range of people means there has to be communication between parents and programs and between programs and community agencies. There should also be some coordination between the various types of programs. To address the coordination issue, some communities have developed child care councils made up of representatives from the various factions of the child care community. Their meetings and discussions focus on the needs of the community, policies regarding quality, ways to facilitate communications, and ways to affect legislative actions. More recently, state and federal departments of education are seeing the need to become involved.

Child Care in the 21st Century

Former Secretary Donna Shalala, U.S. Department of Health and Human Services, gave the keynote address at the Annual State Child Care Administrators Meeting in Washington, DC, on July 29, 1998. She opened her address with a discussion of quality. She expressed her admiration for caregivers, calling them "heroes," but said that even heroes need a helping hand sometimes. She challenged state and county administrators across the country to provide support as well as financial incentives. She pointed to the challenge made by President Clinton's Child Care Initiative and his commitment to providing quality care for all children. To that end, the Child Care Bureau was created, and in turn the bureau has set up a National Child Care Information Center that shares trends and ideas with states and communities. Money has been added to the new welfare law to promote quality care.

Secretary Shalala listed what she believes constitutes quality care:

- good interaction between the provider and parents
- continuous improvement strategy that remains current on child development research
- strong and meaningful relationships with families based on trust and sharing information about children
- teaming up with health experts and building a system where children's health is monitored
- supportive directors who respond to staff needs but also demand accountability
- good working conditions for all providers, meaning decent pay, leave, and family-friendly policies as well as good working space

Shalala further urged her audience to involve the community. She pointed to the wisdom and experience of teachers, parents, clergy, businesses, and law enforcement. She said they should all be a part of decisions about funding, safety, training, eligibility, and access.

On January 8, 2002, George W. Bush signed legislation putting into effect his policy "No Child Left Behind" (NCLB). The NCLB Act expands the federal government's role as outlined in the Elementary and Secondary Education Act (ESEA) of 1965. The NCLB is aimed at disadvantaged students and sets strict requirements and deadlines for participation. There are four main points to NCLB:

- accountability measured by frequent testing
- more flexibility in how states, school districts, and schools use the federal funds
- more options for parents of children from disadvantaged backgrounds
- more use of teaching methods based on scientifically proven research studies selected by government agencies

In addition, the act guarantees that every classroom is staffed by qualified teachers and that the gap between advantaged and disadvantaged children, as reflected in test scores, is narrowed. Although this program does not directly affect what happens in after-school programs, it is important that child care personnel be aware of what is happening in schools. Some aspects of this program are controversial and are being questioned by teachers and professional organizations. More information about the No Child Left Behind policy can be found at the following Web site: http://www.ed.gov/nclb.

Accreditation and Standards
National AfterSchool Association (NAA)

Several years have gone into developing the standards that NAA uses. The pilot statement was drafted in 1995 after several years of research and field testing but revised in 1997.

The latest version grew out of discussions with personnel from pilot sites and school-age care professionals as well as review by the NAA Accreditation Advisory Board. The standards reflect the best practices for children between the ages of 5 and 14. They are meant to be used in group settings where children attend on a regular basis. Programs can use the guidelines for a self-study leading to accreditation.

The professionals who developed NAA standards believe there is a need for an accreditation and improvement process that specifically addresses school-age care. Some of the unique characteristics of programs that serve this population are the following:

- They usually serve a wide range of ages, from age 5 to 14.
- They often share facilities with other programs, preschools, recreational buildings, and elementary schools.
- Staff members may work at other jobs as well as caregiving.
- They often must organize their calendar around school schedules.
- A unique combination of skills is needed to do the work well.

NAA also believes that there is a need for a system that raises public awareness of the importance of out-of-school care and its impact on the future development of children. It was their intent to develop a process whereby centers could use the guidelines to improve quality whether they eventually applied for accreditation or not. Experience has shown that most programs continue to work toward improving quality even after they have completed the accreditation process.

NAA Standards

The standards are divided into six sections. The following paragraphs present a brief summary of each of those sections.

Human Relationships

Interactions between staff and children should be positive and appropriate to the needs of the children. This guideline includes sensitivity to each child's interests and abilities as well as her culture and home language. Interactions should help children to make choices, become more responsible, and learn the skills they need to be successful. Staff members should use positive guidance techniques that encourage children to resolve their own conflicts and to interact with one another in positive ways. This section also has statements about including families and ways that staff should work well together to meet the needs of children.

Indoor Environment

Indoor space should meet the needs of the children they serve, including space for all program activities. The space should be arranged so that a variety of activities can take place and allow children to participate without disruption. Indoor space encourages children to explore their own interests by providing convenient places to store and retrieve materials. Work space should reflect the children's interests.

Indoor space should meet the needs of the children served and be arranged so that a variety of activities can take place.

Outdoor Environment

The outdoor environment meets the needs of school-age children and allows them to be independent and creative. There should be at least 30 minutes of outdoor play for every three-hour block of time, during which children can use a variety of equipment or participate in a variety of activities.

Activities

The daily schedule is flexible, allowing transitions to be smooth and children to go at their own pace. There should be time enough for children to choose from a variety of activities that reflect the mission of the program. There should be enough materials to support those activities.

Safety, Health, and Nutrition

The safety and security of children are of utmost importance. All observable hazards are secured, and systems are in place to protect children from harm. The environment should enhance the health of children, and staff are responsive to individual health needs. Children are supervised in such a way as to maintain safety at all times and in accordance with children's ages, abilities, and needs. All foods served at the facility should be healthy and appropriate for the ages and sizes of the children.

Administration

The number of staff members should vary according to group size, the ages of the children, and the complexity of the activity. There should be a staff plan for maintaining adequate supervision of children at all times. Policies are in place to keep parents informed and support their involvement in the program. Administrative policies should foster cooperation with schools and the community. Administration guidelines also include statements regarding qualifications of staff and the establishment of policies that encourage ongoing training and adequate working conditions.

With the current increase in the need for care for young children when the school day is finished, this seems an optimum time for looking at ways to increase the quality of that time. The NSACA standards are certainly one way to achieve that.

The full text of the standards can be obtained from:

National School-Age Care Alliance
1137 Washington Street
Boston, MA 02124
http://www.nsaca.org

National Association for the Education of Young Children (NAEYC)

NAEYC is a large national professional association that provides a service for accrediting programs that serve children from birth through the elementary years. The program is administered by the National Academy of Early Childhood Programs. The system is voluntary and involves a three-step process: self-study by the director, staff members, and parents; validation visits by trained professionals; and an accreditation decision by a team of early childhood experts. Schools can pace the length of time involved in completing the process, but it usually takes from 4 to 18 months.

The critical step in the process is the self-study. The program administrator pays a fee and then receives an accreditation manual. The director, staff, and parents use the manual to rate the quality of the program in 10 different categories. When the study is completed, a final report is prepared and sent to the academy. Academy personnel review the materials to determine whether the information is complete or whether further information is needed.

Accreditation covers the following categories of center operations:

* interactions among staff and children
* curriculum
* staff/parent interactions
* staff qualifications and development
* administration
* staffing patterns
* physical environment
* health and safety
* nutrition and food service
* evaluation process

Self-study by a committee of staff members and parents is the first step in the accreditation process.

When all materials are ready, the academy appoints one or more validators, and they in turn schedule a visit. The purpose of the visit is to observe the day-to-day operations to verify that they are as described in the report. The final step involves an accreditation commission consisting of three professionals. The commission reviews the information provided by the validators and decides to grant accreditation or defer it until further improvements are made. Deferred centers can appeal the decision. Accreditation is valid for three years, during which time centers must submit annual reports. Before expiration, the accreditation process must be repeated. Further information about accreditation can be obtained from:

National Academy of Early Childhood Programs
1509 16th Street NW
Washington, DC 20036-1426
800-424-2460 202-328-2601
Fax 202-328-1846
E-mail: NAEYC@naeyc.org
http://naeyc.org

National Association for Family Child Care (NAFCC)

According to NAFCC, one million family child care providers care for four million children, some of whom are elementary-school ages. Along with the move to professionalize all child care settings, NAFCC felt it important to develop a process for accrediting home-based child care. Their quality standards for NAFCC accreditation were developed in conjunction with the Family Child Care Project at Wheelock College, Boston, Massachusetts.

The provider reviews the accreditation workbook and identifies areas that need improvement. The next step is to design a professional development plan followed by improvements. When the provider is ready, she notifies NAFCC to schedule a visit. The provider receives an observer visit packet, including a self-observation to complete before the observer visit. The visit is scheduled. The observer scores the visit. If standards are met, accreditation is awarded for three years. If the score is not high enough, accreditation can be deferred until the conditions can be corrected. If a provider moves, the new site must be reaccredited.

The categories used to score a setting for accreditation follow:

- relationships that convey a sense of belonging to children, parents, provider's family, and community
- a welcoming environment with enough materials to engage children and support their interests
- activities that are both child directed and adult directed
- developmental learning goals that are appropriate for the ages of the children
- policies and procedures that ensure the safety and health of children
- professional and business practices that reflect concern for ethics and legality as well as time for professional activities

NAFCC Quality Standards for Accreditation, 1999 edition, can be obtained from:

The National Association for Family Child Care
5202 Pinemont Drive
Salt Lake City, UT 84123
801-269-9338
FAX: 801-268-9509
E-mail: nafcc@nafcc.org
http://www.nafcc.org

Credentials

Child Development Associate

Upgrading the quality of programs can also be accomplished through training and credentialing of teachers. The Child Development Associate (CDA) credential is a nationally recognized credential for early childhood teachers and has been used in preschools, child care, and Head Start programs. The curriculum for attaining the credential was designed by the Council for Early Childhood Professional Recognition and contains a set of goals and a series of graduated experiences. The goals are:

1. to establish and maintain a safe, healthy learning environment
2. to advance physical and intellectual competence

3. to support social and emotional development and provide guidance
4. to establish positive and productive relationships with families
5. to ensure a well-run, purposeful program responsive to participant needs
6. to maintain a commitment to professionalism

These graduated experiences are divided into three phases. Phase I is fieldwork with students participating in the daily activities of a program. They are also required to prepare written work, complete exercises, and read. During Phase II, students attend courses or seminars offered by local colleges, universities, or postsecondary institutions. The final phase, Phase III, is meant to integrate and evaluate the student's experiences. During this period, the student returns to working with children while also completing a series of exercises. The last step in the process is interviews with a council representative in which all the documents are reviewed. If the representative's review is positive, the candidate receives a Child Development Associate credential that is valid for life.

For information about the CDA credential, contact:

Council for Early Childhood Professional Recognition
2460 16th Street NW
Washington, DC 20009-3575
202-265-9090
800-424-4310
Fax: 202-265-9161
http://www.cdacouncil.org

National Institute on Out-of-School Time (NIOST)

Formerly called the School-Age Care Project, NIOST has been working to improve the quality of out-of-school time for 20 years. Their focus has been on five areas: education and training, community development, consultation, research, and public awareness. Their target population has been parents, program staff members, community leaders, and government officials.

NIOST began a project to evaluate innovative approaches to both the care of children and preparation and training of staff. They called the project MOST (Making the Most of Out-of-School Time). Three cities (Boston, Chicago, and Seattle) spent three years implementing and evaluating the project. A consulting firm, Nilsen Associates, was commissioned to write a report on one of the most important questions raised by the MOST initiative (Nilsen, 1999), that of staff preparation and credentialing. The report uses the definition of a credential proposed by Morgan (1998) that a credential is a "formal certificate, permit or document that certifies that an individual has mastered a set of skills and has demonstrated competence in caring for children." Colleges and universities issue credentials, as do some professional associations. Community organizations and even employers sometimes award a credential or certificate to those who complete specified requirements. The question is being raised among school-age care professionals about who is best suited to establish the criteria for a credential.

A national survey conducted by Nilsen found that half of the states already have a credential, are doing a pilot study, or are planning one. About one-third do not have a credential and are not planning one. There were 21 credentialing programs from 17 states that had the following common characteristics:

- Almost half were offered by a college.
- Entry requirements were minimal.
- About 75 percent offer college credit.
- Most require the candidate to pay a fee.
- The program took an average of two years to plan.
- Many community entities participated in the development.
- Most have some paid staff.

The Nilsen survey found that some credentials require little investment in time, from as little as a day, while others that take up to two years. Many states are using the CDA credential even though it is specifically designed for caregivers of children under five years of age. Therefore, the question of what components should comprise a credential is being discussed among child care professionals across the United States.

Report Recommendations

The report made recommendations to both local and national leaders about ways to expedite credentialing efforts for school-age care. The following list is a brief summary of those recommendations.

Locally

- Planning efforts should include as many community individuals and organizations as possible.
- If it all possible, there should be a source of funding for the planning process.
- Planners should think creatively about the relationship with a state licensing agency.

Nationally

- Information should be gathered about who the recipients of credentials are and what the impact on quality outcomes is.
- Some in the school-age child care (SAC) community advocate that NSACA take on credentialing in the same way that the Council for Early Childhood Professional Recognition has done. That would require tremendous resources and would conflict with some of the innovative programs that are already in place.
- There is an expressed need to set guidelines or standards for what a credential should include.
  a. core competencies or bodies of knowledge
  b. number of hours to spend on training
  c. qualifications of instructors
  d. evaluation methods
  e. alternative ways to demonstrate knowledge or competence
  f. provisions for ensuring access to a diverse population in the workforce

The report also recommended that standards be tied to the Advancing and Recognizing Quality (ARQ, Assessing School-Age Quality self-study) and the accreditation process NSACA uses (described in a previous section).

The full Nilsen Associates report and the ARQ can be obtained from:

National Institute on Out-of-School Time (NIOST)
Center for Research on Women
Wellesley College
106 Central Street
Wellesley, MA 02481-8203
781-283-1547
Fax: 781-283-3657
http://www.wellesley.edu

Evaluation

School-Age Care Environmental Rating Scale (SACERS)

Developed by Thelma Harms and her two Canadian colleagues Ellen Jacobs and Donna White, the SACERS grew out of a need to have a method of rating programs that serve the 5 to 12-year age range. Harms, Jacobs, and White drew from a number of sources, starting with the criteria for developmentally appropriate practice. They also used research studies done in Canada and the United States (Galambos & Garbarino, 1983; Vandell & Corasanti, 1988; Vandell, Henderson, & Wilson, 1988). The SACERS is also an adaptation of an earlier rating scale, the Early Childhood Environment Rating Scale, done by Harms.

Specially trained observers use a numerical scale to perform the assessment. Each of the seven categories is rated on a scale of one to seven based on written criteria for each item. The following is a brief description of the items listed in each category.

Space and Furnishings, Indoor Space

The scale assesses whether there is sufficient space for gross-motor activities as well as space for privacy. The room arrangement should have adequate space for all activities: homework, routine care, and learning and recreation. Furnishings should allow for children's relaxation and comfort and gross-motor activities. There should be easy access to the host facility and space for staff.

Health and Safety

This section examines the health policies and practices. Emergency and safety procedures must be in place. Attendance is monitored, and departures are managed to bring about maximum safety for the children. Meal times are planned as a learning experience, and personal hygiene is part of the educational program.

Activities

Eight types of activities are described in this section: arts and crafts, music and movement, blocks and construction, drama/theater, language/reading, math/reasoning, science/nature,

Trained observers use the School-Age Care Environmental Scale to determine whether a program is meeting standards for developmental appropriateness.

and cultural awareness. Assessment is made on the basis of frequency, variety of materials and equipment available, and age-level appropriateness. The cultural-awareness category includes ways that staff encourage acceptance of differences.

Interactions

This section on interactions refers to staff interactions with children, with parents, and with one another. Interactions with children should support autonomous behavior and convey feelings of respect and interest. Staff should also talk to children about ideas related to play activities, helping children to extend their ideas. Parents are informed about policies concerning discipline and also receive information on parenting, health care, sports, and cultural activities for families. Parents are included in decision making as well. The program should promote positive interactions among staff members and classroom teachers.

Program Structure

The schedule of the day should allow smooth transitions and time for children to make choices of activities. Community resources should be used to plan field trips or special-occasion activities. The director and key staff member meet on a regular basis with the host of the program to discuss and resolve any problems.

Staff Development

Staff should have opportunities and support to attend professional conferences or workshops. Staff meetings include planned opportunities for participants to share new ideas and materials. Self-evaluation by staff is an ongoing process.

Special-Needs Supplementary Items

This section is used in conjunction with the preceding items when children with special needs are included in the program. Items address objectives to bring about individualization, appropriate learning opportunities, efforts to promote peer interactions, and ways that staff promote communication.

The full text of this rating scale can be obtained from:

Teachers College Press
Columbia University
1234 Amsterdam Avenue
New York, NY 10027
212-678-3929
Fax: 212-678-44149
E-mail: tcpress@tccolumbia.edu
http://www.tcpress.com

Assessing Children's Progress

An important part of evaluating the overall quality of a program should also include an assessment of individual children. According to Lilian Katz (1997), "Assessment should serve one of the following purposes: to determine progress on significant developmental achievements; to make placement or promotion decisions; to diagnose learning and teaching problems; to help in instruction and curriculum decisions; to serve as a basis for reporting to parents; and to assist a child with assessing his or her own progress." Child care leaders do not need to make decisions concerning children's promotions from one grade level to the next, but all of the other purposes Katz stated are pertinent to the child care setting.

Observation

There are several ways to assess children's progress by observing and recording behaviors. One of these is the anecdotal record. The child is observed in a variety of situations while the adult writes down what he does and what he says. This may not be the most accurate picture of a child's behavior because only a small portion of what is happening can be written down. What is there is what the adult decides is important and may present an incomplete picture. It is also true that two people looking at the same situation may see entirely different actions (Click, 2004). Another form of observation is the event recording. The observer chooses a specific situation in which to observe and record behavior. For instance, if the adult wants to find out how a child reacts during group times, then an observer must see the child in that situation several times.

The time or duration sampling looks at behavior at intervals of time and for a specified period of time, such as every half hour for five minutes. This kind of observation may show the presence or absence of certain behaviors. The method can be especially helpful in detecting the frequency of aggressive outbursts, whether a child spends more time alone or with other children, or a child's attention span.

The most accurate observation occurs when the adult uses a video camera or tape recorder. This method is especially useful because more than one person can observe behavior and make the assessment. Further discussion among the observers can yield more pertinent information.

A checklist can also be used to assess a child's behavior. This is a list of predetermined behaviors to be observed. The observer checks off one of several choices indicating whether the behavior occurred or not. The following is a sample of a checklist regarding a child's interactions with other children.

	Usually	Sometimes	Never
Approaches others			
Uses appropriate language to enter a play situation			
Disrupts the play			
Is cooperative			

Self-assessment

Children should be encouraged to assess their own progress. A conference between the adult and child can result in a list of goals to be reached. What is it that the child wants to improve or what does he need to concentrate more on? Is it his ability to hit more balls during baseball games, or is it his ability to curb aggressive behaviors in order to make friends? These should come from the child with support from the adult to clearly define the goals. Most children, once they reach the school-age years, can be fairly realistic about what they can and cannot expect to do. Katz (1995) also says, "In principle, unless children are consulted about their own views of their own progress, they cannot learn to assume some responsibility for it."

Additional information about assessment can be found at the following Web sites:

Center for the Study of Testing, Evaluation, and Educational Policy: position papers and policy statements.
http://www.csteep.bc.edu
Project Spectrum: lists articles on assessment.
http://pzweb.harvard.edu

Summary

The perception of school-age care has changed from only being a safe place for children to one that is a place for growth, nurture, and life skills. The role of the adult as babysitter has changed to that of a facilitator of positive development. There is a critical need for ways to ensure quality. To that end, in 1998 President Clinton enacted his Child Care 2000, a Vision for the Children. The U.S. Department of Health and Human Services established the Child Care Bureau, which in turn set up a National Child Care Information Center. Secretary Shalala of the Department established a set of quality guidelines.

The National AfterSchool Association (NAA) developed standards that it uses for accreditation or to upgrade programs. The standards are divided into sections: human relationships; indoor environment; outdoor environment; activities; safety, health, and nutrition; and administration. The National Association for the Education of Young Children (NAEYC) also developed a set of standards that can lead to accreditation. The process involves a self-study plus evaluation by professionals. Categories used for the study are the following: interactions among staff and children; curriculum; staff/parent interactions; staff qualifications and development; administration; staffing patterns; physical environment; health and safety; nutrition and food service; and evaluation process.

Family child care providers can also be accredited by the National Association for Family Child Care (NAFCC). The provider designs a professional-development plan followed by any necessary improvements. This is followed by an observation visit, after which the provider can be accredited. The categories used are relationships that convey a sense of belonging, an environment that is welcoming, activities that are both child directed and adult directed, developmental learning goals that are age appropriate, policies and procedures that ensure safety, and professional business practices.

A credential is another way to upgrade quality through the training and education of staff. The Council for Early Childhood Professional Recognition designed the Child Development Associate credential that is used in preschools, child care, and Head Start programs. The credential is based on the following goals: establish and maintain a safe learning environment; advance physical and intellectual competence; support social and emotional development; establish positive relationships with children; ensure a well-run, purposeful program; and maintain a commitment to professionalism. To obtain the credential, the student must complete fieldwork, do written work, attend courses or seminars, apply knowledge in a setting with children, and participate in interviews with evaluators.

National interest in improving quality has prompted the National Institute on Out-of-School Time (NIOST) to focus on becoming an advocate for credentialing or certification. The activities of the organization target local, state, and national sources for developing a credential that will specifically meet the needs of child care professionals.

The last method of upgrading quality discussed in this chapter is evaluation. Thelma Harms and two colleagues developed the School-Age Care Environmental Scale (SACERS). Evaluators use seven categories on which to rate programs: space, indoor space and furnishings, health and safety, activities, interactions, program structure, and staff development. A supplementary section applies to programs that include children with special needs. Assessment of individual children should be part of evaluating overall quality of a program. There are several methods that can be used. Observation is frequently the method of choice, and includes anecdotal records, event recording, time or duration sampling, and a checklist. A video camera or tape recorder can also be used to make a record of behaviors and situations. Children should be encouraged to assess their own progress.

Key Terms

anecdotal record
CDA
checklist
child care councils
event recording
NAA
NAEYC

NAFCC
NIOST
SACERS
self-assessment
time or duration sampling
video camera or tape recording

Student Activities

1. Copy pages from the NAA standards. Work with other students in small groups to discuss one of the sections. If a center where they work or are doing practice teaching were applying for accreditation by this organization, what would it be like?

   Describe the environment, both indoors and outdoors.
   Delineate ways that interactions would be fostered.
   Describe what is being done to foster good health and nutrition.
   What administrative procedures are in place?

2. Ask students to find out which centers in their community are accredited and by whom. Assign small groups to interview selected center directors. Have them ask the following:

   How difficult was it to go through the process?
   Which people were the most helpful in achieving your goal?
   How long did it take?
   What has the result been?
   Was the effort worth it?

   Have each group report to the class on their findings.

Review Questions

1. Discuss the ways public perception of after-school care has changed.
2. What has NAA done to upgrade standards for out-of-school time?
3. Describe the accreditation process NAEYC uses.
4. Can family child care providers be accredited? If so, by whom?
5. List the goals on which the Child Development Associate credential is based.
6. How has NIOST worked toward increasing quality in child care?
7. What is the name of the rating instrument that Thelma Harms and her colleagues developed?
8. List the seven categories Harms used.

Case Study

The director/owner of the Little Oaks Child Care Center has already achieved accreditation for her preschool program. She is very proud of this fact and believes it has helped to fill her enrollment and even to generate a waiting list. She has just returned from a conference where she heard about the National AfterSchool Association. She learned that the alliance has developed a set of standards for school-age programs that can lead to accreditation and has obtained a copy of their material. She wants very much for her after-school staff members to review the standards and start the process leading to accreditation. Most of the caregivers are eager to start, but several are resistant, saying they don't think they need a stamp of approval on their program.

1. Why do you think some staff members resist the idea of accreditation?
2. What would you do about the attitude of the resistors?
3. How can the director help them to be more positive toward the process?

References

California Department of Education. (1996). *School age care in California.* Sacramento: Child Development Division.

Click, P. (2004). *Administration of programs for young children* (6th ed.). Clifton Park, NY: Thomson Delmar Learning.

Galambos, N., & Garbarino, J. (1983). Identifying the missing links in the study of latchkey children. *Children Today, 13,* 2–4.

Halpern, R. (1992). The role of after-school programs in the lives of inner city children. *Child Welfare, 71,* 215–230.

Katz, L. G. (1995). *Talks with teachers of young children: A collection.* Norwood, NJ: Ablex.

Katz, L. G. (1997). *A developmental approach to assessment of young children.* (ERIC Digest ED407172).

Morgan, G. (1998). *Credentialing in out-of-school time programs.* Wellesley, MA: National Institute on Out-of-School time, Center for Research on Women.

National School-Age Care Alliance. (1998). *The NSACA standards for quality school-age care.* Boston: Author.

Nilsen, E. A. (1999). *On the road to SAC professionalism, emerging models, trends, and issues in credentialing: A working paper.* Wellesley, MA: National Institute on Out-of-School Time.

Statistics. http://www.childstats.gov

Vandell, D. L., & Corasanti, M. A. (1988). The relations between third-graders' afterschool care and social, academic, and emotional functioning. *Child Development, 59*(4), 868–875.

Vandell, D. L., & Su, H. (1999). Child care and school-age children. *Young Children, 54*(6), 62–71.

Vandell, D. L., Henderson, V. K., & Wilson, K. S. (1988). A longitudinal study of children with day-care experiences of varying quality. *Child Development, 59*(5), 1286–1292.

Suggested Readings

Marion, M., & Mindes, G. (2004). Resources on assessment. *Young Children, 59*(1), 54–55.

NAEYC. (2004). Where we stand on curriculum assessment, and program evaluation. *Young Children, 59*(1), 51–53.

Web Resources

The National AfterSchool Association http://www.naaweb.org
The National Association for the Education of Young Children http://www.naeyc.org
The National Association for Family Child Care http://www.nafcc.org
Council for Professional Recognition http://www.cdacouncil.org
National Institute on Out-of-School Time http://www.niost.org

APPENDIX

All About Me

_____

Name

Adapted from material written by JoAnn Kosko Simmons.

Full name: _____

I want to be called: _____

Parent(s): _____

Address: _____

_____

Phone number: _____

Vital Statistics!

THEN

Date of birth: _____

Place of birth: _____
          (city, state)

_____
          (hospital)

Weight at birth: _____ pounds, _____ ounces.   Length at birth: _____ inches

Hair color at birth: _____

Eye color at birth: _____

NOW

Height now: _____ feet _____ inches

Hair color now: _____ Eye color now: _____

ABOUT MY FAMILY . . .

Members of my family include: _____

_____

_____

_____

_____

I am told that I look like: _____

Here are some pictures of:

ME   MY FAMILY

MY FRIENDS

The person I consider my best friend is: _____

My newest friend is: _____

The qualities that I admire in friends are: _____

MY MEMORIES

My first memory of my childhood was: _____

_____

_____

The first birthday that I remember was: _____

_____

My first memories of school include: _____

_____

Some of the things that I would like you to know about me are: _____

_____

_____

I think I am: _____

_____

_____

THOUGHTS ABOUT SCHOOL

What is your favorite school subject?_____

What is your least favorite subject? _____

Do you like to read? Why or why not? _____

_____

What do you like to read?_____

_____

What is the best book you ever read or had read to you? _____

Do you usually have homework assignments every day? _____

How much time do you usually need to spend completing your homework?_____

_____

Do you occasionally need help with some subjects?_____

Do you have any special interests or things you like to do? _____

Would you be willing to share your interests with your classmates? _____

If you could plan a day in your after-school program, what would be included?_____

_____

_____

If you could invite two famous people to join our class for a day, they would be:_____

_____and_____

FAVORITE THINGS

Favorite food: _____

Favorite meal: _____

Prepared by: _____

Favorite color:_____

Second favorite color:_____

Favorite group (musical): _____

Favorite song: _____

Favorite board game: _____

Favorite sport to play: _____

Favorite sport to watch: _____

Favorite TV show: _____

Second favorite TV show: _____

Favorite hobby: _____

Favorite season:_____

MY GOALS

This year I want to be able to: _____

FOR PARENTS

Some things that I would like you to know about my child include: _____

_____

He/She has the following talents: _____

He/She has the following strengths as a student: _____

He/She has experienced some difficulty with the following subject(s) in school: _____

_____

_____

My child learns best by: _____

My thoughts on homework are: _____

_____

Other information you should know about my child: _____

_____

A funny/amusing anecdote I would like to share about my child would be the time that:

_____

_____

I would be willing to share my talents/skills with the class for the purpose of enrichment.
My talents/skills include: _____

_____

I would like to get involved with my child's after-school experience in the following way(s):_____

_____

The most convenient time(s) for me to do so are: _____

Should a problem arise with my child, I would like you to handle it in the following manner: _____

_____

_____

If you need to contact me, the best time to do so would be:

_____ at work _____-_____-_____ between _____ and _____

_____ at home _____-_____-_____ after _____ no later than _____

(signature) _____

(date) _____

Internet Links
for Information

The authors and Thomson Delmar Learning affirm that the Web site URLs referenced below were accurate at the time of printing. However, due to the fluid nature of the Internet, we cannot guarantee their accuracy for the life of the edition.

- ADA and Disability Information: http://www.ada.gov
- Administration for Children and Families: http://www.acf.dhhs.gov
- Afterschool.gov: http://www.afterschool.gov
- The American Academy of Pediatrics: http://www.aap.org
- Association for Childhood Education International: http://www.acei.org
- Bureau of Labor Statistics: http://www.bls.gov
- Center for the Child Care Workforce: http://www.ccw.org
- Centers for Disease Control and Prevention: http://www.cdc.gov
- Child Care Bureau: http:www.acf.dhhs.gov select "Child Care Bureau" from Program drop down menu in lower left corner
- Children's Defense Fund: http://www.childrensdefense.org
- Council for Early Childhood Professional Recognition: http://www.cdacouncil.org
- The Council for Exceptional Children: http://www.cec.sped.org
- Day Care Provider's Beginner Page: http://www.oursite.net click on "Daycare Provider's Beginner Page"
- ERIC Clearinghouse on Elementary and Early Childhood Education (ERIC/EECE): http://www.eric.ed.gov
- The Food Allergy & Anaphylaxis Network: http: //www.foodallergy.org
- Food and Nutrition Information Center: http://www.nal.usda.gov/ click on search our website. Type in "Food and Nutrition Information Center" in the search field
- Frank Porter Graham Child Development Center: http://www.fpg.unc.edu
- The Future of Children: http://www.futureofchildren.org
- General Accounting Office (GAO) Reports: http://www.access.gpo.gov
- Harvard Family Research Project, Harvard University: http://gseweb.harvard.edu type "Family Research Project" in search field
- Head Start Bureau: http://www.acf.dhhs.gov select "Head Start Bureau" from program drop down menu in lower left corner
- Health Care Financing Administration (HFCA): http://www.cms.hhs.gov
- I Am Your Child Public Engagement Campaign: http://www.iamyourchild.org
- Library of Congress: http://www.loc.gov
- Military Child Development Program: http://military-childrenandyouth.calib.com
- National AfterSchool Association: http://www.naaweb.org
- National Center for Health Statistics: http://www.cdc.gov type "National Center for Health Statistics" in search field
- National Association of Child Care Professionals: http://www.naccp.org
- National Association for the Education of Young Children (NAEYC): http://naeyc.org
- National Association for Family Child Care: http://www.nafcc.org
- National Child Care Information Center: http://nccic.org
- National Information Center for Children and Youth with Disabilities: http://www.nichcy.org
- National Institute on Out-of-School-Time: http://www.niost.org
- National Network for Child Care: http://www.nncc.org

- National Parent Information Network: http://npin.org
- National Program for Playground Safety: http://www.playgroundsafety.org
- National Research Council: http://www.nas.edu. click on "National Research Council"
- National Resource Center for Health and Safety in Child Care: http://nrc.uchsc.edu
- National SAFEKIDS Campaign: http://www.safekids.org
- Quality Care for Children: http://qualitycareforchildren.org
- School-Age Notes: http://www.schoolagenotes.com
- The Urban Institute: http://www.urban.org
- U.S. Census Bureau: http://www.census.gov
- U.S. Department of Education: http://www.ed.gov
- U.S. Department of Health and Human Services: http://www.os.dhhs.gov
- Welfare Information Network: http://www.financeprojectinfo.org
- World Bank: http://www.worldbank.org

Art Lesson Plans

Newspaper Sculptures

Brief description: Firmly rolled newspapers are taped together randomly to create a three-dimensional structure.

Materials:

> ½-inch dowels, 3 feet long (at least 4)
> Newspaper
> Masking tape
> Large piece of cardboard for the base of the structure

Procedure: Lay newspaper flat. Place dowel on one corner of the paper at an angle. Roll paper tightly around dowel rolling from one corner to the opposite corner. Secure with a small piece of tape. Slide dowel out from paper. Continue making paper rolls (50 or more will be needed).

Begin constructing the sculpture by taping one end of each newspaper roll to the cardboard base. The other end will be taped to other rolls in whatever manner the children decide.

Role of the leader: Gather materials. Most of these can be brought in by children or donated by parents. Dowels can be purchased at your local hardware store. Dedicate ample space for the ongoing sculptures. Encourage children to work in teams.

Extension: Paint the sculpture when completed.

Craft Dough Sculptures

Brief description: Children will make free-form sculptures that can be dried and painted.

Materials:

> 1 cup cornstarch
> 2 cups baking soda (1-lb. box)
> 1¼ cups water
> Tempura paint
> Small paintbrushes
> Wax paper

Procedure: Combine cornstarch, baking soda, and water and cook until thickened to dough-like consistency. Turn mixture out on to a pastry board and knead. Cover with damp cloth or keep in plastic bag. Children will mold piece of dough to desired result. Place sculpture on wax paper. Let air-dry. (May take several days.) Children can paint sculptures when dried.

Role of the leader: Dough must be prepared and cooled prior to use by children. Be available to scaffold for children who struggle implementing their ideas. They may need techniques to use. Encourage children to share their techniques with one another.

Extensions: Experiment with other types of doughs. Advance to modeling clay. Introduce tools used for working with clay. Use tools such as toothpicks, the end of straws, combs, scissors, etc., to make details in dough.

Tissue Paper Art

Brief Description: Children will explore books by Eric Carle to see how he uses tissue paper in his illustrations. They will make their own creations by cutting and layering tissue paper pieces.

Materials:

>   Several colors of tissue paper (cut into pieces about 4 inches square)
>   12 × 18-inch white drawing paper
>   Scissors
>   Thinned white glue
>   Containers to hold thinned glue
>   ½" to 1" wide paintbrushes
>   Books by Eric Carle

Procedure: Children will examine pictures in Eric Carle books, notice the colors used, and make predictions about how they are layered. Children will cut tissue paper into desired shapes. Thinned white glue will be painted onto paper in areas where tissue paper will be placed. Tissue paper shapes will be laid onto the glue to create designs or pictures.

Role of the leader: Prepare materials. Search Internet Web sites for information about Eric Carle's illustrations made from tissue paper. Experiment with making tissue paper art to determine how much to thin the glue.

Extensions: Learn about other illustrator techniques used in children's books. Try some of them and determine if any are appropriate for children's use.

Salt Painting

Brief description: Children will paint a picture or design then sprinkle salt onto the wet paint. The salt gives a unique sheen to the finished painting.

Materials:

>   Variety of brightly colored tempura paint
>   Variety of sizes of easel paintbrushes
>   12 × 18-inch black construction paper
>   Salt in saltshakers

Procedure: Children will paint desired picture or design on paper. When finished they will sprinkle salt onto paint. Finished paper will be placed on a flat surface in the sun for drying.

Role of the leader: Provide ample materials and drying space for painting. Involve children in setup and cleanup of materials including the washing of paintbrushes.

Extensions: Paint on different colors of construction paper. Sprinkle glitter, sand, or soap flakes onto wet paint.

Stencil Art

Brief description: Children will make their own stencil, paint it, and make a print of their stencil.

Materials:

> Clean Styrofoam meat trays (run them through the dishwasher for disinfecting prior to use)
> Blunt pencils
> Small paint rollers
> Two to three colors of tempura paint placed in Styrofoam tray
> Plain newsprint cut into pieces slightly larger than the meat trays

Procedure: Children will use blunt pencil to press into the bottom of the meat tray making a design or picture. Press only hard enough to indent into the Styrofoam, creating an imprinted design. Use the paint roller to apply a thin layer of paint to the entire bottom of the tray. Place a piece of paper on top of the paint; press then lift off. It should be a print of the design. Children will have to work at the technique of getting the right amount of paint to produce a clear stencil.

Role of leader: Leaders will collect materials. Parents can be asked to donate Styrofoam meat trays. Pour a small amount of paint into a Styrofoam tray and spread with a paint roller to get the roller ready for painting. Involve children in cleanup of activity.

Extension: Paper can be placed over stencils and rubbed with the side of crayons to make a crayon rubbing.

Music Lesson Plans

Foot Conducting

Brief description: Children will use instruments to make music by following the directions of a conductor who conducts with his feet.

Materials:

> At least four kinds of instruments
> Hoops approximately 2 feet in diameter (can be made from yarn or tape on the floor; need one hoop for each kind of instrument, that is, five kinds of instruments requires five hoops).
> Instrumental music and CD or record player

Procedure: Children sit in a circle (or semicircle) with the conductor placed in the middle. Distribute instruments to children so that children with the same kind of instrument are sitting next to each other. Place the hoops on the floor, one in front of each group of musicians. The conductor will step in and out of the circles to direct the musicians. Children will accompany the instrumental music by playing their instruments when the conductor has his or her foot in the hoop in front of them.

Role of the leader: Gather instruments and select a variety of instrumental music. The leader will need to model the process of conducting. Select children to take turns conducting the musicians. The leader should continue to facilitate the activity even though children are conducting.

Extensions: Children can learn how to conduct using their hands. Visit a local school band practice or performance.

Who Stole the Cookie Jar Chant

Brief description: Children will work together to clap in rhythm and accompany clapping with a chant.

Materials:

None

Procedure: Children will sit in a circle. Leader will begin clapping rhythm (clap, then slap hands on thighs, clap, slap, etc.). Everyone claps and chants throughout the entire chant. Once class is in rhythm, the leader begins the chant.
"<u>Who</u> <u>stole</u> the <u>cook</u>ie <u>from</u> the <u>cook</u>-<u>ie</u> <u>jar</u>?" (Clap and slap on the underlined words and syllables.)
"<u>(Child's name)</u> stole the cookie from the cookie jar!"
Child responds: "Who me?"
Leader: "Yes, you!"
Child: "Couldn't be!"
Leader: "Then who?"
That child continues with the chant naming another child. The same rhythm continues throughout the chant. Chant continues until all children have been called on to play. The last child responds, "<u>Leader's name</u> stole the cookie from the cookie jar."
Leader: "I stole the cookie from the cookie jar."

Role of the leader: Organize children into a circle. Model the chant and explain the rules. Begin and end the chant.
Extensions: Change the rhythm of the chant. Change the body movements to stomping and finger snapping. Let children chose the body movements or make up new words for the chant.

Stories of Music

Brief description: Children use their imaginations to draw pictures that tell a story based on the music they hear.

Materials:

   Colored markers, one set per child
   Drawing paper, one piece per child
   Instrumental music of varying tempos and instruments
   CD or record player for playing music

Procedure: Children will close their eyes and listen to segments of the music. Leader will ask what the music makes them think of. Leader will play another segment and again ask what it makes the children think of. Then, the children will be given paper and markers to draw what they are thinking as they listen to the entire piece of music. Children will share their stories with the group.
Role of the leader: Choose music and facilitate children's thinking as they listen. The leader will also facilitate children's storytelling to the entire group, in small groups or with one other person.

Extensions: Listen and draw to different kinds of music, especially music from other cultures. Children can move according to how they feel instead of drawing what they think.

Composing to the Beat

Brief description: Children will work in groups of three or four and create rhythm patterns. They will write their rhythms pictorially on paper and play them on instruments. Rhythms can be recorded on a tape player.

Materials:

Instruments, one per child
Paper and pencils or markers
Tape player

Procedure: Leader will introduce the idea of a four-beat rhythm in music and model a few rhythms with an instrument. Children will repeat the rhythms with their instruments. The leader then should elicit ideas from the children about how to pictorially represent the rhythm. The leader can write one of these ideas as an example. Children will be divided into teams to create their own rhythms. They will be encouraged to write their rhythm in whatever manner makes sense to them. The team will practice their rhythm following their written plan. Lastly they will play their rhythm and record it on a tape player.
Role of the leader: Gather enough instruments so everyone has an instrument. Facilitate this activity by modeling and playing rhythms, encouraging children to repeat the rhythms. The leader further facilitates the activity by managing groups as their work on rhythms. Some groups may need additional scaffolding.
Extensions: Children can be exposed to the formal method of recording rhythms by use of whole notes, half notes, etc. Make rhythms with different numbers of beats. Children can listen to patterns in music and try to repeat them.

Bottles of Music

Brief description: Children will experiment with various levels of water in glass containers to make music.

Materials:

Glass bottles or large water glasses (five or more)
Pitcher of colored water (use small amount of food coloring)
Spoon
Measuring cup
Funnel (to assist in filling the bottles if necessary)

Procedure: Children, working in teams of two, will fill containers with different amount of water. One may have ¼ cup, ½ cup in the next, ¾ cup in the next, and so on. Children should note the different levels of water in the glasses and put them in sequential order. Children tap on the side of the containers with a spoon to make musical tones. Children can use the glasses to tap out various known tunes such as "Happy Birthday" or make up their own tunes.

Role of the leader: Leaders will gather materials. It may be possible for parents to donate the bottles. The leader can scaffold the measuring of the liquid for children not yet familiar with the measuring of liquid. Leaders will facilitate the activity, asking divergent questions to guide children's observations and discovery. "Which container gives the highest tone? Why? What would change the tone?"

Extensions: Find other items that can be used for making music such as pan lids, metal bowls, etc. Children can sequence these other items from high to low sounds and again try to make music.

Math Lesson Plans

Bubble Math

Brief description: Children will make bubbles to explore counting, addition, and measurement.

Materials:

Liquid dish soap (⅓ cup to each gallon of water)
Water
Container to hold bubble mixture
Small containers for individual children's bubbles (such as empty yogurt containers)
Bubble wands
Paper and pencil
Measuring tape (as used in construction)

Procedure: Make bubble mixture the day before it is to be used. Pour bubble mixture into individual containers for each child. Children will use bubble wand to blow bubbles. They will work in teams of two to complete the following math tasks:

1. Each team member will blow bubbles and his partner will count the number of bubbles and record the information on paper. Each person will blow bubbles five times. The bubble scores will be added to get a total number of bubbles for each person.
2. Each team member will blow bubbles and the team will watch and follow the bubbles to see which one travels the farthest. The team will measure the distance from where the bubbles were blown to where it was when it disappeared. The distance will be recorded. Each person will blow and measure at least two times.

Role of the leader: Some children may not have had any distance-measuring experience and will need the task scaffolded for them.

Extensions: Other instruments can be used to blow bubbles. Children can determine if there is a relationship between the size of the bubble maker and the number of bubbles that can be blown. Other bubbles makers might include the plastic rings that hold soda cans together, small hoops, or some other item with a hole in it.

Build a School

Brief description: Children will work together using blocks and cardboard to replicate the length, height, and perimeter of their classroom and the school.

Materials:

> Unit blocks of various sizes
> Random sizes of cardboard
> Cardboard scissors
> Clipboards, paper, and pencils

Procedure: Children will work in teams to examine their classroom and draw it on paper. They will then build it with blocks and cardboard. This process will involve discussion about where doors and windows are placed in relationship to the size of walls. Once children understand the process of examining and replicating the classroom, they can move on to larger spaces such as building a model of the entire school or even the city block.

Role of the leader: The facilitation of this activity will require the leader to be available to listen to children as they brainstorm ideas and to provide needed materials. The leader will introduce new vocabulary such as length, width, and perimeter. This activity will take several days so space will need to be dedicated to this work.

Extensions: Create a model on a smaller scale using craft sticks and wood glue with cardboard as a base. Bring in blueprints of buildings for children to examine. Visit a construction site.

Catapults

Brief description: Homemade catapults will be used to launch objects and measure distances of trajectory.

Materials:

> Wooden rulers
> Rubber bands
> Plastic spoons
> Small paper balls (crumpled newspaper densely squashed into a spherical shape)
> Crayons
> Yardsticks or measuring tapes
> Masking tape or sidewalk chalk

Procedure: Children will construct the catapults and paper balls. To construct the catapult, lay a plastic spoon onto a wooden ruler with the bowl of the spoon and about 1 inch of the handle beyond the end of the ruler. Face the bowl of the spoon toward the ruler. Secure with a rubber band tightly wrapped around the spoon handle and ruler. Cut newspaper into pieces about 8 inches square. These will become the paper balls. Color the newspaper with the crayon with large scribble-like lines. (Each child will need his or her own crayon color.) Crumple the newspaper as compactly as possible. To play the game, children will place a paper ball in the bowl of their spoon on the catapult. Holding the spoon and the ball, pull back on the spoon slightly then let go of the spoon. The paper ball will be launched onto the playing field. The playing field consists of an area that is marked off with parallel lines of masking tape every foot. Children can launch five paper balls and then measure the distance of their flights. Additional rulers may be used to measure exact distance between the lines. Children can record their scores on their clipboards.

Role of the leader: The leader will construct the playing field by placing rows of masking tape on the floor 1 foot apart. Use sidewalk chalk to make the lines on concrete or blacktop. The leader should experiment with the catapults to determine the depth of the playing field. The leader will also need to determine the rules, where children will stand, and when there is a no-launch time so children are safe while measuring distances.

Extensions: Experiment with other objects such as cotton balls for launching. Read about catapults.

Pattern Prints

Brief description: Children will design their own pattern and print it on paper.

Materials:

> Variety of rubber stamps
> Ink for stamps (preferably more than one color)
> Drawing paper

Procedure: Children will review the concept of patterns. Each child will create a pattern on the border of his paper. Paper can be used as invitations or placemats. It can serve as the background paper for displaying another piece of artwork in the classroom. Children can be encouraged to print patterns in other ways on their paper. Children will verbalize their patterns (such as frog, frog, snake, frog, frog, snake).

Role of the leader: The leader will need to facilitate a discussion about patterns. Scaffolding may be necessary for some children who aren't familiar with patterns.

Extensions: Examine patterns in wallpaper and have children make their own wallpaper pattern. Examine patterns in wrapping paper. Then encourage children to make patterns on easel paper to be later used as wrapping paper. Use paint or markers to make the patterns.

Sink the Ships

Brief description: Children will play this game in teams of two while they learn about using coordinates. The goal of the game is to find and sink each other's ships.

Materials:

> Graph paper
> Pencils (one per child)
> Marker (one per child)

Procedure: Each child will make his game card in the following manner. (Younger children may need the playing card made for them.) Each player has his own playing graph. To begin, each player places his ships on the graph by letters in the spaces. The letter B is for battleship, C for cruiser, D for destroyer, and S for submarine. Each player will place four battleships (B), three cruisers (C), two destroyers (D), and one submarine (S). Each kind of ship must be in a line vertically, horizontally, or diagonally as displayed in the example. Children play in teams of two. For example, Susie will begin play by calling out coordinates, such as G4. Lena looks to see if that coordinate corresponds to the placement of one of her ships. If it is a hit, then Lena tells what has been hit. "You hit one of my

	1	2	3	4	5	6	7	8	9
J		B	B	B	B				
I									
H			C						
G				C					
F					C				
D							D		
C							D		
B			S						
A									

cruisers." Lena will put a large X on the cruiser that was hit. Susie will write "C" in the G4 space on her paper. Children take turns calling out coordinates until all of one person's ships have been sunk.

Role of the leader: The leader may want to make the game cards ahead of time. These can be easily made on a computer and printed.

Extensions: The coordinate system can be changed to more closely match that used in geometry. Instead of a column of letters, the column could be numbers. The submarine in the above example is at point (3, 2). More advanced children can use an X-Y axis system that incorporates negative numbers.

Science Lesson Plans

Interactive Inventions

Brief description: Children will work in teams to explore objects and their properties to determine how they interact to move objects through the air.

Materials:

Dishpans (one for each team of three to four children)
Objects to interact: cotton balls, clay or dough, clothespins, straws, rubber bands, craft sticks, paper clips, corks, pipe cleaners, plastic gears, string, plastic spoons, scissors, berry baskets, and any other materials available ("found materials")
Easel paper and markers or science journals

Procedure: The leader will introduce the idea of inventions, highlighting that inventions happen as a result of inventor's ideas and that everyone has ideas. Children will work in teams to explore the materials in their tub. The focus of this free exploration is to see how objects can work together to move objects through the air. After a predetermined length of time, teams will work together to report their ideas and discoveries either on a piece of easel paper or in their science journals.

Role of the leader: The leader will gather materials and elicit donations from parents. The leader sets the stage for exploration by talking about inventors and how inventions start. The scope of exploration is further guided by the leader clearly stating the goal of determining how materials work together (interact). The leader will monitor children's progress and, if needed, guide their explorations with questions or personal thoughts such as "I wonder what would happen if. . . ."

Extensions: Children implement their invention ideas and test them by propelling an object such as a cotton ball or dough through the air. Children can read about various inventors.

Solutions and Emulsions

Brief description: Children will experiment with a variety of materials to experience what combinations of matter and water become solutions and what combinations are emulsions.

Materials:

Small clear plastic cups
Teaspoon
Stirring sticks
Pitcher of water
Things to mix with water: vegetable oil, vinegar, sand, salt, sugar, baking soda, flour, cornstarch
Science journals

Procedure: The child will pour a plastic cup half full of water. The child will put one teaspoon of one of the other materials in the cup and gently stir to the count of 15. Let the mixture settle and observe what happened to the matter that was added. If it disappeared, the mixture has become a solution. If it is cloudy or separates, the mixture is an emulsion. The mixture is then dumped into a large container and the experimenter again pours the cup half full of water and tests another material. Each child can record his findings in his science journal after completing the project.

Role of the leader: The leader must have a basic understanding of solutions and emulsions. The leader will explain these two new vocabulary words to children and model the process by pouring a cup half full of water and measuring out a teaspoon of salt. The leader will then ask the children to predict what they think will happen. The leader will elicit a few responses then put the salt back into the salt container, encouraging children to be scientists and make those discoveries themselves.

Extensions: Children can continue exploration of solutions by adding another teaspoon of matter and stirring. If the water is again clear, another teaspoon can be added. Keep adding until no more will dissolve. This means that the solution has reached the saturation point.

Melt the Crayons

Brief description: Children will devise experiments to see what helps crayons melt when placed in the sun.

Materials:

Crayon pieces
Items to place under the crayons: small disposable pie pans, black construction
    paper, white construction paper, foil, wax paper

Procedure: Children will make predictions about what material will help crayons melt the fastest. They will put a crayon piece on five different substances and place them in the sun outside. (Be sure they are placed on a surface that will not be harmed if the crayon melts.) Children will observe their science project every 15 minutes for the next two hours and record their observations in their science journals.

Role of the leader: The leader should be prepared by having completed the activity herself to determine which brand of crayons melts the easiest. This will help set up the children for success. Be watchful of the weather and do this on a sunny, warm day.

Extensions: Melt ice cubes in a similar fashion using items that may absorb or reflect the heat. Discuss heat reflection and absorption as it pertains to clothing.

Shadows in Time

Brief description: Children will work in teams to explore how their shadow changes throughout the day.

Materials:

Sidewalk chalk
Measuring tapes
Clipboards, paper, and pencils

Procedure: Children will work in teams of two tracing each other's shadows. Begin this activity in the morning of a sunny day. Children must work in a place where there is adequate blacktop or concrete to outline the shadows. Trace around the person's shoes and shadow. Measure the distance from the heels of the shoes to the farthest point on the shadow. Record the measurement and the time of day. Children will return to the shadow tracings every one to two hours and stand in their traced footprints. Each time the children will trace the shadows, measure their lengths and record the new measurements. Near the end of the class day (and before the sun goes down), children will trace and measure the last time. Children will examine their tracings of the day and draw conclusions.

Role of the leader: The leader should anticipate the changes in the shadows and be certain that children have enough space between their shadows to allow for the changes. The leader should facilitate the activity by asking children divergent questions to encourage critical thinking. "Why does the shadow change size? Where do you think the shadow will be this afternoon?"

Extensions: Children can do this activity at different times of the year and notice how their shadows change. Further study can help them understand the tilt of the earth on its axis and how it changes the placement of the sun in the sky.

Feed the Ants

Brief description: Children will create an experiment to try to determine what attracts ants.

Materials:

Ant trail (found outside)
Paper plate divided into eight pie-shaped sections (one per team)
Very small portions of food (sugar, vegetable oil, bread, candy, meat, cheese, fruit, vegetables, etc.)

Procedure: On the first day, lead children in a discussion about ants. Who has had them in their house? Why do they come in? What food do they go after? Divide children into teams of four to further discuss what foods they think ants would like. Each team will make a list of the foods. Children are to be encouraged to bring in very small portions of food from home for the experiment. Each team will decide what eight foods they want to offer the ants and place a different type of food on each section of the paper plate. Teams will then search for an ant trail outside and place their paper plate near the trail. Children will observe the plates throughout the day and record any ant activity in their science journals.

Role of the leader: Leaders should gather some background knowledge of ants. They will have to work with each team to be certain that team members have access to needed food items.

Extensions: Children can be encouraged to do Internet searches to learn about different kinds of ants. Other outdoor insects can be explored in a similar fashion.

GLOSSARY

A

AAHPERD   American Alliance for Health, Physical Education, Recreation, and Dance: develops standards for aerobic endurance, muscular strength, and flexibility that indicate fitness

academic approach   an approach to programming that involves determining outcomes that can be measured and then planning a program to help children achieve those goals

accommodations   changes that are necessary when planning activities to include special-needs children

ADA   Americans with Disabilities Act

adjunct learning tool   additional ways to learn that are not part of traditional curriculum activities

adolescence   Freud's stage in which there are changes to sexual organs and in appearance accompanied by strong sexual urges

age appropriateness   programs are planned according to universal, predictable growth and changes that occur in children

anal period   Freud's second stage, in which children increase body awareness and focus of attention is on the anus as a source of pleasure

anecdotal record   written observations of a child in a variety of situations

antibias curriculum   a curriculum that addresses cultural diversity by including gender and differences in physical differences; is based on children's developmental tasks as they construct identity and attitudes; directly addresses the impact of stereotyping, bias, and discriminatory behavior in young children's development and interactions

authentic feedback   a description of a child's real accomplishments

autonomy vs. shame and doubt   Erikson's second stage, in which the focus is to become independent by gaining control over bodily functions

B

biodegradable   objects that disintegrate over time

BMI   body mass index; a measure of the ratio of weight to height

bullying   unprovoked aggression that is intended to inflict injury or discomfort on the victim

C

caregiver   name for an adult in child care when the emphasis is on the caring role

CDA   Child Development Associate, nationally recognized credential for early childhood teachers and caregivers

centering   Piaget's observation that young children focus on only one dimension of a form at a time

checklist   a list of predetermined behaviors to be observed

child care councils   group of representatives from the various factions of the child care community

chronic health conditions   recurring allergies or infections

classical conditioning   conditioning brought about by proximity of stimulus and response

clique   a group of children who have similar characteristics and interests

code-switching   a complete change of language form when addressing adults and when talking to other children

concrete operations   ability to think symbolically and to reverse processes when information is presented concretely

constructing knowledge   children develop their own theories about how the world works

conventional   Kohlberg's second stage of moral development in which there is an emphasis on social rules of the individual's family, group, or nation

convergent thinking   a process of thought that narrows down many ideas into a single focused point

curriculum   a plan of activities that accomplishes the goals of a program

D

developmentalist   name for an adult in child care who is versed in the developmental aspects of the child

divergent questions   questions that have no specific answer and require a child to think critically

divergent thinking   a process of thought or perception that involves considering alternatives, taking a line of thought that is different from the usual

E

educare   a name for an adult in child care reflecting the multifaceted aspect of working with school-age children

ego   in psychoanalytic theory, the rational aspect of personality

elaborated code   a communication that uses a more extensive vocabulary, is correct grammatically, and is longer

emergent curriculum   activities that are planned as a result of caregivers noting the current interests of children or that develop as children play

ethics   a study of right, wrong, duty, and obligation

event recording   observer chooses a specific situation in which to observe a child

extended family   members of nuclear family plus grandparents, aunts, uncles, and cousins

F

Food Guide Pyramid   U.S. Department of Agriculture guide to healthy food choices and number of servings per day

formal operations   ability to consider hypothetical problems without concrete examples

G

gang   a group of children who gather together to be out of the realm of adults but also to be antisocial

H

holistic approach   a curriculum that evolves from children's individual and group abilities and interests

I

id   in psychoanalytic theory, the part of the personality that is the source of pleasure-seeking drives

identity vs. role confusion Erikson's fifth stage, in which adolescents search for their identity as individuals in a society

inclusion placing children with disabilities in settings with same-age peers

individual appropriateness refers to each child's unique pattern and timing of growth

Individualized Education Plan (IEP) set of goals determined by a team of professionals and parents to reflect what the child should accomplish within a year's time

industry vs. inferiority Erikson's fourth stage, in which children expend all their energies on mastering new skills at home, in school, on the playground, and in their neighborhoods

initiative vs. guilt Erikson's third stage, in which children attempt new activities that can result in either pride (initiative) or guilt when unsuccessful

integrated curriculum the linking of two or more subject areas such as literacy and math, or linking an academic subject to the community or vocations

integrated learning interrelated disciplines such as language, math, or science to achieve a goal

intergenerational program child care programs that utilize older persons and young adults or teenagers as volunteers

interracial family marriage between two adults of different races

L

latency period Freud's fourth stage, in which children's sexual urges are unobtrusive and energies are directed toward school activities and sports

lateralization specialization in function of the two hemispheres of the brain

learning processes by which environmental influences and experiences bring about permanent changes in thinking, feeling, and behavior

logical consequence a tool for changing behavior in which the result of a child's misbehavior is related to the behavior

logicomathematical knowledge how objects compare to one another

M

maturation progression of changes that take place as one ages

meaning-based experiences learning experiences that emphasize thinking, cooperative problem solving, decision making, and an opportunity to challenge preconceived ideas

modeling adults exhibit the behaviors that are expected of children

moral realism a stage of moral development in which children believe that rules are determined by an authority figure and they are not to be changed

moral relativism a stage of moral development in which children view punishments as fair or unfair, are more flexible in their thinking, and can discuss moral issues

morality our perception of what is good or right

morality of caring Gilligan's theory that girls are socialized to be caring and nurturing and reluctant to judge right and wrong in absolutes

morality of justice Gilligan's theory that boys will determine what is right or wrong and then follow it with a clear solution when faced with making choices

multipurpose equipment equipment that has many possibilities for play activities

N

NAA National AfterSchool Association has developed standards for the best practices for children ages 5 to 14

NAEYC National Association for the Education of Young Children, a large professional organization that accredits programs for children from birth through the elementary years

NAFCC National Association for Family Child Care; has developed quality standards for accreditation

nature a variety of characteristics that are inherited from parents

negotiable rules rules that are based on choices

NIOST National Institute on Out-of-School Time; focuses on education and training, community development, consultation, research, and public awareness

nonbiodegradable objects that will not disintegrate over time

nonnegotiable rules rules that are used for actions that can be harmful to others or destructive to property and that are not open for discussion

nuclear family mother, father, and children

nurture all the experiences and influences one is exposed to from the moment of conception on throughout a lifetime

O

operant conditioning the process by which children act upon their environment and are reinforced for their behaviors

optional rules things that children can reasonably control themselves

oral period Freud's term for the first stage, in which the infant gains pleasure through sucking

P

phallic period Freud's third stage, during which the genital areas are the focus of pleasure and children become aware of physical differences

physical knowledge how objects behave as a result of their characteristics

postconventional Kohlberg's third stage of moral development, in which there is an emphasis on moral values and principles

preconventional Kohlberg's first stage of moral development, in which there is an emphasis on punishment and rewards

preoperational period ability to begin to think symbolically and to remember experiences and objects independently of the immediate encounter

R

reconstituted or blended family families that include children from previous marriages plus those from the present union

recreational supervisor name for an adult in child care when the emphasis is on the recreational aspects

restricted code communications that are more limited and may rely on gestures and voice intonation to convey meaning

rough and tumble play aggressive behavior, but the children usually have positive facial expressions or may be laughing

S

SACERS School-Age Care Environmental Scale, a method of rating programs that serve children 5 to 12

safety audit survey of all playground structures in comparison to standards, guidelines, and laws set by federal and state agencies

scaffold support system that supports children as they move from one intellectual level to the next

scientific literacy knowledge and understanding of science concepts and process

self-assessment a list of goals that children can use to assess their own progress

self-image our perception of ourselves plus the perceptions conveyed by others

sensorimotor period Piaget's first period, in which infants use all their senses to explore and learn about the world around them

single-gender family two adults of the same gender plus children

single-parent family father or mother and children

single-purpose equipment play equipment that can be used for only one kind of play

social knowledge information children cannot construct for themselves

storage strategies methods children use to increase their memory

superego in psychoanalytic theory, the part of the personality that controls behavior through the development of conscience

T

time or duration sampling observation of a child's behavior at intervals of time and for a specified period of time trust vs. mistrust   Erikson's first stage, in which babies learn to trust that others will take care of their basic needs and that others can be depended upon

typically developing   children without disabilities

V

values   the qualities we believe to be intrinsically desirable and that we strive to achieve in ourselves

video camera or tape recording   most accurate methods of observation

volunteer corps   group of older adults and young persons or teenagers who volunteer in a child care center

Z

zone of proximal development   the hypothetical environment in which learning and development take place

INDEX